Postsecondary Play

Tech.edu
A Hopkins Series on Education and Technology

Postsecondary Play

The Role of Games and Social Media in Higher Education

Edited by
WILLIAM G. TIERNEY, ZOË B. CORWIN,
TRACY FULLERTON, and GISELE RAGUSA

Johns Hopkins University Press
Baltimore

Johns Hopkins Paperback edition 2017
2 4 6 8 9 7 5 3 1

Johns Hopkins University Press
2715 North Charles Street
Baltimore, Maryland 21218-4363
www.press.jhu.edu

The Library of Congress has cataloged the hardcover edition
of this work as follows:
Postsecondary play : the role of games and social media in higher
education / edited by William G. Tierney, Zoë B. Corwin, Tracy Fullerton,
and Gisele Ragusa.

    pages cm
  Includes bibliographical references and index.
  ISBN-13: 978-1-4214-1306-8 (hardcover : alk. paper)
  ISBN-10: 1-4214-1306-x (hardcover : alk. paper)
  ISBN-13: 978-1-4214-1307-5 (electronic)
  ISBN-10: 1-4214-1307-8 (electronic)
  1. Education, Higher—Effect of technological innovations on.
 2. Education, Higher—Social aspects. 3. Play—Social aspects.
 4. Video games. 5. Computer games. 6. Social media.
 I. Tierney, William G.
  LB2395.7.P68 2014
  378.1734—dc23   2013029166

A catalog record for this book is available from the British Library.

ISBN-13: 978-1-4214-2275-6
ISBN-10: 1-4214-2275-1

Special discounts are available for bulk purchases of this book.
For more information, please contact Special Sales at 410-516-6936 or
specialsales@press.jhu.edu.

Johns Hopkins University Press uses environmentally friendly book
materials, including recycled text paper that is composed of at least
30 percent post-consumer waste, whenever possible.

Contents

Acknowledgments

Five years ago we embarked on a collaboration to improve access to college through the creation of game-based tools. Our work on the project informed this edited volume. We are grateful to the University of Southern California (USC) Office of the Provost, TG, The Rosalinde and Arthur Gilbert Foundation, the Bill & Melinda Gates Foundation, and the U.S. Department of Education's Institute for Education Sciences (award R305A110288) for supporting the project. The text does not reflect the views of these organizations.

We are indebted to Lisa Garcia, research associate at the USC Pullias Center, for meticulously editing evolving versions of the book and to Monica Raad and Diane Flores for their effortless administrative support.

Postsecondary Play

Why Games and Social Media?

ZOË B. CORWIN, WILLIAM G. TIERNEY,
TRACY FULLERTON, AND GISELE RAGUSA

In the fall of 2008, faced with the persistent challenge of how to boost college-going rates for low-income students, we embarked on an interdisciplinary collaboration intended to create new technology and game-based college-access tools. With seed funding from the University of Southern California's Office of the Provost, our team of educational researchers, game designers, and outreach practitioners convened to conceptualize these tools. Almost immediately, we involved a group of local high school students from the target audience. Our collective expertise informed the design and development of a series of no-tech, low-tech, and high-tech games designed to engage students in the college preparation process in effective, novel, and fun ways.

During the course of the project, as we prepared proposals for conferences, responded to calls for funding, and conversed with potential funders from philanthropic and business fields, we recognized a significant disconnect between the education and game worlds. Educators and foundations appreciated our efforts to improve college access but were skeptical of how games or social media might help. Gamers liked the concept of what we were developing but were less invested in games for social good. As we wrote about the subject, we lacked a synthesized text that focused on the intersection of these fields. When we talked about our work with varied audiences across the country, we fielded questions that emphasized the need to provide academics and practitioners with a language for discussing games, social media, and higher education.

Technology has always informed social life. Wagons revolutionized the way food was harvested and brought to market. Factory assembly lines transformed industry. Toasters, blenders, and microwaves expedited meal preparation and in turn changed family life. Yet at no other time in history has technological change unfolded as rapidly as in the twenty-first century. Digital technologies are now designed, developed, and adopted within single decades (Palfrey and Gasser 2008). Adoption of new technologies is not only rapid but also expansive. As of 2011, 95% of 12- to 17-year-old U.S. teenagers spent time online, and 80% used social media (Parker, Lenhart, and Moore 2011). Annual growth rates illustrate that the video game industry is a solid market force despite nationwide economic challenges. Whereas the U.S. economy grew at a rate of 1.4% between 2005 and 2009, the video game industry grew at a rate of 10.6% during that same time period and contributed $4.9 billion to the U.S. gross domestic product (Siwek 2010).

Widespread adoption of new media has the potential to facilitate cultural reorganization within organizations as well as in the larger public sphere (Baym 2010). Digital media, for instance, has drastically changed the way that people communicate. Just as the advent of the telegraph and then telephone altered the manner in which people interacted across distances and time, the recent influx of new media—such as texting, emailing, instant messaging, and social networking—influences the way people communicate as a society. Baym (2010, 4) argues that "the separation of presence from communication offers us more control over our social worlds yet simultaneously subjects us to new forms of control, surveillance, and constraint." Changes in communication strategies and access to information are in turn dramatically affecting the way we learn.

Curiously, postsecondary institutions have served as incubators for technological innovation, but those in academe also have traditionally resisted some forms of change. Email, for example, largely began within universities and became ubiquitous earlier among academics than the general citizenry. Changes in postsecondary institutional-level social media use between 2008 and 2012 illustrate the wide-scale and rapid adoption of social media. In the 2008–2009 school year, for instance, only 61% of universities used Facebook, while no universities were active on Twitter or LinkedIn. In a survey of social media use for 2010–2011, though, university usage rates jumped to 98%, 84%, and 47%, respectively, for Facebook, Twitter, and LinkedIn (Parker, Lenhart, and Moore 2011). Within those institutions, traditionally aged college students have been the earliest adopters of social media and the most avid game players.

Despite the prevalence of digital media, the teaching and learning component in colleges and universities has largely remained unchanged. Professors continue to function as the "sage on the stage" in a lecture hall or "guide on the side" seminar facilitators among a relatively small group of students. Technology changes that have become pervasive elsewhere—such as crowd sourcing—remain a relatively rare undertaking in the academy. To be sure, all institutions have websites, and video tours of college campuses are increasingly common. But if one were to examine the most exciting social media experiments in the twenty-first century, the first place to look would not be postsecondary institutions.

Why This Book?

The impetus for this book derives from a multiyear university research project exploring the potential of game-based strategies to push students to think and act differently with regard to applying to college and navigating college experiences. Every year thousands of students from low-income backgrounds are denied the opportunity to attend college because they are not supported during the college preparation process. For some students, college remains an amorphous and out-of-reach experience. Other students aspire to attend college from an early age. Yet, although they perform well in college preparatory courses, when the time comes to enroll, they slip through the cracks. At the same time, students from high-income backgrounds have come to rely more heavily on private college guidance counselors to ensure college enrollment. Private college-support services are now a multimillion-dollar industry in the United States (McDonough 2005).

Some students, once they are accepted, never arrive. Far too many students graduate from high school having committed to a postsecondary institution but do not attend; in effect, there is a "summer melt," as students end up staying home rather than going to college. Of those who arrive, many do not persist to graduation. Many are unprepared academically and socially for college-level work. Close to 60% of freshmen entering the California State University (CSU) system, for example, require remedial coursework (CSU 2011a), and only 50% of these students graduate in six years (CSU 2011b). Other students may be academically prepared, but they lack the "college knowledge" that enables them to navigate large classes and confusing financial and academic hurdles. David Conley and Mary Seburn's chapter in this book posits that to have college success students must be equipped with cognitive strategies consistent with the requirements of given subject areas, understand the structure of knowledge within a discipline, possess a range of skills and techniques necessary to learn effectively and efficiently, and understand the dynamics of the transition from secondary to postsecondary education. Students who have never had a bank account or credit card, though, lack sufficient financial literacy for college success. Others who attended low-performing high schools, or even "dropout factories," may have poor time management skills, which can inhibit their college persistence. These dilemmas result in a nation without sufficient numbers of students applying for and getting into college, and of those who have arrived at college, far too many do not matriculate to graduation in a timely manner.

Over the course of four years and through an extensive iterative design process, our team of researchers, game designers, and students has collaborated on a series of college access and completion games that provide an alternative to existing college guidance resources. The intent was to offer an effective tool for engaging students in scalable ways. The approach was to meet students where they were—playing games and online—and create rich learning experiences that complemented the work of guidance counselors but also extended beyond school environments. We drew from the potential of games outlined in part II of this book to boost aspirations, cultivate strategies, and grow what Jenkins and Kahn, authors in part II, have defined as a "participatory culture."

The games are designed for middle school, high school, and college students and have been effective in cultivating college aspirations, sharing information, and teaching college preparation strategies. The first game, a no-tech card game called *Application Crunch*, reflects students' concerns about balancing academics and extracurricular involvement, managing time, and meeting deadlines. Players role-play a high school senior applying for college. The game relies on standard game mechanics such as "leveling up" to indicate how players will spend their actions in the game. Through collaborative play, players become familiar with terms and behaviors associated with successful college applications. For example, students learn the differences between various types of postsecondary institutions, the importance of applying to scholarships, and the value of specializing in an extracurricular activity.

The second game in the series, *Mission: Admission*, translates the card game into a digital format. Using Facebook as a platform, the game focuses on the college application process and makes use of students' actual online social networks to facilitate dialogue about college. Many of the first-generation students we work with through our outreach program in the Pullias Center have high college aspirations but know very little about college. Their confusion extends to not even knowing what questions to ask. Players have the option of posing questions to their friends who are playing the game. Questions are generated by the game and are intended to stimulate dialogue among players not only online but also between face-to-face peers and teachers. The game takes place in real time and occurs over the course of a week. Players choose an avatar and are responsible for managing that character's time and activities (i.e., should their character spend time studying at the library or conducting science experiments), determining which deadlines to work toward, and making sure they request letters of recommendation in advance (requested letters incubate over time and are not readily available to use during gameplay—just like requests for letters of recommendation require advance solicitation in the real world). Both the card and Facebook games have been shown—through mixed-methods research—to significantly increase college-going self-efficacy and build college knowledge.

The third game, *FutureBound*, targets middle school students. Three major foci of the game are: (1) emphasizing that actions and decisions in middle school affect future opportunities, (2) illustrating the value of reaching out to people who can provide support, and (3) staying away from negative influences. The game is designed to illustrate the value of building skills related to passions, and how those skills can lead to a variety of career options. In the game, students guide their self-designed avatars through a series of fun and challenging obstacle courses that change as the scenario unfolds to simulate real life. Students answer questions about college and career, fight "doubts" that strip powers from students, and gain college and career "passions" by speaking with teachers and peers about their career interests, ultimately helping to fuel their goals to win the game.

A fourth game focused on cultivating financial aid knowledge, teaching financial literacy, and building decision-making skills around determining a sound college fit is under development. We have identified the need for games to cultivate college knowledge and college aspirations in elementary school students, games that target nontraditional students such as veterans or adult learners, games that target particular groups of students such as foster youth, and games to ease the first-year transition to college and increase the likelihood of persistence.

Our involvement in the interdisciplinary game project revealed a general lack of attention paid to games and social media in the college access literature. At the same time, game and new media literacy theories did not focus on higher education or issues of access. When we applied to conferences or for grant funding, we sought a common-ground literature and found virtually none. We also learned that scholars, practitioners, foundation officers, and game designers lacked a common language and shared understanding when discussing games for college access (Corwin and Tierney 2012). This book is an attempt to address these important gaps.

Why Now?

The technological and digital landscape has been changing dramatically during the writing of this book—in ways that are impossible to predict. From the first to the final manuscript, for instance, MOOCs (massively open online courses) had grown from an obscure acronym to a viable course type and had become a massively popular, albeit controversial, aspect of the postsecondary landscape. Projections into the next decade are even more difficult to determine. Over the next few years, will movies still be streamed normally? Will traditional newspapers have been eliminated? Will bookstores still exist? Will scholarly journals all be open access and online? We anticipate that hybrid learning environments incorporating online instruction with traditional approaches will have increased and that tablets and mobile devices will have been incorporated widely into classrooms at all levels.

Social media and games are currently transforming multiple aspects of mainstream lives in general, and university life in particular. Take, for example, the way that information is created. Before the internet, information was primarily accessed through print journals and books. To publish, authors had to write, edit, and undergo extensive peer review and a lengthy publication process. Consumers of such texts ventured into libraries or bookstores to find printed materials, or they ordered journals, magazines, and newspapers delivered to their homes. The production of knowledge is now much less centralized; traditional gatekeepers are less powerful, and the process of knowledge construction is significantly much more fluid (Palfrey and Gasser 2008). Open Education Resources (OER) and Open Learning Networks (OLN) have gained wide prevalence. By blogging, commenting on online content, and contributing to websites such as *Wikipedia*, more and more people have access to creating information—and knowledge—in far simpler ways. In 2008, for example, 64% of teenagers had created content online (Palfrey and Gasser 2008), a percentage that most definitely has grown in recent years. Web 2.0 is changing the way that knowledge is developed, critiqued, and disseminated. An examination of social media and games is applicable to a tremendous array of topics: K–12 learning, the global work force, military advancements, and civic engagement. The decision to focus our discussion on higher-education and college access stems from a collective investment in educational equity and leveling the post-secondary playing field. In addition, while the genres of games and social media are applicable to many fields, we felt that a focus on postsecondary education and access would offer a particular lens through which to explore these topics. We are not alone in our concern over improved access to college. President Obama has stated that in order for the United States to compete in the global economy the United States once again needs to have the highest proportion of college graduates in the world (Obama 2009). Laura Perna's chapter discusses the need for programs that increase access and degree completion for particular groups of students: those from low-income families, African Americans, and Hispanics. Her chapter describes the potential of social media and games for addressing the barriers that continue to limit college enrollment and completion, particularly the barriers facing students from groups that have been traditionally underrepresented in higher education.

Higher education is at a critical juncture. As tuition prices rise and unemployment plagues our nation, debates have surfaced over the explicit value of a college education. With rapid technological change, there is also an increased demand for more educated workers. The slowdown of educational attainment is the most important factor in increasing wage differentials and in lessening family income inequality (Goldin and Katz 2008). While college attendance rates have increased in the United States over the past few years, college completion rates remain stagnant. The United States lags in the middle of the pack among Organisation for Economic Co-operation and Development (OECD) countries (Goldin and Katz 2008). As technology becomes more skill-based, K–12 schools and universities are challenged to meet the need to address those demands.

In the MacArthur Foundation report *Re-imagining Learning in the 21st Century*, the foundation asserts that "we are on the cusp of one of the significant transformations in media and potentially in the nature of public participation. Young people are the best ones through which to look at this transformation" (8). High school and college students are frequently the earliest adapters to technology. As James Gee, Henry Jenkins, and Adam Kahn explain later in this volume, youth actively learn through interest-driven spaces and popular culture. Younger and younger children are asserting a greater level of control over their media use in more and more sophisticated ways (Rideout, Vandewater, and Wartella 2003). Hence we can learn from them. An important portion of the people reading this book will be "digital immigrants," people born before 1980 who have learned how to use email and various web tools later in life. Many in this group approach games and social media differently from those who have grown up with computer and mobile technologies. As we move toward a more fluid informational infrastructure, digital immigrants will continue to adapt to the ever-changing digital landscape. Schools and universities are in the midst of a significant shift in the way students learn. Learning is predominantly occurring not just in the traditional classroom but all around us (Thomas and Brown 2011).

Play, Games, Social Media

Games and social media are tremendously varied. Games are not a panacea, and not all games are effective. Not all social media are conducive to college success. In fact, social media can easily detract from learning and, in some cases, be quite harmful to students. Consider the student who is consumed by online activities to the detriment of missing out on participating in on-campus study groups—or, as Zoë Corwin and Gisele Ragusa point out in their chapters, by extreme cases of cyberbullying. At the same time, as Jenkins and Kahn discuss, online communities are reinvigorating the way we engage in civic activities and learn through collective knowledge sharing. Our intention throughout the book is to unpack these concepts, explicate how they relate to higher education, and suggest ways that we can evaluate and make use of each genre moving forward. The structure of this text is flexible. Chapters are organized into three parts but can be read as stand-alone essays. The overarching goal is to explain key concepts and illustrate ways in which games and social media interface with higher education; we even provide a glossary of common terms for digital neophytes.

The spectrum of games is wide. Games can be premised entirely on fantasy or grounded in real-world performance. Games have been shown to positively influence aspirations, empower learners, increase motivation, and promote learning through social mediation (Gee 2007; Kirkley and Kirkley 2005; Reese 2007). Games can also facilitate reflective practice (Gee 2007). Through role-playing activities, players have the opportunity to probe a virtual world, form a hypothesis about what things mean given particular scenarios, reprobe the world with a new hypothesis in mind, and rethink their original hypothesis. This process mirrors how children learn. Games have been shown to teach strategy, encourage problem solving, foster engagement in socially cognitive rich interactions, and deepen understanding of complex issues (Gee 2007; Jenkins 2004). Furthermore, "games that require students to solve complex social problems lay the groundwork for them to develop 21st century skills. In addition to systems thinking, those skills include teamwork, creative problem solving, and time management" (MacArthur Foundation 2010, 20). Through situated cognition, players learn to recognize patterns and develop mastery in those patterns. Humans tend to reason more effectively when basing their rationale on patterns as opposed to abstract principles detached from experience (Gee 2007).

Social media is also tremendously varied and difficult to define. In most general terms, social media refer to web-based and mobile tools that facilitate communication. Social media are characterized by user-generated content and fluid structure. According to *Wikipedia*, a social media "collaborative project," social media services focus on some or all of seven functional building blocks (identity, conversations, sharing, presence, relationships, reputation, and groups). Common social media tools include email, instant messaging, crowd sourcing, blogs and microblogs (e.g., Twitter), content communities (e.g., YouTube), virtual games (e.g., *World of Warcraft*), wikis, and podcasts.

And finally a word about play is in order. A playful orientation might at first seem inappropriate to our readers. We may joke in class or devise interactive classroom exercises, but universities are not generally viewed as playful environments. Salen and Zimmerman (2004) distinguish between three categories of play: (1) *gameplay*—the formalized interaction that occurs within the structure of a game; (2) *ludic activities*—informal play activities that do not necessarily take place within the confines of a game; and (3) *being playful*—a mindset or attitude that extends beyond physical activities and speaks to a spirit of playfulness that can be incorporated into speech, writing, or activities. In chapters 5 and 8, Tracy Fullerton and Katie Salen highlight the complexity of defining, understanding, and evaluating the implications "play" has on how universities foster learning, innovation, and citizenship through games and social media. It is our hope that understanding the value of play pushes readers to rethink how teaching occurs in postsecondary settings and the implications of playful approaches on learning at multiple levels.

What's in the Book?

Despite the potential of institutions of higher education to harness innovation, until now colleges and universities have shied away from addressing the growth of games and social media. The rapid pace of change affects all postsecondary stakeholders. Hence, we put together a group of contemporary thinkers in the fields of higher education, games and social media, and evaluation to frame key issues and stimulate dialogue in an ever-changing digital landscape. Over the course of the book, educational researchers, game theorists, and learning assessment experts reflect on the role of games and social media in higher education and how they envision changes in the future. Collectively, we address the following questions: How might games and social media address the challenges facing postsecondary institutions? What do school administrators, professors, and related practitioners need to know in order to evaluate how they might benefit from games and social media? When might stakeholders capitalize on social media or games to more effectively engage students? What salient concerns exist when integrating games and social media into postsecondary learning environments?

Part I of the book focuses on the current landscape of postsecondary education. Authors establish a foundation for examining the challenges facing postsecondary institutions, the complex nature of increasing degree attainment for various populations, approaches to boosting college readiness across students, and the role that games and social media are currently playing in higher education and college access fields.

In chapter 1 Bill Tierney argues that higher education is undergoing the most significant changes it has faced since World War II. Although previous eras have caused economic downturns and momentary stagnation, this era is particularly noteworthy. The recession and constricted state budgets have caused many states to provide less revenue to public institutions. At the same time, there is a pressing need for more students to participate in some form of postsecondary education. We have seen the rapid rise of for-profit higher education. Technology is also transforming the delivery of college courses and degrees. As the number of online universities increases, there is a dilemma about how to gauge their effectiveness: Should they be encouraged to expand or be overregulated to constrict their growth? The chapter outlines the challenges in the postsecondary sector, considers the forces that are reshaping higher education, and suggests where these changes may lead. Ultimately, Tierney calls into question the role of disruptive technologies in transforming higher education, university governance, and academic freedom. He concludes the chapter with suggestions for how to move forward given a disruptive future.

Laura Perna in chapter 2 adds to the discussion by highlighting calls from multiple fronts to increase educational attainment of the U.S. population in order to meet global competitiveness goals and associated work force needs. Not all, however, agree with the need for increased educational attainment. After reviewing arguments on both sides of this important higher-education debate as well as trends in college access, completion, and attainment, the chapter concludes that the United States must improve educational attainment particularly for students from low-income families, blacks, and Hispanics. Perna underlines the importance of fostering academic preparation and easing concerns about college affordability. But she also suggests that a possible way to improve access is through decreasing informational barriers. She draws a connection between college access and digital technology by suggesting that the latter might offer solutions to ensuring broader access to college information to underserved communities. The chapter culminates by outlining the forces that must be addressed in order to improve educational attainment among these important, historically marginalized groups.

David Conley and Mary Seburn's chapter asserts that being prepared to succeed in postsecondary education is more complex and multidimensional than simply enrolling in challenging classes, getting good grades, and scoring well on college entrance or placement exams. Students must be equipped with cognitive strategies that include a range of disciplinary, transitional, and self-regulatory skills necessary to learn effectively and efficiently in postsecondary education. Students who are proficient in these areas are more likely to succeed in college than their peers. How high school programs of study and classroom instruction can be designed to address the necessary components of college and career readiness is an emerging issue in research. Student control and ownership of learning that enables the independence and self-reliance necessary to succeed beyond high school is of critical importance. This chapter offers suggestions that are framed within the larger conceptual framework of the four keys to college and career readiness. Conley and Seburn acknowledge that social media have come to play a significant role in how students learn about and select colleges. They also discuss the potential that games and simulations might play in cultivating more nuanced understandings of college selection and career awareness.

In the fourth chapter, Corwin provides an overview of the types of games and social media prevalent in postsecondary education as they pertain to students, faculty, librarians, and administrators. Exploring the tools available to each stakeholder group gives way to a broader discussion about how games and social media are changing the way we communicate, socialize, recruit, learn, assess, and create knowledge within institutions of higher education. Corwin poses the question: Given a rapidly changing postsecondary landscape with multiple moving parts, how do we rethink the role of colleges and universities in structuring opportunities for students to interact with each other, professors, and other institutional agents in meaningful ways? As social media evolves and games gain prevalence, we are forced to rethink social interactions, learning, and the production of knowledge. Corwin argues that fostering digital literacy and digital citizenship should become an integral component of K–16 education.

Part II shifts the focus onto games, social media, participatory culture, and play. Chapters can be read independently in order to gain insight into particular themes. Read together, part II orients the reader to the complex and dynamic ways in which games, social media, and play can cultivate learning. Chapter authors draw links to higher education through concrete examples of games and social media from the postsecondary sector and broader examples targeting K–12 or intergenerational audiences. Contributors portray games and play as multifaceted and share a critical analysis of what makes a good game. When games are tasked with simply delivering information such as that found in a textbook, they become dry and static, removed from their engagement potential. And when they are created to mimic a classic skill drill or other traditional teaching methods that lack playful interaction, they become the worst kind of "edutainment." But if we take the time to investigate what games do well, rather than trying to make them fill the same purpose as a book or examination, we find that they contain their own kind of potentials—potentials that are deeply connected to learning. For example, some actions for which games are well suited include providing players with the opportunity to engage in complex situations; building capacity for problem solving; defining questions and interests around subject matter; and developing identity, social connections, and aspirations both in and out of the play space. Bringing games to compelling learning environments radically changes not only the learning process but what is learned and the emotional connection to that learning. Through connected, collaborative play experiences, social interaction, and peer mentorship, players can grapple with ideas in a dynamic environment and relate their current educational situation to future possibilities. It is our hope that the chapters in part II will push readers to think about how innovative and playful approaches might be integrated into postsecondary education and used to address the challenges described in part I.

In chapter 5, Tracy Fullerton points out that games clearly offer great potential for learning and assessment, but those who look to them to scale existing teaching methods or to communicate traditional curricular content are apt to be disappointed; because what games offer to learners is not better access to old school methods and content, but rather a reformulation of the entire learning experience—its dynamics, pedagogical approaches, content, and outcomes. Fullerton grounds her discussion in real-life examples of meaningful gameplay. This chapter defines key attributes of games that can become effective learning situations and explores how playful interactions lead to mastering concepts and strategies embedded within game mechanics. Fullerton challenges the reader to examine the motivation of learners and to devise ways to lure them into challenging and evocative learning experiences. In doing so, we can harness the potential of games and craft meaningful playful experiences.

In chapter 6, Henry Jenkins and Adam Kahn call attention to the mismatch between informal learning that occurs outside of schools and the more formalized learning that universities recognize and reward. They offer reflections on the uncharted territory of "open laptop" exams as a means to explore how faculty are responding to changes in learning resulting from networked environments. This tangible example pushes educators to consider how to cultivate skills in students for sharing knowledge, trusting knowledge shared by others, and capitalizing on diverse expertise and backgrounds of their colleagues. The authors discuss how collective intelligence, transactive memory, and affinity spaces offer a framework for addressing the complexity of open laptop exams and related implications for learning in general. The chapter pushes readers to consider how we constitute the classroom as a knowledge community and what conditions should be present in university courses so that they facilitate effective learning.

James Gee highlights in chapter 7 how institutions of higher education might learn from well-designed, well-mentored problem-solving spaces found in certain online games. Gee argues that passionate affinity spaces (PAS) connect people by common interests and passion, provide opportunities to interact around complex issues in a space that values high-quality content, and foster meaningful interactions. Accordingly, they offer the potential for intergenerational learning, participation from a spectrum of participants (novice to experts), fluidity in leadership, and reciprocal participation. Gee encourages the reader to draw connections between the potential for learning and the creation of knowledge inherent in these spaces, and he questions how universities might structure learning opportunities to take advantage of the passion of their students.

Katie Salen's chapter extends beyond games for learning in the traditional sense of designing games with educational content. Instead, Salen explores strategies for using the fundamentals of game design and play as the basis for a vision of learning that is student centered, engaging, social, and problem based; in other words—situated and game-like. This approach to learning draws from what we know games do best: situate players into inquiry-based, complex problem spaces that are scaffolded to deliver just-in-time learning and to use data that assist players in understanding how they are doing, what they need to work on, and where to go next in learning processes. It is an approach that creates, above all else, a need to know—a need to ask why, how, and with whom? Reimagining teacher practice within such a model is critical, and the chapter examines new forms of collaboration with game designers—producing new learning tools, activities, and assessments. Salen speculates on how game-like learning might be leveraged to change the way we think about the purposes of education and the challenges young people face to survive and thrive in an increasingly complex, globalized world.

In parts I and II, chapter authors provide an overview of the current state of higher education and of the potential of games and social media to foster learning. Part III contributors offer nuanced ways to consider evaluating games and social media in higher-educational contexts. Authors tackle the utility of games and social media by highlighting specific aspects of gameplay, among them, how gender, social capital, and effective design influence learning. The perspectives shared in part III are intended to inform readers' critical understanding of the issues and provide them with scaffolding for informed evaluation of games and social media—and their usefulness in practice.

In chapter 9, Valerie Shute, Matthew Ventura, Yoon Jeon Kim, and Lubin Wang explain how transformative digital learning tools have the potential to support the development of a variety of knowledge and skills with potential for the global workplace. The authors outline several core principles of good video games, overview theoretical approaches that support video games as vehicles for learning, and provide ample examples to guide readers. For example, the authors propose that persistence and collaboration fostered through gameplay mirror skills and attributes necessary for success in higher education and career. The chapter proposes a framework for evaluating the effects of games on learning. Authors argue that competencies cultivated through gameplay—such as causal reasoning and systems thinking—have significant ramifications for twenty-first-century work force skills and should be considered as viable tools in educational settings. They share various models of assessment including stealth assessment and the value of conscientiousness and persistence on learning.

Nicole Ellison, Donghee Wohn, and Carrie Heeter suggest in chapter 10 that games have the potential to support college access and academic success goals because they can encourage the development of communication and knowledge-acquisition skills in meaningful and engaging ways. The social skills and relationships that players develop through and around gameplay can teach numerous social skills and strategies including teamwork, leadership, social support provision and requests, collaborative learning, and information seeking, which are critical components of college access and success. This chapter employs a communication-focused perspective to illuminate the opportunities social games afford as potential sites for social capital exchange and formation through processes such as informal learning, knowledge sharing, and relationship development. The authors outline several aspects of gameplay that might promote these dynamics, such as shared goals, reciprocal helping activities within the game, and social interactions outside of the game. Authors suggest how socially relevant interaction with both weak ties and close connections leads to opportunities for social capital accrual both within and outside of the game. Connected to the themes of play described in part II—and tremendously applicable to enhancing postsecondary experiences—this chapter also asserts the benefits derived from having *fun* through sociable gaming. The chapter concludes with thoughts on the implications of social network games for the higher-education community.

In chapter 11, Gisele Ragusa suggests that games have great potential to support learning through collaboration, although gender impacts this collaboration and its interaction. The chapter takes an advocacy stance and posits that social media and games can play an important and transformative role in equalizing the playing field across genders. Role-based assumptions have the potential for influencing the power relationships among game players. Social networking sites are seen as opportunities for girls and women to be mentored using equity pedagogy so that they are empowered to succeed in college and ultimately the workplace. Gameplay may serve as an optimal learning "environment" for analyzing the experiences that enable equity among genders and opportunities for both women and men to learn and practice equity through role-play and character (or avatar) identity development. This chapter explores the relationship among gender, role assignment, power relationships, and gameplay. In particular, Ragusa explores the role of stereotypic factors including hypersexuality in characterization, gender roles, and their influence on peer relationships, and cyberbullying. Ragusa focuses on what is optimal for learning interactions for boys and girls via mediation.

In chapter 12, Steven Weiland offers a distinct perspective and calls into question the popularity of digitally inspired reform. Weiland problematizes the intersection of literacy, learning, and technology by challenging the evidence for the educational "transformation" inspired by digital resources. He reflects on how we *really* know if students are learning as a result of games or social media. Weiland offers contrasting student experiences of technology. In one poignant example, he underlines the value of book reading, given the overwhelming migration of postsecondary reading to tablets, laptops, and mobile devices. Weiland voices concern over the ramifications for students of being "continually connected" and the devaluing of autonomous work. He challenges the reader to consider the scale, speed, and logistics of how we adopt technology and foster new literacies—a theme that harkens back to Tierney's discussion of disruptive technologies in chapter 1.

Throughout the volume, contributors discuss the challenges inherent in implementing policy and practice related to games and social media. We address contemporary issues including ways that universities may respond to the continuous and rapid pace of change related to games and social media. We do not intend for this book to outline a formula for implementing technology or games into higher-education curricula. Rather we hope to stimulate dialogue about positive attributes of games and social media as well as highlight the dilemmas associated with digital tools. In doing so, we aim to move debate about the best ways to ensure higher rates of college completion to the forefront, including a focus on relevant and engaging teaching and learning pedagogies.

Individuals frequently assume that certain aspects of daily life always have been part of daily life. If "digital immigrant" readers of this book had said when they were in college, "my mouse died," they would most likely have been referring to a pet (albeit a strange pet). Two generations ago, if someone talked about the "web," they most likely were referring to spiders. YouTube is less than a decade old. As we embarked on writing this book, Facebook had just gone public with 845 million active monthly users, 2.7 billion likes and comments per day and 100 billion friendships. A few months later, when we were copyediting the first draft of the book, Facebook users had already surpassed 900 million. Fast-forward several more months to our second round of revisions: monthly Facebook users topped one billion. In a letter to investors, Mark Zuckerberg outlines how the social mission of Facebook was "inspired by technologies that have revolutionized how people spread and consume information" (Kessler 2012). Zuckerberg points out that the printing press and television did not merely make communication more efficient but transformed society by giving people a voice and fostering progress. Ultimately, Zuckerberg suggests, these innovations "changed the way society was organized. They brought us closer together" (Kessler 2012). In many ways, universities fulfill a similar function; by cultivating and disseminating new knowledge, by pushing innovation, and by facilitating collaborations, they bring people together in ways that change society. In what follows, we explore how postsecondary institutions, digital tools, and play converge to push an agenda that has the potential of improving higher education.

REFERENCES

Baym, Nancy. K. 2010. *Personal Connections in the Digital Age: Digital Media and Society Series.* Malden, MA: Polity Press.

California State University (CSU). 2011a. "California State University, Fall 2010, Regularly Admitted, First-Time Freshmen Proficiency, and Remediation Combined Campus and Systemwide." Last modified May 24. http://www.asd.calstate.edu/performance/combo /2010/index.shtml.

———. 2011b. "Graduation Rates by Campus, First-Time Full-Time Freshmen." Last modified October 3. http://www.asd.calstate.edu/csrde/ftf.htm.

Corwin, Zoë B., and William G. Tierney. 2012. *Interdisciplinary Collaboration for College Access and Success in an Age of Technological Innovation.* Arlington: Center for K–16 Education Policy and Research, University of Texas.

Gee, James Paul. 2007. *What Video Games Have to Teach Us about Learning and Literacy.* New York: Palgrave Macmillan.

Goldin, Claudia, and Lawrence F. Katz. 2008. *The Race between Education and Technology.* Cambridge, MA: Harvard University Press.

Jenkins, Henry. 2004. "The Cultural Logic of Media Convergence." *International Journal of Cultural Studies* 7:33–43.

Kessler, Sarah. 2012. "Zuckerberg to Potential Shareholders: Facebook Is on a Social Mission." Accessed March 1. http://mashable.com/2012/02/01/facebook-ipo-letter/.

Kirkley, Sonny E., and Jamie R. Kirkley. 2005. "Creating Next Generation Blended Learning Environments Using Mixed Reality, Video Games and Simulations." *TechTrends for Leaders in Education & Training* 49(3):42–89.

MacArthur Foundation. 2010. *Re-imagining Learning in the 21st Century.* Chicago.

McDonough, Patricia. 2005. *Counseling and College Counseling in American's High Schools.* Arlington, VA: National Association for College Admission Counseling.

Obama, Barack H. 2009. "Remarks of President Barack Obama." Address to Joint Session of Congress, February 24.

Palfrey, Jeffrey, and Urs Gasser. 2008. *Born Digital: Understanding the First Generation of Digital Natives.* New York: Basic Books.

Parker, Kim, Amanda Lenhart, and Kathleen Moore. 2011. *The Digital Revolution and Higher Education: College Presidents, Public Differ on Value of Online learning.* Washington, DC: Pew Research Center. Accessed May 10, 2012. http://www.pewsocialtrends.org/2011/08 /28/the-digital-revolution-and-higher-education/.

Reese, Debbie. D. 2007. "First Steps and Beyond: Serious Games as Preparation for Future Learning." *Journal of Educational Multimedia and Hypermedia* 16:283–300.

Rideout, Victoria. J., Elizabeth A. Vandewater, and Ellen A. Wartell. 2003. *Zero to Six: Electronic Media in the Lives of Infants, Toddlers and Preschoolers*. Washington, DC: Henry J. Kaiser Family Foundation. http://www.kff.org/entmedia/upload/Zero-to-Six-Electronic -Media-in-the-Lives-of-Infants-Toddlers-and-Preschoolers-PDF.pdf.

Salen, Katie, and Eric Zimmerman. 2004. *Rules of Play: Game Design Fundamentals*. Cambridge, MA: Massachusetts Institute of Technology.

Siwek, Stephen E. 2010. *Video Games in the 21st Century: The 2010 Report*. Washington, DC: Entertainment Software Association. Accessed April 12, 2012. http://www.theesa.com /facts/pdfs/VideoGames21stCentury_2010.pdf

Thomas, Douglas, and John S. Brown. 2011. *A New Culture of Learning: Cultivating the Imagination for a World of Change*. Scotts Valley, CA: CreateSpace.

PART ONE

What Is the Current Landscape of Higher Education?

CHAPTER ONE

The Disruptive Future of Higher Education

WILLIAM G. TIERNEY

Many have spoken about the changes that academe faces, but these changes often have been phrased in terms of some distant future. How we construct time in an age-old organization frequently gets measured in decades rather than days. A university's review of the general education curriculum, for example, may seem thoughtful and deliberative to the faculty and administration if it extends over a year or two and gets enacted a few years after the final committee has agreed to the changes. Any changes to the curriculum also are usually more modest than dramatic. Some courses may get added or subtracted, or a new theme may be created, but the new plan looks like an updated, possibly improved, old plan.

Strategic plans or reviews of programs have followed a similar trajectory. Administrators propose a study to improve the institution or to provide direction, and members of the faculty study the problem during the academic year with an appropriate interlude over the summer. Eventually recommendations arrive, and they are critiqued and modified by the vice president or president and finally become policy. Changes that frequently appear exceedingly modest to an outsider may have engendered earnest and outraged debate by those involved in the undertaking.

More recently, postsecondary institutions have been hit with a wave of fiscal problems because of the Great Recession. Because states have had to cut their budgets, the postsecondary sector has had to respond to less revenue than had been anticipated. The response, however, has been incremental change rather than sweeping reform. Tuition has risen. Enrollments have been cut. Course size has increased. Summer sessions have been cut or eliminated.

More out-of-state students have been accepted because they pay more than in-state students. I do not mean to belittle such actions, and I am fully aware of the belt-tightening that has occurred.

But such responses are in keeping with the traditional ways that higher education has functioned. A downturn in the economy and, in turn, state revenue suggests to postsecondary leaders and the faculty that a few modest changes begrudgingly must be enacted. The changes will continue until the latest economic storm has passed, and then our postsecondary institutions can return to business as usual. But what if the current state of higher education is the new normal? What if the changes that have been talked about as someday happening at some future moment when all of us are retired is about to happen tomorrow? The purpose of this chapter is to begin an argument that Laura Perna and Zoë Corwin extend in their chapters: these changes are about to happen, or actually are happening now, and they are necessary if America is to remain competitive. The changes will impact everyone—from how students study to how teachers teach and what administrators do and oversee.

I wish to consider how one particular aspect of higher education—social media—might be used to grapple with the new normal. What I mean by the "new normal" is my focus here. The point is less that administrators will need to use social media, although it is certainly true, and more that the technology of learning is undergoing a reformation. We now have the ability to go beyond the classroom, and to expand the modalities of how we teach. In doing so, our reach can be exponential. If learning, as the central activity of any postsecondary institution, is going to undergo revolutionary changes, then the infrastructure and administrative tasks and functions that support and surround learning of necessity will need to change.

Current Constraints on the System
Capacity and Fiscal Constraints

The United States has, or soon will have, a postsecondary crisis on its hands. High-wage jobs demand an educated work force. By 2025, the country faces an estimated shortfall of 23 million workers with skills learned in college (Lumina Foundation for Education 2009). In a previous era, such a prediction might have led to an increase in the country's existing public colleges and universities as well as plans to build new campuses. States, when in good economic shape, once sought ways to expand via new campuses and increased postsecondary participation. In California, for example, in 2002 when the state was flush with funds and still thought in a traditional manner about the delivery of teaching, California State University (CSU) Channel Islands opened as the twenty-third campus in the CSU system, and in 2005 the University of California (UC) system opened a new campus in Merced.

Much has changed in the past decade. Demand has outpaced capacity, and the fiscal resources of states have evaporated. The result is that most of the public postsecondary sectors in our states are over capacity with regard to enrollment. Even the states' newer campuses and branch campuses face fiscal constraints which prevent them from expanding in a manner that will solve the enrollment-capacity dilemma.

To exacerbate the problem, as President Obama and others have pointed out, the United States now lags behind other industrialized countries with regard to college participation and attainment (see table 1.1). For 2006, the most recent year for which there are complete data, the United States was ranked third in the percentage of the population aged 25–64 that had earned a degree, but fourteenth in the percentage of graduates among traditionally aged students (OECD 2009, 2010). The country is falling behind in the global race for human capital development, and that places the country at risk. The president, as well as the Lumina Foundation and the Bill and Melinda Gates Foundation, have called for the United States to regain competitiveness over the next decade and to once again be the number one nation in the world in terms of college access and attainment. For the United States to reach such an ambitious goal, the states and their institutions must change in numerous ways—and not only by increasing the number of students who attend a postsecondary institution. Postsecondary institutions also need to work with high schools to increase the number of students who are college ready, increase the number of students who are retained once they are in college, increase the number of students who transfer from two- to four-year institutions, and increase the number of students

TABLE 1.1

United States Tertiary Education Performance and Ranking, 2009–2010

Indicator	Percentage	Ranking
Attainment rate, ages 25–64	39.5	3rd
Entry rate, first-time entrants as % of population	64.0	9th
Graduation rate, as % of graduates to population at typical age of graduation	35.5	14th

Source: OECD 2009, 2010.

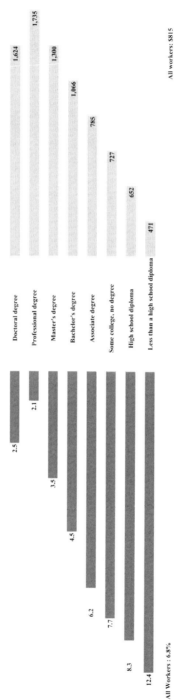

Unemployment rate in 2012 (%)

Median weekly earnings in 2012 ($)

	Unemployment	Median earnings
Doctoral degree	2.5	1,624
Professional degree	2.1	1,735
Master's degree	3.5	1,300
Bachelor's degree	4.5	1,066
Associate degree	6.2	785
Some college, no degree		727
High school diploma	7.7	652
Less than a high school diploma	8.3	471
	12.4	

All Workers : 6.8%

All workers: $815

Figure 1.1. Unemployment rate and median weekly earnings by education level, 2012. (*United States Bureau of Labor Statistics* 2013)

who spend less time in college. In other words, our institutions must be more efficient while they improve upon the product that the consumer (aka student) is getting—a college education.

Why does the country need more workers with postsecondary certificates or college degrees? The United States Bureau of Labor Statistics (2012) has pointed out that unemployment rates are much lower for college graduates and wages are substantially higher (see Figure 1.1). College graduates, for example, earn almost twice as much per hour as high school graduates. Not only do college graduates earn more, but the need for a better-educated work force will continue to grow. If the country does not address this need immediately there will not be enough working adults with some form of postsecondary education to meet the projected demand for workers with more than a high school degree.

Such news is not new. Consider, for example, employment projections and needs for a state such as California (table 1.2). The Georgetown University Center on Education and the Workforce, for example, projects that by 2018 California will need 61% of its workers to have some form of a postsecondary education in order to meet work force demands. Because of the expected retirement of well-educated workers, the assumption is that California will have 3.3 million jobs requiring postsecondary credentials. Current projections, however, show that the state will have a supply of only 2.2 million workers. Deficits in participation in higher education and attainment of a college degree are most stark among the state's racial and ethnic minorities. African American and Latino students remain the most at risk of dropping out of high school, not transitioning to college, or not completing a postsecondary degree (see figures 1.2 and 1.3,

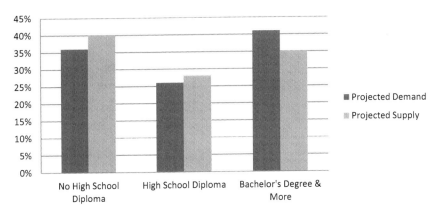

Figure 1.2. California work force needs for various education levels in 2025. (*Johnson 2012*)

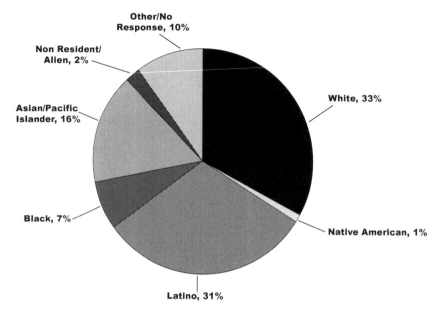

Figure 1.3. California enrollment: Access and equity. (*California Postsecondary Education Commission* 2012)

and tables 1.2 and 1.3). The implications for the country are significant. Because of this lack of skilled workers, the country will fall short in economic competitiveness.

The need for growth of participation in higher education in the United States requires considering various options. With sufficient funding through tax revenues or bonds, a state could, for example, build more campuses; but in addition to the cost that would be incurred, campus construction is a slow, deliberative process that would take the better part of a decade if discussions began today. For example, the University of California Regents voted to begin planning for a new campus in 1988. After expenditures of $500 million, the first day of classes at UC Merced was 17 years later, in 2005, and the addition to capacity was very slight; projections for them to complete the campus suggest that they need an additional $500 million, and even with this increase in funding the state would not see a dramatic increase in enrollment from new campus construction. Thus, to meet the enrollment needs that exist today and in the immediate future, a new campus seems unlikely because of fiscal constraints and inefficient because of immediate demands.

Increasing enrollment at existing campuses is unfortunately not possible given current funding realities and the structure of course offerings at our public

TABLE 1.2
Studies Projecting Shortfalls in Educated Workers in California

Source	Out-Year	Basis for the Goal	Degree Mix	Age Group	Target Goal	Gap in California above Current Production Levels
PPIC	2025	Labor force and California rank relative to other U.S. states	BA and above only	25–64	41%	1 million
Georgetown Center for Workforce and Economy	2018	Labor force	Some postsecondary, all credentials and degrees	25–64	61%	1,327,000
Lumina Foundation "Big Goal"	2025	International leadership	Some postsecondary, all credentials and degrees	25–34	60%	3.4 million
Obama administration	2020	International leadership	Some postsecondary, all credentials and degrees	25–34	California's share of a national goal to get to 60%, adjusted to reflect state variations in attainment	1.13 million
California Workforce Advisory Board	2016	California Workforce/skill needs	All skill areas, including on-the-job /certificate/degree	24–64	Not expressed as a target, good source for occupation-specific areas	California's needs for replacement workers as great as new job growth

Source: Tierney and Hentschke 2011.

TABLE 1.3
California Graduates, Dropouts, Higher Education Enrollment, 2009–2010

Classification	Amount
Grade 12 enrollment	488,388[a]
High school graduates	405,087
Graduation % of grade 12 enrollment	84.7%
Grade 9 to Graduate Rate	74.3%
Dropout Rate—4-year derived (grades 9–12)	17.5%
Dropout Rate—1-year rate (grades 9–12)	4.6%
California Higher Education Enrollment	284,446[b]

Source: California Department of Education 2012.
[a]Indicates data taken from 2010–2011, the latest year available.
[b]Indicates data taken from 2008–2009, the latest year available.

institutions. Fiscal constraints and programmatic inefficiencies disable students from completing their academic programs in a timely manner owing to the unavailability of courses needed for graduation. In fact, although studies show that during periods of economic downturn postsecondary enrollment demand increases (Taylor et al. 2010; Taylor et al. 2009), because of how the state funded public higher education and how the postsecondary institutions responded to the cutbacks, public postsecondary enrollment decreased between the 2008–2009 and 2009–2010 academic years at the California community colleges and the California State University and marginally increased at the University of California (see figure 1.4). The problem is lack of seats (supply), not lack of demand. The wrenching operational and cultural shifts needed to enable dramatic increases in public higher education appear impossible given the current policies and practices of its public-sector boards, administrators, and faculty.

Without an infusion of funding and changes to current scheduling practices that retard student progress through programs, the country's historical public and private campuses are unable to increase capacity significantly. Indeed, because of an inability to staff enough courses in a required major, many campuses now have "impacted" (oversubscribed) majors. These majors have additional admissions criteria for eligibility, requiring students to be admitted to the campus in an alternate major, or to work to meet supplementary admission criteria for their desired oversubscribed major. Similarly, because the community college system has experienced an influx of students, it lacks the means to enable them to complete their degrees or transfer in a timely manner. As a result, the time to achieve graduation exceeds five years on many campuses, and transfer rates from a community college to a four-year institution remain abysmally low.

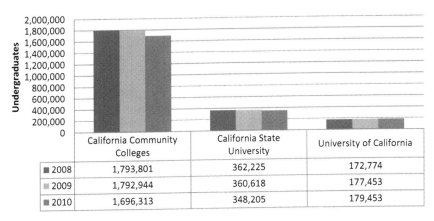

	California Community Colleges	California State University	University of California
▪ 2008	1,793,801	362,225	172,774
▪ 2009	1,792,944	360,618	177,453
▪ 2010	1,696,313	348,205	179,453

Figure 1.4. California year-to-year enrollment comparison. (*California Postsecondary Education Commission 2012*)

Many students transfer among institutions. However, among students enrolled in two-year institutions in Pennsylvania, only 13% graduated from a four-year institution (National Center for Public Policy and Higher Education 2011). Unfortunately, in recent years only a minority of students nationally who enrolled in a community college made it to upper-division coursework; 15% of students who started at two-year institutions enrolled in a four-year institutions four years later.

Clearly, there are internal decisions that education systems need to face over the next decade, all of which affect adjacent systems. More students need to graduate from high school. Alignment between what students take in high school and what students need in college must improve. Most of those who graduate from high school need to be college ready. The number of transfers from a community college to a four-year institution needs to increase proportionately and absolutely. Time-to-degree at four-year institutions needs to decrease. Retention in all institutions needs to increase. All of these trends suggest that changes around the edges, or doing more of what has been done in the past, will be an insufficient response to the enormous pressures the country faces.

Learning and Temporal Constraints

Although academic work certainly has changed in the past century, the same cannot be said for how teachers have taught college students. That is, the advent of the internet has created pervasive use of it, as well as related changes in the manner in which academics undertake research. The wealth of information that now sits at one's fingertips, the ability to communicate with one's colleagues in real time, and the manner in which data get accumulated, tracked, stored, and disseminated all have contributed significantly to the revolution in academic work. It is fair to say that Emile Durkheim, the father of modern sociology, Franz Boas, Durkheim's counterpart in anthropology, or Louis Pasteur and his counterparts in science would not recognize how their successors do their work today. What once took weeks or even years to accomplish now may take a matter of minutes or hours.

The same, however, cannot be said about college teaching. If John Dewey were to find himself in front of a classroom in any of America's college classrooms, he would likely know precisely what to do. A century ago two modalities existed with regard to college teaching, and those two forms have been maintained. Either the "sage on the stage" lectures in front of college students or the sage has a smaller seminar where he or she engages in Socratic dialogue with the students. To be sure, the accoutrement of college teaching have changed— from a chalkboard to a white board, from handwritten lecture notes to notes buttressed by PowerPoint presentations and the like. Minor changes always have occurred in the standard pedagogies, or what I define later as sustainable technology, that faculty employed to teach their students. What has not occurred is the transformation we have seen in the research arena.

We also have seen very little change with regard to the academic calendar, the timing and sequencing of classes, and the manner in which degrees are awarded. The largest temporal battles over the past half century have been rather minuscule. From time to time, members of the faculty have been consumed with epic arguments suggesting that their institution needs to shift from the semester system to the quarter system, or vice versa. Other arguments have ranged around whether to add or subtract a week to the academic calendar, or to give the Wednesday before Thanksgiving off and the like. When one is involved in such battles, they seem significant, and the ability to change them is a Herculean task often taking longer than a calendar year.

When compared to the contact hours per class that a course is supposed to meet in order to be considered a course, the changes in the academic calendar have been significant. That is, the credit hour, the core of academic life, is seemingly fixed in concrete. One three-credit course at an institution that has a semester that meets for 15 weeks will have 45 contact hours. Although a professor may try to be creative with the contact hours, the norm is that a professor will meet the class for the allotted time. The time of the class is largely determined by the registrar. That is, a three-unit class may meet for one three-hour bloc, or two 90-minute blocs, or perhaps three one-hour blocks. However, if a professor believes that a class should meet five days a week for two weeks, then skip a week, and the next week meet for one full day, such a plan would be a scheduling nightmare. Any campus has a set number of classrooms and a set number of classes. The result is that courses actually get scheduled around the availability of physical space rather than any pedagogical logic. The result is that my class schedule from 1975 at Tufts University does not look very different from the classes undergraduates take today at the University of Southern California.

For traditional undergraduates classes are more often offered Monday through Friday (or actually Thursday, since students and faculty do not like classes on Fridays). Evening classes and weekend classes are exceptions to the norm, and a class that met after 10:00 p.m. and before 8:00 a.m. would likely be newsworthy for its unique temporal structure. Similarly, most students do not take classes in the summer, and there is frequently a disincentive for faculty to teach during the summer. The teaching load of faculty as stipulated by contact occurs between September and June.

A framework such as this inevitably places the instructor at the core of the undertaking. The assumption was that all students, more or less, learned the material at the same pace, and the grade a professor provided served as a proxy for learning. A student who received an "A" did better than a student who earned a grade of "B" or lower. Once a student had accumulated the stipulated number of credits—based on seat time and the professors' evaluations—then the student was deemed to have been educated and could graduate.

Such a structure may once have worked, especially when there were few options. If classes are seat bound within a physical setting, over a particular time frame, then what we have done makes sense. If the only way to assess learning is via the teacher in the class, which results in the accumulated assessments of a student's teachers and classes, then the credit hour makes sense. The assumption, of course, is that all students learn in similar fashion, and if they do not, then they need to adapt their learning styles to the few choices that are provided to them. The assumption of those of us who have chapters in this book is that the status quo cannot hold much longer in our traditional postsecondary institutions. We freely acknowledge that during the twentieth century the United States created a postsecondary system that was the envy of the world. The challenge in the twenty-first century, however, is how one might adapt to the changing realities of the marketplace by utilizing new technologies that already have transformed other markets such as the news media.

Disrupting the System
Defining Disruptive Technology

Although I have bemoaned the incremental and slow pace of change in the academy, I would be mistaken if I portrayed postsecondary institutions as static entities that never change. Postsecondary organizations have changed, albeit insufficiently for the times. Such a point is important because organizations always change; the question is what kind of changes are occurring and are they enabling the institutions to respond adequately to the various forces that exist. Clayton Christensen and colleagues have written about one particular form of change and termed it "sustaining" innovation (Christensen et al. 2011; Christensen, Horn, and Johnson 2008). When typewriters went from manual to electronic models, the customers looked on the change as a significant improvement. As Christensen explains, "Companies introduce what for them are sustaining innovations; as long as an innovation helps a company make better products that it can sell for better profits, the company figures out a way to get it done" (Christensen, Horn, and Johnson 2008, 49). The company is not looking for a product that has not been invented or desperately needed. Rather, the company is simply trying to meet the needs of its consumers and hopefully expand its market share. A better product means that the consumers will be happier and presumably more consumers will buy it.

Traditional colleges and universities might be thought of as organizations that call upon sustainable technologies. Course readers, for example, were once mimeographed and then photocopied. Students once went to a bookstore and waited in long lines to buy books, whereas today they can buy them online. Faculty used to have to go to the university library to get a book, and today the book can be ordered over the internet and delivered to one's office. PowerPoint replaced audiovisual equipment to buttress class lectures. These sorts of examples are improvements on what once existed, and the consumers (students and faculty) have looked on these changes as an improvement from what once took place.

Disruptive technology, however, is entirely different. The consumer and customer are not looking for a new technology because they cannot envision it. Those who typed on manual typewriters celebrated the creation of an electronic typewriter, but they did not wonder if computers might make life even better. Customers who used the telegraph enjoyed its improvement and expansion, but did not wonder about how to speak to someone on a telephone. Disruptive technology, according to Christensen, follows a similar path: inventors develop something that is unrefined, expensive, and of interest to very few. Eventually, the small cadre of people who are working on the technology is able to improve the product and bring down cost. The result is that the technology spreads rapidly; the previous product loses its appeal and the company is likely to go out of business. Once the disruptive technology takes hold, however, usually with a new company, then sustainable technology occurs again. Consider the trajectory of the personal computer—customers had no idea what to expect, and very few became interested in the new product at first. However, within a matter of years computers swept the country, and typewriters went out of fashion. The first portable computer weighed about 20 pounds; when the weight went down, customers rejoiced just as they had done when the manual typewriter went electronic.

Disruptive technology also starts at the margins. Automobile companies, for example, produced a line of cars from inexpensive to luxury. When a new company entered the market, it produced only one cheap version. Established companies such as General Motors and Ford did not think it was worth their while to compete with Toyota's compact car, the Corona. The major car companies ceded that territory to Toyota, which in turn, enabled the new company to turn a profit and to bring the price of its cars down, which generated further sales. Eventually the company branched out into larger cars, and today it has a full array of cars from compact models to its luxury brand, the Lexus.

The same sort of pattern has happened for more than a century. The telephone started slowly and then swamped the telegraph. Whereas at one point only a privileged few had a telephone or one went to a center to make a phone call, in a relatively short time frame telephones became ubiquitous. The telegraph still existed but became secondary. Televisions originally were expensive until a breakthrough technology enabled them to be made smaller and more cheaply. In a matter of years the middle and working classes were able to own something that had been in the province of the rich. A decline in cost enabled greater numbers to buy the product, which in turn enabled more emphasis to be placed on improving the technology.

Thus, disruptive technology involves a product or sector of interest at first to only a select group of individuals, because the product is either expensive or cumbersome to operate, but which then undergoes improvements to the point that the innovation becomes easy to operate and relatively inexpensive.

The result is that more individuals buy the product, the cost drops even more, further improvements occur, and eventually the new product overwhelms the market. Those who built their reputations on the previous technology are unprepared for the new competitors and unable to bring their traditional product in line with the disruptive technology. Most often such technologies occur in new or stand-alone companies rather than in traditional ones. As Christensen explains, "Plugging a disruptive innovation into an existing business model never results in transformation of the model; instead, the existing model co-opts the innovation to sustain how it operates" (Christensen et al. 2011, 3).

Well-run existing organizations try to do what they are supposed to do: meet the needs of the consumer. They develop sustaining technologies that improve the current product and satisfy the customer. Customer satisfaction suggests that customers will return and bring new customers with them. The problem for existing organizations is that they neither try to nor can deal with disruptive innovations. Why would a company try to disrupt what they are doing well? Indeed, disruption requires the invention of a new product that involves processes that are different from those of a sustainable company. "That's not the way we do things around here" may make good sense in a profitable company, but such an observation is not the kind of comment one hears if disruptive technologies are being created. The consequences are often quite significant. Western Union fades as a company, and AT&T arrives. Smith Corona and Olivetti go out of business, as Microsoft and Apple become gigantic companies. Newspapers leave the stage, as Google and Facebook enter.

An additional observation is that disruptive technologies tend to occur in organizations that have a fundamental business model. Simply stated, business models are meant to serve and foster a particular business. A consulting firm consults; the consultants are trying to find a solution to a problem that has been identified. Faculty research might be thought of in this vein. Some external unit provides an individual or team the financial resources to study a problem. Such an undertaking is quite different from a service organization that offers a product to improve the quality of life of its customers. "Satisfaction guaranteed" might be something seen in a service organization but not a solution-focused organization. Colleges and universities also offer a service—the consumer presumably is better off after using the product. Finally, a membership organization has a fee for service. Christensen calls such organizations "facilitated user networks." The network itself is the vehicle, but the exchange value occurs through interactions of the customers with one another.

Disruptive technology generally occurs within a specific business, not a plethora of them. Traditional organizations, however, evolve. Different value propositions that derive from different business models are able to coexist with one another because the individuals involved in the undertaking are serving the various interests of the organization. Universities once were primarily teaching organizations (service), but throughout the twentieth century research, or the desire for constituents to undertake research, rose in importance (solutions). Recall, too, that regardless of institutional type, all four-year institutions reward research more than teaching. Thus, by the turn of the twenty-first century postsecondary institutions had conflated two business models where there once was one. Networked activities among students and faculty only added to the complexity of the organization.

The point is not that a mixture of business models is necessarily bad or fatal for all organizational types. Complex organizations such as Harvard or Stanford are not only successful at what they do but they also have served as organizational prototypes. Two problems have arisen, however. First, because these organizations have been so successful virtually all other postsecondary organizations have tried to evolve in a similar fashion. The result is a mixture of business models in all of our public and private postsecondary institutions and a conflation of institutional mission such that all postsecondary organizations are trying to move up the academic food chain. Imagine if the same sort of mimicry occurred in the service industry. McDonald's, Taco Bell, and other franchises would try to be Michelin-rated restaurants. Second, disruptive technology is least capable of happening in organizations that have multiple business models.

The moral of the story is that well-run companies that try to please their customers are always at risk of disruptive technology. Innovation in well-run organizations frequently occurs when individuals "think outside the box" to use a commonplace metaphor. Rather than routinize work and repeat what worked yesterday, analysts tend to applaud companies that are innovative and creative. However, disruptive technology is not simply creative and innovative. The point is less to think outside the box and instead to create a new box—or to question if it even is a box. Most traditional companies are not very good at creating new boxes because they are intent on improving upon the box that already exists; those who work in the organization also have become socialized in a manner that orients them toward maintaining the box. Further, new boxes do not happen very often. "Disruption" assumes that normal processes are in place and work relatively well. Thus, it is easy to dismiss those who say that significant change is coming as little more than Chicken Little saying that the sky is falling. And, quite frequently, those who claim the sky is falling are wrong—until it does.

Disruptive Technology in the Academy

The idea of disruptive technology is not a perfect fit onto the terrain of postsecondary education. Some will suggest, for example, that traditional organizations and disruptive organizations can certainly exist side by side rather than one driving out the other. Such an observation, however, might be said of disruptive technology in the automobile, computer, and other industries. While it is true that academe faces a capacity problem, one might wonder why a system in need of expansion cannot simply add more providers. The assumption might be that rather than one entity swamping another, the potential exists that old entities will maintain their customer base, while new ones create new customers. Ford and General Motors made that assumption about Toyota, as did Olivetti and Smith-Corona about the nascent computer industry.

Disruptive technology also refers to a technology; online learning and social media might be considered the technology, but certainly traditional colleges and universities are already using the technology. Some of the examples I have provided pertain to how traditional institutions have incorporated the technology into their daily interactions. Online courses are not entirely eschewed in traditional institutions, and the change over the past generation has been gradual and visible rather than abrupt and out of sight. One might analyze these changes, however, as more sustainable than disruptive.

Disruptive technology conceivably might need to be different if it were to sweep through postsecondary education. The use of technology certainly has the potential to disrupt the system, but not if the organizations embrace that technology rather than merely adapt it to their teaching and learning frameworks. For disruption to occur, two additional components need to take place. First, organizations may survive through adaptation, but in doing so, their core services and providers are entirely transformed or overwhelmed. Second, alternative providers may be more adept at providing a product in an entirely different manner that forces traditional organizations to appear outmoded and their product unsatisfactory. My sense is that both components are occurring.

Traditional colleges and universities came of age in the twentieth century, and faculty provided the primary means by which teaching and learning occurred. The faculty was also a central part of the governance of the institution. Faculty members were hired on tenure lines ostensibly in order to protect academic freedom. Technology, coupled with financial downturns, is in the process of transforming the academy. We now hire more adjunct and part-time faculty than full-time tenure-track faculty. In 2009–2010, only 48.7% of full-time faculty were tenured; during the same period, 47.8% of higher-education systems had tenure systems (United States Department of Education 2011). One outcome of having fewer tenure-track faculty on campus is that participation in governance has gone down. Of consequence, the importance of the faculty's voice has been lessened. Concomitantly, the idea of academic freedom as a central tenet of the academy is being brought into question or pushed to the side. Genteel universities where scholarly discourse was the coin of the realm are being supplanted by stripped-down, lean organizations that aim to bring students in, have them amass what they need to learn in as efficient a manner as possible, and then get them out the college door and into a job. Although individuals may still give lip service to critical inquiry or college as a time when a student "finds ones-self," such sentiments seem misplaced at a time when alternative providers are better able to recruit students and the traditional postsecondary provider—the state government—is less likely to provide fiscal support.

In the meantime, for-profit higher education has become the fastest-growing organization in the postsecondary universe. Career colleges have existed for more than a century but until the 1970s were still a microscopic part of the higher-education universe. In 1967 approximately 7 million students attended degree-granting institutions in the United States; fewer than 22,000 of these students, or less than one-third of 1%, attended for-profit institutions (Tierney and Hentschke 2007). Indeed, the term "for-profit college" was not generally employed; instead they were called career and technical colleges. The career colleges were privately owned and largely operated below higher education's radar screen. They were mostly unaccredited, seeking neither federal nor state financing. The situation began to change with the founding of the University of Phoenix in 1976—now America's second largest postsecondary institution, with more than 400,000 students (Tierney and Hentschke 2011).

Today, the mom-and-pop career shops of a half century ago still exist, but they are swamped by Phoenix and other publicly traded entities such as Corinthian Colleges Inc. and DeVry University, with more than 80,000 students each. They now account for more than 12% of the college-going population when a decade ago they were half that size. Although the for-profits have certainly come in for their fair share of criticism, they also are the companies best able to adapt to online technologies. Some companies, such as the University of Phoenix, have put literally hundreds of millions of dollars into creating online platforms, and they are adapting their teaching to online courses (Hentschke, Lechuga, and Tierney 2010). As opposed to having to train individuals such as tenured faculty wedded to previous methods, the for-profits simply hire (and fire) people according to the needs of the company. Their ability to scale up and down based on consumer need is remarkably swifter than most traditional institutions that spend a great deal of time determining if a program should be created and frequently never terminate a program—the result of which is a never-ending curricular expansion.

Phoenix and other institutions began to experiment with the meaning and purpose of higher education in ways that highlight a group trying to disrupt the system. Adults who work part-time are not simply the main focus of the institutions—they are a potentially huge customer base that traditional higher education has either ignored or disdained. These students do not need a campus and the related accoutrement—fitness and student centers, athletics, and so on. Rather than a smorgasbord of courses whose utility for future work is not apparent, such students take a finite number of classes, offered at convenient times and in convenient locations, and in as efficient and focused a manner as possible.

Faculty life is also very different. Tenure, shared governance, and academic freedom are absent. In traditional institutions the professor creates his or her syllabus, which results in the same course having very different foci, objectives, and goals, depending on the instructor. At the for-profits, the syllabi and teaching styles are standardized. Further, for-profit admissions practices are also entirely different from how traditional postsecondary institutions function. Rather than engage in a leisurely admissions process that begins in the summer prior to twelfth grade and culminates with an acceptance letter in the spring and a financial aid award letter soon after, the for-profit institutions speed up the process. They find potential consumers, try to convince them of the worth of the product, explain the financing that will enable them to attain it, and get them to sign up. Courses may begin in a manner of days.

When the for-profit industry started to grow, its intent was not to compete with traditional institutions—just as other disrupters did in other industries. The for-profits never went after traditional students or tried to emulate the traditional college model. Instead, they chose the low end of the market and have called upon a different metric of performance—the ability of the customer to get a job rather than a degree. Even today many in the traditional sector find any discussion of comparing how for-profits and traditional institutions function as absurd. Such observations, however, could be made in the same manner with regard to previous disruptive technologies. Those working on computers did not think their purpose was to drive typewriters out of business. Those who worked on typewriters saw little comparison between typewriters and what initially were gigantic mainframe computers. Few in the newspaper industry thought that the *Huffington Post* or the birth of blogging was going to supplant a centuries old profession. Those who began the *Huffington Post* were more interested in making use of a new technology rather than trying to kill an old one. Why, then, should those of us in higher education simply dismiss out of hand the growth of the for-profit industry, or assume that the processes involved in creating and delivering this new product will not also transform the traditional industry—or kill it?

Further, alternative providers are not only developing as for-profit organizations. Individuals are offering online courses on a scale that was unheard of only a decade ago. The thought, for example, that someone such as Peter Norvig from Stanford University might teach a mini-class to hundreds of thousands of students was unthinkable. Today, however, various individuals are endeavoring to offer such courses in ways that go far beyond the traditional "sage on a stage." StraighterLine is a company which is offering self-paced courses online and will offer students certificates. A former Stanford professor has given up his teaching position to start a company that will offer low-cost online courses. A recent list of the world's ten greatest players dealing with innovations in education listed only one educational organization—and that was a community college (Fast Company 2013). Such changes, if successful, suggest not only an alternative to traditional forms of teaching and learning but a revolution in how postsecondary education gets offered.

One strength of for-profits is that they do not mix business models, whereas traditional institutions do. Very few for-profits are complex entities. They do not do research; the reward structure for the faculty pertains to how good they do teaching their students. The institutions do not have a multitude of services that meet the needs of multiple clients. Even the course offerings are limited and finite rather than the comprehensive nature of so many traditional public and private colleges and universities. For-profits, then, have the potential for being the purveyors of disruptive technology, which in this case is online learning.

The growth of the for-profit industry, certainly not without criticism—often justified—has brought the companies significant profits. Many of those profits have gone back into improving the technology. The University of Phoenix, for example, spends more than $300 million a year on course improvement and improving its platform. By contrast, consider how little income gets put into improving teaching at a traditional college every year. Centers for teaching excellence on college campuses are famous for the low regard in which they are held and the meager incomes on which they operate.

One of the more confusing aspects of the higher-education industry, however, is that much of it is in the public domain. In 2009, more than 14 million students who participate in higher education attend a public institution (United States Department of Education 2011). Although the for-profit market has increased to 12%, the remaining 88% of the clientele attends non-profit institutions, public or private. The assumption has been that as a public good profit is not something to be calculated into how education gets offered. Coupled with the ethical lapses of some for-profits, the portrait is unclear about how traditional institutions might best respond.

One stance has been to simply ignore the upstart for-profits and assume that their growth is unrelated to the traditional postsecondary sector. Another stance is to function a bit like a cartel that keeps out new entities through regulatory procedures otherwise known as accreditation. Both stances have been the norm through the first decade of the twenty-first century. On the one hand, traditional institutions whether they are small liberal arts colleges or nationally ranked public and private institutions assumed that for-profit institutions had nothing in common with them. On the other hand, those who looked askance at postsecondary education being offered in shopping malls in unconventional ways have accrediting agencies at their disposal that had a particular definition of what the format, structure, and function of a traditional institution should be.

If for-profit institutions simply had a different business model or appealed to a new constituency, then one might not think of them as disruptive providers. However, as a sector they are arguably better than all other postsecondary institutions at understanding and utilizing the potential of social media and online learning. My assumption is that those of us in the traditional sectors ignore for-profits and social media at our own risk. Technology does not get cordoned off once it becomes disruptive; it will have implications for all of teaching and learning whether that occurs in a community college or a research university. And if formats, structures, and functions change, then it is the accrediting organizations that, rather than trying to keep the new barbarians out, are going to need to adapt. Hence, a purpose of this book is to look at how games and social media might function in the universe of postsecondary institutions.

Adapting to a Disruptive Future

Thomas and Brown (2011) have asked, "What happens to learning when we move from the stable infrastructure of the 20th century to the fluid infrastructure of the 21st century?" (7). The assumption of the authors in this book is that a great deal happens. Not only will our contemporary notions of play, games, and imagination change but so will the manner in which the university gets structured and the way it functions. An information network that provides unlimited access and resources to learn about anything cannot but shape how teaching and learning occur in the academy. And when nontraditional providers such as for-profit companies are leaders in developing this disruptive technology, then traditional providers such as public and private colleges and universities need to consider the implications not from a vantage point of disinterest but with the assumption that significant transformations are upon us.

The chapters that follow discuss how games and social media might function in the academy, and how they might be judged and evaluated. As academics, we are not so much cheerleaders for a new technology as we are innovators or observers of what we consider to be a disruptive technology. Most of us work in traditional colleges and universities; all of us have received diplomas from these institutions and, to varying degrees, have a great deal of respect and enthusiasm for academic organizations. We are convinced, however, that the academic "center cannot hold," to use Yeats's phrase from an earlier time. With that in mind, three suggestions might guide those of us involved in academic work: develop nontraditional partnerships, disrupt academic norms, and increase quality and decrease cost.

Develop Nontraditional Partnerships

Postsecondary organizations are too insular. Professors develop courses and argue among themselves what should be taught and how the courses should be structured. If we are to accept the implications of the following chapters, one logical outcome is that those who are most adept at utilizing social media need to be able to work with those in the academy, but not in a manner that stifles creativity or demands that nontraditional modes of inquiry fit within the traditional format. Fortunately, examples exist of what I am suggesting. Daniel Cohen, for example, at George Mason University, works in the Center for Digital History and New Media that reaches 16 million people. Burke Smith, of StraighterLine, and Sal Khan, of the Khan Academy, are the sort of entrepreneurs whom colleges and universities need to partner with rather than simply watch as they develop massive followings.

I am suggesting that the "go-it-alone" approach for which academics are so famous needs to be reversed if we heed the comments of the ensuing chapters. The strength of the academy is that we are deliberative and that we are able to conduct careful research to inform how effectively particular teaching pedagogies function. However, the future lies in cross-organization partnerships that will necessitate the academy departing from long-cherished norms about teaching and learning.

Disrupt Academic Norms

The traditional caution that the faculty has toward change will need to be refashioned. Familiar concepts such as a major, credit hours, contact hours, semesters, and terms are all going to need to be rethought. If one accepts the implications of the ensuing chapters, then how academic content gets delivered will need to be dramatically reconfigured. Those who change—significantly—will survive. For all but an elite few, those who do not change will not survive.

Perhaps such a dramatic statement seems unwarranted or overblown. Unfortunately, those on the losing end of other disruptive innovations—from the telegraph to the typewriter—most likely would have made the same argument. As I noted, a resistance or ignorance of disruptive technologies by no means implies that the company is being lackadaisical. Most often such companies are trying to improve their product through sustaining technology. But we are now at a moment when online learning is going to force a redefinition of college life, and how we deal with the sorts of arguments made in the next sections will suggest hard times or a newly developed academic plan that can take us into the future.

Increase Quality, Decrease Cost

Recall that the pattern of a disruptive technology is that in its infancy it is clunky and cumbersome; eventually the technology improves to a point where a mass market exists, so that resources can be put into improving the technology and lowering the cost. Higher education, however, has never worked that way. Costs always go up. Quality is elusive largely because it is in the mind of the professor who teaches the course. The assumption is that the student is knowledgeable because the professor says so.

Online learning, however, is now at the point where its increased usage will enable those who focus on developing the platforms to improve the delivery system even further. The creation of games has a high-end cost at the front end but then has the potential to drop in cost significantly as the game goes viral. Think of how many people use social media such as Facebook or LinkedIn today; rather than assume that such vehicles have no academic uses, consider how their potential might be harnessed by our institutions. If traditional postsecondary institutions are not able to figure out ways to utilize this new technology so that their costs go down as well, then they will be at risk. Similarly, as learning becomes more tied to skills needed for the job market, simply receiving a good grade in a class will be insufficient. A different metric of performance needs to be developed that will ensure that the customer-cum-student has the requisite skills to do a job. Overhead costs need to go down, and a better understanding of the correct business model to utilize needs to be put in place. Rather than try to do a multitude of tasks so that all institutions strive to be Harvard, a better understanding of one's value propositions will enable organizations to better meet the changing realities of the marketplace.

REFERENCES

Christensen, Clayton M., Michael B. Horn, Louis Caldera, and Louis Soares. 2011. *Disrupting College: How Disruptive Innovation Can Deliver Quality and Affordability to Postsecondary Education.* Washington, DC: Center for American Progress.

Christensen, Clayton M., Michael B. Horn, and Curtis W. Johnson. 2008. *Disrupting Class: How Disruptive Innovation Will Change the Way the World Learns.* New York: McGraw Hill.

Fast Company. 2013. "The World's Top 10 Most Innovative Companies in Education." Last modified February 11. http://www.fastcompany.com/most-innovative-companies/2013/industry/education.

Hentschke, Guilbert C., Vincente M. Lechuga, and William G. Tierney. 2010. *For-Profit Colleges and Universities: Their Markets, Regulation, Performance, and Place in Higher Education.* Sterling, VA: Stylus.

Lumina Foundation for Education. 2009. *Lumina Foundation's Strategic Plan: Goal, 2025.* Indianapolis. http://www.luminafoundation.org/wp-content/uploads/2011/02/Lumina_Strategic_Plan.pdf.

National Center for Public Policy and Higher Education. 2011. *Policy Alert: Affordability and Transfer; Critical to Increasing Baccalaureate Degree Completion.* San Jose, CA.

Organisation for Economic Co-operation and Development (OECD). 2009. *OECD Factbook, 2009: Economic, Environmental and Social Statistics.* Paris. doi:10.1787/factbook-2009-en.

———. 2010. *OECD Factbook, 2010: Economic, Environmental and Social Statistics.* Paris. doi:10.1787/factbook-2009-en.

Taylor, Paul, Richard Fry, Gabriel Velasco, and Daniel Dockterman. 2010. *Minorities and the Recession-Era College Enrollment Boom.* Washington, DC: Pew Hispanic Research Center.

Taylor, Paul, Richard Fry, Wendy Wang, Daniel Dockterman, and Gabriel Velasco. 2009. *College Enrollment Hits All-Time High, Fueled by Community College Surge.* Washington, DC: Pew Hispanic Research Center.

Thomas, Douglas, and John Seely Brown. 2011. *A New Culture of Learning: Cultivating the Imagination for a World of Constant Change.* Charleston, SC: CreateSpace.

Tierney, William G., and Guilbert C. Hentschke. 2007. *New Players, Different Game: Understanding the Rise of For-Profit Colleges and Universities.* Baltimore: Johns Hopkins University Press.

———. 2011. *Making It Happen: Increasing College Access and Participation in California Higher Education: The Role of Private Postsecondary Providers.* La Jolla, CA: National University System Institute for Policy Research.

United States Bureau of Labor Statistics. 2013. "Employment Projections: Education Pays . . ." Last modified on March 28, 2013. http://www.bls.gov/emp/ep_chart_001.htm.

United States Department of Education. 2011. *Digest of Education Statistics.* Washington, DC.

CHAPTER TWO

The Need to Increase College Enrollment and Completion

LAURA W. PERNA

This book describes the potential role of social media and games in improving college enrollment and completion. But do we really need to invest time, energy, and other finite resources into new approaches for addressing these outcomes? Although some (Adelman 2007) argue that the nation has solved the college access problem, this chapter concludes, after a review of available data and research, that the answer to this question is an emphatic *yes*. We agree with Tierney that for reasons of international competitiveness, work force readiness, and social justice, more work is required to improve college enrollment, as well as college degree completion and ultimate educational attainment. Greater attention is also needed to reduce the gaps in college enrollment and completion that continue to exist on the basis of students' family income, race or ethnicity, and other demographic characteristics. Moreover, the persisting need to improve college enrollment and completion for all students and to reduce gaps in these outcomes across groups suggests that traditional approaches for accomplishing these goals are not sufficient; innovative approaches that more effectively address the underlying barriers are required.

Approaches that take advantage of the pervasiveness of social media in today's society hold particular promise for addressing a primary force limiting college enrollment and completion, particularly for youth from groups that are historically underrepresented in higher education: the lack of relevant, usable, and appropriate information about college-related outcomes, processes, and requirements. Social media take multiple forms, including collaborative

Seher Ahmad assisted with gathering background materials for this chapter. I am grateful for her assistance.

projects (e.g., *Wikipedia*), "blogs, content communities, social networking sites, virtual game worlds, and virtual social worlds" (Kaplan and Haenlein 2010, 60). As Kaplan and Haenlein (2010) assert in an article on the challenges and opportunities of social media for businesses: "Social media allow firms to engage in timely and direct end-consumer contact at relatively low cost and higher levels of efficiency than can be achieved with more traditional communication tools" (67). Indeed, as Gee and Fullerton point out in their chapters in this volume, social media are not merely an effective tool for communication; games are "social" and provide the opportunity for learning in ways that have not been present in traditional teaching and learning environments.

To be effective, however, an approach that involves social media must recognize that access to and use of computers, the internet, and social media vary across groups. Despite the recent rapid growth in the availability and usage of the internet and related technologies, rates of access and usage continue to be lower among those from groups that could benefit most—namely the groups that are now relatively underrepresented in higher education.

Why Must We Increase Educational Attainment?

Efforts to increase the educational attainment of the U.S. population are not without controversy. A *Chronicle of Higher Education* (2009) article provides a useful summary of the range of perspectives on this issue. Some (e.g., Daniel Yankelovich) argue that all should attend, asserting that a postsecondary education is required for success in today's economy. But others (e.g., Bryan Caplan) believe that only those who are most academically qualified should enroll, given the low rates of completion for those who enter. And still others (e.g., Richard Vedder) believe that a college education is not necessary for most new jobs and thus assert that too many individuals are currently enrolling. In another useful synthesis of various dimensions of the debate, William Zumeta (2010) notes the reasons why some argue that efforts to produce a substantial increase in college graduates are not worthwhile. These reasons include the views that higher education does not increase the productivity of workers but merely sends a signal to employers that a college-educated individual has the characteristics and aptitude of a successful worker; and employers are inflating the level of education that is actually required for available jobs (Zumeta 2010).

Underlying both sides of the debate, however, is agreement about many of the basic facts (Zumeta 2010). While disagreeing about the implications of these facts, both sides recognize the importance of increasing educational attainment in order to improve the nation's international competitiveness, ensure that workers are ready for available jobs, and increase equity and social justice (Zumeta 2010).

As noted in chapter 1, the country needs to increase its degree production. To raise degree production to the level of leading nations, the United States must improve educational attainment of not only traditional-age students but also adults. The Council for Adult and Experiential Learning (CAEL 2008) warns that "32 states cannot catch up to the educational attainment levels of the best performing countries internationally by relying solely on strategies related to traditional-age students . . . educating adults must be part of the solution" (7). About one-third of the U.S. adult population (more than 59 million individuals) has no postsecondary education, and 20% of U.S. adults have some postsecondary education but no college degree (CAEL 2008).

Others argue that the educational attainment of the U.S. population must be raised to ensure that the nation's workers possess the education required to perform current and future jobs. While noting the challenges of classifying jobs by level of required education, Osterman (2008) concludes from his examination of available data that the demand for more highly skilled and educated workers is growing in the United States. Projections from the Bureau of Labor Statistics (BLS) also show the increasing educational requirements of future jobs (Zumeta 2010). Growth over time in the earnings premium that accrues to those who have earned a college degree rather than only a high school degree further suggests the value that employers place on a college education is increasing (Zumeta 2010).

Drawing on data from the BLS and its assumptions about the continued "upskilling" of current jobs (Zumeta 2010), Anthony Carnevale, Nicole Smith, and Jeffrey Strohl (2010) quantify the growth in the educational attainment of current and future jobs in their *Help Wanted* report. They project that 63% of jobs in 2018 will require education beyond high school, up from just 28% in 1973. Carnevale and colleagues also estimate that, at the current rate of degree production, the demand for workers with at least an associate's degree will exceed the supply by 3 million by 2018. They estimate that meeting the projected demand for college-educated workers will require a 10% annual increase in degree production (Carnevale, Smith, and Strohl 2010).

Although less commonly stressed in the current rhetoric, increasing educational attainment is also important for equity and social justice reasons. With higher levels of educational attainment come numerous economic and social benefits for both society and individuals (Baum, Ma, and Payea 2010; Hout 2011; Perna 2003; Psacharopoulos 2006). For society, increased educational attainment is associated with increases in taxes paid, higher labor force participation and employment rates, lower reliance on social support programs, and higher rates of volunteerism and civic engagement, as well as greater economic growth and other benefits (Baum, Ma, and Payea 2010; Hout 2011; Psacharopoulos 2006). Goldin and Katz (2009) conclude from their review that increases in educational attainment are a primary driver of reductions in wage inequality over time.

For individuals, higher levels of education are associated with higher annual earnings, greater job satisfaction, lower rates of unemployment and poverty, greater likelihood of employer-provided health insurance, better health, greater family stability, and improved educational outcomes for their children, as well as other benefits (Baum, Ma, and Payea 2010; Hout 2011; Zumeta 2010). Figure 2.1 shows that, in 2009, median annual earnings of year-round, full-time workers were substantially higher for men and women who had attained a bachelor's degree ($62,440 and $46,830, respectively) than for men and women who had finished only high school ($39,480 and $29,150, respectively) (National Center for Education Statistics 2011). Moreover, the economic benefits of higher education to individuals have increased over time. Since the early 1990s, the wage premium associated with holding a bachelor's degree rather than an associate's degree, some college, or a high school diploma has grown (Baum, Ma, and Payea 2010; Carnevale, Smith, and Strohl 2010).

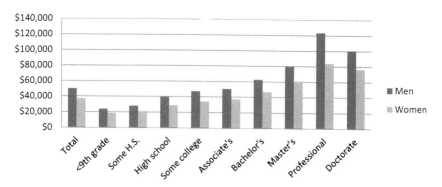

Figure 2.1. Earnings of year-round, full-time workers 25 years of age and older, by educational attainment and sex, 2009. (*National Center for Education Statistics 2011*)

Available data also suggest that, for individuals, the benefits of attending college far exceed the costs, with one report estimating that an individual who enrolls in a four-year college at age 18 and earns a bachelor's degree will have "earned enough by age 33 to compensate for being out of the labor force for four years, and for borrowing the full amount required to pay tuition and fees without any grant assistance" (Baum, Ma, and Payea 2010, 13).

Nonetheless, the likelihood of realizing the many economic and societal benefits varies according to an individual's demographic characteristics. Educational attainment is lower, on average, for blacks and Hispanics than for whites, and for students from lower than higher socioeconomic status. Among adults age 25 and older in 2006–2008, only 17.2% of blacks and 12.6% of Hispanics held at least a bachelor's degree, compared with 30.4% of whites and 49.7% of Asians (National Center for Education Statistics 2011). Only 12.3% of students who were in the lowest quartile of socioeconomic status when they were high school sophomores in 1990 had attained at least an associate's degree by 2000, compared with 65.4% of those who were in the highest socioeconomic status quartile in 1990 (National Center for Education Statistics 2011). Even more dramatically, only 9.6% of 1990 high school sophomores whose parents had not earned a high school diploma had earned at least an associate's degree by 2000, compared with 77.4% of 1990 high school sophomores whose parents had a professional or doctoral degree (National Center for Education Statistics 2011).

Identifying ways to effectively raise the educational attainment of blacks and Hispanics is even more important when considered in light of demographic trends. In short, the United States cannot achieve the levels of educational attainment required to achieve international competitiveness goals or work force needs unless it raises educational attainment especially among Hispanics. The nation's Hispanic population not only averages lower rates of college enrollment, college completion, and educational attainment than whites do but also is growing dramatically. Between 2000 and 2008, nearly all (83%) of the nation's population growth was among blacks, Hispanics, and Asians, rather than whites (Frey 2012). Between 2004–2005 and 2014–2015, the numbers of Hispanics and blacks graduating from the nation's public high schools were projected to increase by 54% and 3% respectively, compared with a 32% increase among Asians and an 11% decline among whites (Western Interstate Commission on Higher Education 2008). In 2010, racial or ethnic "minority" groups already represented at least 50% of the population in the District of Columbia (65%) as well as several states: California (60%), Hawaii (77%), New Mexico

(60%), and Texas (55%). Nonwhites now represent more than 40% of the population in other states, including Arizona (42%), Florida (42%), Georgia (44%), Maryland (45%), Mississippi (42%), Nevada (46%), New Jersey (41%), and New York (42% (Humes, Jones, and Ramirez 2011).

Where Is the Pipeline to Educational Attainment Leaking?

Increasing educational attainment requires improving several junctures in the pipeline, including enrollment in a postsecondary education institution and completion of the postsecondary educational program or degree. Over the past several years, the attention of many government and foundation leaders has shifted away from emphasizing the need to improve participation in college toward stressing the importance of increasing degree and program completion among those who enroll.

Along these lines, some (e.g., Adelman 2007) argue that the United States does not have an access problem, given the high number of students who are enrolling in higher education. A cursory review of college enrollment trends suggests the merits of this perspective. In fall 2009, more than 20.4 million students were enrolled in degree-granting postsecondary educational institutions, 38% more than the nearly 14.8 million enrolled a decade earlier (i.e., fall 1999) and nearly twice as many as were enrolled 35 years earlier (10.2 million in 1974) (National Center for Education Statistics 2011, table 197). Most of these enrollments (86% in fall 2009) are at the undergraduate rather than the postbaccalaureate level (National Center for Education Statistics 2011, table 202).

Despite the dramatic increase in college attendance, however, problems remain. One continued challenge is the disparity in the likelihood of college enrollment across groups. College-enrollment rates have been increasing over time among all racial and ethnic groups. Remarkably, 70.1% of all recent high school graduates were enrolled in college in 2009, up from 62.9% in 1999, 59.6% in 1989, and 49.3% in 1979 (National Center for Education Statistics 2011). Yet, despite these increases, gaps across groups in college enrollment persist. Only 55.7% of black recent high school graduates and 62.3% of Hispanic recent high school graduates were enrolled in college in 2008, compared with 71.7% of their white peers (National Center for Education Statistics 2011, table 209). College enrollment rates also continue to increase with family income, as just 55% of recent high school graduates in the lowest family income quintile were enrolled in college in 2008, compared with 80% of recent high school graduates in the highest family income quintile, a 25-percentage-point gap (Baum, Ma, and Payea 2010). Research also shows the role of differences in economic resources other than family income in determining students' educational attainment. Using data from the Panel Study of Income Dynamics, Nam and Huang (2009) found that, after controlling for demographic and household characteristics, cognitive skills and other variables including parental income, parental assets—particularly liquid-asset ownership—were positively related to measures of their children's educational attainment, including high school graduation, college attendance, and total number of years of schooling.

College enrollment rates also vary based on other dimensions, such as the characteristics of the high school that a student attends. Table 2.1 shows that the percentage of high school graduates enrolling in a four-year college is higher, on average, for those who graduate from private rather than public high schools (66.5% vs. 39.5%). Four-year college-enrollment rates are also considerably higher for students attending schools with relatively few poor students than for students attending schools with a high rate of poverty. In 2007–2008, 52.1% of graduates from public high schools where no more than 25% of students qualified for free or reduced price lunch were enrolled in four-year colleges, compared with only 26% of graduates from public high schools where more than 75% of students qualified for this program (National Center for Education Statistics 2011).

Also noteworthy is the stratification of students from different groups across various types of postsecondary educational institutions. When they do

TABLE 2.1
Four-Year College Attendance Rates of Those Who Graduated High School in 2006–2007, %

Selected High School Characteristic	College Attendance Rate of 2006–2007 Graduates in 2007–2008 at Four-Year Institutions
Public high schools	39.5
Students approved for free or reduced-price lunch	
School does not participate	25.4
0–25%	52.1
26–50%	41.5
51–75%	33.2
76–100%	26.0
Private high schools	66.5
Students approved for free or reduced-price lunch	
School does not participate	68.3
0–25%	73.2
26–100%	46.7

Source: National Center for Education Statistics 2011, table 210.

enroll, students from the lowest income families are relatively concentrated in for-profit and public two-year institutions. In 2007–2008, dependent students in the lowest family income quartile (i.e., family income less than $40,000) represented 54% of all dependent students attending private for-profit institutions and 35% of dependent students attending public two-year colleges, but only 17% of dependent students attending private four-year universities. In contrast, dependent students in the highest family quartile (i.e., $120,000 or higher) represented only 6% of all dependent students attending private for-profit institutions and 10% of dependent students attending public two-year colleges, but 34% of students attending private not-for-profit universities (Baum, Ma, and Payea 2010). Following a similar pattern, blacks and Hispanics represented higher shares of undergraduate students enrolled in for-profit institutions (24.7% and 21%) and public two-year institutions in 2007–2008 (14.3% and 14.8%, respectively) than of undergraduates enrolled in public four-year institutions (11.4% and 12%) and private four-year institutions (11.6% and 11.5%) (Staklis and Chen 2010). Differences in the type of college or university in which students enroll are of concern, as the magnitude of the benefits that result from higher education depends on the characteristics of the institution attended (Thomas and Perna 2004; Zhang 2005).

Although necessary, improvements in college enrollment and reductions in gaps in enrollment across groups are not sufficient to increasing educational attainment; improvements in program and degree completion are also required. The conventional metric for assessing college completion rates, that is, the percentage of first-time full-time students who complete their program within 150% of the defined program length, is not without limitations. For one, this metric reflects completion rates only for those who first enroll in a college or university on a full-time basis even though fewer than two-thirds (63%) of all undergraduates were enrolled full-time in fall 2009 (National Center for Education Statistics 2011, table 202). Attention only to full-time students is particularly problematic for measuring completion rates at community colleges, as a substantially smaller percentage of undergraduates attending two-year rather than four-year institutions are enrolled full-time (43% vs. 79% in fall 2009) (National Center for Education Statistics 2011, table 202). This metric also defines successful completion as finishing a degree or credential at the institution in which a student first enrolls, ignoring the reality that many students now transfer from one institution to another and that not all students enter with the goal of completing a degree. More than one-fourth (28.9%) of students who first entered a public two-year college in 1995–1996 transferred to a four-year institution by 2001 (Hoachlander, Sikora, and Horn 2003). Only about half (48.9%) of students who first enrolled in a public two-year college in 1995–1996 were expecting to earn an associate's degree; 15.6% were not seeking any credential, 10.8% were expecting to earn a certificate, and 24.8% were expecting to earn a bachelor's degree or transfer to a four-year institution (Hoachlander, Sikora, and Horn 2003).

These limitations notwithstanding, available data paint a troubling picture of the likelihood that a student who enrolls in a postsecondary educational program will persist to completion. Table 2.2 shows that only 36.4% of students who first enrolled full-time in a four-year college or university in fall 2002 completed a bachelor's degree within four years and only 57.2% completed a bachelor's degree within six years. Although substantially more students complete a bachelor's degree within six years than four years, longer periods of enrollment often translate into higher direct costs of attendance, higher indirect costs associated with additional earnings foregone while enrolled, and lower benefits of attendance as the individual has fewer years to realize the increase in earnings that typically results from degree or program completion. These negative implications are even greater for the sizable share of students—42.8% of students who first enrolled full-time in 2002—who do not complete a bachelor's degree within six years of first enrolling. The very low rates of certificate and associate's degree completion for those who first enroll full-time in a two-year institution (table 2.2) raise similar concerns.

The type of institution that a student attends is related not only to the magnitude of resulting benefits (as described earlier in this chapter) but also to the likelihood of completing an educational program or degree. Table 2.2 shows that six-year bachelor's degree completion rates are lower, on average, for students who first enroll in a for-profit four-year institution (22%) than for students who first enroll in a public four-year institution (54.9%) or private not-for-profit four-year institution (64.6%) (National Center for Education Statistics 2011). Suggesting the importance to degree completion of both students' academic readiness for college and institutional characteristics, table 2.2 also shows that bachelor's degree completion rates increase with institutional selectivity. Among those who first enrolled in 2002, six-year bachelor's degree completion rates rose from 27.1% at open-admissions institutions and 45.9% at institutions where at least 90% of applicants are admitted to 82.8% at institutions where fewer than 25% of applicants are admitted. The likelihood of completing a certificate or degree also varies according to students' demographic characteristics. For instance, six-year bachelor's degree completion rates are

TABLE 2.2

Graduation Rates of First-Time Postsecondary Students Who Started as Full-Time Degree-Seeking Students, by Sex, Race/Ethnicity, and Level and Control of Institution Where Student Started, %

Level and Control of Institution	Total	Male	Female	White	Black	Hispanic	Asian/Pacific Islander	American Indian/Alaska Native
Completing bachelor's degrees in 4 years (2002 start)								
All 4-year institutions	36.4	31.3	40.5	39.3	20.4	26.4	42.8	20.5
For-profit institutions	14.2	17.0	11.6	17.5	10.0	19.1	29.4	11.2
Public institutions	29.9	24.5	34.3	32.3	16.9	20.1	35.8	16.0
Not-for-profit institutions	51.0	46.3	54.7	54.0	29.4	44.1	61.0	36.6
Completing bachelor's degrees in 6 years (2002 start)								
All 4-year institutions	57.2	54.1	59.7	60.2	40.1	48.9	67.1	38.3
For-profit institutions	22.0	23.6	20.5	25.5	16.3	27.5	35.5	17.1
Public institutions	54.9	51.7	57.5	57.4	39.4	46.3	64.7	35.7
Not-for-profit institutions	64.6	61.9	66.7	67.2	44.9	59.5	75.3	49.8
Open admissions	27.1	25.4	28.6	32.9	18.4	25.8	30.3	13.6
90 percent or more accepted	45.9	42.5	48.8	48.2	30.4	33.8	53.1	35.4
75.0–89.9% accepted	54.6	51.3	57.2	57.0	40.5	47.0	55.6	34.0
50.0–74.9% accepted	59.9	56.4	62.7	62.8	43.7	51.9	65.1	45.8
25.0–49.9% accepted	73.1	71.0	74.7	78.8	47.2	62.1	82.3	67.2
Less than 25.0% accepted	82.8	82.3	83.5	84.5	57.5	83.6	93.1	76.0
Completing certificates or associate's degrees within 150% normal time (2005 start)								
All 2-year institutions	27.5	25.3	29.3	28.5	22.6	25.7	31.5	24.9
For-profit institutions	57.7	57.7	57.7	62.9	47.8	61.4	65.8	55.8
Public institutions	20.6	19.9	21.2	22.9	12.1	15.6	25.8	18.2
Not-for-profit institutions	48.2	44.5	51.3	52.3	41.6	47.3	41.6	14.8

Source: National Center for Education Statistics 2011, table 341.

considerably lower for American Indians or /Alaskan Natives (38.3%), blacks (40.1%), and Hispanics (48.9%) than for whites (60.2%) and Asian/Pacific Islanders (67.1%) (National Center for Education Statistics 2011).

The lack of progress in improving degree completion rates is also problematic. Over the past five years, bachelor's degree completion rates improved only marginally, with four-year degree completion rates rising only from 34.5% to 36.4% and six-year bachelor's degree completion rates rising from just 56.4% to 57.2%. Over the same period, the percentage of first-time full-time students completing certificates or associate's degree completion rates within 150% of the extended timeframe actually declined from 30% to 27.5% (National Center for Education Statistics 2011).

What Are the Primary Barriers Limiting College Enrollment and Completion?

Although many forces play a role, a review of available data and research demonstrates the unequivocal importance to college enrollment and completion of academic preparation and financial resources (Perna 2006a). Although most studies focus on the predictors of college access and success for traditional-age students (Perna 2006a), available data and research also point to the role of academic and financial barriers for adult students. One report estimates that more than 3 million of the 45 million adults nationwide with no college degree face the following three barriers to improving their educational attainment: no high school diploma, very low income (i.e., less than 200% of the poverty level), and limited English-language proficiency (CAEL 2008). Of the 45 million U.S. adults without a college degree, 32 million earn less than a living wage (CAEL 2008).

Research consistently shows that measures of academic preparation and achievement are strong positive predictors of a host of college-related outcomes (Perna 2005), including high school graduation rates (Cabrera and La Nasa 2000), college entrance examination scores (Horn and Kojaku 2001), college enrollment rates (Perna 2000; Perna and Titus 2004), attendance at more selective colleges and universities (Horn and Kojaku 2001), rates of transfer from a two-year to a four-year institution (Cabrera, La Nasa, and Burkam 2001), college grades (Warburton, Bugain, and Nuñez 2001), college persistence (Horn and Kojaku 2001; Warburton, Bugarin, and Nuñez 2001), and college completion (Adelman 2006; Cabrera and La Nasa 2000; Cabrera, La Nasa, and Burkam 2001). Improving academic readiness for college may be especially important to raising college enrollment rates for students from lower-income families (Cabrera, La Nasa, and Burkam 2001) and bachelor's degree completion rates for African Americans and Latinos (Adelman 2006). In an examination of how to "double the number" of low-income students completing associate's and bachelor's degrees, Goldberger (2007) concluded that improving academic readiness for college would disproportionately benefit high school students from low-income families and result in an additional 53,700 degree-earners from low-income families per year. And as the chapters in part III show, one way to increase academic readiness is via the use of games and related tools that utilize social media.

The inadequacy of current levels of adequate preparation is further indicated by the high rates of participation in remedial or developmental education, and the negative consequences of this participation for degree completion. About one-fifth of all first-year undergraduates took at least one remedial course in 2007–2008, with 10.9% of all first-year undergraduates taking at least two remedial courses that year (National Center for Education Statistics 2011, table 241). Using descriptive and multivariate analyses of data collected as part of the Achieving the Dream: Community Colleges Count Initiative, Bailey, Jeong, and Cho (2008) found that about half of students assigned to developmental coursework left the institution before completing the first developmental course. Only 16% of students who were referred to remedial math courses two or three levels below the college level completed the developmental math sequence within three years. Students who were male, black, older, part-time, and on a vocational track were less likely than other students to advance through the recommended sequence of remedial courses.

As suggested by the positive relationship between family income and measures of college enrollment and degree completion described earlier in this chapter, "money" also continues to matter to educational attainment. Research consistently shows a positive relationship between family income and the likelihood of enrolling in a two-year or four-year institution (Ellwood and Kane 2000; Hossler, Schmit, and Vesper 1999; Kane 1999; Perna 2000) as well as the total number of years of schooling completed (Hofferth, Boisjoly, and Duncan 1998). Research also shows that the enrollment of individuals with low family incomes is more sensitive than the enrollment of individuals with higher family incomes to changes in college costs, as measured by tuition, student financial aid, and the unemployment rate (Avery and Hoxby 2004; Heller 1997; Kane 1999; Long 2004). On the basis of his comprehensive review and synthesis of prior research, Heller (1997) concluded that, although enrollment generally declines if tuition increases or financial aid decreases, the effects of these changes on enrollment are greater among students from low-income families than among other students.

Many public policies and institutional practices have been implemented with the goal of improving students' academic readiness for college and students' ability to pay college costs. As the authors in part II discuss, social media and games have a potentially significant role to play in improving readiness on multiple levels. Current academic reforms include efforts to improve the alignment of K–12 and higher-education curricula and assessments (e.g., Achieve 2007), as well as initiatives designed to increase the availability of academically rigorous courses in high schools (e.g., Advanced Placement, International Baccalaureate, dual enrollment). The federal government, state governments, and colleges and universities invest substantial dollars each year in student financial aid programs designed to reduce the financial barriers to college attendance (see the College Board's [2011] report for detailed information on changes over time in the availability of student financial aid from these sources).

Nonetheless, the persistence of gaps in college enrollment and degree completion across groups, as well as the generally low rates of degree completion overall, suggest that existing interventions and approaches to improving academic preparation and financial resources are not enough, which is why some suggest that games and social media may be able to meet the needs that exist. One reason that traditional approaches may be insufficient is that they do not adequately recognize the information barriers that limit the effectiveness of these interventions (Perna 2010). The extent to which these and other programs and practices can serve as levers that effectively improve students' academic preparation and ensure the availability of sufficient financial resources likely depends, at least to some extent, on whether students are knowledgeable about and appropriately take advantage of these resources (Perna 2010).

Although little is known about students' understandings of the academic preparation required to enroll and succeed in college (Perna, Rowan-Kenyon, and D'Alconzo 2008), existing reports and studies consistently document the absence of accurate knowledge of college prices and financial aid among high school students and their families (e.g., Grodsky and Jones 2004; Horn, Chen, and Chapman 2003; Perna and Steele 2011). Levels of awareness and understanding of college prices and financial aid are particularly low among Latino students and parents (Immerwahr 2003; Tomás Rivera Policy Institute 2004) and among parents who have no direct personal experience with college (Hossler, Schmit, and Bouse 1991).

Information challenges may limit the effectiveness of existing practices and programs in several ways. Consistent with a human capital approach to understanding college enrollment (Perna 2006a), existing research suggests that students make college-related decisions on the basis of their perceptions of the availability of student financial aid (Tierney and Luna De La Rosa 2007). As a result, incomplete or inaccurate information likely compounds the barriers associated with academic preparation and financial resources, as students who do not believe that they can pay college prices may be less likely to become academically ready for college (Perna 2010; St. John, Hu, and Fisher 2011; Tierney and Venegas 2009). Students typically do not learn the amount or types of need-based financial aid they will receive, or the total out-of-pocket expenditure required to pay college costs, until they engage in other steps, including deciding to enroll in college, applying for admission, completing a financial aid form, and being accepted for admission (Kane 1999). Because students lack early information, most existing need-based student financial aid programs can influence only one narrow and discrete part of the attainment process: the actual decision to enroll.

One recent study illustrates the benefits to students' college-related outcomes of creating early awareness of student financial aid eligibility and awards. In short, using an experimental design, Bettinger and colleagues (2009) showed that simplifying the student financial aid process and providing assistance with completing the financial aid application form can improve college-related outcomes for individuals from low- to moderate-income families. Specifically, individuals from low- and moderate-income families who received assistance with completing and submitting the federal financial aid application form and personalized estimates of the net costs of attending a nearby public college or university were more likely to submit a financial aid application, enroll in college, and receive need-based financial aid than individuals who received only personalized estimates of the net costs or who received no information.

Efforts to improve students' knowledge of financial aid have been hampered by several forces (Perna 2010). One challenge is the complexity of the formula used to calculate eligibility for need-based student aid and determine students' need-based financial aid awards. Although awarding financial aid on the basis of academic criteria is less effective at promoting college enrollment than awarding financial aid because of financial need (Perna and Titus 2004), the relatively simple and transparent eligibility and award criteria of merit-based aid appears to have some knowledge-related benefits (Perna and Steele 2011). Using case study analyses of 15 schools, three in each of five states, Perna and Steele (2011) found that, although knowledge of financial aid was low at schools in all five states, students and parents attending the high schools in Florida and Georgia, two states with extensive state-sponsored merit-based aid programs, were aware of the availability of the aid and the criteria for receiving the aid. The analyses point to differences between the state need- and merit-based aid programs in the transparency and simplicity of available information as a potential reason for the differences in knowledge. Suggesting the importance of students' perceptions of their eligibility for aid to college enrollment, Ness and Tucker (2008) used logistic regression analyses to show that perceived eligibility for state student aid had a greater influence on the decision to enroll in college for African American and low-income students than for other students.

A second challenge in improving knowledge of student financial aid is the large number of different sources and types of financial aid (Perna 2010). The federal government is still the primary source of student financial aid, providing 74% of the $177.6 billion awarded to undergraduate students in 2010–2011 (College Board 2011). Nonetheless, other entities also offer sizable amounts of student financial aid. In 2011, state governments were the source of 5% of all aid awarded to undergraduates, while other sources included colleges and universities (17% of aid awarded to undergraduates) and employers and other private organizations (4%) (College Board 2011). Financial aid also comes in different forms, including grants, loans, work-study, and tax credits. In 2010–2011, about half (52%) of all aid awarded to undergraduates from all sources was in the form of grants, 39% was in the form of loans, 1% was in the form of work-study, and 8% was in the form of tax credits (College Board 2011). These different sources and types of aid vary in terms of application procedures, eligibility criteria, award amounts, and terms (e.g., whether the aid must be repaid, or whether students must work for an institutionally sanctioned employer). Appropriately counseling students about the intended use of loans to pay college costs is especially challenging, given differences in students' willingness to borrow to pay higher-education expenses (Perna 2008) as well as the potential negative consequence of borrowing if students should fail to complete the degree program and have a loan to repay (Gladieux and Perna 2005).

A third challenge to increasing knowledge of student aid is identifying the information that is culturally relevant and appropriate to students with particular backgrounds and needs (Perna 2006b; Tierney and Venegas 2009). Information about student financial aid is seemingly widely available; the greater challenge is to make the information understandable and accessible, given an individual's worldview (Perna 2006b).

Research demonstrates the importance of providing individually tailored information that recognizes a student's cultural background and other contextual forces (Perna 2010). For instance, in an ethnographic study of 12 high-achieving rural high school students who had immigrated from Mexico, Valadez (2008) found that these students made their college-enrollment decisions by negotiating their own agency and preferences with the norms and expectations of their structural (e.g., high school) and cultural (e.g., family) contexts. The findings highlight the need for high school counselors to pay greater attention to the cultural perspectives and values, as well as the particular knowledge requirements, of immigrant students, when providing college-related information. Other research shows that tuition costs and financial aid are much more important to the college application and enrollment decisions of low-income than high-income students (e.g., Lillis 2008), suggesting variations in the types of financial information required by students from these different backgrounds.

Students, especially students from groups that are historically underrepresented in higher education, generally lack access to culturally relevant and individually tailored information. Obtaining relevant and usable information about college-going requirements, expectations, and processes is particularly challenging for students whose families have no prior direct experience with higher education and for students who attend high schools with relatively few resources and structures to support college going (McDonough 1997; Perna et al. 2008; Tierney and Luna De La Rosa 2007; Valadez 2008). High schools often have too few counselors to provide college-related information (McDonough 1997, 2005; Perna et al. 2008). College-related counseling is even less available in schools with predominantly low-income or minority student populations than in other schools (McDonough 1997, 2005).

Even when available, counselors are often unable to devote much attention to providing college counseling to high school students, as this type of counseling is typically only one of a counselor's many responsibilities (McDonough 2005; Perna et al. 2008). Other forces, including the short-term duration of most interactions between counselors and students and the fact that counselors are generally not trained in the nuances of college and financial aid processes, also limit the quality and quantity of college-related counseling that is available in most high schools (Perna et al. 2008).

Within high schools, the availability of college advising varies on the basis of student characteristics. Counselors are more likely to encourage students with higher socioeconomic status than students with middle and lower socioeconomic status to attend a four-year college or university (Linnehan 2006). College counseling is more common for students in Advanced Placement, honors, and college preparatory curricular tracks than for students in other tracks (McDonough 2005; Venezia and Kirst 2005). Using hierarchical logistic regression analysis and data from the 2002 Educational Longitudinal Survey, Bryan and colleagues (2009) found that, after controlling for other variables, students attending schools with fewer students, more counselors, and fewer poor students were more likely to contact a school counselor for college information. Female and African American students were more likely than other students to contact a school counselor for college-related information (Bryan et al. 2009).

Other research demonstrates that the availability of resources and structures to support or encourage college going also varies across schools (Perna et al. 2008). Using data from the High School Effectiveness Study of the National Educational Longitudinal Study, Hill (2008) conceptualized three types of strategies that high schools use to assist students with college-related processes: *traditional*, characterized by limited availability of school resources to promote college enrollment; *clearinghouse*, characterized by the availability of resources to promote college enrollment but a limited commitment to proactively connecting these resources to students and families; and *brokering*, characterized by both the availability of considerable resources to promote college going and a norm of proactively connecting these resources to students and their families. These three strategies are associated with different college-going outcomes as the multilevel analyses revealed that students who attend schools with either a brokering or clearinghouse strategy are substantially more likely than students who attend schools with a traditional strategy to enroll in a four-year rather than a two-year college. The analyses also revealed variations in the relationship between these strategies and college enrollment based on students' race or ethnicity. A school's use of a clearinghouse strategy was associated with a greater likelihood of no enrollment rather than two-year college enrollment for Latinos than for whites, suggesting that Latinos may benefit more than other students from a strong school commitment to promoting students' college going.

Other research points to the absence of systematic initiatives that provide college-related information to adult learners. An exploration of the ways that precollege outreach programs may be promoting the college enrollment of the parents of students who participate in these programs suggests that, although programs generally have relevant information available, they typically provide this information only when proactively requested by interested parents (Perna, Walsh, and Fester 2011).

Why Does Attention to Social Media and Games Hold Promise for Improving College Enrollment, Completion, and Attainment?

Over the past several decades, numerous public policies and institutional programs have been developed with the goal of improving college access and completion. Each year, the federal government, state governments, colleges and universities, and other entities invest substantial financial resources into these efforts (College Board 2011). Nonetheless, despite the substantial annual investment in these and other efforts, the data and research described in this chapter suggest that these efforts are insufficient for improving college enrollment and completion.

An approach to improving college access and completion that capitalizes on the pervasiveness of social media and games in the lives of today's youth (as described in the introduction to this volume) offers promise for addressing these persisting problems. While social media and games may take multiple forms, the most effective forms of each for improving college enrollment, completion, and attainment are likely those with the greatest social presence. Drawing on theories from the field of media research, Kaplan and Haenlein (2010) conceptualize social presence as reflecting the degree of intimacy and immediacy, and they assert that the social influence of a particular form of social media increases with the intensity of social presence. They also note differences in the richness of social media, defining richness as "the amount of information they allow to be transmitted in a given time interval" (61). Virtual social worlds and virtual game worlds have high social presence and richness, whereas blogs and *Wikipedia* have low social presence and richness. Social media, especially those forms characterized by high social presence and richness, may be especially effective for addressing the structural barriers that now limit the ability of students, especially students who have the lowest levels of educational attainment, from obtaining the information needed to enroll in and complete college.

Access to and engagement with the internet have increased rapidly in recent years. For example, in just nine months (between May 2011 and February 2012), the share of adults who reported owning a smartphone increased from 35% to

46% (Smith 2012). Using the internet is now a regular component of most teen-agers' (age 12 to 17) daily lives. In 2009, 63% of teenagers reported going online every day, with 36% reporting going online several times each day (Lenhart et al. 2010). About three-fourths of teenagers own a cell phone, with higher rates of cell phone ownership among those who are age 17 (83%) than for those who are 12 (58%) or 13 (73%) (Lenhart et al. 2010). Most teens now also own comput-ers (69%), iPods or MP3 players (79%), and portable gaming devices (80%) (Lenhart et al. 2010).

Even more relevant to this book chapter, as Corwin suggests in chapter 4, is that most teens are using the internet in general and social media in particular. In 2009, 93% of teens (age 12 to 17) reported using the internet (Salmond and Purcell 2011). About three-fourths (73%) of teens who went online reported used social networks in September 2009, up from just 55% in November 2006 (Lenhart et al. 2010). Between 2006 and 2009, increasing shares of teens were using social networking sites (21% to 25%), as well as text messaging (27% vs. 54%) and calling on cell phones (34% vs. 38%) (Salmond and Purcell 2011). At the same time, declining shares of teens were talking on a landline phone (39% vs. 30%), instant messaging (28% vs. 24%), and emailing (14% vs. 11%) (Salmond and Purcell 2011).

Nonetheless, the ability to go online continues to vary across groups. Rates of access and usage are generally lower among groups that have lower rates of college access and success. For instance, smaller shares of lower-income (less than $30,000) adults than high-income ($75,000 or more) adults report own-ing a cellphone (75% vs. 95%), desktop computer (42% vs. 79%), laptop com-puter (38% vs. 79%), MP3 player (32% vs. 70%), game console (34% vs. 54%), book reader (3% vs. 12%), or tablet (2% vs. 9%) in 2010 (Jansen 2010). Similarly, the share of adults who owned a smartphone in February 2012 increased from 34% among those from low-income households (less than $30,000) to 68% among those with household incomes above $75,000 (Smith 2012). Similarly, the rate of smartphone ownership was substantially lower for those with less than a high school education (25%) than for those who were high school gradu-ates (39%) or college graduates (60%) (Smith 2012). Cell phone ownership rates are also substantially higher among teens (age 12 to 17) who are from families with incomes above $75,000 than for teens with family incomes below $30,000 (87% vs. 59%) (Lenhart et al. 2010).

Other indicators point to the challenges of an approach that relies on access to and usage of social media for improving college access and success for both traditional-age and adult students from historically underrepresented groups. On the basis of their many surveys of teens, researchers from the Pew Internet & American Life Project conclude that teens who have the greatest access to the internet are disproportionately white, with college-educated parents, and from households with incomes exceeding $50,000 (Salmond and Purcell 2011). Smaller shares of adults from low-income families (less than $30,000) than adults from high-income families ($75,000 or more) have broadband access at home (40% vs. 87%), use the internet (57% vs. 95%), and own a cellphone (75% vs. 95%) (Jansen 2010). Among those who go online, smaller shares of lower-than higher-income adults use the internet to search for a map (12% vs. 20%), research a product (19% vs. 40%), get online news (25% vs. 50%), purchase products (51% vs. 81%), and make travel reservations (47% vs. 83%) (Jansen 2010).

Although the share of adults owning smartphones does not vary among whites, blacks, and Hispanics (Smith 2012), other indicators of technology access and use do vary across racial or ethnic groups. For instance, smaller shares of black and Hispanic teens than of white teens report going online several times each day (33% and 26% vs. 39%) (Lenhart et al. 2010). Preferred social networking sites also appear to vary across racial or ethnic groups, with some evidence suggesting that white adults tend to prefer Facebook and LinkedIn, while adults from racial or ethnic minority groups prefer MySpace (Lenhart et al. 2010).

An approach that relies on social media is also likely to reach a smaller share of adult than traditional-age students, in light of current patterns of access to and use of technology. Smartphone ownership rates are particularly low among older adults with low household incomes or low levels of educational attainment. Among adults with household incomes below $30,000 only 42% of those age 30 to 49 own a smartphone compared with 58% of those age 18 to 29 (Smith 2012). Similarly, among adults who have attained no more than a high school education, only 43% of those age 30 to 49, but 63% of those age 18 to 29, own a smartphone (Smith 2012).

Following the same pattern, rates of access to and use of the internet are also somewhat lower among older than younger adults. About 86% of adults age 34 to 45 report going online, compared with 95% of adults age 18 to 33 (Zickuhr 2010) and teens age 14 to 17 (Lenhart et al. 2010). Rates of access to broadband at home and wireless use are also lower for adults age 34 to 45 than for adults age 18 to 33 (73% vs. 81% and 71% vs. 82%, respectively) (Zickuhr 2010). Older adults (34 to 45) also report lower rates than younger adults (age 18 to 33) do of using social network sites (62% vs. 83%) and playing online games (38% vs. 50%) (Zickuhr 2010).

Nonetheless, while differences persist, the use of social media has increased rapidly in recent years among all groups. Over the short two-year period between December 2008 and May 2010, the percentage of adults reporting use of social network sites increased substantially from 67% to 83% among adults age 18 to 33 and from 36% to 62% among adults age 34 to 45 (Zickuhr 2010). These patterns and trends suggest that social media may offer a viable mechanism for delivering college-related information even for older adults.

Summary

Capitalizing on the current and growing pervasiveness of social media holds promise for reaching critical national goals, including raising educational attainment in the United States to the level of its international competitors, ensuring that workers have the education and skills required for current and future jobs, and improving equity in the receipt of the many economic and social benefits that result from higher education. To be effective, however, an approach to delivering information via social media must recognize that access to computers and the internet, and usage of social media, continues to vary across groups. Importantly, both access and usage are generally lower among the groups that could benefit most from the information that social media could provide, that is, the groups that now have lower rates of educational attainment. As researchers from the Pew Internet & American Life Project conclude, greater access to broadband for those from white, college-educated, higher-income households translates into "greater overall engagement in online activities, particularly activities like social media" (Salmond and Purcell 2011, slide 5). Approaches involving social media must also recognize that the information needs, and patterns of access and use of internet technology, are different for potential and current traditional-age college students than for adult students. Nonetheless, an approach that relies on social media holds great potential for addressing the nation's need to raise the educational attainment of the population and eliminate persisting gaps in college-related outcomes across groups.

REFERENCES

Achieve, Inc. 2007. *Aligning High School Graduation Requirements with the Real World: A Road Map for States.* Washington, DC.

Adelman, Clifford. 2006. *The Toolbox Revisited: Paths to Degree Completion from High School through College.* Washington, DC: U.S. Department of Education.

———. 2007. "Do We Have an Access Problem?" *Change* 39(4):48–51. http://www.carnegie foundation.org/change/sub.asp?key=98andsubkey=2385.

Avery, Christopher, and Catherine M. Hoxby. 2004. "Do and Should Financial Aid Packages Affect Students' College Choices?" In *College Choices: The Economics of Where to Go, When to Go, and How to Pay for It*, edited by Catherine Hoxby, 239–302. Chicago: University of Chicago Press.

Bailey, Thomas, Dong Wook Jeong, and Sung-Woo Cho. 2008. *Referral, Enrollment, and Completion in Developmental Education Sequences in Community Colleges*. Community College Research Center Working Paper Series. New York: Teacher's College, Columbia University.

Baum, Sandra, Jennifer Ma, and Kathleen Payea. 2010. *Education Pays 2010*. Washington, DC: College Board. http://trends.collegeboard.org/downloads/Education_Pays_2010.pdf.

Bettinger, Eric P., Bridget T. Long, Philip Oreopoulos, and Lisa Sanbonmatsu. 2009. *The Role of Simplification and Information in College Decisions: Results from the H&R Block FAFSA Experiment (NBER Working Paper No. 15361)*. Cambridge, MA: National Bureau of Economic Research. http://www.nber.org/papers/w15361.

Bryan, Julia, Cheryl Holcomb McCoy, Cheryl Moore-Thomas, and Norma L. Day-Vines. 2009. "Who Sees the School Counselor for College Information? A National Study." *Professional School Counseling* 12:280–291.

Cabrera, Alberto F., and Steven M. La Nasa. 2000. "Understanding the College-Choice Process." In *Understanding the College Choice of Disadvantaged Students*, edited by Alberto F. Cabrera and Steven M. La Nasa, 5–22. San Francisco: Jossey-Bass.

Cabrera, Alberto F., Steven M. La Nasa, and Kurt R. Burkam. 2001. *Pathways to a Four-Year Degree: The Higher Education Story of One Generation*. Unpublished report. University of Wisconsin–Madison.

Carnevale, Anthony, Nicole Smith, and Jeffrey Strohl. 2010. *Help Wanted: Projections of Jobs and Education Requirements through 2018*. Washington, DC: Georgetown Center on Education and the Workforce. http://www9.georgetown.edu/grad/gppi/hpi/cew/pdfs/FullReport.pdf.

Chronicle of Higher Education. 2009. "Are Too Many Students Going to College?" *The Chronicle Review*, November 8. Accessed August 7, 2012. http://chronicle.com/article/Are -Too-Many-Students-Going/49039/.

College Board. 2011. *Trends in Student Aid 2011*. Washington, DC: Author. http://trends .collegeboard.org/downloads/Student_Aid_2011.pdf.

Council for Adult and Experiential Learning (CAEL). 2008. *Adult Learning in Focus: National and State-by-State Data*. http://www.cael.org/pdf/publication_pdf/State_Indicators _Monograph.pdf.

Ellwood, David T., and Thomas J. Kane. 2000. "Who Is Getting a College Education? Family Background and the Growing Gaps in Enrollment." In *Securing the Future: Investing in Children from Birth to College*, edited by Sheldon Danziger and W. J. Danziger, 283–324. New York: Russell Sage Foundation.

Frey, William H. 2012. "Race/Ethnicity." In *The State of Metropolitan America*, 50–63. Washington, DC: Brookings Institute. http://www.brookings.edu/metro/StateOfMetroAmerica .aspx.

Gladieux, Lawrence, and Laura W. Perna. 2005. *Borrowers Who Drop Out: A Neglected Aspect of the College Student Loan Trend*. San Jose, CA: National Center for Public Policy and Higher Education.

Goldberger, Susan. 2007. "Doing the Math: What it Means to Double the Number of Low-Income College Graduates." In *Minding the Gap: Why Integrating High School with College Makes Sense and How to Do It*, edited by Nancy Hoffman, Joel Vargas, Andrea Venezia, and Marc S. Miller, 27–41. Cambridge, MA: Harvard Education Press.

Goldin, Claudia, and Lawrence F. Katz. 2009. "The Future of Inequality: The Other Reason Education Matters So Much." *Milken Institute Review.* http://www.milkeninstitute.org/publications/review/2009_7/26-33mr43.pdf.

Grodsky, Eric, and Melanie Jones. 2004. "Real and Imagined Barriers to College Entry: Perceptions of Cost." Paper presented at the annual meeting of the American Education Research Association, San Diego, California, April 13–17.

Heller, Donald E. 1997. "Student Price Response in Higher Education: An Update to Leslie and Brinkman." *Journal of Higher Education*, 68:624–659.

Hill, Lori D. 2008. "School Strategies and the 'College-Linking' Process: Reconsidering the Effects of High Schools on College Enrollment." *Sociology of Education* 81:53–76.

Hoachlander, Gary, Anna C. Sikora, and Laura Horn. 2003. *Community College Students: Goals, Academic Preparation, and Outcomes (NCES 2003-164)*. Washington, DC: National Center for Education Statistics.

Hofferth, Sandra L., Johanne Boisjoly, and Greg J. Duncan. 1998. "Parents' Extrafamilial Resources and Children's School Attainment." *Sociology of Education*, 71:246–268.

Horn, Laura J., Xianglei Chen, and C. Chapman. 2003. *Getting Ready to Pay for College: What Students and Their Parents Know about the Cost of College Tuition and What They Are Doing to Find Out*. Washington, DC: U.S. Department of Education.

Horn, Laura, and Lawrence Kojaku. 2001. *High School Academic Curriculum and the Persistence Path through College (Report No. NCES 2001-163)*. Washington, DC: U.S. Department of Education.

Hossler, Don, Jack Schmit, and Gary Bouse. 1991. "Family Knowledge of Postsecondary Costs and Financial Aid." *Journal of Student Financial Aid* 21:4–17.

Hossler, Don, Jack Schmit, and Nick Vesper. 1999. *Going to College: How Social, Economic, and Educational Factors Influence the Decisions Students Make*. Baltimore: Johns Hopkins University Press.

Hout, Michael. 2011. "Social and Economic Returns to College." *Annual Review of Sociology* 37:1–45.

Humes, Karen R., Nicholas A. Jones, and Roberto R. Ramirez. 2011. *Overview of Race and Hispanic Origin: 2010 (C2010-BR-02)*. Washington, DC: U.S. Census Bureau. http://www.census.gov/prod/cen2010/briefs/c2010br-02.pdf.

Immerwahr, John. 2003. *With Diploma in Hand: Hispanic High School Seniors Talk about Their Future (National Center Report No. 03-2)*. San Jose, CA: National Center for Public Policy and Higher Education, and Public Agenda.

Jansen, Jim. 2010. *Use of the Internet in Higher-Income Households*. Washington, DC: Pew Internet & American Life Project. http://www.pewinternet.org/~/media//Files/Reports/2010/PIP-Better-off-households-final.pdf.

Kane, Thomas J. 1999. *The Price of Admission: Rethinking How Americans Pay for College*. Washington, DC: Brookings Institution Press.

Kaplan, Andreas M., and Michael Haenlein. 2010. "Users of the World, Unite! The Challenges and Opportunities of Social Media." *Business Horizons* 53:59–68.

Lenhart, Amanda, Kristen Purcell, Aaron Smith, and Kathryn Zickuhr. 2010. *Social Media and Mobile Internet Use among Teens and Young Adults*. Washington, DC: Pew Internet & American Life Project.

Lillis, Michael P. 2008. "High-Tuition, High Loan Financing: Economic Segregation in Post-secondary Education." *Journal of Educational Finance* 34:15–30.

Linnehan, Frank. 2006. "High School Guidance Counselors: Facilitators or Preemptors of Social Stratification in Education?" Paper presented at the annual meeting of the Academy of Management, Atlanta, Georgia, August 11–16.

Long, Bridget T. 2004. "How Have College Decisions Changed over Time? An Application of the Conditional Logistic Choice Model." *Journal of Econometrics* 121:271–296.

McDonough, Patricia M. 1997. *Choosing Colleges: How Social Class and Schools Structure Opportunity*. Albany, NY: SUNY Press.

———. 2005. "Counseling and College Counseling in America's High Schools." In *State of College Admission*, edited by David A. Hawkins and J. Lautz, 107–121. Washington, DC: National Association for College Admission Counseling.

Nam, Yunju, and Jin Huang. 2009. "Equal Opportunity for All? Parental Economic Resources and Children's Educational Attainment." *Children and Youth Services Review* 31:625–634.

National Center for Education Statistics. 2011. *Digest of Statistics, 2010*. Washington, DC. http://nces.ed.gov/pubsearch/pubsinfo.asp?pubid=2011015.

Ness, Erik C., and Richard Tucker. 2008. "Eligibility Effects on College Access: Under-Represented Student Perceptions of Tennessee's Merit Aid Program." *Research in Higher Education* 49:569–588.

Osterman, Paul. 2008. *College for All? The Labor Market for College Educated Workers*. Washington, DC: Center For American Progress.

Perna, Laura W. 2000. "Differences in the Decision to Enroll in College among African Americans, Hispanics, and Whites." *Journal of Higher Education* 71: 117–141.

———. 2003. "The Private Benefits of Higher Education: An Examination of the Earnings Premium." *Research in Higher Education* 44:451–472.

———. 2005. "The Key to College Access: A College Preparatory Curriculum." In *Preparing for College: Nine Elements of Effective Outreach*, edited by William G. Tierney, Zoë B. Corwin, and Julia E. Colyar, 113–134. Albany, NY: SUNY Press.

———. 2006a. "Studying College Choice: A Proposed Conceptual Model." In *Higher Education: Handbook of Theory and Research*, vol. 21, edited by John C. Smart, 99–157. New York: Springer.

———. 2006b. "Understanding the Relationship between Information about College Costs and Financial Aid and Students' College-Related Behaviors." *American Behavioral Scientist* 49:1620–1635.

———. 2008. "Understanding High School Students' Willingness to Borrow to Pay College Prices." *Research in Higher Education* 49:589–606.

———. 2010. "Toward a More Complete Understanding of the Role of Financial Aid in Promoting College Enrollment: The Importance of Context." In *Higher Education: Handbook of Theory and Research*, vol. 25, edited by John C. Smart, 129–180. New York: Springer.

Perna, Laura W., Heather Rowan-Kenyon, and Alyssa D'Alconzo. 2008. "Understanding Perceived Academic Preparation for College: The Role of the School and State Context." Paper presented at the annual meeting of the American Educational Research Association, New York, March 24–28.

Perna, Laura W., Heather Rowan-Kenyon, Scott L. Thomas, Angela Bell, Robert Anderson, and Chunyan Li. 2008. "The Role of College Counseling in Shaping College Opportunity: Variations across High Schools." *Review of Higher Education* 31:131–160.

Perna, Laura W., and Patricia Steele. 2011. "The Role of Context in Understanding the Contributions of Financial Aid to College Opportunity." *Teachers College Record* 113:895–933.

Perna, Laura W., and Marvin Titus. 2004. "Understanding Differences in the Choice of College Attended: The Role of State Public Policies." *Review of Higher Education* 27:501–525.

Perna, Laura W., Erin Walsh, and Rachel Fester. 2011. "Promoting the Postsecondary Educational Attainment of Adults: The Potential Role of Pre-college Outreach Programs." *Educational Policy* 25:935–963.

Psacharopoulos, George. 2006. "The Value of Investment in Education: Theory, Evidence, and Policy." *Journal of Educational Finance* 32:113–136.

Salmond, Kimberlee, and Kristen Purcell. 2011, February 9. *Trends in Teen Communication and Social Media Use: What's Really Going On.* Webinar presented jointly by the Girl Scouts and Pew Internet & American Life Project. http://www.pewinternet.org/~/media/Files/Presentations/2011/Feb/Pew%20Internet_Girl%20Scout%20Webinar%20PDF.pdf.

Smith, Aaron. 2012. *46% of American Adults Are Smartphone Owners.* Washington, DC: Pew Internet & American Life Project. http://pewinternet.org/~/media//Files/Reports/2012/Smartphone%20ownership%202012.pdf.

Staklis, Sandra, and Xianglei Chen. 2010. *Profile of Undergraduate Students: Trends from Selected Years, 1995–96 to 2007–08 (NCES 2010-220).* Washington, DC: U.S. Department of Education.

St. John, Edward P., Shouping Hu, and Amy S. Fisher. 2011. *Breaking through the Access Barrier: How Academic Capital Formation Can Improve Policy in Higher Education.* New York: Routledge.

Thomas, Scott L., and Laura W. Perna. 2004. "The Opportunity Agenda: A Reexamination of Postsecondary Reward and Opportunity." In *Higher Education: Handbook of Theory and Research,* vol. 19, edited by John C. Smart, 43–84. Dordrecht, Netherlands: Kluwer.

Tierney, William, and Mari Luna De La Rosa. 2007. *Breaking through the Barriers to College: Empowering Low-Income Communities, Schools, and Families for College Opportunity and Student Financial Aid.* Los Angeles: University of Southern California, Center for Higher Education Policy Analysis.

Tierney, William G., and Kristan M. Venegas. 2009. "Finding Money on the Table: Information, Financial Aid, and Access to College." *Journal of the Higher Education* 80:363–388.

Tomás Rivera Policy Institute. 2004. *Caught in the Financial Aid Information Divide: A National Survey of Latino Perspectives on Financial Aid.* Reston, VA: Sallie Mae Fund.

Valadez, James R. 2008. "Shaping the Educational Decisions of Mexican Immigrant High School Students." *American Educational Research Journal* 45:834–860.

Venezia, Andrea, and Michael W. Kirst. 2005. "Inequitable Opportunities: How Current Education Systems and Policies Undermine the Chances for Student Persistence and Success in College." *Educational Policy* 19:293–307.

Warburton, Edward C., Rosio Bugarin, and Anne-Marie Nuñez. 2001. *Bridging the Gap: Academic Preparation and Postsecondary Success of First-Generation Students (Report No. NCES 2001-153).* Washington, DC: U.S. Department of Education.

Western Interstate Commission on Higher Education. 2008. *Knocking at the College Door.* Boulder, CO. http://www.wiche.edu/knocking.

Zhang, Liang. 2005. *Does Quality Pay? Benefit of Attending a High-Cost, Prestigious College.* New York: Routledge.

Zickuhr, Kathryn. 2010. *Generations, 2010.* Washington, DC: Pew Internet & American Life Project. http://pewinternet.org/~/media//Files/Reports/2010/PIP_Generations_and _Tech10.pdf.

Zumeta, William. 2010. "Does the U.S. Need More College Graduates to Remain a World Class Economic Power?" Paper prepared for National Discussion and Debate Series, Miller Center of Public Affairs, University of Virginia.

CHAPTER THREE

Transition Readiness

*Making the Shift from High School to College
in a Social Media World*

DAVID CONLEY AND MARY SEBURN

A successful transition from high school to postsecondary education depends on many individual, social, and institutional factors. Throughout high school, students must develop and nurture an identity that evolves from "high school student" to "college student" or "employee." They must be willing and able to adapt to an academic or workplace culture and to learn and adhere to norms that are specific to that culture. They need to learn and navigate the complex processes through which eligibility, financial support, and admissions are obtained for college or through which desired positions are obtained in the workplace. Once out of high school, they must be able to identify and utilize financial, housing, tutoring, health, recreational, and advising resources as needed, and mature into their own academic and professional advocates. They need to do all of this while keeping current goals, interests, and strengths in mind and with an eye to future career options and advancement. Being poorly prepared along any of these dimensions makes the transition more difficult and decreases the likelihood the student will complete the transition successfully. Together, these experiences, skills, and strategies constitute *key transition knowledge and skills*.

The knowledge and skills necessary to make a successful transition from high school to college are often obscure, unclear, and difficult for many students to access. A host of factors in schools and in the transition process itself conspires to make it more difficult for many students to know what they need to do to be ready to make a successful transition from secondary to postsecondary educational environments. Social media offer the potential to make access to necessary information more convenient and equitable. However, this is still more of an aspiration than a reality. We discuss in this chapter the range of factors related to a successful transition, some examples of ways social media could conceivably support more successful transitions, and acknowledge the challenges present in using social media in educational settings in ways that allow all students more equitable access to the knowledge and skills necessary for a successful transition.

Limitations of the Current Approach

Although schools have long grappled with how to prepare students for a productive and successful life after high school, college and career readiness as a goal for most schools is a relatively recent focus. President Obama's "Race to the Top" challenge, the Common Core State Standards, and the two consortia of states designing assessments of the Common Core are all united by the goal that many more students graduate from high school and are college ready (Common Core State Standards 2012; Partnership for the Assessment of Readiness for College and Careers 2012).

Historically, high schools have been called upon to make students eligible for college, not necessarily ready. Eligibility has long been defined by the titles of courses completed, grade point averages, and admissions test scores (Conley 2005, 2010, 2012). Relying on standardized high school course titles without any quality guarantees for course and curriculum content results in significant variation in students deemed eligible for college, and test scores add little to the equation (Wagner 2006).

In short, the current model based on eligibility is fundamentally broken when it comes to ensuring students are in fact ready for college. Some evidence of the extent to which it is broken includes the following:

- Test scores used as current measures of postsecondary readiness (SAT and NAEP) have not increased significantly in the past 20 years (College Board 2011; National Center for Education Statistics 2011).
- Only 25% of high school seniors taking the ACT in the four core subject areas demonstrated the content knowledge necessary to enter college-level courses without remediation (ACT Policy Report 2011), and only 43% of the seniors taking the SAT met the College Board's benchmark for college and career readiness (College Board 2011).
- From 70% to 75% of high school students graduate from high school, of whom only 65% enroll directly in a two- or four-year college (Aud et al. 2011; Bureau of Labor Statistics 2012).

- A majority of college faculty indicates dissatisfaction with students' ability to read and comprehend complex material (70%), ability to think analytically (66%), work and study habits (65%), writing quality (62%), ability to do research (59%), and ability to apply what they learn to solve problems (55%) (Achieve, Inc. 2005).
- Remediation rates remain steady, with 40% of first-year college students taking at least one remedial course in college at a significant cost annually (Adelman 1999; Attewell et al. 2006; Howell, Kurlaender, and Grodsky 2010).
- Employers who hire recent high school graduates report dissatisfaction with graduates' basic written and verbal communication skills, mathematics and computer skills, problem-solving skills, and overall demeanor and work ethic (Massachusetts Business Alliance for Education 2006).

College admissions and placement tests are not without value—they do contribute to predictions of first-year grade point average (GPA) (Astin, Tsui, and Avalos 1996; Bridgeman, McCamley-Jenkins, and Ervin 2000; Camara and Echternacht 2000; Kuncel and Hezlett 2007; Kuncel, Ones, and Sackett 2010; Ramist, Lewis, and McCamley-Jenkins 1994; Willingham 1985; Wilson 1980) and beyond. However, several studies suggest that such tests are somewhat useful only in predicting individual college students' first-year grades or success after college (Allensworth and Easton 2007; Geiser 2009; Niu and Tienda 2010). Given the limited predictive power of the tests, the overreliance on ACT or SAT scores as predictors should be of concern—especially when 30% of students fail to return after the first year of college (Knapp, Kelly-Reid, and Ginder 2010) for a variety of factors not assessed by these examinations, such as deficiencies in transition knowledge and skills.

Improving student preparation for life after high school requires a shift from eligibility and prediction to a comprehensive definition of college and career readiness that specifies student skills and strategies associated with college success in greater detail (Conley 2005, 2007, 2010). A broader definition of readiness would include four key areas: the cognitive strategies students possess to interpret and apply content knowledge, their understanding of the structure of knowledge within academic disciplines, their mastery of the skills and techniques necessary to learn effectively and efficiently, and their understanding of all the aspects of the transition from secondary to postsecondary education.

The Four Keys to College and Career Readiness

Although this chapter focuses on only one area—transition knowledge and skills—college and career readiness is much more complex than that. The four keys to college and career readiness (Conley 2012) is a comprehensive and multidimensional model for understanding all aspects of college and career readiness that lays out this complexity in a systematic fashion. Each key is described briefly here (see Figure 3.1).

The *key cognitive strategies* are the cognitive skills and strategies that allow students to consolidate and deepen their understanding of content knowledge. Students who possess a range of cognitive strategies are able to think strategically and insightfully about the work they do. They are able to think well.

Key content knowledge encompasses the structure of knowledge and the interplay with student characteristics that determines how students interact with knowledge. Students need to possess grade-appropriate content knowledge but also to be engaged and motivated to learn and connect relevant facts, terms, linking ideas, concepts, and principles. They understand that knowledge has a structure that organizes its diverse elements and that academic disciplines reflect ways of knowing and understanding the world.

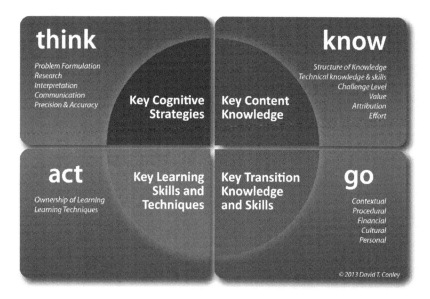

Figure 3.1. The four keys to college and career readiness. (*Conley 2013*)

Key learning skills and techniques are the tools that students use to take ownership of their learning as well as a host of methods for learning efficiently and effectively. Students need to be able to set goals, monitor their performance, seek help when needed, be motivated, and possess learning techniques such as study skills, strategic reading, time management, and technological proficiency.

Key transition knowledge and skills are necessary to adjust to and perform successfully within a postsecondary environment. Students who possess such knowledge and skills are able to thoughtfully explore their options, identify and obtain the necessary resources, and complete the numerous steps necessary to pursue their chosen postsecondary path, and they are prepared for the challenges that come with adapting successfully to the new environment of postsecondary education. We use the term *transition readiness* to describe the level of preparation students need to reach upon completing high school to be ready to enter the workplace or college successfully. The remainder of this chapter focuses on this fourth key and how social media might help students prepare for a successful transition to postsecondary education.

Key Transition Knowledge and Skills: Know How to Go

Six key transition skills are role and identity, postsecondary awareness, postsecondary costs, matriculation, career awareness, and self-advocacy. We provide an overview of each of the six and then discuss the role that technology and social media might play to help more students make a successful transition to college.

1. Role and Identity

Transition readiness hinges on the development and evolution of an *identity* that is academically or career oriented and on a clear set of postsecondary objectives. Students' identities define them as individuals and reflect the beliefs, values, and attitudes of their families, cultures, and—especially during adolescence—peer groups. *Roles* describe the parts individuals play within their social environment. *Role models* provide support and grounded visions of imagined possible future identities and roles. *Role conflicts* complicate the transition for students who feel they must choose between conflicting versions of their future selves.

DEVELOPING AN ACADEMIC IDENTITY: SCHOLARS
INSTEAD OF STUDENTS

Fluid and malleable, identity evolves over time on the basis of intimate associations with others. Identity refers to the defining characteristics that make individuals distinct from and similar to others from the same culture, and it changes to adapt to new environments, communities, and relationships (Gee 2002; Gosine 2002). The nature of the self (i.e., who we are) depends to a large extent on the context within which we live.

The transition to college presents a prime opportunity for students to redefine, or perhaps define, who they are. Even "good" high school students must change to become "good" college students. Because the roles and environments differ in independence, structure, autonomy, and complexity, the identities necessary to navigate successfully through each differ, too.

The attitudes, beliefs, and emotions that students maintain about themselves as learners are critical to their motivation, academic achievement, and success with the transition from high school (Lefkowits et al. 2010). College freshmen who believe that individual attributes are changeable and controllable are happier, better adjusted, and receive more social support than those who believe that individual attributes are fixed and uncontrollable (Tamir et al. 2007). Students with a strong sense of academic identity involve themselves in a wider range of academic activities, interact more with faculty and other students, expend more effort to learn and grow, and are more likely to be self-evaluative, skeptical of their own self-constructions and world views, demonstrate openness to new ideas, and have cognitively complex coping and problem-solving strategies (Adams, Stover, and Whitlow 1999; Berzonsky and Kuk 2000).

SOCIAL MEDIA, ROLE, AND IDENTITY

As Gee and others note in part II, social media provide engaging, authentic, and cognitively complex learning opportunities that can elicit higher-order thinking, problem solving, and decision making in ways that are not as available in traditional classrooms (Bransford, Brown, and Cocking 2002). Social media and simulated environments provide opportunities for identity development and self-exploration by allowing students to interact with others on a global scale and by enabling them to experience virtual events and cultures that are outside the local community.

The I Have A Dream Foundation provides a localized program aimed at increasing transition readiness in first-generation and low-socioeconomic-status

(SES) students. Programs are implemented for cohorts of students in schools or housing authorities. Advancement via Individual Determination (AVID) seeks to increase access and preparation of underrepresented and underprepared students for postsecondary success. Although evaluation results of the classroom-based program suggest effectiveness, incorporating social media and technology might further increase its impact (Lozano, Watt, and Huerta 2009; Mendiola, Watt, and Huerta 2010; Watt et al. 2008).

Road Trip Nation helps students explore possible career and life pathways they never knew existed by interviewing and video-recording people in career areas of interest to them and then creating a final project in the form of a brief video. All student videos are collected into Road Trip Nation's online database, which can be accessed by all students. The website also has opportunities for social interactions around the videos (Road Trip Nation 2012).

CHANGING ROLES: NOT ALL SUCCESSFUL HIGH SCHOOL STUDENTS ARE SUCCESSFUL COLLEGE STUDENTS

Because identity and cognition are embedded in and expressed by language, our discourse influences the way we perceive and understand the world (Vygotsky 1986). Language allows students to assimilate into a new postsecondary culture as well as internalize and communicate ideas, expectations, and perceptions present in that culture. As students gain proficiency in academic discourse, they develop "academic literacy," which is the ability to use and apply the type of language expected in a college environment (White and Lowenthal 2011).

As students become more competent in their academic identity, fully embrace the role of college student, and become fluent in academic literacy, they are better poised for success in their academic pursuits. Self-confidence, achievement motivation, and academic self-efficacy are strong nonacademic predictors of college GPA (Bandura 1997; Eccles and Wigfield 2002; Elias and Loomis 2002; Linnenbrink and Pintrich 2002). Moving away from family and friends to attend college is especially difficult for students who have not been exposed to the conventions of academic discourse and who have underdeveloped academic identities (Bailey, Hughes, and Karp 2002; Hertel 2002; Jay and D'Augelli 1991).

Some minority groups are more likely to belong to and identify with cultures that embody uniquely specific discourse styles. These students may feel that adopting a new language is a betrayal to their cultural identity and may thus be especially reluctant to abandon their "native language" (Heath 1983; Willis 1977). Lacking a common language with others once they arrive in college, some students are unable to communicate effectively with their peers and instructors and, as a result, tend not to feel like legitimate members of the culture. This feeling is often experienced by the student as impostor syndrome (Clance and Imes 1978), the phenomenon of not feeling that one's accomplishments and qualifications are genuine or sufficient.

Students may also experience role conflict. For minority and first-generation students, adopting an academic identity created by and associated with a mostly white, middle- and upper-class culture is not only unfamiliar but can be perceived as negating one's own culture or "acting white," and is often resisted (Apple 1995; Erickson 1987; Giroux 1982; Huffman 2001; Ogbu 2004; Tyack 1976; Willis 1977). The resulting academic illiteracy and resistance to adopting an academic identity in college, coined "cultural suicide" by Tierney (1999), is alienation and disengagement, which are frequently cited as key reasons for student attrition. Similar challenges apply to the career transition, where assimilation into the work world requires mastering the culture and language of the trade.

One strategy to reduce the cultural shock is to give students opportunities to experience a college identity while still in high school. Dual enrollment programs offer opportunities to take college classes while still in high school. This strategy aims to nurture academic identities through exposure to college in much the same way as internships serve to develop professional identities. Evidence is emerging that indicates the positive effects dual enrollment programs can have (Bailey, Hughes, and Karp 2002; Karp et al. 2007; Rogers and Kimpston 1992; Swanson 2008).

ROLE MODELS: HOW IMPORTANT ARE THEY AND DO THEY IMPACT FUTURE SUCCESS?

Role models provide good examples of desirable behaviors and of what is possible. They demonstrate attributes that others want to emulate and achievements others can seek to duplicate. For the college transition process, role models are those who provide guidance or information or are examples of how others from similar backgrounds to the role model might transition successfully. Traditionally, they include parents, recent graduates who come back to the high school and talk to students about college aspirations, teachers who share their college experiences and inspire others to similar aspirations, and public figures or celebrities for whom students aspire to be like.

Having role models can benefit high school students in multiple ways. Role models are associated with increased interest in college for first-generation college students (DuBois et al. 2002), increased undergraduate academic performance and retention (Campbell and Campbell 1997; Crisp and Cruz 2009; Sum et al. 2010; Terenzini, Psacarella, and Blimling 1996), and increased self-reported perceptions of preparedness for college and the workplace (Gandara and Mejorado 2005; Schlosser et al. 2003; Stanton-Salazar 2001). Historically, minority students face a far more difficult transition to college than do white, middle-class students (Tinto 1996, 1998, 1999; Tinto and Pusser 2006), and they also tend to have fewer academically oriented role models than do white students (Perna 2000; Rice, Cole, and Lapsley 1990; Swail, Redd, and Perna 2003; Wimberly 2002).

Mentoring is especially promising as a means to increase the transition readiness of high school students with few role models, especially those with low GPAs, low motivation, and little family support (Center for Higher Education Policy Analysis 2009). Few mentoring programs utilize social media (e.g., icouldbe.org and MentorNet). Most are limited to the locally available mentoring pool. Although the use of online mentoring is increasing, evidence of its effectiveness is still limited (Ensher, Heun, and Blanchard 2003; Knouse 2001).

2. Postsecondary Awareness

Adolescence is a time of creating, trying out, and refining self-concept, identity, and aspirations (Marcia 1991). As young people explore different roles and identities, they imagine possible futures. Sometimes these imagined futures are unrealistic or are inconsistent with abilities, skills, or behaviors, making the college decision-making process and transition more difficult (Schneider and Stevenson 1999). But for students to be college and career ready, they must develop self-knowledge sufficient to establishing goals for themselves that extend beyond high school, familiarize themselves with the postsecondary environment(s) to which they aspire, and know how best to prepare themselves for their desired future.

ASPIRATIONS: WHAT ISN'T ASPIRED TO CAN NEVER BE ACHIEVED
Aspirations develop from many factors and drive goal attainment behaviors. Higher aspirations are consistently associated with beneficial outcomes including high levels of cognitive and emotional development and attainment, increased leadership, and higher salaries as adults (Csikszentmihalyi 1990; Finn 1989; Finn and Rock 1997; Kirsch 1986; Quaglia 1989; Steinberg 1996).

Because students are unlikely to attain goals to which they do not aspire, those with college aspirations are also more likely to attend college than are students without college aspirations. High school seniors who aspire to earn a college degree are 28% more likely to apply to a four-year institution than are students who do not, and seniors aspiring for an advanced degree are 34% more likely to apply to college (Cabrera and La Nasa 2001). High-aspiring students are more likely to get accepted into college (Bennett and Xie 2003; Flint 1992; Perna 2000; Solozorano 1991) and are more likely to persist and succeed once in college than are their peers with lower aspirations (Bickel 1989; Bickel and Lange 1995).

Student aspirations have increased in recent decades. In 1980 only 40% of tenth graders wanted to go to college, but current measures indicate as many as 93% of eighth graders say they want to go to college (Roderick et al. 2008), but only 70% to 75% graduate from high school, and of those, only 65% enroll immediately in a two- or four-year college. The rate is 85% for students whose parents attended college and 47% for students whose parents did not attend college (Aud et al. 2011; Bridgeland, DiIulio, and Morison 2006; Kao and Thompson 2003). Unfortunately, college aspirations slowly decline between middle school and high school for many students (Csikszentmihalyi and Schneider 2000). This dropoff is largest for students from low-income backgrounds, members of ethnic minority groups, and those who would be first in their family to attend college.

This pattern suggests that recent efforts to instill the importance of a college education in students well before high school have been successful but that it takes more than exhortations to students for them to sustain a focus on college readiness, particularly for groups historically underrepresented in college. This is why the work of Ellison, Wohn, and Heeter in chapter 10 offers such possibilities; games and social media have the potential to connect students in new ways that heretofore did not exist.

POSTSECONDARY NORMS AND CULTURE: COLLEGE KNOWLEDGE

Norms are the unspoken social rules that define acceptable and expected behaviors within a specific environment. College and workplace norms and culture differ significantly from high school norms and culture. In high school, students tend to be passive recipients of an education—they are provided with class schedules, are reminded repeatedly of deadlines, and are corrected when they fail to meet the behavioral or academic expectations of the institution and are rewarded for the right kind of effort, regardless of the outcome. In college, students abruptly become the active owners of their education—they schedule their own courses; structure how much time they spend studying and socializing; determine if they are on track to meet course and degree requirements; and monitor, determine, and adjust the correctness of their own behavior. In both college and the workplace, people are judged primarily on products and outcomes, and much less on effort expended.

Transition preparedness requires an awareness, understanding, and acceptance of postsecondary norms and culture. Students lacking exposure to college life are unable to anticipate or prepare for this adjustment and are more likely to feel alienated, isolated, or disengaged. Incidentally, these are among the most frequent reasons given for college attrition in the first year (Bean and Metzner 1985; Billson and Terry 1982; Pantages and Creedon 1978; Terenzini et al. 1996; Tinto 1975, 1993).

Interpreting the differences between high school and college culture is a task that has fallen on parents who have already gone to college. Increasingly, however, perceptions of college culture are reaching young people via the media, from sources such as "reality" television (e.g., MTV's *My College Life*, BET's *College Hill*, NBC's *Tommy Lee Goes to College*). With recent advances in games and simulations, as Tracy Fullerton points out in chapter 5, it becomes more possible to provide students with more realistic and engaging exposure to postsecondary culture. For example, Educational Simulations *Real Lives 2010* (www .educationalsimulations.com) could be adapted to simulate college life on a variety of campuses, allowing students the opportunity to experience college culture vicariously. Simulations could mimic the acceptance or rejection process and base decisions on actual high school qualifications. The fiscal implications of taking on loans rather than pursuing grants or scholarships can easily be demonstrated, along with course selection choices, impact on grades of time spent studying versus socializing, benefit of participating in social groups, ways to communicate with professors, advantages of using an adviser, and many others.

3. Postsecondary Costs

Choices made as high school juniors and seniors come with significant, lifelong fiscal effects. On average, a four-year college degree costs $70,532, and the average student debt incurred is $23,300 and rising (Federal Reserve Bank of New York 2012). However, not going to college also has a cost. Employees with a bachelor's degree earn nearly twice as much as employees with a high school degree (Day and Newburger 2002). This is a difference of a million dollars over the course of their work lives (Wirt et al. 2003).

Financial aid programs help make postsecondary education more accessible to all, regardless of ability to pay, but they work only when students and families know how to take advantage of them.

TUITION AND FINANCIAL AID: WHAT DO HIGH SCHOOL STUDENTS KNOW AND HOW DOES WHAT THEY DON'T KNOW HURT THEM?

Students tend to decide whether they will attend college between grades 8 and 10 (Choy 2001). Under the current system, many students learn about college tuition and financial aid in grades 11 or 12, after they have already made their decision about college (Fitzgerald 2006; Heller 2006). Compounding the problem, students most in need of financial aid learn about it the latest (Ikenberry and Hartle 1998). On average, students from households earning more than $75,000 first hear about financial aid at the age of 14, while students from families earning less than $25,000 first hear about financial aid at 16 (Sallie Mae Fund and Harris Interactive 2003). When students who want to go to college are not introduced to financial aid until late in high school, they are often overwhelmed and unable to complete the FAFSA (Free Application for Federal Student Aid) process in time and subsequently miss grant and scholarship deadlines (American Council on Education [ACE] 2004; Dynarski and Scott-Clayton 2006).

Students consistently overestimate what college will cost, more so for two-year than for four-year colleges. They estimate three times the actual costs for community colleges and two times the actual cost for colleges and universities (Venezia, Kirst, and Antonio 2003). Not only are college costs overestimated, but financial aid options are overlooked. When asked to identify sources of financial aid, more than two-thirds of students failed to identify grants, scholarships, or loans as options (Sallie Mae Fund and Harris Interactive 2003). These inflated perceptions of college costs and lack of familiarity with funding options can discourage students from aspiring and applying to college. In fact, approximately half of all college-ready low-income high school students do not attend college for financial reasons (Advisory Committee on Student Financial Assistance [ACSFA] 2002; Goldrick-Rab 2006).

Low-income and minority parents overestimate college costs the most, by as much as 228% and, as a result, can conclude that their children should not aspire to college (Goldrick-Rab 2006; Grodsky and Jones 2004; Horn, Chen, and Chapman 2003; Zarate and Pachon 2006). The parents of college-aspiring students are only slightly more knowledgeable about identifying sources of financial aid than are students; fully three-fifths failed to identify grants, scholarships, and loans as options (Sallie Mae Fund and Harris Interactive 2003). Parents' understanding of college costs increases with income, making the parents who are least able to pay also the least educated about postsecondary costs (Horn, Chen, and Chapman 2003). Parental influence is the most important factor affecting college aspirations, and parents who understand financial aid have higher expectations for their students (Horn, Chen, and Chapman 2003; Luna De La Rosa 2006).

College and financial aid eligibility misperceptions present another barrier, particularly for students most in need of financial support. Many students believe that their grades are too low or that their families make too much money to be eligible for any financial aid (Zarate and Pachon 2006). In 1999–2000, only 50% of all students enrolled in credit-granting postsecondary institutions offering a Federal Title II aid program completed a FAFSA, and only one in four students eligible for a Pell Grant applied for financial aid (ACE 2004). Others, especially those underrepresented in higher education, believe that education is important but not worth what it costs, especially when attendance requires debt (Rodriguez et al. 2000; Zarate and Pachon 2006).

EDUCATING STUDENTS AND FAMILIES ABOUT FINANCIAL AID BETTER?

The more students know and understand financial aid, the less money becomes a factor in (or a barrier to) determining postsecondary plans, and the more likely they are to apply to and enroll in college (Berkner and Chavez 1997; Ekstrom 1992; Freeman 1997; Hossler, Hu, and Schmit 1999; King 1996; Terenzini, Cabrera, and Bernal 2001).

Most students (85%) learn about financial aid from counselors, teachers, and coaches, making school-based efforts to demystify financial aid essential (Art and Science Group, Inc. 2000; Luna De La Rosa 2006). Students from low-SES families are particularly disadvantaged because they learn about college costs later then their higher-SES peers and because their school and peers are more than twice as likely to be their only sources of information about financial aid (Luna De La Rosa 2006; Terenzini, Cabrera, and Bernal 2001; Tierney and Venegas 2006).

Financial aid offers—regardless of the amount of the offer—are associated with college enrollment and persistence (Bresciani and Carson 2002; Jackson 1978). Funding postsecondary education with loans alone, however, is associated with lower persistence and graduation rates (Dowd and Coury 2006), and students most in need of financial support to attend college are often the most reluctant to go into debt to do so (Burdman 2005; McDonough and Calderone 2004). In fact, financial indebtedness is negatively associated with persistence and completion. Students with loans persist less than do students without loans (Dowd and Coury 2006). Other research suggests that a willingness to pay, and not the ability to pay, for college is a determining factor in college selection (Hu and Hossler 2000).

Games and social media could be motivating factors if used as a planning process that starts in middle school with students learning about financial aid options and then progresses to simulated offers. Schools should direct such opportunities to learn about financial aid to low-SES, first-generation, and less academically competitive students. Although evidence of effectiveness is yet to be firmly established, online counseling and mentoring programs are emerging options. The internet is an increasingly valuable and utilized source of financial aid information for both students and families (Luna De La Rosa 2006; Tornatzky, Cutler, and Lee 2002).

4. Matriculation

The likelihood of enrolling in postsecondary education is strongly related to parents' education even when other factors are taken into account. Among 1992 high school graduates whose parents had not gone to college, 59% had enrolled in some form of higher education by 1994. This rate increased to 75% among those whose parents had some college experience, and 93% among those who had at least one parent with a bachelor's degree (Choy 2001). Low-income students and students of color are less likely to transition directly into college after graduating from high school (Venezia, Kirst, and Antonia 2003). Fewer than half (47%) of students whose parents did not go to college enrolled in any postsecondary institution the year after graduating from high school compared to 85% of students whose parents had college degrees (Berkner and Chavez 1997). Not all who are qualified attend. Only 69% of students meeting college qualifications criteria such as the requisite GPA, class rank, aptitude test scores, and SAT and ACT scores enrolled in college, while only 9% of unqualified students enrolled (Cabrera and La Nasa 2001).

ELIGIBILITY: WHAT DO HIGH SCHOOL STUDENTS KNOW ABOUT COLLEGE REQUIREMENTS?

Eligibility refers to the extent that students meet postsecondary criteria for admission. High school students often share a set of common misperceptions about eligibility, including thinking that graduation from high school alone makes one eligible for college, that the senior year does not matter, or that taking easy courses to get good grades improves one's chances of getting into college (Venezia, Kirst, and Antonia 2003).

Although most students want to go to college, they often take an unenthusiastic approach to college preparation and application, resulting in misperceptions and poorly informed decisions. Although schools and counselors provide information about college requirements, events such as college nights are often poorly attended. Further, students also do not know the course requirements or the admissions and placement test policies for local colleges and universities. Fewer than 12% of students knew the high school courses required for admission to the local college nearest their high school and fewer than half could identify the tests that were required (Conley 2006; Venezia, Kirst, and Antonia 2003).

While students can be inundated with information online and materials from colleges and counseling offices, some may have difficulty understanding the materials intended to help them. College admissions materials are written at a reading level expected of an upper-level college student or college graduate, and high school students applying to colleges often do not understand the terminology used in college applications and admissions materials (Johnson and Chapman 1979). Students who are uncertain in their plans understand this terminology the least, while those with older siblings in college understand it the best. Presenting information through technical formats familiar to today's students, such as social media, may make it easier for them to understand and be more helpful to them in the transition process.

Some innovators are capitalizing on the opportunity to apply social media and gaming as a transition tool—particularly for students lacking other means of developing the key transition skills and strategies. For example, the games *Application Crunch* and *Mission: Admission*, developed collaboratively between the University of Southern California's Pullias Center for Higher Education and Game Innovation Lab, challenge students to apply for, gain entry to, pay for, and succeed in college. To win, players must get into college, save money to pay for tuition and other expenses, and build the kind of personal characteristics that can succeed in their chosen school (collegeology.usc.edu/games).

PROGRAM SELECTION: MATCHMAKING STUDENTS TO FUTURES

The process of selecting and applying to college requires considerable planning, self-knowledge, and preparation. Many traditional programs and tools aimed at supporting students and families with college selection are well intentioned and provide valuable and helpful information but often do not incorporate emerging technical advances. For example, although countless online databases containing college selection criteria exist, they provide the same information that has been listed in the two-inch-thick bound books available before the internet and offer little in terms of interactivity beyond rudimentary matching with the same traditional search criteria that has been provided to earlier generations of college applicants (e.g., total enrollment, average tuition, geographic region, average test scores, and ethnicity of student body).

Not only do existing databases provide the same limited set of college characteristics as they have for decades, but they are not directly aligned to what students find the most helpful when selecting a college. The most important considerations prospective students have cited when choosing among colleges include the perceived credentials of faculty and high institutional standards (Baird 1976); the academic reputation of the institution (more than cost) (Spies 1978); the availability of desired majors; the opinions of parents, guardians, and friends; guidance center materials (Galotti and Mark 1994); family input; and cost (Kim 2004).

Not surprisingly, technology is increasingly important to students selecting a college. Students rely on social media for networking and exploring schools, majors, and careers, particularly the unfiltered and authentic media, such as student-run blogs, university Facebook page likes, events and updates, YouTube videos, Foursquare check-ins, and Twitter feeds. All provide an insider's view into student culture on campus that is more authentic than official websites and brochures. One out of five students has dropped a prospective college from consideration after having an unsuccessful visit to the school's website, and 57% of students reported being more interested in colleges after seeing great websites (Noel-Levitz 2011). College selection can also be driven by social and status factors, such as the reputation of the sports teams. Applications from prospective football and basketball players increase at institutions in the years following championship wins, as do applications from academically highly qualified candidates (Letawsky et al. 2003; Toma and Cross 1998).

Social media data have great potential to facilitate the college selection process by better connecting institutions and programs to prospective applicants on the basis of student study habits, recreational pursuits, and aspirations that can be inferred from their status updates, online profiles, and check-ins. Although students rarely make decisions about where to attend college from pe-rusing a school's social media site, once the decision has been made, social media can be helpful in the transition from home to college campus by facilitat-ing the necessary identity change (from high school student to college student) and by forming new college-level social networks (Stageman 2011).

Although gaming and simulations could be applied to the college selection and application process, no applications are currently available. One example of a possible application is Cisco's series of simulated gaming environments de-signed to prepare students for certification exams (e.g., *Aspire* and *MindShare* available at learningnetworkstore.cisco.com). Aspire is a simulated IT envi-ronment that provides "gamers" with real-world network set up, routing and trouble-shooting situations, problems, and decisions as practice for working in IT fields. Correct decisions are rewarded with tokens that can be used to unlock new "contracts" and gain additional and increasingly complex virtual experi-ences. A simulated environment that allows students to try out college choices might benefit students by showing the implications different decisions have on virtual futures.

Happiness with one's choice of college is related to success in college. Stu-dent commitment to and satisfaction with their college correlates with re-tention and GPA (Richardson, Abraham, and Bond 2012; Robbins et al. 2004). Many college students say their current college was their first choice, but agree-ment differs by ethnicity. Between 68% and 79% of whites, Latinos, and African Americans report that their current college was their first-choice institution, but only 55% of Asian Americans do so (Kim 2004). Additional research evalu-ating how happy students are with their ultimate college choice would be useful in identifying effective college selection practices.

5. Career Awareness

The four keys apply to both college and career readiness. Despite recent de-bates identifying the similarities and differences between college and career readiness, the two have significant overlap in elements found in all four of the keys. Ultimately, employers want many of the same skills colleges do. Ad-missions offices and employers both want candidates with core academic skills, higher-order thinking skills, the ability to learn, and personal qualities such as self-direction, persistence, and motivation (Kuncel, Ones, and Sackett 2010).

The most effective career exploration programs are those that start early (elementary school) and continue through high school (Rogers et al. 1995). Participation in these programs is associated with positive postsecondary outcomes (Benz, Yovanoff, and Doren 1997) and increased student achievement, particularly when career exploration is integrated with academic subjects (Baker and Taylor 1998; Evans and Burck 1992).

Social media, and gaming in particular, present opportunities to expose students to different careers in interactive online learning environments. For example:

- *Go North!* (www.polarhusky.com), an interactive adventure learning distance education approach, provides students with opportunities to explore real-world issues in geology, geography, economics, and ecology through authentic learning experiences within collaborative learning environments.
- *Zapitalism* (http://www.zapitalism.com/) is a simulated business strategy game where players make deals with the locals, invest in stocks and bonds, corner the market, and build megastores. The player building the largest empire wins.
- *Earthducation* (lt.umn.edu/earthducation/) provides a series of interactive, virtual expeditions to eco-sensitive areas of the world on every continent to create a global community-driven narrative of the dynamic intersections between education and sustainability.
- *Boulevard* (fugazo.com/games/time/bistro) lets players hire staff, build a menu, experiment with ingredients to create new recipes, redecorate, and upgrade a small diner into a five-star restaurant. Players assume the role of general manager of a series of restaurants.
- *GeoThentic* (lt.umn.edu/geothentic/) applies geospatial technology to the online exploration of real-world problems through "cognitive apprenticeships" in ecology, biology, and demography.
- *EcoMuve* (ecomuve.gse.harvard.edu) and *RiverCity* are simulated and mobile interactive outdoor learning environments that allow students to mimic the steps a scientist would take in the field to explore complex real-world problems.
- *Virtual U* (designed by Enlight Software, the Jackson Hole Higher Education Group, and the Institute for Research on Higher Education) is a virtual college campus, where players take on higher education administration as administrators, deans, and university donors.

6. Self-Advocacy and Help Seeking

Self-advocacy refers to an individual's ability to effectively communicate, convey, negotiate, or assert his or her own interests, desires, needs, and rights. Effective self-advocacy involves proactively making informed decisions and taking responsibility for those decisions (Izzo and Lamb 2002; Rotter 1975). Being able to self-advocate assumes an awareness of one's interests, desires, needs, and rights and the determination to negotiate and pursue these interests.

Although much of the research on self-advocacy focuses on students with disabilities, self-advocacy is essential for all students. Being an effective self-advocate is related to academic performance, persistence, and achievement (Brown and Lent 1996; Lent, Brown, and Larkin 1984). Self-efficacy beliefs predict college outcomes (performance and persistence) by 10% to 15% above and beyond the prediction provided by standardized achievement and placement tests (Kahn and Nauta 2001; Multon, Brown, and Lent 1991; Pajares and Miller 1995). Being aware of and able to advocate for their best interests is a key predictor of success among college students with disabilities (Brinckerhoff 1994; Lock and Layton 2001; Vogel and Adelman 1992) and is associated with increased persistence and retention (Izzo and Lamb 2002), increased educational opportunities (Aune 2000; Durlak and Rose 1994), and positive outcomes after school (Wehmeyer and Schwartz 1995). Additionally, greater self-efficacy has been associated with higher goals, greater motivation to achieve those goals, and better coping with stress during taxing times (Bandura 1997; DeAndrea et al. 2011).

Students tend not to utilize the resources available on college campuses, including library and career centers, do not ask faculty for help, and do not know when to ask for help (National Association of Colleges and Employers 2011; Ryan, Gheen, and Midgley 1998). In recent documentaries on the college transition process (Declining by Degrees: Higher Education at Risk [2005] and First Generation [2011]), students provide compelling vignettes about falling behind and not recognizing they needed help until it was too late.

Programs sponsored by the U.S. Department of Education, such as TRIO and GEAR UP, have successfully supported underrepresented and first-generation college students in part by educating them about the resources available in postsecondary education. However, they use technology in a very limited fashion. Games could help teach potential college students about the resources and supports available and when it is appropriate to use them. As part of the enrollment process, new students could play a campus game, similar to Application Crunch or Mission: Admission that identifies common issues and needs and that introduces them to available resources (e.g., student union, office of dean of students, bursars office, advisers, campus writing center, tutoring services, counseling center, career services, financial aid office, and student activities).

Geosocial applications, such as the "Foursquare for Universities" program (www.foursquare.com/universities), may help students identify and obtain resources. The program assists students, alumni, and staff in finding and sharing information about classes, building hours, campus activities, and traditions. Augmented reality and geotagging programs have great potential as well. Imagine a walking tour around campus, augmented by a mobile device similar to *CultureClic* (www.cultureclic.fr), or *New York Nearest Subway* (http://www.acrossair.com/apps_newyorknearestsubway.htm), which overlay culturally significant locations or subway stops onto the map on a mobile device, but instead superimpose the traditions, purpose, services, and hours over each building as a student passes by it. New students could collect "badges" for completing tasks during a virtual tour (e.g., visit the adviser office, sign up at the gymnasium, pick up an events schedule the student union) and receive an engaging and interactive tour of available resources while they tour the physical campus.

Conclusion

It is clear that the transition process is complex and information intensive, consisting of a great deal of "privileged knowledge." Providing equal access to this knowledge to groups historically underrepresented in postsecondary education can help level the playing field by enabling more high school students to do what it takes to be both eligible and ready for college.

While an argument can be made that the true solution is to make the system itself more transparent and streamlined, unless and until this occurs, the next best strategy is to get more information to students and their parents, and get it to them in forms that engage them, make college seem to be a realistic goal, connect them with others facing similar challenges, guide and support them, teach them what it takes to make a successful transition, and then shepherd them through the process. In this way, technology can help to overcome the knowledge differential present between different groups in society regarding what it takes to get into and persist in college.

Today's students think about technology as a natural extension of much of what they do in their daily lives. It has changed how they interact with one another, how they gather, how they share and use information in real time, and how they learn and think. There is no reason it should not have just as much of a transformative effect on how students make successful postsecondary transitions.

Technology has changed the way today's students interact with the learning process and with one another around shared learning goals or activities. Consider some of the ways that students can effect such interaction:

- Contribute to class discussions, not by raising one's hand and speaking out loud but by posting on classroom blogs, chat rooms, or Pinterest pages, or via an avatar in a simulated lecture hall interacting with other student and instructor avatars
- Attend lectures in person and online via UStream, SecondLife, take proctored exams online via ProctorU, and check their assignments and grades on ChalkBoard
- Access information and resources 24 hours a day, 7 days a week, on mobile devices
- Create and share multimedia content by posting and following others' status on Facebook and Twitter and by connecting via Meet Up, Foursquare, or Skype
- Share documents, photographs, music, and web pages, anywhere, any time, on DropBox, InstaGram, and Pandora
- Find and rate things to do, places to go, and food to eat on UrbanSpoon, FoodSpotting, and Yelp
- Communicate instantly via email, instant messaging, and text messaging
- Read electronic versions of magazines, newspapers, and books on e-readers instead of print versions
- Interview people in a wide range of occupations to learn more about what it is like to work in those areas, and then develop and post videos online and comment on those videos
- Choose from among online tools such as those offered by Naviance, College Board, or ConnectEdu to make choices about colleges, construct a digital portfolio of materials necessary to apply for college, and assemble all the materials necessary to apply

The K–12 educational system has been a slow adopter of new technologies and has actively fought the incursion or inclusion of almost all social media platforms. The transition process from high school to college has immense potential to benefit from technology-mediated interactive tools. However, the transition process lags behind in incorporating technology that students use in other aspects of their lives. Overcoming the institutional barriers schools place on social media and the fiscal, technical, and human issues associated with infusing new technologies into schools is a daunting proposition. However, these issues must be confronted and addressed if technology is to play a central role in equalizing opportunities for students to prepare for the transition from high school to college.

Technology can be as much of a barrier as a help to students and parents. Poorly designed and implemented websites with forms that are difficult or impossible for parents or students to complete can become an insurmountable barrier to those not accustomed to dealing with such challenges. The FAFSA is perhaps the best example of this phenomenon. However, colleges need to pay careful attention to the user friendliness of their sites and online resources. Selective schools do a somewhat better job in this regard, with community colleges often lagging behind in terms of site design and maintenance, which is unfortunate because students attending community college are more often likely to be in need of support in using online resources.

Also a challenge is the opportunity to use many of these online tools and systems in school. Social media in support of transition will require time for interactions and thoughtful responses, rather than the casual, superficial, and often trivial nature of social interaction online. Social media systems will need to find their place in the school day if they are to be fully integrated and supported. Where will they fit? Are they a part of a class or an independent assignment? Are students required to use social media, expected to do so, encouraged to do so, or some combination of all of these? Right now, who takes advantage of the social media opportunities to enhance and smooth the transition process is entirely hit or miss.

Technology generally and social media tools specifically offer new possibilities for solutions, not just another requirement to be met in the transition process. Technology, in the form of social media, games, and simulations, provides a unique opportunity to address the historical challenges and inequalities in transition facing students, and particularly underrepresented students.

Currently lacking are development efforts in the many areas identified in this chapter. Few companies have been able to develop profitable apps or platforms in this space yet. Given the dramatic increase in college-going students that has occurred over the past 30 years and that will likely continue into the future, the commercial potential of this space seems unlikely to be overlooked indefinitely. Whether it is via numerous small startups or concerted large-scale projects, transition readiness would appear to be an area in which extensive technological development will occur, the result of which will be more students ready to make a successful transition from high school to college.

REFERENCES

Achieve, Inc. 2005. *Rising to the Challenge: Are High School Graduates Prepared for College and Work?* Washington, DC.

ACT Policy Report. 2011. *The Condition of College and Career Readiness, 2011.* Iowa City, IA: ACT. http://www.act.org/readiness/2011.

Adams, Marsha H., Lynn M. Stover, and Joy F. Whitlow. 1999. "A Longitudinal Evaluation of Baccalaureate Nursing Students' Critical-Thinking Abilities." *Journal of Nursing Education* 38:139–141.

Adelman, Clifford. 1999. *Answers in the Toolbox: Academic Intensity, Attendance Patterns, and Bachelor's Degree Attainment.* Washington, DC: Office of Educational Research and Improvement.

Advisory Committee on Student Financial Assistance (ACSFA). 2002. *Empty Promises: The Myth of College Access in America.* Washington, DC.

Allensworth, Elaine M., and John Q. Easton. 2007. *What Matters for Staying On-Track and Graduating in Chicago Public High Schools.* Chicago: Consortium on Chicago School Research, University of Chicago.

American Council on Education (ACE). 2004. *Missed Opportunities: Students Who Do Not Apply for Financial Aid.* Washington, DC.

Apple, Michael W. 1995. *Education and Power.* 2nd ed. New York: Routledge.

Art and Science Group, Inc. 2000. "Internet Now Pervasive and Powerful Element in College Choice: Promises to Become Decisive Factor in Near Future." *Student Poll* 4(1):1–12.

Astin, Alexander, Lisa Tsui, and Juan Avalos. 1996. *Degree Attainment at American Colleges and Universities: Effect of Race, Gender, and Institutional Type.* Los Angeles: UCLA Higher Education Research Institute.

Attewell, Paul, David Lavin, Thurston Domina, and Tania Levey. 2006. "New Evidence on College Remediation." *Journal of Higher Education* 77:886–924.

Aud, Susan H., Kena G. William, Kevin Bianco, Lauren Frohlich, Jana Kemp, and Kim Tahan. 2011. *The Condition of Education, 2011 (NCES 2011-033).* Washington, DC: U.S. Government Printing Office.

Aune, Betty. 2000. "Career and Academic Advising." *New Directions for Student Services* 91:55–67.

Bailey, Thomas R., Katherine L. Hughes, and Melinda K. Karp. 2002. *What Role Can Dual Enrollment Programs Play in Easing the Transition between High School and Postsecondary Education?* New York: Community College Research Center and Institute on Education and the Economy, Teachers College, Columbia University.

Baird, Leonard L. 1976. *Using Self-Reports to Predict Student Performance.* New York: College Board.

Baker, Stanley M., and John G. Taylor. 1998. "Effects of Career Education Interventions: A Meta-Analysis." *Career Development Quarterly* 46:376–385.

Bandura, Albert. 1997. *Self-Efficacy: The Exercise of Control.* New York: W. H. Freeman.

Bean, John P., and Barnara S. Metzner. 1985. "A Conceptual Model of Nontraditional Undergraduate Student Attrition." *Review of Educational Research* 55:485–540.

Bennett, Pamela R., and Yu Xie. 2003. "Revisiting Racial Differences in College Attendance: The Role of Historically Black Colleges and Universities." *American Sociological Review* 68:567–580.

Benz, Michael R., Paul Yovanoff, and Bonnie Doren. 1997. "School-to-Work Components that Predict Post-School Success for Students with and without Disabilities." *Exceptional Children* 63:151–165.

Berkner, Lutz, and Lisa Chavez. 1997. *Access to Postsecondary Education for 1992 High School Graduates.* Washington, DC: National Center for Education Statistics.

Berzonsky, Michael D., and Linda S. Kuk. 2000. "Identity Status, Identity Processing Style, and the Transition to University." *Journal of Adolescent Research* 15:81–98.

Bickel, Robert. 1989. "Post-High School Opportunities and High School Completion Rates in an Appalachian State: A Near-Replication of Florida Research." *Youth and Society* 21:61–84.

Bickel, Robert, and Linda Lange. 1995. "Opportunities, Costs, and High School Completion in West Virginia: A Replication of Florida Research." *Journal of Educational Research* 88:363–370.

Billson, Janet M., and Margaret B. Terry. 1982. "In Search of the Silken Purse: Factors in Attrition among First-Generation Students." *College and University* 58:57–75.

Bransford, John D., Ann L. Brown, and Rodney R. Cocking. 2002. *How People Learn: Brain, Mind, Experience, and School.* Washington, DC: National Academy Press.

Bresciani, Marilee J., and Lewis Carson. 2002. "A Study of Undergraduate Persistence by Unmet Need and Percentage of Gift Aid." *NASPA Journal* 40:104–123.

Bridgeland, John M., John J. DiIulio Jr., and Karen Burke Morison. 2006. *The Silent Epidemic: Perspectives of High School Dropouts.* Washington, DC: Civic Enterprises.

Bridgeman, Brent, Laura McCamley-Jenkins, and Nancy Ervin. 2000. *Predictions of Freshman Grade Point Average from the Revised and Recentered SAT I: Reasoning Test (College Board Research Report No. 2000-1).* New York: College Entrance Examination Board.

Brinckerhoff, Loring C. 1994. "Developing Effective Self-Advocacy Skills in College-Bound Students with Learning Disabilities." *Intervention in School and Clinic* 29:229–237.

Brown, Steven D., and Robert W. Lent. 1996. "A Social Cognitive Framework for Career Choice Counseling." *Career Development Quarterly* 44:354–366.

Burdman, Pamela. 2005. *The Student Debt Dilemma: Debt Aversion as a Barrier to College Access.* Berkeley: Project on Student Debt, Institute for College Access and Success.

Bureau of Labor Statistics. 2012. *College Enrollment and Work Activity of 2011 High School Graduates (Press Release).* http://www.bls.gov/news.release/hsgec.nro.htm/.

Cabrera, Alberto F., and Steven M. La Nasa. 2001. "On the Path to College: Three Critical Tasks Facing America's Disadvantaged." *Research in Higher Education* 42:119–149.

Camara, Wayne J., and Gary Echternacht. 2000. *The SAT I and High School Grades: Utility in Predicting Success in College (College Board Research Notes RN-10).* New York: College Entrance Examination Board.

Campbell, Toni A., and David E. Campbell. 1997. "Faculty/Student Mentor Program: Effects on Academic Performance and Retentions." *Research in Higher Education* 38:727–742.

Center for Higher Education Policy Analysis. 2009. *Mentoring Scaffoldings: Do They Promote College Access?* Los Angeles: Rossier School of Education, University of Southern California.

Choy, Susan P. 2001. *Students Whose Parents Did Not Go to College: Postsecondary Access, Enrollment, and Persistence (NCES 2001-126)*. Washington, DC: National Center for Education Statistics.

Clance, Pauline R., and Suzanne A. Imes. 1978. "The Impostor Phenomenon among High Achieving Women: Dynamics and Therapeutic Intervention." *Psychotherapy Theory, Research, and Practice* 15:241–247.

College Board. 2011. *2011 College-Bound Seniors: Total Group Profile Report*. New York: College Board Publications. http://professionals.collegeboard.com.

Common Core State Standards Initiative. 2012. "About the Standards." Accessed June 21. http://www.corestandards.org.

Conley, David T. 2005. *College Knowledge: What It Really Takes for Students to Succeed and What We Can Do to Get Them Ready*. San Francisco: Jossey-Bass.

———. 2006. *What We Must Do to Create a System That Prepares Students for College Success: Policy Perspectives*. San Francisco: WestEd. http://www.wested.org/online_pubs/pp-06-01.pdf.

———. 2007. *Redefining College Readiness*. Eugene, OR: Educational Policy Improvement Center. http://www.aypf.org/documents/RedefiningCollegeReadiness.pdf.

———. 2010. *College and Career Ready: Helping All Students Succeed beyond High School*. San Francisco: Jossey-Bass.

———. 2012. *A Complete Definition of College and Career Readiness*. Eugene, OR: Educational Policy Improvement Center. https://www.epiconline.org/publications.

Crisp, Gloria, and Irene Cruz. 2009. "Mentoring College Students: A Critical Review of the Literature between 1990 and 2007." *Research in Higher Education* 50:525–545.

Csikszentmihalyi, Mihaly. 1990. *Flow: The Psychology of Optimal Experience*. New York: Harper and Row.

Csikszentmihalyi, Mihaly, and Barbara Schneider. 2000. *Becoming Adult: How Teenagers Prepare for the World of Work*. New York: Basic Books.

Day, Jennifer C., and Eric C. Newburger. 2002. *The Big Pay Off: Educational Attainment and Synthetic Estimates of Work-Life Earnings (Current Population Report P23-210)*. New York: U.S. Census Bureau.

DeAndrea, David C., Nicole B. Ellison, Robert LaRose, Charles Steinfield, and Andrew Fiore. 2011. "Serious Social Media: On the Use of Social Media for Improving Students' Adjustment to College." *Internet and Higher Education*. Accessed September 10, 2012. doi:10.1016/j.iheduc.2011.05.009.

Declining by Degrees: Higher Education At Risk. 2005. Produced by John Merrow. PBS Video, DVD.

Dowd, Alicia C., and Tarek Coury. 2006. "The Effect of Loans on the Persistence and Attainment of Community College Students." *Research in Higher Education* 47:33–62.

DuBois, David L., Bruce E. Holloway, Jeffrey C. Valentine, and Harris Copper. 2002. "Effectiveness of Mentoring Programs for Youth: A Meta-analytical Review." *American Journal of Community Psychology* 30:157–197.

Durlak, Christine M., and Ernest Rose. 1994. "Preparing High School Students with Learning Disabilities for the Transition to Postsecondary Education: Teaching the Skills of Self-Determination." *Journal of Learning Disabilities* 27:51–59.

Dynarski, Susan M., and Judith Scott-Clayton. 2006. *The Cost of Complexity in Federal Student Aid: Lessons from Optimal Tax Theory and Behavioral Economics*. Cambridge, MA: Harvard University, John F. Kennedy School of Government.

Eccles, Jacquelynne S., and Allan Wigfield. 2002. "Motivational Beliefs, Values, and Goals." *Annual Review of Psychology* 53:109–132.

Ekstrom, Ruth B. 1992. *Attitudes toward Borrowing and Participation in Postsecondary Education.* New York: College Board.

Elias, Steven M., and Ross J. Loomis. 2002. "Utilizing Need for Cognition and Perceived Self-Efficacy to Predict Academic Performance." *Journal of Applied Social Psychology* 32:1687–1717.

Ensher, Ellen A., Christian Heun, and Anita Blanchard. 2003. "Online Mentoring and Computer-Mediated Communication: New Directions in Research." *Journal of Vocational Behavior* 63:264–288.

Erickson, Frederick. 1987. "Transformation and School Success: The Politics and Culture of Educational Achievement." *Anthropology and Education Quarterly* 18:335–356.

Evans, James H., and Harman D. Burck. 1992. "The Effects of Career Education Interventions on Academic Achievement: A Meta-analysis." *Journal of Counseling and Development* 71:63–68.

Federal Reserve Bank of New York: Research and Statistics Group. 2012. "Quarterly Report on Household Debt and Credit: May." Accessed July 15. http://www.newyorkfed.org/creditconditions/.

Finn, Jeremy D. 1989. "Withdrawing from School." *Review of Educational Research* 59:117–142.

Finn, Jeremy D., and Donald A. Rock. 1997. "Academic Success among Students At-Risk." *Journal of Applied Psychology* 82:221–234.

First Generation. 2011. Directed by Adam Fenderson and Jaye Fenderson. Market Street Productions. Film.

Fitzgerald, Brian K. 2006. "Lowering Barriers to College Access: Opportunities for More Effective Coordination of State and Federal Student Aid Policies." In *Expanding Opportunity in Higher Education: Leveraging Promise*, edited by Patricia Gandara, Gary Orfield, and Catherine L. Horn, 53–74. Albany, NY: SUNY Press.

Flint, Thomas A. 1992. "Parental and Planning Influences on the Formation of Student College Choice Sets." *Research in Higher Education* 33:689–708.

Freeman, Kassie. 1997. "Increasing African Americans' Participation in Higher Education: African American High School Students' Perspectives." *Journal of Higher Education* 68:523–550.

Galotti, Kathleen M., and Melissa C. Mark. 1994. "How Do High School Students Structure an Important Life Decision? A Short-Term Longitudinal Study of the College Decision-Making Process." *Research in Higher Education* 35:589–607.

Gandara, Patricia, and Maria Mejorado. 2005. "Putting Your Money Where Your Mouth Is: Mentoring as a Strategy to Increase Access to Higher Education." In *Preparing for College: Nine Elements of Effective Outreach*, edited by William G. Tierney, Zoë B. Corwin, and Julia D. Colyar, 89–110. Albany, NY: SUNY Press.

Gee, James Paul. 2002. "Literacies, Identities, and Discourses." In *Developing Advanced Literacy in First and Second Languages: Meaning with Power*, edited by Mary J. Schleppegrell and M. Cecilia Colombi, 159–175. Mahwah, NJ: Lawrence Erlbaum Associates.

Geiser, Saul. 2009. "Back to the Basics: In Defense of Achievement (and Achievement Tests) in College Admissions." *Change: The Magazine of Higher Learning* 41(1):16–23.

Giroux, Henry. 1982. "Literacy, Ideology, and the Politics of Schooling." *Humanities in Society* 4(4):20–36.

Goldrick-Rab, Sara. 2006. *Promoting Academic Momentum at Community Colleges: Challenges and Opportunities (CCRC Working Paper No. 5)*. New York: Community College Research Center, Teachers College, Columbia University.

Gosine, Kevin. 2002. "Essentialism versus Complexity: Conceptions of Racial Identity Construction in Educational Scholarship." *Canadian Journal of Education* 27:81–100.

Grodsky, Eric, and Melanie Jones. 2004. "Real and Imagined Barriers to College Entry: Perceptions of Cost." *Social Science Research* 36:745–766.

Heath, Shirley B. 1983. *Ways with Words: Language, Life, and Work in Communities and Classrooms*. Cambridge: Cambridge University Press.

Heller, Donald E. 2006. "Early Commitment of Financial Aid Eligibility." *American Behavioral Scientist* 49:1719–1738.

Hertel, James B. 2002. "College Student Generational Status: Similarities, Differences, and Factors in College Adjustment." *Psychological Record* 52:3–18.

Horn, Laura J., Xianglei Chen, and Chris Chapman. 2003. *Getting Ready to Pay for College: What Students and Their Parents Know about the Cost of College Tuition and What They Are Doing to Find Out (NCES 2003-030)*. Washington, DC: National Center for Education Statistics.

Hossler, Don, Shouping Hu, and Jack Schmit. 1999. "Predicting Student Sensitivity to Tuition and Financial Aid." *Journal of Student Financial Aid* 29:17–31.

Howell, Jessica S., Michal Kurlaender, and Eric Grodsky. 2010. "Postsecondary Preparation and Remediation: Examining the Effect of the Early Assessment Program at California State University." *Journal of Policy Analysis and Management* 29:726–748.

Hu, Shouping, and Don Hossler. 2000. "Willingness to Pay and Preference for Private Institutions." *Research in Higher Education* 41:685–701.

Huffman, Terry. 2001. "Resistance Theory and the Transculturation Hypothesis as Explanations of College Attrition and Persistence among Culturally Traditional American Indian Students." *Journal of American Indian Education* 40(3):1–39.

Ikenberry, Stanley O., and Terry W. Hartle. 1998. *Too Little Knowledge Is a Dangerous Thing: What the Public Thinks about Paying for College*. Washington, DC: American Council on Education.

Izzo, Margo Vreeburg, and Peg Lamb. 2002. *Self-Determination and Career Development: Skills for Successful Transitions to Postsecondary Education and Employment (White Paper)*. Honolulu: National Center for the Study of Postsecondary Educational Supports (NCSPES), University of Hawai'i at Manoa. http://www.ncset.hawaii.edu/publications/pdf/self_determination.pdf.

Jackson, Gregory A. 1978. "Financial Aid and Student Enrollment." *Journal of Higher Education* 49:548–574.

Jay, Gina M., and Anthony R. D'Augelli. 1991. "Social Support and Adjustment to University Life: A Comparison of African American and White Freshmen." *Journal of Community Psychology* 19:95–108.

Johnson, Russell H., and David W. Chapman. 1979. "An Assessment of College Recruitment Literature: Does the High School Senior Understand It?" *Research in Higher Education* 11:309–319.

Kahn, Jeffrey H., and Margaret M. Nauta. 2001. "Social-Cognitive Predictors of First-Year College Persistence: The Importance of Proximal Assessment." *Research in Higher Education* 42:633–652.

Kao, Grace, and Jennifer S. Thompson. 2003. "Race and Ethnic Stratification in Educational Achievement and Attainment." *Annual Review of Sociology* 29:417–442.

Karp, Melinda Mechur, Juan Carlos Calcagno, Katherine L. Hughes, Dong Wook Jeong, and Thomas R. Bailey. 2007. *The Postsecondary Achievement of Participants in Dual Enrollment: An Analysis of Student Outcomes in Two States.* St. Paul: National Research Center for Career and Technical Education, University of Minnesota.

Kim, Dongbin. 2004. "The Effect of Financial Aid on Students' College Choice: Differences by Racial Groups." *Research in Higher Education* 45:43–70.

King, Jacqueline E. 1996. *The Decision to Go to College: Attitudes and Experiences Associated with College Attendance among Low-Income Students.* Washington, DC: College Board.

Kirsch, Irving. 1986. "Early Research on Self-Efficacy: What We Already Know without Knowing We Knew." *Journal of Social and Clinical Psychology* 4:339–358.

Knapp, Laura G., Janice E. Kelly-Reid, and Scott A. Ginder. 2010. *Enrollment in Postsecondary Institutions, Fall 2008; Graduation Rates, 2002 and 2005 Cohorts; and Financial Statistics, Fiscal Year 2008 (NCES 2010-152).* Washington, DC: National Center for Education Statistics.

Knouse, Stephen B. 2001. "Virtual Mentors: Mentoring on the Internet." *Journal of Employment Counseling* 38(4):162–169.

Kuncel, Nathan R., and Sarah A. Hezlett. 2007. "Standardized Tests Predict Graduate Students' Success." *Science* 315(5815):1080–1081.

Kuncel, Nathan R., Deniz S. Ones, and Paul R. Sackett. 2010. "Individual Differences as Predictors of Work, Educational, and Broad Life Outcomes." *Personality and Individual Differences* 49:331–336.

Lefkowits, Laura, Carolyn Woempner, John Kendall, and David Frost. 2010. *A McREL Report Prepared for Stupski Foundation's Learning Center: College Readiness.* San Francisco: Stupski Foundation.

Lent, Robert W., Steven D. Brown, and Kevin C. Larkin. 1984. "Relation of Self-Efficacy Expectations to Academic Achievement and Persistence." *Journal of Counseling Psychology* 31:356–362.

Letawsky, Nicole R., Raymond G. Schneifer, Paul M. Pederson, and Carolyn J. Palmer. 2003. "Factors Influencing the College Selection Process of Student-Athletes: Are Their Factors Similar to Non-athletes." *College Student Journal* 37:604–610.

Linnenbrink, Elizabeth A., and Paul R. Pintrich. 2002. "Motivation as an Enabler for Academic Success." *School Psychology Review* 31:313–327.

Lock, Robin, and Carol A. Layton. 2001. "Succeeding in Postsecondary Education through Self-Advocacy." *Teaching Exceptional Children* 34:66–71.

Lozano, Aliber, Karen M. Watt, and Jeffrey Huerta. 2009. "A Comparison Study of 12th Grade Hispanic Students' College Anticipation, Aspirations and College Preparatory Measures." *American Secondary Education* 38:92–110.

Luna De La Rosa, Mari. 2006. "Is Opportunity Knocking? Low-Income Students' Perceptions of College and Financial Aid." *American Behavioral Scientist* 49:1670–1686.

Marcia, James. 1991. "Identity and Self-Development." In *Encyclopedia of Adolescence (Vol. 1)*, edited by Richard R. Lerner, Anne C. Petersen, and Jeanne Brooks-Gunn. New York: Garland.

Massachusetts Business Alliance for Education. 2006. *Preparing for the Future: Employer Perspectives on Work Readiness Skills.* Boston.

McDonough, Patricia M., and Shannon Calderone. 2004. "The Meaning of Money: Perceptual Differences between College Counselors and Low-Income Families about College Costs and Financial Aid." *American Behavioral Scientist* 49:1703–1718.

Mendiola, Irma Doris, Karen M. Watt, and Jeffery Huerta. 2010. "The Impact of Advancement via Individual Determination (AVID) on Mexican American Students Enrolled in a 4-Year University." *Journal of Hispanic Higher Education* 9:209–220.

Multon, Karen D., Steven D. Brown, and Robert W. Lent. 1991. "Relation of Self-Efficacy Beliefs to Academic Outcomes: A Meta-analytic Investigation." *Journal of Counseling Psychology* 38:30–38.

National Association of Colleges and Employers. 2011. *The Class of 2011 Student Survey Report.* Bethlehem, PA. http://www.naceweb.org/uploadedFiles/NACEWeb/Research/Student/student.pdf.

National Center for Education Statistics. 2011. *The Nation's Report Card: Reading, 2011 (NCES 2012-457).* Washington, DC: Institute of Education Sciences, U.S. Department of Education.

Niu, Sunny X., and Marta Tienda. 2010. "Minority Student Academic Performance under the Uniform Admission Law: Evidence from the University of Texas at Austin." *Educational Evaluation and Policy Analysis* 32:44–69.

Noel-Levitz. 2011. "2011 E-Expectations Report: The Online Expectations of Prospective College Students and Their Parents." http://blog.noellevitz.com/2011/07/19/online-expectations-prospective-college-students-parents/.

Ogbu, John U. 2004. "Collective Identity and the Burden of 'Acting White' in Black History, Community, and Education." *Urban Review: Issues and Ideas in Public Education* 36:1–35.

Pajares, Frank, and M. David Miller. 1995. "Mathematics Self-Efficacy and Mathematics Performance: The Need for Specificity of Assessment." *Journal of Counseling Psychology* 42:190–198.

Pantages, Timothy J., and Carol F. Creedon. 1978. "Studies of College Attrition: 1950–1978." *Review of Educational Research* 48:49–101.

Partnership for the Assessment of Readiness for College and Careers (PARCC). 2012. "About PARCC." Accessed June 21. http://www.parcconline.org.

Perna, Laura W. 2000. "Differences in the Decision to Attend College among African Americans, Hispanics, and Whites." *Journal of Higher Education* 71:117–141.

Quaglia, Russ J. 1989. "Student Aspirations: A Critical Dimension in Effective Schools." *Research in Rural Education* 6:7–10.

Ramist, L., Charles Lewis, and Laura McCamley-Jenkins. 1994. *Student Group Differences in Predicting College Grades: Sex, Language, and Ethnic Groups (College Board Research Report No. 93-1).* New York: College Entrance Examination Board.

Rice, Kenneth G., David A. Cole, and Daniel K. Lapsley. 1990. "Separation-Individuation, Family Cohesion, and Adjustment to College: Measurement Validation and a Test of a Theoretical Model." *Journal of Counseling Psychology* 37:195–202.

Richardson, Michelle, Charles Abraham, and Rod Bond. 2012. "Psychological Correlates of University Students' Academic Performance: A Systematic Review and Meta-analysis." *Psychological Bulletin* 138:353–387.

Road Trip Nation. 2012. "About." Accessed September 10. www.roadtripnation.com.

Robbins, Steven B., Kristy Lauver, Huy Le, Daniel Davis, Ronelle Langley, and Aaron Carlstrom. 2004. "Do Psychosocial and Study Skill Factors Predict College Outcomes? A Meta-analysis." *Psychological Bulletin* 130:261–288.

Roderick, Melissa, Jenny Nagaoka, Vanessa Coca, Eliza Moeller, Karen Roddie, Jamiliyah Gilliam, and Desmond Patton. 2008. *From High School to the Future: Potholes on the Road to College.* Chicago: Consortium on Chicago School Research at the University of Chicago.

Rodriguez, Adele L., Florence Guido-DiBrito, Vasti Torres, and Donna Talbot. 2000. "Latina College Students: Issues and Challenges for the 21st Century." *NASPA Journal* 37:511–527.

Rogers, Anne M., Susan Hubbard, Ivan Charner, Bryna Shore Fraser, and Richard Horne. 1995. *Learning from Experience: A Cross-Case Comparison of School-to-Work Transition Reform Initiatives.* Washington, DC: National Institute for Work and Learning, Academy for Educational Development.

Rogers, Karen B., and Richard D. Kimpston. 1992. "Acceleration: What We Do vs. What We Know." *Educational Leadership* 50(2):58–61.

Rotter, Julian B. 1975. "Some Problems and Misconceptions Related to the Construct of Internal versus External Control of Reinforcement." *Journal of Consulting and Clinical Psychology* 43:56–67.

Ryan, Allison M., Margaret H. Gheen, and Carol Midgley. 1998. "Why Do Some Students Avoid Asking for Help? An Examination of the Interplay among Students' Academic Efficacy, Teachers' Social-Emotional Role, and the Classroom Goal Structure." *Journal of Educational Psychology* 90:528–535.

Sallie Mae Fund and Harris Interactive. 2003. *Caught in the Financial Aid Information Divide.* Fishers, IN.

Schlosser, Lewis Z., Sarah Knox, Alissa R. Moskovitz, and Clara E. Hill. 2003. "A Qualitative Examination of Graduate Advising Relationships: The Advisee Perspective." *Journal of Counseling Psychology* 50:178–188.

Schneider, Barbara, and David Stevenson. 1999. *The Ambitious Generation: America's Teenagers, Motivated but Directionless.* New Haven, CT: Yale University Press.

Solozorano, Dg. 1991. "Mobility Aspirations among Racial Minorities, Controlling for SES." *Sociology and Social Research* 75:182–188.

Spies, Richard R. 1978. *The Effect of Rising Costs on College Choice: A Study of the Application Decisions of High-Ability Students.* New York: College Entrance Examination Board.

Stageman, Amanda. 2011. "Consulting Social Media in the College Transition Process: Experiential Accounts of the Class of 2014." Master's thesis, Marquette University.

Stanton-Salazar, Ricardo D. 2001. *Manufacturing Hope and Despair: The School and Kin Support Networks of U.S.-Mexican Youth.* New York: Teachers College Press.

Steinberg, Lynn. 1996. "A Simple Lack of Manners Imperils Civilized Society." *Plain Dealer*, January 14.

Sum, Andrew, Ishwar Khatiwada, Joseph McLaughlin, Sheila Palma, Jacqui Motroni, Neil Sullivan, and Nahir Torres. 2010. *The College Success of Boston Public School Graduates from the Classes of 2000–2008: Findings from a Post-Secondary Longitudinal Tracking Study and the Early Outcomes of the Success Boston College Completion Initiative.* Boston: Center for Labor Market Studies, Northeastern University.

Swail, Watson S., Kenneth E. Redd, and Laura W. Perna. 2003. *Retaining Minority Students in Higher Education: A Framework for Success. ASHE-ERIC Higher Education Report.* Hoboken, NJ: John Wiley.

Swanson, Joni L. 2008. "An Analysis of the Impact of High School Dual Enrollment Course Participation on Post-Secondary Academic Success, Persistence and Degree Completion." Paper presented at the meeting of the National Association for Gifted Children, Tampa, Florida, and the National Alliance of Concurrent Enrollment Partnerships, Kansas City, Missouri.

Tamir, Maya, Oliver P. John, Sanjay Srivastava, and James J. Gross. 2007. "Implicit Theories of Emotion: Affective and Social Outcomes across a Major Life Transition." *Journal of Personality and Social Psychology* 92:731–744.

Terenzini, Patrick T., Alberto F. Cabrera, and Elena M. Bernal. 2001. *Swimming against the Tide: The Poor in American Higher Education.* New York: College Board Publications. http://research.collegeboard.org/publications/content/2012/05/swimming-against-tide-poor-american-higher-education.

Terenzini, Patrick T., Ernest T. Pascarella, and Gregory S. Blimling. 1996. "Students' Out-of-Class Experiences and Their Influence on Learning and Cognitive Development: A Literature Review." *Journal of College Student Development* 37:149–162.

Terenzini, Patrick T., Leonard Springer, Patricia M. Yaeger, Ernest T. Pascarella, and Amaury Nora. 1996. "First-Generation College Students: Characteristics, Experiences, and Cognitive Development." *Research in Higher Education* 37:1–22.

Tierney, William G. 1999. "Models of Minority College-Going and Retention: Cultural Integrity versus Cultural Suicide." *Journal of Negro Education* 68:80–91.

Tierney, William G., and Kristan M. Venegas. 2006. "Fictive Kin and Social Capital: The Role of Peer Groups in Applying and Paying for College." *American Behavioral Scientist* 49:1687–1702.

Tinto, Vincent. 1975. "Dropout from Higher Education: A Theoretical Synthesis of Recent Research." *Review of Educational Research* 45:89–125.

———. 1993. *Leaving College: Rethinking the Causes and Cures of Student Attrition.* 2nd ed. Chicago: University of Chicago Press.

———. 1996. "Reconstructing the First Year of College." *Planning for Higher Education* 25(1):1–6.

———. 1998. "Colleges as Communities: Taking Research on Student Persistence Seriously." *Review of Higher Education* 21:167–177.

———. 1999. "Taking Retention Seriously: Rethinking the First Year of College." *NACADA Journal* 19(2):5–9.

Tinto, Vincent, and Brian Pusser. 2006. *Moving from Theory to Action: Building a Model of Institutional Action for Student Success.* Washington, DC: National Postsecondary Education Cooperative. http://nces.ed.gov/npec/pdf/Tinto_Pusser_Report.pdf.

Toma, J. Douglas, and Michael E. Cross. 1998. "Intercollegiate Athletics and Student College Choice: Exploring the Impact of Championship Seasons on Undergraduate Applications." *Research in Higher Education* 39:633–661.

Tornatzky, Louis G., Richard Cutler, and Jongho Lee. 2002. *College Knowledge: What Latino Parents Need to Know and Why They Don't Know It.* Los Angeles: Tomas Rivera Policy Institute (TRPI).

Tyack, David. 1976. "Ways of Seeing: An Essay on the History of Compulsory Schooling." *Harvard Educational Review* 46:355–89.

Venezia, Andrea, Michael W. Kirst, and Anthony L. Antonio. 2003. *Betraying the College Dream: How Disconnected K–12 and Postsecondary Education Systems Undermine Student Aspirations.* Stanford, CA: Stanford Institute for Higher Education Research.

Vogel, Susan A., and Pamela B. Adelman. 1992. "The Success of College Students with Learning Disabilities: Factors Related to Educational Attainment." *Journal of Learning Disabilities* 25:430–441.

Vygotsky, Lev S. 1986. *Thought and Language.* Cambridge, MA: MIT Press.

Wagner, Tony. 2006. "Rigor on Trial." *Education Week* 25(18):28–29.

Watt, Karen W., Dennis Johnston, Jeffery Huerta, Irma Doris Mendiola, and Ersan Alkan. 2008. "Retention of First-Generation College-Going Seniors in the College Preparatory Program AVID." *American Secondary Education* 37:17–40.

Wehmeyer, Michael, and Michelle Schwartz. 1995. "Self-Determination and Positive Adult Outcomes: A Follow-Up Study of Youth with Mental Retardation or Learning Disabilities." *Exceptional Children* 63:245–255.

White, John Wesley, and Patrick R. Lowenthal. 2011. "Minority College Students and Tacit 'Codes of Power': Developing Academic Discourses and Identities." *Review of Higher Education* 34:283–318.

Willingham, Warren W. 1985. *Success in College: The Role of Personal Qualities and Academic Ability.* New York: College Entrance Examination Board.

Willis, Paul E. 1977. *Learning to Labour: How Working Class Kids Get Working Class Jobs.* Farnborough, England: Saxon House.

Wilson, Kenneth. 1980. "The Performance of Minority Students beyond the Freshman Year: Testing the 'Late-Bloomer' Hypothesis in One State University Setting." *Research in Higher Education* 13:23–47.

Wimberly, George L. 2002. *School Relationships Foster Success for African American Students* (Report 050802040). Iowa City: ACT.

Wirt, John, Susan Choy, Stephen Provasnik, Patrick Rooney, Anindita Sen, Richard Tobin, Barbara Kridl, and Andrea Livingston. 2003. *The Condition of Education, 2003 (NCES 2003-067).* Washington, DC: Government Printing Office.

Zarate, Maria E., and Harry P. Pachon. 2006. *Perceptions of College Financial Aid among California Latino Youth.* Los Angeles: Tomas Rivera Policy Institute.

CHAPTER FOUR

From Communication to Community

How Games and Social Media Affect Postsecondary Stakeholders

ZOË B. CORWIN

Social media and games have begun to infiltrate most aspects of college life. From preparing for college to navigating freshman year to interacting with faculty, the postsecondary landscape is dramatically different from what it was a decade ago. Students now learn about colleges through social media, get to know their prospective roommates through Facebook, and quickly learn how to communicate with their professors through online tools such as Blackboard. For students who enroll in online courses, most—if not all—faculty-student interactions are mediated through technology. Games have also gained prevalence in postsecondary settings. Some games are more formal, with clearly articulated structures; others are informal and more organic in nature. Games might involve technology such as icebreaker activities in dorms; other games masquerade as business incentives such as reward programs offered by credit card companies. Students informally might convene in response to games such as an impromptu Wii tournament; at other times, games structure interactions such as the extended freshman orientation alternate reality game Tracy Fullerton describes in chapter 5. This chapter provides a snapshot of games and social media common in postsecondary educational settings. Examining how students, professors, administrators, and librarians engage with games and social media points to the changing ways in which individuals and groups are learning, communicating, interacting, and creating knowledge.

Most college students are "digital natives," born after 1980 into an era where their lives have been mediated by digital technologies (Palfrey and Gasser 2008). Considering that a large percentage of professors are "digital immigrants," people born before 1980 who learned how to use email, social networks, and online games later on in life, a potential schism exists with how both groups view and use online technologies. To dichotomize the two groups is oversimplified, of course, as individual's interactions with media are highly personalized and are influenced by level and time of exposure to technology (Whitton 2010). The ways individuals engage with technology are affected by media ideologies—a set of beliefs and perceptions that shape how people use and experience communication technologies (Gershon 2010). To be sure, a senior professor might exhibit a deep fluency in how to play massively multiplayer online games (MMOGs) in comparison to a freshman student with little experience in participating in online game environments. In most situations, however, the adoption of new technologies tends to manifest generational differences. Compared to when digital immigrants were the same age, digital natives experience friendships differently, express creativity in different ways and mediums, and perceive information and knowledge in more fluid ways (Palfrey and Gasser 2008).

As noted by Laura Perna in chapter 2, postsecondary education involves the investment of multifaceted stakeholder groups. Consequently, understanding the effects of games and social media on higher education entails examining various "players" and stages of the college process. Students anchor the group at all stages. K–12 teachers, college preparation practitioners, and guidance and college counselors play significant roles in the postsecondary landscape. College recruiters, college mentors, financial aid advisors, and lenders contribute to the critical moments leading up to college enrollment. Professors, academic advisers, residential life staff, coaches, religious leaders, and librarians—among others—have an impact on how students transition to college and navigate their postsecondary educational experience as well as their likelihood of completing college and successfully transitioning to careers. Family members or guardians tend to figure significantly in all phases of a student's K–16 journey, university administrators play an indirect role in most facets of the postsecondary education, and peer groups figure strongly in college preparation and postsecondary experiences.

This chapter highlights how four different postsecondary stakeholder groups interface with social media and games and the related effects of each on learning. I suggest that new media are changing the way colleges and universities serve students. Neither do I argue for decreased or increased use of social media or games nor do I assume that the experiences of stakeholder groups are unique to each specific group. My aim, rather, is to highlight the experiences of students, professors, administrators, and librarians in relation to games and social media in order to turn attention to the changing nature of how we communicate, interact, learn, and create knowledge at the postsecondary level. Ultimately, I intend to illustrate that the way different stakeholder groups experience games and social media are intertwined and require those of us in the academy to reconceptualize the meaning of postsecondary learning.

Students
Communication and Social Interactions

Before starting my freshman year in college, my new roommate and I spoke once. We compared notes on who would bring various items: a mini refrigerator, a popcorn machine, a cassette player. When we finally met in person, we basically started to get to know each other from scratch. Today, college roommates connect via Facebook, communicate frequently, and learn a tremendous amount about each other before meeting in person. Before the advent of social media, most college students eased into their new postsecondary social environment by attending orientation and mixers in dorms. Most communication was face-to-face and location-specific. College students now capitalize on social media and games when navigating their college experience. Social and mobile technologies provide the opportunity for students to share their lives with their friends and acquaintances and expand their reach beyond traditional boundaries (Panteli 2009). Often, youth bond with individuals they may never meet. They move seamlessly between online and offline spaces. Digitally rich and multimodal texts, free from in-class or out-of-class binaries, lead to experimentation and exploration. As a consequence, young people's communicative practices are undergoing significant change (Vasudevan, DeJaynes, and Schmier 2010).

Humans are social creatures. As individuals navigate the social world, they attempt to connect with others in varied ways—through strong and weak relationships, from long-lasting to brief encounters, and in multiplex (across spaces and time) and uniplex settings (Chayko 2002). Today's youth are connected, accessible, social, and vulnerable (Watkins 2009). Traditional social interactions still exist, but the benefit of social media and gameplay is that both offer the opportunity for users to share their lives with close friends and acquaintances across space and time (Watkins 2009). Whether communicating through Facebook or interacting through one of the games mentioned in parts II and III of this book, the predominant form of communication among students and professors and other postsecondary staff has changed dramatically over the past decade. Before email, a student waited to speak with a professor before or after class or during office hours. Now, a question to a professor is more normally sent via email—and at any time of the day. Because humans are social and language is the core communicative practice of culture, the way people communicate with each other has implications for understanding, comfort, and growth (Barnes 2001; Wood 1992). Communicative practices are complex and can be unpredictable. One student might feel less intimidated communicating with a professor through a social media site, whereas another might feel alienated from the professor with few face-to-face interactions. One professor might lament the disconnect she feels to students she never meets in person, while another might relish the flexibility and creativity of communication through social media or games.

The structure of communicative technologies and the relationship of a particular medium to another matters (Gershon 2010). Email might appear as a quick and nimble way to communicate when compared to letter writing, but slow and more cumbersome when compared to texting or communication via Facebook. Without experience in texting or without avid use of Facebook, however, the comparison is limited. If professors are not using the same technologies or playing the same games as their students, norms and perceptions of communication can be confusing. In addition, people tend to understand and interlink media in relation to the other forms of media they employ (Bolter and Grusin 1999). On the one hand, college students explained to Gershon (2010) that they viewed email as a formal way to correspond. Gershon's (2010) take on the same medium differed as he stated that he generally used email for informal interactions, using shorter sentences and a relaxed tone. The distinction is important because the medium ends up affecting the message—in both execution and reception.

A potential intergenerational challenge comes into play when oral features and written text intertwine and change the symbolic form of written language (Barnes 2001). For example, a college student might send an email that he believes is entirely understandable by a professor including abbreviations such as "TBH" (to be honest) or "SPST" (same place same time); the professor, however, has no idea of the meaning and is expected to respond appropriately and immediately. When someone sends a letter, however, the language employed is more traditional, and the receiver has time to reflect on the content and language. Messages communicated over message boards or texts differ in style, formality, and content. Yet if professors and university staff are not familiar with those terms or modes of communication, they run the risk of miscommunication. As of May 2012, there were 1,359 text or chat abbreviations listed on the Webopedia (2012) site under "Text Abbreviations," quite an enormous number to keep up with if the abbreviations are not a common part of one's communication. At the same time, if students are not familiar with more formal styles of writing, they run the risk of sending email correspondence that might seem disrespectful. In the Pullias Center's college mentoring program, after witnessing far too many emails with misspellings and informal language written to professors, we now include a lesson on email etiquette for the summer program we run for first-generation college students.

Community

Just as the nature of office hours has changed, so has the nature of study groups. In-person study groups still exist—a walk through any university library during finals week will find the conference rooms full of students—and are governed by a type of communication and interpersonal dynamic generally reliant on verbal and nonverbal communication. Cyber study spaces function differently. In computer or technology mediated spaces, participants most often use written language to communicate (Barnes 2001). When studying with an online group, students are likely to draw from a much wider base of knowledge than exists in an in-person study group, especially if the group is expansive. Yet participants are also less likely to develop supportive face-to-face friendships that potentially contribute to a student's socioemotional well-being and subsequent college persistence.

In her book on how social bonds and communities form in the internet age, Chayko (2002) explores social interconnectedness in situations where people never meet. She underscores the complexity of social bonds and illustrates that face-to-face interactions do not necessarily foster close social bonds. Nor do internet interactions necessarily lead to weak social connections. The mind, Chayko (2002) explains, is powerful. Just as someone might feel close to a deceased relative but distant from a co-worker, a person can perceive of a relationship nurtured online as close and supportive. She describes three types of relationships: long-lasting *sociomental bonds*, weaker and more fleeting *sociomental connections*, and *communities of the mind*, where people group together according to shared sociomental bonds or connections. Technology creates new opportunities to both connect *and* avoid interacting (Baym 2010). Consider, for example, the ease of sending a question to a co-worker on a different floor versus taking the time to walk over and pose the question in person—and how the product of those interactions differs depending on delivery. In chapter 2,

Laura Perna outlined serious challenges to promoting educational attainment. In the struggle to improve college completion rates, considering Chayko's characterization of relationships and the ways in which postsecondary institutions structure interactions—especially with increased use of social media and technology—is valuable.

Identity

In September 2010, Tyler Clementi, a Rutgers University freshman, committed suicide after his roommate secretly filmed his private, sexual encounter with another male. In an example of a tragic misuse of social media in a postsecondary setting, the roommate used his computer webcam to remotely record the encounter and then broadcast the video to his social network through iChat and Twitter. Clementi reached out for help to a residential adviser but did not recover from the incident. Roommate confrontations, even those of this harsh nature, are not uncommon or new. As soon as students arrive at a college or university, they navigate a wide range of social relationships inside and outside of the classroom—some positive, others negative. How students respond and react to various social situations and relationships contributes to their identity formation. But Tyler Clementi's case is a painful example of how social media introduces a new element into the challenges students have to negotiate. As his case illustrates, "Social media can mirror and magnify teen friendship practices. Positive interactions are enhanced through social media while negative interactions are also intensified" (boyd 2010, 114). The dynamic introduced by the public nature of social media potentially has serious implications for identity formation and student well-being; colleges and universities can no longer ignore its effects on students.

Juxtaposed to the preceding severe example, the mundane and prevalent nature of social media also has an impact on identity formation. Perpetual contact, argue Katz and Aakhaus (2002), both entraps and empowers individuals. New media blur boundaries between the personal and the private. At the center of boundary flux is confusion over what is virtual, what is real, and what is simulation. As college and university students navigate their postsecondary experiences on a daily basis, they simultaneously develop and experiment with their emerging adult identity. Facebook and other forms of social media now factor into the identity development of college-aged youth.

Consider the concepts of *play* and *playfulness* as discussed by Fullerton in chapter 5 and Salen in chapter 8. As children, imaginary play contributes to an evolving sense of self; children's experimentation with different personas leads to critical thinking and more nuanced clarity about fantasy and realistic roles (Wandell and Beavers 2010). With full anonymity, individuals can play more freely and engage in self-discovery. Wandell and Beavers (2010) outline the types of play inherent in Facebook—where users communicate via wall postings, send virtual gifts, and decorate Facebook pages with banners and links to various affiliations. Without full anonymity, however, individuals are more constrained as they experiment with emerging understandings of self. Lack of anonymity or partial anonymity lends itself to a "restraint of accountability" where individuals edit the representations of self they publish in front of friends (Wandell and Beavers 2010). When creating and maintaining a Facebook profile, users are faced with a countless number of choices. They think about which profile picture to post, who to include as friends, what to make public, what to keep private, what links to share, and what posts to like. Before Facebook, performances and personal understandings of identity evolved at a slower pace and in more nuanced and individualized ways. Today, identity development appears more malleable, changes more rapidly, is much more public, and is less individualized. Individuals send out status updates to represent how they conceive of themselves and select a relationship status from a list of preordained choices. And when they do, their entire online social network is able to see the posts immediately.

Facebook has created a new forum for negotiating identity that has implications for college students' individuality. Historically, concern has been placed on fragmentation of identity—or how role switching affects identity. The way a student might present herself in an honors seminar might differ, for example, to the way she presents herself at a sorority party or at a schoolwide protest against tuition hikes. What happens then, when a person plays out these roles, positions, or personas in full view of the people she used to be able to keep compartmentalized? Before Facebook, she might have conveyed a different emerging identity to a sibling, professor, and potential employer. Now, if each of those individuals are Facebook friends of the person, they all potentially have access to the way the student presents herself online—and at the same moment.

Much of traditional college and university living occurs in small communities such as dormitories or fraternities and sororities. Not only do these living situations affect identify formation; social media also affect how people present themselves within the collective. Groups tend to hold people accountable for how they express their individuality—they either justify their uniqueness or change. To illustrate how tight-knit communities affect identity and individuality, Wandell and Beavers (2010) discuss the possible self-restriction imposed by members of a fraternity who succumb to pressure to fit in. "It is a social fact," they state, "that one can be somewhat different but too much difference amounts to a loss of credibility" (94). Obviously students can impose a variety of privacy settings and screen who is able to read their posts, but the point is that students now have to factor their digital profiles into how they experience their new college lives.

Professors, university staff, and administrators also communicate, interact, form community, and develop identity in similar ways but do so at a developmental life stage different from most students'. Faculty have grappled with which images to post on the university website, how much to self-censure when posting on Facebook, and how to nurture community when more and more communication is done over social media. The issues presented in this section on students apply to all postsecondary stakeholder groups, just as the following discussion focuses on professors but also are applicable to students and others in postsecondary settings.

Professors
Learning and Instruction

With low- and high-tech game-based and social media approaches, the potential to shake up traditional classroom learning grows. As Henry Jenkins and Adam Kahn illustrate in chapter 6, a massive and evolving digital infrastructure provides students and professors access to a tremendous array of online resources. Social media facilitate the connection of people around those resources. Consequently, the infrastructure of learning and resources is in a constant state of flux as information is shared, connections are made, and learning occurs in seamless environments in and out of the classroom. Thomas and Brown (2011) suggest that a "new culture of learning" has emerged that has the potential to augment traditional forms of learning. In this new culture, play, questioning, and imagination, coupled with the collective nature of inquiry, cultivate citizenship and curiosity. Participants in this type of learning have the freedom to make the general personal and share personal experience with a wide audience, thus adding to the flow of knowledge. They describe play as "the tension between the rules of the game and the freedom to act within those rules. But when play happens within a medium for learning—much like a culture in a petri dish—it creates a context in which information, ideas, and passions grow" (Thomas and Brown 2011, 18). This type of learning can take place without teachers, books, or classrooms. Facebook, *Wikipedia*, YouTube, and online games are examples of the bounded yet free environments in which this type of learning occurs. How are postsecondary institutions responding?

Approaches to learning, argue Thomas and Brown (2011), have evolved at a very slow pace. Memorization, for example, is a good skill for topics that do not change. As Tierney noted in chapter 1, most colleges and universities still function with a professor in the front of a class or facilitating group work. Students then illustrate what they have learned through exams and papers. Yet hybrid models and online programs are expanding rapidly and make use of social media and game-based tools. So while a professor lectures or holds a seminar, he also utilizes some form of social media in his course. As Henry Jenkins and Adam Khan discuss in their chapter, changes in how we learn pose challenges to how we assess what we learn given new media. Thomas and Brown (2011) outline three guiding principles for the new culture of learning: traditional ways of learning cannot keep up with the changing nature of information and learning, new media forms make peer-to-peer learning more interesting and more natural, and the collective nature of participation with new media is key.

James Gee, in chapter 7 and various other publications (Gee 2007a, 2007b), discusses the many ways that games have the potential to foster strategy development, team building, and other forms of learning. When playing MMOGs, for example, college students participate in networks of players, spread across physical locales. Because of the nature of gameplay, gamers tend to evaluate and assess a situation with a focus on the bottom line, value the power of diversity as diverse talents and abilities help solve problems, thrive on change in a constantly changing virtual world, see learning and tackling challenges as fun, and take risks and explore innovation and radical alternatives (Thomas and Brown 2011). In part II of this volume, authors expand on the potential of games to affect learning. And while it is not the norm for professors to incorporate games into the curriculum, it is important to recognize that today's college students are familiar with this different type of learning and engagement—and that game-based lessons have the potential to enhance the craft of teaching and subsequent learning.

Office Hours

A decade ago, most extraclass interactions between students and professors would occur during a set time in a professor's office. As noted earlier, interactions now often occur via email or through other online technologies such as Black-board. There are advantages and disadvantages to each approach. Faculty members are more readily available to students who work during the day, for example. At the same time, for some students and some faculty written feed-back pales in comparison to feedback offered through a dialogue. Face-to-face communication, as Barnes (2001) explains, is "dynamic and transactional, the direction or flow of information goes back and forth between the participants as senders and receivers exchange positions during the communication pro-cess" (9). There are obvious advantages to face-to-face communication that oc-curs in one location and involves the five senses.

Communication that is not delivered in person is mediated. Mediated com-munication can take many forms, from mass communication (where senders and receivers cannot alternate roles) with high degrees of anonymity to video conferencing where participants can hear and see each other. Mediated com-munication can be verbal, written, or a combination of the two forms. Because of technology, mediated communication can occur asynchronously, involve participants from remote locations, facilitate communication among multiple participants (i.e., when several individuals can compose or edit a Google doc), and often produces a record of points addressed. The advantages for global and interdisciplinary collaboration are significant.

Evaluations

Before the internet, students relied on word of mouth to identify which profes-sors to take and which to avoid. At the institutional level, students were—and still are—afforded the opportunity to evaluate professors and courses by filling out instructor evaluations at the end of the course. Evaluations tend to include standardized reports and open-ended questions. While these evaluations offer students a voice, they are not available as a tool for students when determining which classes to take. At most institutions, it is questionable how evaluations are used by the institution to monitor faculty. How seriously professors (and students) take evaluations is highly individualized. Word of mouth still figures into students' course selection, but now a variety of social media sites exist that offer students the opportunity to evaluate professors. One particular site, RateMyProfessors.com (2012), houses a national and open (students can add professors) database of professors. The site is now produced by mtvU and MTV Networks and hosts ratings on professors at more than 7,500 schools in the

United States, Canada, and the United Kingdom. The site boasts 14 million student-generated comments about 1.7 million professors. As the website explains, the service is widely popular and responds in a digitally relevant way to a postsecondary dynamic that has existed for ages. Users can rate professors on overall quality, helpfulness, clarity, easiness, and then of course the additional category of "hotness." Students also list open-ended critiques. Professors can post rebuttals to student critiques. Selected professor rebuttals are highlighted in quick videos produced by MTV. The advantage of such sites is that they are accessible, public, and track students' perspectives over time. The disadvantage is that the users who post are self-selecting and the criteria for evaluating teacher effectiveness are not aligned with learning objectives (did I mention the category of "hotness"?). What is still to be seen is how these sites influence how professors teach and students learn, if at all. Nevertheless, social media are creating novel informational systems to inform how students approach class selection. Beyond class selection, the vastly different and evolving postsecondary informational landscape is clearly illustrated by how libraries and library scientists now operate.

Librarians: Knowledge and Information

Some readers might remember the process for requesting an article from another institution if the college or university did not subscribe to a particular journal. A process that could take weeks now transpires within a few clicks of the keyboard. Book stacks and archives still exist, but the internet has influenced how libraries and librarians function. How information is reviewed, edited, received, shared, and revised has changed dramatically with the advent of social media (Walther et al. 2011). The production of information has become decentralized; the traditional gatekeepers of information have become less powerful. Professors and students now have other options to share thoughts and research besides through a lengthy peer-review process and the constraints of physical library resources.

The fluidity of knowledge has been influenced by Web 2.0 and the growing prevalence of virtual social networks. Virtual social networks facilitate the creation and maintenance of social interactions across space and allow for multi-mediated, massive, and multiplayer interactions (Panteli 2009). Multimediated networks made possible by Web 2.0 bring together varied forms of media such as blogging, videos, and audio files. Panteli (2009) explains that when multiple media interact in unpredictable ways, outcomes are also unpredictable and expansive. In a MacArthur Foundation white paper, Henry Jenkins and colleagues (2009) elaborate on the participatory nature of

> a culture with relatively low barriers to artistic expression and civic engagement, strong support for creating and sharing one's creations, and some type of informal mentorship whereby what is known by the most experienced is passed along to novices. A participatory culture is also one in which members believe their contributions matter, and feel some degree of social connection with one another (at the least they care what other people think about what they have created). (3)

The implications and possibilities for professors and students who are proficient in multiple media are significant; with access and proficiency, opportunities for collaboration and communication unfold. Without proficiency, people are excluded. The scenarios are complex. If professors do not know how to navigate a media form, they might miss an opportunity to interact with students in meaningful ways. For college students without strong digital literacies, they might be presented with another level of challenge to transitioning to or persisting in college. This possibility is particularly concerning for students from low-income backgrounds who may not have been exposed to as robust digital preparation as their higher-income peers.

The fact that virtual social networks are massive affects how knowledge is produced. The quality of information posted online without a peer-review process is debatable and context specific. In an extensive study comparing the content of *Wikipedia* (an online reference with entries created by users) and the *Encyclopaedia Britannica* (a traditional and highly esteemed hard-copy encyclopedia), researchers found that the margin of error in content was not as drastic as expected; *Wikipedia* entries held up well in comparison to the traditional encyclopedia (Giles 2005). Through social media, individuals working as a collective have the power to influence culture, information, and knowledge.

How young people interact with information is rapidly changing. Web 2.0 brought the internet from something individuals consume to something that they produce (Watkins 2009). The problem becomes what do individuals do with all the information they have access to? How do students—or librarians or professors, administrators, or staff—determine the criteria of "quality" information? Palfrey and Gasser (2008) suggest that the relationship individuals have to information influences how they process that information; the context of information is key. Take, for example, the group of low-income high school students I currently work with on the college access game intervention mentioned in the introduction and in chapter 5. The attention they dedicated online to college-related matters changed dramatically over the course of the year. Now that they are high school seniors, they pay closer attention to Facebook posts from peers announcing college deadlines and scholarships. They respond differently to college-related posts now from how they did earlier in their junior year.

With the internet as a tool, librarians are empowered to help students find resources beyond what a campus library offers but are also challenged to help students sort through a vast expanse of information and resources. A visit to the library to compile a reading list for a research project can be quite intimidating to undergraduates who are not familiar with either libraries or writing term papers. A university library in Texas is experimenting with how to orient students to the library by hosting photo-based library scavenger hunts. Professors can sign students up to participate in the interactive, high-energy orientation. Qualitative responses indicate that students found the new orientation effective and believe the library—and librarians—to be accessible. Professors have lauded the library's efforts, and professor-initiated participation in library orientation has increased.

With the vast quantity of information available, all postsecondary stakeholders are challenged to edit, select, and evaluate useful information and resources. Palfrey and Gasser (2008) question whether learners tend to surround themselves with information and content that they like. They suggest that education and filtering can serve as a solution to information overload. Research has illustrated that children use different techniques to sort through information, employing "chunking" and "twigging" to avoid information overload (Palfrey and Gasser 2008). College students and professors are faced with similar challenges—as are administrators.

Administrators

As Tierney discusses in chapter 1, the disruption of higher education involves responding to market forces that are driving an extreme and continual stream of innovation. Postsecondary institutions have reacted slowly in their response to technological innovation, but are now beginning to experiment with innovations based on social media and games in order to facilitate a smoother transition to college, higher likelihood of college completion, and higher profit margins. The online college industry has blossomed, although without much oversight. Several innovations elevate the field whereas others pose cause for concern. During a two-month period alone while writing this book, for example, the following postsecondary developments surfaced, among others:

- iTunesU: Apple launched free software for students to download or create textbooks and for professors to create digital curriculum.
- MITx: Massachusetts Institute of Technology shared plans to create a self-service learning system where students could take online tests and earn certificates online.
- StraighterLine: The online postsecondary program announced it would be offering Collegiate Learning Assessments that could serve as indicators of proficiency in subject areas to employers or postsecondary institutions.
- Udacity: A new company created by a Stanford University professor opened to offer highly scalable, low-cost online courses.
- TedEd: The hugely popular Ted talks expanded to include a curated collection of lessons designed by top-notch educators and animators designed for teachers and individual users.

In the time between drafting the manuscript and the revision process, MOOCs (massively open online courses) have become the hot topic in postsecondary learning, monopolizing the attention of university administrators and professors alike.

Postsecondary institutions are experimenting with other innovations based on social media and games in order to facilitate a smoother transition to college. Administrators are paying attention to how social media and games might bolster recruitment efforts and ease transitions to college for incoming students. In another example of capitalizing on social media, the company Inigral has successfully appealed to colleges and universities with its promise to "build community, boost enrollment, and retention" through "creating a private, branded community" that allows students "to meet their future classmates, ask questions, share interests, and get excited about their college experience" (Inigral 2012). Through the use of Facebook networks and services specific to schools, Inigral claims to have dramatically improved yield rates and deposit rates and decreased summer melt rates of incoming freshmen. The site offers a way to measure social media engagement in order to track yield and retention.

The trend toward online instruction does not go only in one direction. As more and more colleges and universities offer traditional courses online and textbooks are more readily available online, Yale University recently published a series of hard copy books based on online lectures. The series' editors take online lectures, edit and reformat them, and make them available to an international audience (Howard 2012).

Moving Forward: Digitally Literate Stakeholders

The concept of teachers learning from students as much—if not more—as students learning from them is not new. From the Babylonian Talmud to the methods of Socrates to the pedagogy of Paulo Freire, the value and power of a teacher and student learning from each other is clear. While social media and games have not introduced these concepts into our lexicon, each is pushing the boundaries of how holistic and authentic learning occurs in modern society. Students, professors, librarians, and administrators—as well as many other postsecondary stakeholders such as residential staff, coaches, religious leaders, and community service leaders—are all engaged in a shifting landscape where communication, information, knowledge, and community are being reconfigured in ways that call into question traditional roles of those stakeholder groups.

In her study of Webkinz, blogs, and avatars, Janie Cowan (2010) shares lessons learned from adolescents applicable to college-aged students. Her analyses illustrated that in virtual worlds, teaching and learning occur simultaneously and in fluid motion. Roles shift between teacher and learner. Collaboration and communal participation are key. When navigating virtual worlds, youth draw on nontraditional literacies to solve problems. Thus far, educational institutions are behind the times in capitalizing on the types of learning and interaction prevalent in virtual spaces.

Given a rapidly changing postsecondary landscape with multiple moving parts, how do we rethink the role of colleges and universities in structuring opportunities for students to interact with each other and with professors and other institutional agents in meaningful ways? Vasudevan, DeJaynes, and Schmier (2010) found that when youth are immersed in virtual spaces, physical location matters. They suggest that "educational institutions must become spaces that can more readily accommodate and encourage literacy experimentation, exploration, and discovery" (22). And yet even turning attention to bolstering the physical space of learning is complicated. In his analysis of how mobile technologies are affecting postsecondary institutions, Quinn (2012) proposes the utility of mobile devices in enhancing students' learning experiences—and critiques campuses for slow adoption of innovative mobile platforms.

Digital Literacy and Digital Citizenship

There is no doubt that all postsecondary participants can learn from each other—but how do we wade through the onslaught of new products, platforms, and ideas in order to select and capitalize on effective games and social media? Part III of this book turns attention to evaluating and assessing games and social media. I posit that the starting point, however, begins with developing digital literacy. Digital literacy includes the ability to "use technology competently; interpret and understand digital content and assess its credibility; and create, research, and communicate with appropriate tools" (Common Sense Media 2011, 2).

A salient challenge to digital literacy arises when students have not been mentored in how to communicate formally through social media—a particular problem for the youth from low-income communities discussed by Laura W. Perna in chapter 2 and David Conley and Mary Seburn in chapter 3. The concept of the "digital divide" initially referred to inequitable access to physical resources such as computers. What has now come to be known as the "participation divide" moves beyond a focus on machinery to issues of access to quality training and education (Watkins 2009). Kline, Dyer-Witheford, and De Peuter (2003) write that, "as with other domestic technologies, access to interactive play has been marked by great unevenness and deep digital divides falling along lines of class, gender, race, and age" (183). A Pew Internet & American Life Project's (Lenhart et al. 2008) report indicates that lower-income teens from families earning under $50,000 are more likely to play racing, adventure, or survival horror games as opposed to games that foster critical thinking. Pandey, Pandey, and Shreshtha (2007) found that "electronic literacy is clearly embedded in the family's educational and economic background" (46).

Building digital ability, knowledge, and ultimately citizenship can be approached in varying degrees of intensity—but not if programs fail to acknowledge the importance of such work. Understanding the implications of digital literacy and the closely related concept of digital citizenship has significant practical ramifications at both the K–12 and postsecondary levels. Digital citizenship applies ethics and responsibility to the use of social media and other digital resources. Cultivating digital literacy prior to college will better equip students to capitalize on digital resources and help students mediate their online interactions. Once students enroll in college or university, their digital citizenship remains vitally important as students navigate complex peer and institutional dynamics as well as prepare for the work force.

The value in improving digital literacies extends beyond students. Fostering more robust digital literacies among stakeholder groups offers the possibility of harnessing innovation in how we teach, recruit, retain, and nurture each other on college and university campuses. Postsecondary stakeholders will then grapple with how best to create and sustain educational spaces—physical or virtual—where people with common interests can connect in meaningful and productive ways.

REFERENCES

Barnes, Susan B. 2001. *Online Connections: Internet Interpersonal Relationships.* Cresskill, NJ: Hampton Press.

Baym, Nancy, K. 2010. *Personal Connections in the Digital Age.* Malden, MA: Polity Press.

Bolter, Jay D., and Richard Grusin. 1999. *Remediation: Understanding New Media.* Cambridge, MA: MIT Press.

boyd, danah. 2010. "Friendship." In *Hanging Out, Messing Around, and Geeking Out,* edited by Mizudo Ito, Sonja Baumer, Matteo Bittanti, danah boyd, Rachel Cody, Becky Herr-Stephenson, Heather A. Horst, Patricia G. Lange, Dilan Mahendran, Katynka Z. Martinez, C. J. Pascoe, Dan Perkel, Laura Robinson, Christo Sims, and Lisa Tripp, 79–114. Cambridge, MA: MIT Press.

Chayko, Mary. 2002. *Connecting: How We Form Social Bonds and Communities in the Internet Age.* Albany, NY: SUNY Press.

Common Sense Media. 2011. *Digital Literacy and Citizenship in the 21st Century: Educating, Empowering, and Protecting America's Kids.* San Francisco. http://www.commonsensemedia.org/sites/default/files/DigitalLiteracyandCitizenshipWhitePaper-Mar2011.pdf.

Cowan, Janie. 2010. "Webkinz, Blogs, Avatars: Lessons Learned from Young Adolescents." In *Adolescents' Online Literacies: Connecting Classrooms, Digital Media, and Popular Culture,* edited by Donna. E. Alvermann, 27–50. New York: Peter Lang.

Gee, James P. 2007a. *Good Video Games and Learning: Collected Essays on Video Games, Learning, and Literacy.* New York: Peter Lang.

———. 2007b. *What Video Games Have to Teach Us about Learning and Literacy.* New York: Palgrave Macmillan.

Gershon, Ilana. 2010. *The Breakup 2.0: Disconnecting over New Media.* Ithaca, NY: Cornell University Press.

Giles, Jim. 2005. "Internet Encyclopedias Go Head to Head." *Nature* 438:900–901. Accessed August 13, 2012. doi:10.1038/438900a.

Howard, Jennifer. 2012. "At Yale, Online Lectures Become Lively Books." *Wired Campus*, April 26. Accessed August 13, 2012. http://chronicle.com/blogs/wiredcampus/at-yale-online-lectures-become-lively-books/36162?sid=wcandutm_source=wcandutm_medium=en.

Inigral. 2012. "How It Works." Accessed March 7. http://www.inigral.com.

Jenkins, Henry, Katie Clinton, Ravi Purushotma, Alice J. Robison, and Margaret Weigel. 2009. *Confronting the Challenges of Participatory Culture: Media Education for the 21st Century*. Boston: MIT Comparative Media Studies Program. http://digitallearning.macfound.org/atf/cf/%7B7E45C7E0-A3E0-4B89-AC9C-E807E1B0AE4E%7D/JENKINS_WHITE_PAPER.PDF.

Katz, James E., and Mark Aakhaus. 2002. "Introduction: Framing the issues." In *Perpetual Contact: Mobile Communication, Private Talk, Public Performance*, edited by James E. Katz and Mark Aakhaus, 1–14. New York: Cambridge University Press.

Kline, Stephen, Nick Dyer-Witheford, and Greig De Peuter. 2003. *Digital Play: The Interaction of Technology, Culture, and Marketing*. Quebec: McGill-Queen's University Press.

Lenhart, Amanda, Joseph Kahne, Ellen Middaugh, Alexandra Rankin Macgill, Chris Evans, and Jessica Vitak. 2008. *Teens, Video Games, and Civics*. Washington, DC: Pew Internet & American Life Project. http://www.pewinternet.org/~/media//Files/Reports/2008/PIP_Teens_Games_and_Civics_Report_FINAL.pdf.pdf.

Palfrey, John, and Urs Gasser. 2008. *Born Digital: Understanding the First Generation of Digital Natives*. New York: Basic Books.

Pandey, Iswari P., Laxman Pandey, and Angish Shreshtha. 2007. "Transcultural Literacies of Gaming." In *Gaming Lives in the Twenty-First Century: Literate Connections*, edited by Cynthia L. Selfe and Gail E. Hawisher, 37–52. New York: Palgrave Macmillan.

Panteli, Niki. 2009. "Virtual Social Networks: A New Dimension for Virtuality Research." In *Virtual Social Networks: Mediated, Massive and Multiplayer Sites*, edited by Niki Panteli, 1–17. New York: Palgrave Macmillan.

Quinn, Clark N. 2012. *The Mobile Academy: mLearning for Higher Education*. San Francisco: Jossey-Bass.

Rate My Professors. 2012. "Home." Accessed April 4. http://www.ratemyprofessors.com/About.jsp.

Thomas, Douglas, and John Seely Brown. 2011. *A New Culture of Learning: Cultivating the Imagination for a World of Change*. Charleston, NC: CreateSpace Self-Publishing, Douglas Thomas and John Seeley Brown.

Vasudevan, Lalitha, Tiffany DeJaynes, and Stephanie Schmier. 2010. "Multimodal Pedagogies: Playing, Teaching and Learning with Adolescents' Digital Literacies." In *Adolescents' Online Literacies: Connecting Classrooms, Digital Media, and Popular Culture*, edited by Donna E. Alvermann, 5–26. New York: Peter Lang.

Walther, Joseph, Caleb T. Carr, Scott Seung W. Choi, David C. Deandra, Jinsuk Kim, Stephanie T. Tong, and Brandon Van der Heide. 2011. "Interaction of Interpersonal, Peer, and Media Influence Sources Online: A Research Agenda for Technology Convergence." In *A Networked Self: Identity, Community, and Culture on Social Network Sites*, edited by Zizi Papacharissi, 17–38. New York: Routledge.

Wandell, Tamara, and Anthony Beavers. 2010. "Playing Around with Identity." In *Facebook and Philosophy: What's on Your Mind?*, edited by D. E. Wittkower, 89–96. Chicago: Open Court.

Watkins, S. Craig. 2009. *The Young and the Digital: What the Migration to Social Network Sites, Games, and Anytime, Anywhere Media Means for Our Future*. Boston: Beacon Press.

Webopedia. 2012. "Text Messaging and Online Chat Abbreviations." Last modified May 18. http://www.webopedia.com/quick_ref/textmessageabbreviations.asp.

Whitton, Nicole. 2010. *Learning with Digital Games: A Practical Guide to Engaging Students in Higher Education.* New York: Routledge.

Wood, Julia T. 1992. *Spinning the Symbolic Web: Human Communication and Symbolic Interaction.* Norwood, NJ: Ablex.

PART TWO

What's in a Game?

CHAPTER FIVE

What Games Do Well

Mastering Concepts in Play

TRACY FULLERTON

In the past several years there has been a growing interest in "using" games to "do things" (Bogost 2007, 2011; McGonigal 2011). The virtues of games as intrinsically motivating systems has been extolled, rather ironically, right alongside the excitement around creating extrinsic reward systems, such as badge and achievement systems in social media (Digital Media and Learning Competition 2011). These systems, often called *gamification*, though they are actually only peripherally related to games, have sparked the public's imagination toward what social goods we might accomplish using the game form. I have been involved in designing games with goals beyond entertainment, such as goals for learning, for activism, and for expression (Fullerton 2008b; Fullerton et al. 2009). The value of the experiments seems clear enough: finding novel ways to engage learners and improve educational outcomes using compelling media experiences such as games and social media comes from a good intention and in part relates to the needs Tierney, Perna, Conley and Seburn, and Corwin speak about in part I. At the same time, to have greater expectations for the outcome of such media to accomplish these goals seems unrealistically optimistic, even utopian. Games are not a magic bullet that can solve all of the problems outlined in part I, but they can help. In order to be helpful, however, we have to understand the limits of social media and the potential (see Weiland's chapter for the former and the discussions of Gee and Jenkins and Kahn in their ensuing chapters for the latter).

The notion that games and social media might help us improve our methods and systems of education is little more than an inkling at this point, although there have been studies and discussion about this inkling for a few years (e.g.,

Gee 2007; Jenkins, Squire, and Tan 2003; Salen et al. 2011). It is primarily founded in observations about games and play: we suspect it might be true because we see that games involve the voluntary acquisition of new information and skills, even though that process may be difficult. Also, we wonder if the method of acquisition may be better than that of traditional methods because it is self-initiated and is driven by engagement and social interaction, rather than force or extrinsic motivation. Additionally, the methods found in games hold great interest because they *seem to be* reducible to technologies that might scale more effectively than traditional learning situations (brick and mortar, faculty). And finally, the methods also seem to offer a path toward more sophisticated assessment of the desired learning, through digital surveillance, data collection, and timely—possibly automated—intervention in the feedback cycle.

If what we suspect is true, that games and social media have an important connection to learning, then how can we harness the qualities that make these forms attractive (self-motivating, engaging, social, scalable) and use them to affect the kind of learning we are interested in? This is the catch, because even though games may indeed have a relationship to learning, they also have relationships to entertainment, idleness, sociability, solitude, and many other parts of culture and modes of being, including those that are not currently seen as important to the learning process. If it is true that games are related to learning, they are not necessarily related to *efficient* learning, or *standardized* learning, what James Gee (2008) has called the "content fetish." Also, games are truly not reducible to technology, and therefore not necessarily as scalable as we might imagine. While most games may be built using technologies, and while games may be an important part of our discourse around the digital technologies of today, they are not primarily systems designed to provide mechanical advantage, productivity, or scalability. The goal of a game is not to provide players with the most efficient experience possible. Rather, they are purposefully imperfect systems, with intentional slippage in their mechanics that allows for players to optimize their own behavior to take advantage of those imperfections—in other words, to play.

In many ways, it is this imperfection in games that makes them such good learning environments. For example, because resources are hard to find in a game, the concept of scarcity can be understood in a way that is personally meaningful to the player. Because resources are needed to accomplish the game goals, players are pushed to create strategies to acquire them. Those strategies are an example of creative and critical thinking skills about the issue of scarcity and viable responses to it. So, a game might model resources in our current world economy, like oil and access to it by various entities. Depending on the design of the game, the conflicts spurred between these entities in order to respond to that scarcity may be highly illustrative of a particular set of learning goals. Notice that I say illustrative and not instructive. The structure of a game system may illustrate in the abstract a particular situation or set of concepts, and players may actively engage with that situation; they may even be able to articulate the tensions and risks or rewards of that situation very clearly, but that is just a step to instruction. It seems that what the game situation provides is a meaningful illustration of a dynamic situation in this case. What it does not provide, and should not provide, is the instruction on how to handle that situation, or how to interpret and transfer that instruction to other situations. Instruction is not provided because games are systems that must be played or they are meaningless. If the game provides too much instruction, it will be simply playing itself for the player, and all of its pleasures and suspected benefits will be lost.

Thus, while I am intellectually aligned with those who suspect that games and social media do, indeed, have a deep relationship to learning, I am perhaps more strongly aligned with those who suspect that the connections we seek are fragile and may be broken if we do not respect the aspects of games that also make them unlike traditional learning and education. When we look to games to take on the desired learning goals of our current systems, we transfer some of the problematic aspects of those systems to games, and we deprive them of their own methods. It seems clear that trying to make games more like education does a service to neither. Using games to instruct does not take advantage of those qualities that made us suspect them to be good learning environments to begin with. As a game designer, I am increasingly concerned by the weight of expectations that are being placed on games to "fix" education, learning, and reality itself (McGonigal 2011). Games have been a part of all human cultures since their earliest beginnings (e.g., Avedon, Morton, and Sutton-Smith 1971; Callios 1961; Huizinga 1955). If games have not "fixed" these things by now, perhaps there is a reason. That reason, it may be assumed, is that one form of learning is not the antidote to another, and should not be placed in the position to be so. The core interest in including games as part of educational programs comes from a good impulse, however, and there are things that we can learn from what games do well that can inform both the design of so-called learning games and redesigns of educational situations themselves (Salen et al. 2011).

This chapter looks at some of these aspects of games, not from a technological standpoint, but from an aesthetic one. For those readers who have not yet designed games, or perhaps even played games deeply, and are curious about the form or just beginning to design games for learning, it is an attempt to shed light on some of those aspects of game systems that designers use, sometimes unconsciously, to invite players in, get them engaged in play, keep them coming back, deepen their understanding of the system, reward and rechallenge them, and finally, frame the narrative of how they share that experience with friends and other players. I will use examples from several projects I have been involved in to discuss some of the core attributes of games, especially those attributes I see missing in our discussions of learning and games. I have, in other writings, been more comprehensive as to the formal aspects of game systems for designers (Fullerton 2008a). In this chapter, I focus on aesthetic elements of games that I think are particularly important for games and learning. Unlike the examples presented in other chapters that are more focused on K–12 or global audiences, the games I refer to specifically relate to postsecondary institutions and the challenges of increasing access mentioned in chapters 2 and 4. These are not intended as a taxonomy but rather as the acknowledgment that there is an artistry to game design that cannot be thrown off in our rush to use games for specific purposes—what Eric Zimmerman (2011) has called "instrumentalizing games." I am arguing that this artistry, this inefficiency, in the design of games is as important to their potential for learning as are the more recognized values of technological systems.

The Lure: Attracting Players to the Game

The *lure* is that aspect of a game that compels a player to take it on willingly. The question of what the lure of a particular game to a player might be does not have a simple answer. It could be the promise of a specific kind of gameplay or the appeal of a world or the characters. It could be the physical or social appeal, the tone, or sensibility. A real-time strategy game like *Starcraft 2* might offer to present the player with a tightly balanced array of choices to be made in quick succession, testing his or her intellectual skills. A social card game like bridge might offer an evening of conviviality mixed with tempered competition. These each make a kind of promise to the player. It is a promise that, should they engage, they will be rewarded with an experience equal to that lure. Obviously, the notion of a lure is not specific to games; we experience this with all forms of voluntary entertainment, but when it comes to educational experiences, we do not feel the need to craft such a promise. Why is that?

As educators, we have the authority to tell students to do assignments. We regularly hand out assignments with little to no aplomb, no mystery, and no sense of expectation or promise. The authority and the seriousness of the classroom are one kind of lure, of course, but one that does not create appeal for every learning situation. As game designers, we cannot rely on the kind of compelled participation we see in classrooms. If we were to assume that authority, we would quickly find ourselves without players, because our players' engagement with a game must be voluntary, or the very sense of playfulness is lost. Yes, there may be outside influences: the fact that all our friends are playing, or that we have read about the game in a magazine and are convinced of its appeal; the drive to complete or win may even keep us playing beyond our initial interest. But those influences are really just reflections of the basic lure. Designing that lure, understanding what will attract players to a game, and taking the time to craft the lure as an invitation to play rather than an assignment is one of the real differentiators between game design and more formal learning situations.

The game *Reality Ends Here* offers an example of how a lure might work as a game for learning. The game, designed for the incoming freshman class at the University of Southern California (USC) School of Cinematic Arts, was meant to reboot the typical freshman experience, which is filled with formal orientations, lists of requirements, big lectures, and the like. Students come to the cinema school with energy, excitement, and dreams—dreams that include becoming part of the school's infamous history. But the reality of their initial classes includes invisibility within a large group and the kind of passive learning that pervades large lecture halls. When we started out to design this game intervention, there were many well-meaning suggestions about how we could, for example, make the game *part of a class* or have *assignments* where players completed game challenges. The design team kindly pushed back on these suggestions, which derive from the way most educators think about education: that you should clearly identify the learning experience to all students, because they will be responsible for participating, and that you should be open with assignment information because students are expected to complete them. But those values, well meaning as they are, worked against the kind of lure we knew this game needed to attract participation. So, rather than operating in the open, and creating game-like assignments, we *hid* the game from students. We gave out *random* clues, to only some students. A selection of students found postcards in their orientation folders pointing them to a game website, others noticed a strange flag in the cinema courtyard with an unusual logo on it. Students who posted about the flag received another unusual communication with a puzzle and another clue. As a small number of students began to realize that "something was going on," social groups began forming immediately around the experience, working together to solve these initial puzzles. Later, as the core gameplay became clear, these groups transitioned into creative teams.

In this case, the lure was one of mystery. There are of course many other ways to create an attraction for players to willingly join a game, but the important takeaway here for designers of games for learning, or game-like learning, is that the lure itself, the invitation itself, should be enough to convince players to participate. The appeal of a game is not made more imperative to players by assignment or force. In fact, a game's appeal, as I have suggested, is a fragile thing, something that can be broken if the authority of an instructor is insinuated. The lure of a game is not universal, and neither is it constant. What is appealing to a freshman entering the cinema school may not be appealing to a graduate student or a medical student. Designing the lure of a game has much to do with understanding the preexisting motivations of the target community. In the case of the *Reality Ends Here* game, we were relying on the intense desire of students to become part of the storied history of the cinema school. The invitation from a secret committee to play a game came with the promise: "The more you participate, the more the (game) will work to connect you with unique experiences and active alumni in areas of the media industry and academia that are relevant to you. Even engaging just a little will open up new opportunities and discoveries" (Reality Ends Here 2012).

In another set of games, designed for high school students about to navigate the college application process, in which playing promises to give insights and strategies for understanding that process, the lure is more straightforward, but again, purposefully not framed as a requirement. The *Application Crunch* card game and its online counterpart *Mission: Admission* do not use mystery to attract players but still tap into the desires and existing motivations of their players. Students want to know more about the college application process, but they do not necessarily know the questions to ask or have a counselor or mentor to approach with questions. Also, static information about the process is simply boring and cannot help them develop working strategies for making their way through a complicated and dynamic set of choices. The appeal of these games are in their safe, nonjudgmental space for learning and practicing strategies that, while simplified, have a deep similarity to those they are about to face in the real application process (Collegeology Games 2011).

The Occasion: When and Where to Play?

Because playing a game requires our time and attention, there must be an occasion to play. Traditionally, a game designer assumes that this occasion might be a social situation such as a family get-together or hanging. The number of players required and the physical setup reflects this assumption. For more structured game experiences, like sports leagues, the occasion to play a game might be a more formal appointment, such as a playoff schedule. But more often in today's digitally connected world, occasions to play are being integrated in and among our other responsibilities. We carry devices that allow us to play while waiting in line, or while taking a short break at work. Checking in to social sites like Facebook often involves playing our stored up energy in one or two games. This does not take long, and the games are designed to get us in and out, like a drive-thru, so that we can get back to our daily tasks.

The occasion to play is something of a battlefield when it comes to education. In many K–12 institutions, games and technologies that play them, such as mobile phones, are restricted or disallowed (Obringer and Coffey 2007). In college classrooms, phones are not generally disallowed, but students are often told to turn them off before class begins to discourage interruptions. Where I teach, at USC, some professors will even ask that laptops be turned off to gain the students' full attention. When games are brought into classrooms, it is often as a special case, perhaps requiring a special trip to where the technology is. This separation of classroom and play, classroom and technology, preserves the authority of the traditional classroom and relegates games and play to the feel of a "rainy day" activity, something detached from normal, everyday learning. There are, of course notable experimental exceptions to this, such as those described in Katie Salen's chapter, and others at campuses like Duke where technologies such as the iPod have become the focus of experimental learning situations (Dean 2004).

In the game examples that I have been discussing, *Reality Ends Here* and *Mission: Admission*, the occasion to play was purposefully left open-ended. For example, *Mission: Admission* has been introduced to students in some Los Angeles schools by counselors as part of our project goals. This introduction included some scaffolding about the college application process and will provide a local community for discussion about that process. The game itself is a free-to-play Facebook game, however, so students will most likely access it from home or other environments out of school. Like most Facebook games, it is designed to promote short play sessions and restarts every week so that a student cannot get too far out of sync with his or her friends, even if they have a week when they do not have time to play. Each week, a student chooses a new high school student as a character, with unique aspirations and background. The goal is to help this character on his or her way to college. The player has energy to spend to level up in activities that make the character a better applicant. As with many Facebook games, once the player spends energy, a student has to wait to earn more, making each play session a short burst of decision making that the player can look forward to when he or she has the occasion to play.

Reality Ends Here, as mentioned, was a "secret" experience, so the occasion was necessarily vague. The game, however, was designed to capitalize on the fact that it was played in a community that inhabited the same campus, the same buildings, the same classrooms, sometimes the same dorms most of its days. The local nature of the community—incoming freshmen in the USC School of Cinematic Arts—called for a face-to-face core gameplay mechanic at the heart of the design that would provoke players to interact in person and form real-world social ties. That core game mechanic was a deck of trading cards, which served as a procedural prompting system. The students were lured into the game using puzzles and mysterious messages. Once they found the "game office," a room in the cinema complex filled with artifacts of media making—old cameras, a Moviola editing machine, and the like—they were initiated into the game by a group of graduate students who claimed to be in the employ of a mysterious committee called the Reality committee. (In actuality, the students were the creative director and co-designers of the game.)

Reality Ends Here players were each given a manila envelope with 10 random trading cards and swore an "oath of DIY media" in which they promised to play safely and yet be fearless in their creativity. The cards were part of an interlocking system that allowed players to create prompts—called "deals" in the game—for interesting projects they could make. These projects ranged from short films to games to radio plays to salon events. All of them provoked a need for collaboration with other students who were also playing the game. This need for collaboration was inherent in the game mechanics: first, each card used in a deal added to the overall point value of the deal—more cards, the higher the value of the deal; and second, every player who participated in the deal would score the total value of the deal. Since every player had only 10 cards to start, he immediately saw the value of forming creative groups to create larger deals. Once those groups started working together, its members discovered more creative possibilities among their various skill sets, and their combined cards opened up more deal options—which could be thought of as more occasions to play the game.

The Feel of Fun: Testing, Teasing, Exploring

As with the concept of a lure, the feel of fun in a game is not something that translates naturally to most traditional learning environments. In her chapter, Salen also calls out the need for this quality of playful potential; she discusses principles for game-like learning, noting the importance that it "kind of feels like play." Salen is working with K–12 students, of course, and in that environment the sensibility of play makes obvious sense. This might not seem as clear a need when dealing with games in and around higher education. The feel of a game, however, is an aesthetic property of its experience that makes it attractive and engaging. Once players have followed the lure, accepted the promise of play, and found occasion to engage in play, that promise must be fulfilled.

As already described, the system of a game is an imperfect one, one that does not drive the player directly to closure or success. Rather, the system includes opportunity for inefficacies, testing, teasing, exploring, and seeing how actions provoke consequences. In his book on the concept of game "feel," designer Steve Swink (2008) discusses the aesthetics of game feel in real-time simulated environments. He describes the pleasures of controlling virtual objects, the sense of extension of identity, including the joy of mastery over controls that previously felt clumsy and unfamiliar. This kind of sensibility is one way to think of the feel of play. But one might more broadly identify the feel of fun as being linked to a player's perception of opportunity, her sense of ability within the constraints of the system. We see someone hit a ball with a bat, and we think: "Can I do that?" We watch the activity some more, perhaps we swing a bat ourselves to test the feel, and we think: "I can do that!" Suddenly, it looks like fun.

This property of games, their "feeling of fun," is twofold: it has to do not only with the actual pleasure associated with the designed activity but also with how that activity displays itself as being pleasurable and achievable, though not without challenge. Visual puzzles are a good example of this quality—they are crafted to show their complexity and to tease their solvability at the same time. Think of a Rubik's cube: at first glance, it is a jumble of colors that looks complex and interesting. Watching a person play with it, you might see her solve a face of the cube. Suddenly, it looks doable; you might have an idea on how to proceed. Even playing with the object, your sense of both its complexities and its constraints are clear in the tactile nature of the interface—an interface that feels playful and allows you to test and tease out potential solutions. Most games are not "solvable" in the same way that puzzles are, but well-designed playful systems have that same combination of an underlying complexity accessed by a simple visual interface that allows for pleasurable exploration and playful testing of strategies.

For example, in *Reality Ends Here*, the card-based prompts were constrained by a very simple visual system. Each card had several connectors on its sides; the connectors varied by color and direction. One card could be connected to another card if they had connectors with matching colors and matching "flow." But the real pleasure of the system was actually more than just the successful linkage of cards into a deal. On each card was a piece of content. For example, on green cards, of which there could be only one in each deal, were project types that formed the goal of the prompt. As already described, these included short films, games, radio plays, faux products, character artifacts, and more. Also in the deck were pink cards that made the project more specific. For example, a green card calling for the players to make a "silent film short" could be modified with the pink card "using the quality of solitude." Another pink card might be connected to the deal calling for the silent short to also involve "the everyman." As already noted, the more cards added to the deal, the more points it was worth. There were about 300 total cards in the game deck, each with different connectors, point values, and content. As larger deals were put together, the creative challenge became harder and harder to meet. It might seem that this would deter players, however, just the opposite. As the game progressed, teams solidified, and bigger and bigger collaborations were formed, using more and more cards. The highest scoring deal of the semester included 74 cards in its prompt.

What made the *Reality Ends Here* system have the feel of fun for its players? One facet of the appeal is that each player clearly had access to only a small set of cards; however, it was obvious that there was a vast universe of cards out there to be found and played with. A feature on the game's website showed players a random "card of the moment" and offered a look-up feature, but nowhere was there simply a directory of cards, library, or index. This piqued so much interest that a group of players spent hours of time compiling its own list of cards (SCA Reality Card Compilation on Facebook 2011). By making the cards coveted objects—part of a large complex interconnected system—we imbued them with a sense of mystery that fulfilled on the promise of our initial lure. By giving them a simple, tactile interface, we allowed players the testing and exploring potential uses in each prompt. And, by adding evocative content to each card ("the last of their kind," "regarding fact and fiction," "starring a toy animal"), we constrained the players in their creative thinking, but in ways that effectively boosted their creative output. Again, we see the combination of a complex underlying system, accessed with a simple visual interface that allows for pleasurable exploration of ideas.

The Grasp of It: The Feeling of Understanding

As is likely becoming evident, however complex a game system may be, players will ultimately begin to grasp its organization. In fact, this sense of understanding and mastering a game's underlying structure may be the ultimate driver for many players: to gain the highest level, to explore every land, to max out stats, to collect all badges. Understanding the patterns in a game system, as well as optimizing play to take advantage of those patterns, is part of the pleasure of play. Whether it is optimizing a resource system, or developing just the right skills to execute a precise play, developing this grasp of the system's opportunities is as much a part of the pleasure of play as the moment-to-moment mechanics. It follows therefore that designing the system for this kind of discovery is also critical. If a system is too thin and is completely visible from the outset, it denies players the opportunity to make these discoveries and, perhaps as importantly, to share them. As articulated by James Gee in chapter 7, having and sharing knowledge of this kind in what he has termed "passionate affinity spaces" (Gee and Hayes 2011) provide an opportunity to develop the kinds of twenty-first-century learning skills that have become more and more critical in education.

In the games I have been using as examples, the systems were designed so that grasping the structure of the game would eventually lead to an understanding of important learning goals. Articulating that understanding becomes a form of transfer. For example, in the *Application Crunch* card game and *Mission: Admission* Facebook game, understanding the underlying structure of the games leads to a grasp of important concepts in the college application process. As part of the research around the use of the games, for example, the team conducted play sessions where high school students played the game several times. During the first sessions, students were learning the basics of the system such as how to manage time and what activities to focus on for their applications. During later rounds, the players who had grasped the basics began to articulate their knowledge to their peers: "Don't forget to turn in your FAFSA!" became a common warning among all the players. Students also cautioned each other about getting enough letters of recommendation, or focusing all their efforts on getting into one school. The design of the game supported this gradual building of knowledge about the game system, and in this case that knowledge became understanding that could be transferred back to their real-world situations.

In *Reality Ends Here*, the system was developed to lead players to an understanding about the kind of twenty-first-century media makers we hoped they would become. As already described, the basic mechanics emphasized collaboration across disciplines and a proactive, self-initiating attitude about creative activities. The projects and their supporting justifications and cards were all available to the local community via the game website, where they were discussed and lauded. However, the system had other hidden elements that were not revealed on the site. These consisted of "serendipitous encounters" with alumni and other professional media artists who met and mentored small groups of students. Each week, the mysterious "reality" committee contacted several students, generally the top scorers of the week in a variety of categories. They would be instructed to meet a town car on a specific street corner, or to go to a location near campus. At the location, they would meet their mentor participant. Mentors included prominent people in the industry such as writer-director John Singleton, indie game developers Jenova Chen and Kellee Santigo, cinematographer Dante Spinotti, screenwriter John August, game designer Frank Lantz, and Professor Henry Jenkins. These rewards were personal and unique, as the students and mentors had time to talk and sometimes brainstorm creative ideas together. As the game progressed, it became clear to the students that the structure of the game was proving an important point about media making: action begets opportunity. All they had to do was dive in and starting working on projects and amazing opportunities would open up before them. The message of the game was inherent in its structure, discoverable by its players, and transferable to their real-world goals.

Managing Challenge: Incrementally Exposing Complexity

Virtually everyone who has written about the nature of games and what makes them work, myself included, has written about challenge (Fullerton 2008b;

Salen and Zimmerman 2004). In chapter 9, Valerie Shute and colleagues review this principle of games in respect to its ability to engage players and enhance learning. In chapter 8, Katie Salen also refers to this quality as an underlying similarity between game design and the effect of good learning environments in her discussion of Quest to Learn. In each of these discussions, challenge is approached as an experience of the player rather than as a designed state of the system. These are valuable and important ways of understanding challenge. But there are equally valuable ways to understand challenge as a component of design. If we look at challenge in regard to the lure and the feeling of fun we have been examining, we can see that as expressed as a component of design rather than a state of play, challenge is the aspect in the design where the pleasurable, playful interface exposes that underlying complexity. From a designer's perspective, the challenge of a game is the flipside of the lure: it is the actuality of what the player faces in order to achieve its promise. Like a hiker who can see only the rise in front of him, rather than the whole trek to the top of the mountain, challenge is best exposed to the player in increments. Educators would call this scaffolding; game designers often think of challenge in term of levels or stages of a game. There is indeed a deep relationship between this aspect of games and the design of learning environments, but what is important to keep in mind about the difference here is that the challenge of a game is framed by the promise of the lure and the pleasure of that feeling of fun. When we say that "challenge motivates players," we are collapsing the effect all of these aspects of design: the fact that the lure appeals to an existing motivation or proclivity, that the feel of the game has an intrinsic pleasure all its own, and that the challenge presented is carefully structured to reveal just the right amount of complexity to be faced at that moment.

As an example of how challenge is controlled in a game, we can look at a simple illustration of these concepts. In the card game version of the college application game, *Application Crunch*, players are faced with a stream of deadlines to be met. These model real-world milestones like filling out the FAFSA (Free Application for Federal Student Aid) form and applying to scholarships and various schools. Early deadlines such as "appointment with a college counselor" or "attend a college fair" are easy to meet and require little preparation. But the complexity soon begins to ramp up, and players need to think strategically about which deadlines to aim for and how best to prepare for them. Players have limited "time" in the sense that they can take only so many actions per turn. They must divide that time between academics, extracurriculars, service activities, and work. Preparing for deadlines is a challenge that becomes more and more layered as the game progresses, and the game exposes more aspects of the complex system it is modeling. This complexity is one of the reasons that a game may have good replay value. The sense that a player gets as she glimpses that complexity is that there is much more here to be explored in future sessions. Suddenly, challenge can be owned by the player, rather than doled out by the system. This kind of a moment, which we call mastery, is a reward in itself and begins to get at our original suspicion of why we believe that games may have something powerful to add to educational methods.

Sometimes it is not the system itself that provides new challenges but rather the activity of other players. In the example of *Reality Ends Here*, the game website was the instrument through which this occurred. As already described, players of the game quickly formed creative teams to develop projects that answered their procedurally generated "deals." These teams worked on their own to develop short films, games, scripts, character artifacts, and more. Once a project was finished, the group submitted it to the site for scoring and display to the entire community. Additionally, the group could submit behind-the-scenes pictures of the team working on the project for extra points, and players would routinely do so, often posting images as they worked through late nights. In order to finalize a project, the team came to the game office with all the cards used in the deal. The deal was laid out showing that all the cards, indeed, could be included under the rules, and a photo was taken of it and uploaded alongside the project. Last, the team had to explain the use of every card in the deal, in a verbal "justification" shot using a webcam and uploaded with the project and the cards. Because of this, every deal that went on the site was accompanied by evidence of its underlying complexity. Many of the comments in the game forum spoke to the growing sense in the community that the real challenge of the game was becoming a sort of one-upsmanship of who could pull off the most elaborate, complex deals. The point system and leaderboard made this challenge possible, but it was this sense of challenge issued and owned by the players themselves that inevitably drove the game community.

Success and Failure: Assessment and Feedback

One of the themes of our strong interest in games and technology for learning is the ability to automate and scale personalized assessment and feedback to both students and teachers. The argument for digital games as assessment tools usually centers on the fact that we can collect data about a player's actions that allow us to know what she knows about the "content" of a game. If the content encompasses the learning goals, then we can assess her progress along those goals and provide feedback and timely intervention if there is trouble (Delacruz 2011; Wainess, Koenig, and Kerr 2011). Other, more complex arguments center on the notion that games themselves are learning environments, so that the real innovation is not to add "learning content" to games, but to recognize what games are already teaching and that they are already assessing a certain degree of situated understanding about subjects like physics for example, as discussed by Gee in chapter 7. Researchers such as Zoran Popovic and his team are focusing on games as instruments for assessing not final learning goals but best teaching methods (Anderson et al. 2010).

It seems important to restate here that games are not naturally efficient systems. They are purposely inefficient in their designs. As already discussed, this creates a kind of intentional slippage or play in their workings that allows players to act creatively, spontaneously, and perhaps ineffectively and to test the success or failure of those actions according to the feedback they get from the system. Because the game is a safe place to do that testing, the players assume there will be no repercussions. This produces a paradox in the way that we traditionally think about assessment. If a game is a place to make safe choices and to learn how those choices might compare among a range of choices, then how can we expect to judge student players by their performance in a game?

In the *Application Crunch* and *Mission: Admission* games, the design purposefully distances the player from the game character. Rather than playing your own avatar, you play a randomly generated character with unique aspirations and background. This was done to preserve the sense of a safety zone for players. If their characters do not get into the college of their choice, it is not a comment on the future plans of the players. If you decide to send a student who hopes to be a computer scientist to a culinary school, you may have fun doing so, and you may enjoy the fact that the student sends you sad letters home from school, complaining about the mismatch. In this example, the feedback (letters from the unhappy character) serves to let the player know that what he has done has consequences, but it may or may not be a true reflection of his understanding of the college application process. We can assess a player's changing strategies over time; perhaps next week he decides to send a character who wants to be a screenwriter to a small liberal arts school. This closer match of ambition to college choice may or may not mean that the player has learned from his earlier actions. The key here is that the game is meant to be *played with,* and the assumption that play takes a direct route from one point to another, from lack of knowledge to use of knowledge, is a highly biased assumption that does not take into account the way that successful games encourage us to take risks, employ failure as a strategy, and damn the repercussions, so to speak.

A counterexample might better illustrate the issue. At one time, I was part of a team asked to design a set of games that would teach basic math principles and assess how students were learning as part of their play of the game. The design team included math education experts. One of the key points of discussion between the education experts and the game designers came around a discussion of failure. The game designers wanted players to be able to make bad or less efficient decisions as part of their play. The education experts felt this would teach "bad habits." No matter how long this discussion went on, the education experts and the game designers stood on two sides of a vast chasm of beliefs: What does failure mean in terms of play versus what does it mean in terms of learning? Because we were framing this experience as a game, we eventually settled on allowing a certain amount of "bad decision making" or at least inefficient decision making that would still achieve the game's goals. This kind of gulf between how we think of education and how we think of play remains with me as a touchstone whenever I begin to design a game that has goals beyond entertainment.

The Currency: Sharing What You Know

I began this discussion of what games do well with the notion of a lure, an attraction to what a game offers. When a game has delivered on that lure and made good on its promise, and when a player has met its challenges and has a grasp on the nuances of its system, that knowledge becomes a kind of social currency. Giving players the need and the opportunity to share such knowledge in a venue where that currency has value leads to the reinvestment of players in that original lure and the development of a community around a game that in many ways may be where the real learning potential lies (Gee 2007). As Henry Jenkins and Adam Kahn discuss in chapter 6 on the open laptop exam, however, our concepts of sharing knowledge in the learning process have limits. In a game, sharing strategies is not considered cheating, and even strategies that might be considered cheating by hard-core players have their place in games culture (Consalvo 2007). Sharing the understanding of a games system is part of a complex economy of play that needs to be considered as part of the game design, not shut down because it does not easily support individual assessment.

In my example games *Mission: Admission* and *Application Crunch*, each has a question-asking feature that encourages players to discuss college knowledge. In each case, one player chooses to ask a question of the others. In *Mission: Admission*, this is done using an in-game message function that sends the question to all of her Facebook friends who are playing the game. In *Application Crunch*, the player simply asks the question of the players at the table. In both cases, the question is provided by the game, but the players judge the resulting answers. This allows a kind of social informality to the knowledge sharing that would be lost if it were judged by the system, or if the questions were posed as true or false or multiple-choice sets. The goal of both question mechanics is to encourage discussion and sharing around the topics rather than focusing on correct or incorrect answers. All players can answer, and in the end, both the player with the best answer and the player who asked the question are rewarded, incentivizing both roles.

In *Reality Ends Here*, the online community was called "the bullpen" after an infamous location in the original cinema buildings. The original bullpen was a messy, communal editing space with walls covered in graffiti from students. By naming the online community space after this historical space, the game lauded a kind of irreverent, playful, disorderly approach to media making. "This space belongs to you" the top of the online bullpen announced, and students took it at its word with more than 4,400 status updates and tweets posted by the players over the 15 weeks of play. Additionally, because the game was designed for players who were also taking classes together and sometimes living together in dormitories, there were immeasurable opportunities for knowledge sharing outside of the online community. In fact, this was one of the key design features of the game. As articulated by Ben Stokes and colleagues (2012) in their discussion of "situated engagement," a focus on local community, even when using mobile or online technologies, provides a kind "human-centric framework" for engagement that may be otherwise missing in large scale, online communities. The online bullpen awarded a few points for players to make posts and comments, and when measured against the scores awarded for submitting projects, it quickly became clear to players that productivity was more highly valued than social interaction within the game. While some players found this problematic, it brought to the surface a discussion of the values of the game, which ultimately was a game about making, not talking. The few points that were awarded for participating in the online social space could not take the place of participating in projects; however, it could—and often did—act as a tiebreaker. So making deals and also sharing ideas in the online bullpen became the ultimate strategy. And, of course, players who enacted this strategy were ultimately embracing the learning goals of the game. They had been lured into playing by their existing motivations as aspiring media makers, they had found both the occasion to play and the fun of it, they had met the challenges and had a real understanding of the system, and now they were eager to share their experiences.

Conclusion

I began this chapter not only with an acknowledgment that games and social media have a deep connection to learning and offer the potential to play an important role in our current rethinking of educational methods and systems but also with the caution that our assumptions about the benefits of that connection might contain some traps. Throughout this chapter, I have described some of the aesthetic qualities of games—qualities that do not necessarily scale or automate learning and assessment but that certainly engage and make social learning situations. What I hope I have shown by this discussion is that our need to create systems that engage learners deeply has led us dangerously close to the desire to instrumentalize games, but that by doing so, we may neuter their very potential. Assigning students to play a game may be proved at some point to be as effective as assigning them to read a textbook—not wholly inefficient, and yet not imbued with the kind of passion that lures players to games naturally. Similarly, occasions to play need not be appointments or opportunities separated forcefully from the classroom or the learning environment. The feel of fun cannot be taken for granted; awarding badges or recognizing achievements for activities without this sense is not a replacement for designing a system that is evocative and pleasurably challenging in its own right. And, while ramping up the difficulty may be one of the few places that educators and game designers have a similar understanding of player needs, it is in the elegance of the interface to the underlying complexity where a game's artistry lies. This same artistry is found in the flexibility of a game to allow for playful exploration and the freedom to fail. All of this leads to the ability for players to come to an understanding of the game system, to use that knowledge to master it, and to share that knowledge with others.

In chapter 1 of this volume, William Tierney describes the need for "disruptive technology" that may completely upset the educational practices and market forces around higher education. As a designer of games, I feel the need to question if this "disruptive technology" we are looking for will really reach its potential if it is conceived of as scalable e-learning solutions on the one hand, or a kind of neutered game replacement for textbooks on the other. In his discussion of the potential for simulations and learning, Clark Aldrich (2003) has compared e-learning solutions to the fast-food industry—providing a cost-effective, efficient, standardized, and scalable solution to food but at the cost of nutrition and quality. As Tierney points out, e-learning solutions for higher education are clearly seen as "less than" alternatives by their traditional counterparts. And now games for learning, when instrumentalized to the extent that they have none of the artistry described here, are in danger of having effectively the same "nutritional value" as a fast-food burger. Games and social media undoubtedly have powerful potential for learning, but not because they are a cost-effective, efficient, standardized, and scalable solution to education. If we are truly to harness their potential, we must focus on the kind of artistic, crafted experiences that attract and engage players naturally, and that have prompted us to this connection between the experiences of learning and play in the first place. It is important to ask ourselves not "how can we inject traditional learning goals into games and assess how they are taken up by the players," but rather "how can we better understand the motivations of learners, lure them with interesting and challenging play, and craft engaging and evocative learning experiences?" Market forces in education are as strong as they are in the food industry, and ultimately, we may not be in a position to entirely resist the drive-through of learning solutions. I hope, however, that some of the aesthetic qualities of games that I have highlighted here, and the examples of games designed *as games*, may give us the impetus to look for solutions that are scalable and local, high tech and high touch, ones that take advantage of the fact that the best education is one that requires a give-and-take between success and failure and are energized by the person-to-person interaction found within the vibrant social activity of game communities.

REFERENCES

Aldrich, Cark. 2003. *Simulations and the Future of Learning: An Innovative (and Perhaps Revolutionary) Approach to e-Learning.* San Francisco: John Wiley & Sons.

Andersen, Erik, Yun-En Liu, Ethan Apter, François Boucher-Genesse, and Zoran Popovic. 2010. "Gameplay Analysis through State Projection." Paper presented at Foundations of Digital Games, Monterey, California, June 19–21.

Avedon, Elliot Morton, and Brian Sutton-Smith. 1971. *The Study of Games*. New York: John Wiley & Sons.

Bogost, Ian. 2007. *Persuasive Games: The Expressive Power of Videogames*. Cambridge, MA: MIT Press.

———. 2011. *How to Do Things with Videogames*. Minneapolis: University of Minnesota Press.

Collegeology Games. 2011. "Collegeology Games." Accessed December 17. http://www.collegeologygames.com.

Consalvo, Mia. 2007. *Cheating: Gaining Advantage in Videogames*. Cambridge, MA: MIT Press.

Dean, Katie. 2004. "Duke Gives iPods to Freshmen." *Wired*, August 20. Accessed January 6, 2011. http://www.wired.com/entertainment/music/news/2004/07/64282.

Delacruz, Girlie C. 2011. *Games as Formative Assessment Environments: Examining the Impact of Explanations of Scoring and Incentives on Math Learning, Game Performance and Help Seeking [CRESST Report 796]*. Los Angeles: UCLA, National Center for Research on Evaluation, Standards, and Student Testing.

Digital Media and Learning Competition. 2011. "About." Accessed January 7. http://dmlcompetition.net.

Fullerton, Tracy. 2008a. "Documentary Games: Putting the Player in the Path of History." In *Playing the Past: Nostalgia in Video Games and Electronic Literature*, edited by Zach Whalen and Laurie Taylor, 215–238. Nashville, TN: Vanderbilt University Press.

———. 2008b. *Game Design Workshop, Second Edition: A Playcentric Approach to Creating Innovative Games*. Burlington, MA: Morgan Kaufmann Publishers.

Fullerton, Tracy, Laird M. Malamed, Nahil Sharkasi, and Jesse Vigil. 2009. *Designing History: The Path to Participation Nation*. Sandbox 2009, New Orleans, Louisiana, August 4–6.

Gee, James Paul. 2007. *Good Video Games and Good Learning*. New York: Peter Lang.

———. 2008. "Game-Like Learning: An Example of Situated Learning and Implications for Opportunity to Learn." In *Assessment, Equity, and Opportunity to Learn*, edited by Pamela A. Moss, Diana C. Pullin, James Paul Gee, Edward H. Haertel, and Lauren Jones Young, 200–221. Cambridge: Cambridge University Press.

Gee, James Paul, and Elisabeth R. Hayes. 2011. *Language and Learning in the Digital Age*. New York: Routledge.

Huizinga, Johan. 1955. *Homo Ludens: A Study of the Play Element in Culture*. Boston: Beacon Press.

Jenkins, Henry, Kurt Squire, and Philip Tan. 2003. "'You Can't Bring That Game to School!'" In *Design Research: Methods and Perspectives*, edited by Brenda Laurel, 244–252. Cambridge, MA: MIT Press.

McGonigal, Jane. 2011. *Reality Is Broken: Why Games Make Us Better and How They Can Change the World*. New York: Penguin Press.

Obringer, S. John, and Kent Coffey. 2007. "Cell Phones in American High Schools: A National Survey." *Journal of Technology Studies* 33:41–47.

Reality Ends Here. 2012. "About." Accessed January 20. http://reality.usc.edu.

Salen, Katie, Robert Torres, Loretta Wolozin, Rebecca Rufo-Tepper, and Arana Shapiro. 2011. *Quest to Learn: Growing a School for Digital Kids*. Cambridge, MA: MIT Press. Accessed September 4, 2012. http://dmlcentral.net/sites/dmlcentral/files/resource_files/Quest_to_LearnMacfoundReport.pdf.

Salen, Katie, and Eric Zimmerman. 2004. *Rules of Play: Game Design Fundamentals.* Cambridge, MA: MIT Press.

SCA Reality Card Compilation on Facebook. 2011. Accessed January 20. http://www.facebook.com/pages/SCA-Reality-Card-Compilation/218257968240289?sk=wall.

Stokes, Ben, François Bar, George Villanueva, Otto Khera, Teresa Gonzalez, and Cesar Jimenez. 2012. "Situated Engagement." Last modified March. http://www.partour.net/situated-engagement.

Swink, Steve. 2008. *Game Feel: A Game Designer's Guide to Virtual Sensation.* Burlington, MA: Morgan Kaufman Publishers.

Wainess, Richard, Alan Koenig, and Deirdre Kerr. 2011. *Aligning Instruction and Assessment with Game and Simulation Design* [*CRESST Report 780*]. Los Angeles: UCLA, National Center for Research on Evaluation, Standards, and Student Testing.

Zimmerman, Eric. 2011. "Let the Games Be Games: Aesthetics, Instrumentalization & Game Design." Presentation at Game Developers Conference, San Francisco, March 25–29.

CHAPTER SIX

The Open Laptop Exam

Reflections and Speculations

HENRY JENKINS AND ADAM S. KAHN

When Henry Jenkins relocated to the University of Southern California (USC) several years ago, his new teaching obligations required him to oversee a large lecture hall course on new media and culture, the first such course he had taught in many years. He was surprised by his students' responses to practices that had once seemed unproblematic. Specifically, he planned to give an open-note, open-book final exam, one where students would have access to the questions ahead of time but which would require them to enter their responses under the time pressures of a scheduled exam. Past experience had suggested that this approach lowered stress, allowing students to feel more in control as they were preparing for and taking the exam. In practice, a few students worked really hard, writing out their answers in advance. Others studied their notes, prepared an outline, and improvised on the exam. And some, for their own reasons, did not study and performed badly on the exam.

No sooner did Jenkins announce this policy than he got a question from a student wondering whether "open book, open note" meant "open laptop" given that all class readings had been posted online (instead of using a course reader). Given the class was about technology and culture, Jenkins started to break down the computer into two elements. First, the computer acts as a stand-alone word processing machine and source for the course readings and previously taken notes. He had no great objections to students using the computer to write their answers or access their materials. But, the laptop, in a wireless classroom, is also a networking device. Allowing students to use a laptop would mean students could access any information anywhere on the web and more significantly, trade information with each other throughout the test in ways which would be extremely difficult to monitor. An open-laptop exam only seemed to make sense when these potentials were honestly and openly factored into the assessment process.

Jenkins became intrigued by the challenges of designing a meaningful test under those circumstances. What would it mean to create an exam that could be taken not by individual students but by networked study groups? Could collective intelligence be incorporated into test design? Could challenges be created that allowed students to demonstrate their mastery of the material through the search strategies they deployed and the knowledge they produced together? In theory, such an exam holds promise, as more and more jobs require the capacity to collaborate with others to solve complex problems. One could argue that learning how to mobilize expertise under these conditions should be core to our educational process. But would students raised in a culture where grades are based on individual performance know how to act fairly in a context where grades are based on group performance?

As Jenkins began to contemplate these issues, he started to choke. As much as he wanted to be the cool, open-minded teacher, the model pedagogue for the digital age, there was no way he could work through the implications of this radical shift in classroom practice in time to apply it that first semester. Ironically, having failed to create opportunities for collaboration inside the exam space, the students did what might easily have been predicted: they formed study groups outside class and worked through responses together. Many students had written entire answers to the preprovided questions in advance and simply copied their prewritten answers into a blue book. In some cases, as many as 30 or 40 students got the same question wrong and in the same way, which suggests just how expansive the study network (scarcely a study group) had become. The experience illustrated that the question may no longer be whether learning is going to be networked but rather how much control teachers are able to exert over the networks where learning and studying take place.

We offer this chapter as a provocation that derives from the topics raised throughout this book. Our hope is to raise some core questions and spark debates about the nature of testing and assessment in a world that is increasingly shaped by the networked production and exchange of knowledge. In doing so, we highlight how social media are changing the nature of teaching and learning in the academy. This chapter draws on the current literature on collective intelligence, transactive memory systems theory, and affinity spaces to reimagine the open-book exam. As we do so, we recognize that there can be no one-size-fits-all solution to these challenges, so we should be clear that the type of exam on which we focus is for a large lecture hall, introductory-level undergraduate exam—the kind that is widely deployed, alas, across many public and private universities.

Some aspects of collective intelligence are already deployed within smaller-scale classes, especially graduate seminars, but have proved harder to apply to the scope and scale of the lecture hall. In the closing section of the chapter, we outline what a test designed to apply collective intelligence principles in this context might look like and what would need to be done to prepare students to perform well under these conditions. This essay is designed as a thought experiment (suggesting the implications of current research on how knowledge is being produced and shared in a networked society) and partially a pragmatic activity (suggesting principles that might inform our own classroom practices). We may still not be able to address the seemingly innocent question posed by Jenkins's student, but we will at least be able to explain why educators at all levels will not be able to dodge this question much longer.

This chapter, itself, is an example of the knowledge pooling we shall talk about, as Henry Jenkins is a senior scholar with an expertise in cultural studies and many years of teaching experience, whereas Adam Kahn is a doctoral student with an expertise in quantitative social science and only three years of experience as a teaching assistant. Neither one of us would be able to write this provocation alone, nor would the theories we are individually familiar with be able to produce some of our conclusions alone.

A Changing Context

A significant mismatch exists between the learning that occurs outside of schools in recreational or professional contexts and the learning that universities recognize and reward. A growing body of scholarship (Ito et al. 2009; Knobel and Lankshear 2010) has described the informal learning taking place in fan communities and gaming guilds, around the creation of *Wikipedia* entries, and through social networks. In these environments, knowledge gets produced rapidly because each participant contributes what he knows for the group's collective benefit, and each may also draw from the pooled knowledge to address questions of immediate concern. These spaces are characterized by fluid exchanges among participants with different needs, skills, goals, and interests.

These sites empower members to address questions beyond the capacities of any given individual.

Through their involvement in such communities, young people are forming expectations that this is the way they will be working together in the future. In his book *The Penguin and the Leviathan: How Cooperation Triumphs over Self-Interest*, law professor Yochai Benkler (2011) describes future workplaces:

> The most successful [companies] know that innovation happens everywhere. Not just in the executive boardrooms, or R&D labs, but everywhere—from the factory floor to the sales desk to the tarmac of an airport. These companies also know that continuous learning and innovation can't happen in an organization which treats its members like mindless robots. It can only happen in an organization that welcomes and taps the diverse insights, skills, and talents of every human being it employs. Only those organizations that have figured out how to motivate their employees intrinsically and how to engage them in the enterprise as a community of shared interest and common purpose, will survive. (212)

Benkler's analysis of what motivates collaboration and cooperation within organizations has much to teach educators. We need to prepare our students to function in such an environment—teaching them how to share knowledge, how to trust the knowledge shared by others, how to make unique contributions, and how to value diverse expertise.

Young people can acquire many of these skills through their activities as fans, gamers, Wikipedians, and Facebookers. Here, for example, is James Paul Gee (2008) on the experience of playing a multiplayer game:

> Guilds orchestrate organization, planning, and the enforcement of norms and values at a high level—for example, choosing who goes on what raids and how specialized skills (like being a Priest) are to be learned and played out in practice.... *World of Warcraft* is all about social organization for high performance of just the sort that workplaces pay consultants to refine, and workers find stressful. Such games hold out the potential for the discovery of new forms of social organization, new ways of solving social problems (e.g., the free-rider problem), and new ways of researching and testing collaborative learning, knowledge building, and performance. (34)

Since the exam is where we practice our core assumptions about what kinds of learning matter and how students should be assessed, it appears many classrooms embody almost the opposite set of values. The flow of knowledge is hierarchical (top to bottom) and does not respect diverse ways of knowing. Knowledge is standardized (everyone is expected to learn the same things and answer the same questions) and knowledge is autonomous (sharing information and pooling knowledge is primarily seen as a form of cheating). This is why it is crucial for us to think—and debate—how the exam is designed in today's college lecture hall.

Basic Definitions

Let us begin by offering some initial definitions of the key terms we deploy across this chapter. First, *collective intelligence* can refer to a range of different, competing, and sometimes contradictory theories about the ways networked computing supports the collaborative production of knowledge. The French philosopher Pierre Lévy's ([1994] 1999) book *Collective Intelligence: Mankind's Emerging World in Cyberspace* defines collective intelligence as "a form of *universally distributed intelligence*, constantly enhanced, coordinated in real time, and resulting in the effective motivation of skills" (13). He describes the notion of universally distributed intelligence as "no one knows everything, everyone knows something, all knowledge resides in humanity. There is no transcendent store of knowledge and knowledge is simply the sum of what we know" (13–14). While some efforts to characterize collective intelligence (e.g., those used by the MIT Center for Collective Intelligence or those implicit in many discussions of Web 2.0) would include the anonymous aggregation of data (often described as "the wisdom of crowds"), Lévy's original definition stressed how participants deliberate when they consciously share what they know with others. While many college faculty members now engage in collaborative research processes, they often still apply very individualistic notions to their instruction. By this, we mean that faculty members are more likely to assign individual papers than group assignments and that they see discussion sections in lecture hall classes as a means to an end—self-mastery—rather than as producing unique insights on their own terms.

Second, transactive memory is a group's shared division of cognitive labor for the learning, storage, and use of knowledge in order to achieve a goal. Originally proposed by Daniel Wegner (1987), a transactive memory system resembles Lévy's idea of a universally distributed intelligence: it is not important that a group member learn, store, and use every piece of information relevant to a task as long as she knows who in the group holds the most relevant expertise;

and, in return, others in the group can rely on her to learn, store, and use the information most relevant to her expertise (hence the transactive nature). Transactive memory systems form when group members divide cognitive labor according to their knowledge of each other's specializations. Wegner's original study found that when romantic couples were asked to remember together facts, individuals not only recalled facts better when relevant to one's personal expertise but also recalled better facts they knew fell outside their partner's expertise. Similarly, Andrea Hollingshead (2000) found that individuals learned and recalled more information in their own specializations when they perceived that their partners (whom they previously had never met) had an expertise different from rather than similar to their own.

Moreover, individuals learned and recalled more information outside of their areas of expertise when they perceived that their partners had similar rather than different expertise. Transactive memory systems theory has been extended beyond memorization tasks in dyads. It has been shown to exist in ad hoc teams whose members are trained together on a performance task (Lewis, Lange, and Gillis 2005; Liang, Moreland, and Argote 1995; Moreland and Myaskovsky 2000) and in field studies of more long-term, established groups and organizations (Austin 2003; Lewis 2003, 2004). In addition, recent research has suggested that technology can serve as a source of transactive memory (Sparrow, Liu, and Wegner 2011; Yuan, Fulk, and Monge 2007; Yuan et al. 2010). Instead of an individual learning and recalling a piece of information, she need learn and recall only where the information can be retrieved. Some of transactive memory research has been relevant to the university setting. Among the longitudinal groups studied have been MBA teams working on a project for real-world clients (Lewis 2004), undergraduate teams working on a class project (Jackson and Moreland 2009), and undergraduate lab partners writing up lab reports (Michinov and Michinov 2009). However, so far, no studies have extended this research to consider exams.

Third, the concept of "affinity space" comes from recent research on informal learning often within gaming or fan communities, virtual worlds, and other shared online activities. The term *affinity space* was originally coined by James Paul Gee (2007) to describe the ways gamers come together online, sometimes trading goods and services, sometimes exchanging information or learning from each other, with the shared goal of enhancing their play experience. Mizuko Ito (2005) used similar language to describe what she calls "otaku culture," the interest-driven, transnational fan network surrounding Japanese popular culture—especially comics (manga) and animation (anime):

Otaku translate and subtitle all major anime works, they create web sites with hundreds and thousands of members, stay in touch 24/7 on hundreds of IRC channels, and create fan fiction, fan art, and anime music videos that rework the original works and sometimes brilliantly creative and often subversive alternative frames of reference. . . . To support their media obsessions otaku acquire challenging language, skills, and media production crafts of scripting, editing, animating, drawing, and writing. And they mobilize socially to create their own communities of interest and working groups to engage in collaborative media production and distribution. (10)

As Ito's account stresses, shared goals and interests motivate members to work harder, dig deeper, ask new questions, and innovate new forms of cultural production. Writers in game studies (Bartle 2003) have described how different players' interests and activities combine into a self-sustaining play ecology. T. L. Taylor (2008) describes rapid technological innovations within the guild structure of *World of Warcraft*, as players develop, test, modify, and deploy tools as well as monitor and improve their gameplay and coordinate their raids. Researchers disagree as to whether the properties of an affinity space might operate within a formal educational setting, which places far greater constraints on participant interactions. Unlike standardized testing regimes, affinity spaces depend, for example, on the capacity of the members to define their own goals and pursue their own interests with multiple paths toward success.

Gee (2004) specifically framed his concept of affinity space in contrast to the notion of communities of practice. Many sites popular among gamers assume a shared activity but not necessarily strong social bonds. John Seeley Brown and Doug Thomas (Jenkins 2011a) make a similar argument: "Anyone who joins a collective looking for a sense of belonging is going to wind up disappointed, because that is not how they function. Collectives are more social platforms than social entities. Communities may form within a collective, but they need not form in order for the collective to function." By contrast, work on fan communities (Busse and Hellekson 2006; Jenkins 1992, 2006a) has stressed notions of reciprocity and affective bonds. As we think about whether a classroom can become an affinity space, a key question is to what degree students need to experience some kind of social bond or shared identity in order to care about each other's success. Conversely, taking the test may simply be a shared activity requiring only the most minimal investment in a group apt to dissolve as soon as the semester ends. Even if they are less communal than fandoms, class study groups do need to develop what transactive memory researchers call *cognitive interdependence*, a concern we return to later in this chapter. Recognize, however, that these questions are both old and new for the academy. On the one hand, we are asking about how students are engaged in a classroom, which is a question that has been asked about traditional classrooms for over a generation. On the other hand, because of the changes in social media, the nature and context of our questions are new and predicated on the assumptions outlined in part I.

What Are We Testing For?

Any testing regime makes assumptions about what kinds of knowledge matter. In the best circumstances, those standards have some relationship to the kind of learner this educational system wants to produce and to the expectations of the society that the learner is going to enter. So our current testing regime makes the following assumptions:

- The knowledge that matters will be determined hierarchically: what the instructor believes matters is often based on what some larger body (a professional or governmental organization) believes matters. So, today's testing regime believes that there are standards that must be met across many classrooms and that, within the classroom, the instructor should define the objectives and the criteria for meeting them.
- Every student will be measured on how well one masters the standardized knowledge rather than how much one develops an individualized expertise. In other words, success is achieved if every student knows the same thing, not if every student has something meaningful to contribute to the group's combined knowledge.
- The knowledge that matters is what can be recalled at a particular moment in time under test conditions—not what the student may have learned in the past or may learn in the future and not what the student knows how to access and deploy.
- The knowledge that matters, matters innately, because it is important to know, and not in relation to any particular context or circumstances where the group might need to know things in order to solve an immediate problem. It is timeless knowledge and not "just in time" knowledge.
- The knowledge that matters exists as a kind of credential that acts as a surrogate for those who cannot directly observe the individual's performance

but must make a decision about whether to hire that person to perform particular tasks. This focus on certifying knowledge for outside parties becomes one of the biggest obstacles to adopting alternative assessment mechanisms, since such assessments may not measure the things employers are looking for, or since outside parties may not agree on how to read and appraise alternative certificates.

Typical test design reflects these core assumptions: the teacher sets questions every student must address; there is a minimal amount of flexibility about which questions the student chooses to answer (pick one of two questions). The test design emphasizes memorization and recall (closed book, closed note). The test design encourages abstract signs of mastery as opposed to applied signs of access and deployment. The test takes place on a specific date and time independently of any given learner's state of development. We can modify these requirements—so that an open-book, open-note exam is designed to lower the stress on memory and recall. We may allow more room for personal expertise on individual projects and written assignments, much less on exams. Most of these assumptions reflect what Paulo Freire (1970) has called the "banking" model of learning and most reinforce what Peter Walsh (2004) has called the "expert paradigm."

New Models of Expertise

Lévy ([1994] 1999) draws an important distinction between shared knowledge and collective intelligence: "The knowledge of a thinking community is no longer a shared knowledge for it is now impossible for a single human being, or even a group of people, to master all knowledge and skills. It is fundamentally collective knowledge, impossible to gather together into a single creature" (214–215). Shared knowledge refers to information known by all group members. It might, for example, include core information about the kinds of problems the group is confronting, the range of options available to the group, or perhaps the shared values that hold the group together. Much of what we learn in early grades falls broadly into this category of shared knowledge. Collective intelligence, by contrast, is the sum total of the knowledge available to the group on a "need to know" basis—what the group collectively knows rather than what every member individually knows.

A knowledge community would be impoverished if every member knew exactly the same things and only those things; heterogeneity of skills and knowledge allows the group to tackle more complex problems. Gee (2008) makes a similar distinction in his account of guilds in *World of Warcraft*:

> Each group member must learn to be good at his or her special skills and also learn to integrate these skills as a team member into the performance of the group as a whole. Each team member must also share some common knowledge about the game and game play with all the other members of the group— including some understanding of the specialist skills of other player types—in order to achieve a successful integration. (33)

Traditional notions of higher education have emphasized a movement from mastering core knowledge to being able to make an original contribution; the doctoral candidate is asked to demonstrate her expertise through exploring a unique problem or domain. A model of education based on collective intelligence might assume that some specialization should come much earlier. The student learns how to mobilize her own distinctive expertise and to engage meaningfully with others who bring something different to a problem. Education in the social sciences, sciences, and engineering is more apt to encourage working as part of a collaborative research group, while humanistic fields value a high level of independence.

This dispersion and differentiation of expertise occurs spontaneously in many affinity groups. In a fan discussion list, participants may align themselves around particular characters or share professional and personal knowledge throughout the discussion. Game designer and theorist Jane McGonigal (2008) argues that the deployment of different kinds of skills and knowledge is built into alternative reality games, which involve large teams of players solving puzzles together:

> This abundance of pliable data provided inexhaustible ways for players to take differentiated action, whether it was to perform calculations, make maps, conduct Web searches, or visit real world locations. . . . At the same time, there was enough structure and specificity of data to make the application of data processes a challenging, time-consuming affair. (214)

Testing Our Collective Intelligence

Some colleges and universities are experimenting with the pedagogical potentials of these large-scale collaborative games but, so far, mostly outside of formal instruction. In 2011, for example, the USC School of Cinematic Arts launched *Reality Starts Here* (Jenkins 2011b), an alternate reality game designed for entering undergraduates discussed at length in Tracy Fullerton's chapter. *Reality Starts Here* involved collecting and exchanging cards, which helped identify themes, topics, and approaches that student teams must deploy through their own video and film productions. The more of these themes they connected together via their projects, the more points they received; winners were regularly rewarded with a range of unique experiences, including encounters with famous alumni or trips to local Los Angeles attractions. The game's goals were to make students more aware of the school's resources, to connect undergraduates more closely with faculty, staff, and alumni, to foster a deeper understanding of the school's research, and to create social ties across the more specialized divisions. Playing was voluntary, and the game was not officially acknowledged; students found their own points of entry as existing players sought to recruit new participants for their teams.

Since 1980, MIT has run an annual Mystery Hunt which requires students to pool what they know across disciplines. The team that wins one year designs and implements the next year's challenge, ensuring sustainability. During one recent hunt, teams spent more than 60 hours solving over 100 puzzles, including "crosswords, anagrams, cryptograms, number puzzles, multimedia puzzles, geometrical puzzles, physical challenges, mystery trails, scavenger hunts, inter-team games, or anything else that the hunt organizers can think up. The puzzles may or may not be obvious, may or may not have instructions, may or may not be solvable!" (MIT Mystery Hunt 2012).

If only students found exams to be equally compelling, offering as many different ways to contribute and alternative routes to a solution. On one end of a spectrum, exams might consist of questions the students themselves have identified as especially compelling, and the students would be appraised on their ability to frame useful inquiries. On the other end, the instructor might frame large, open-ended questions mobilizing a large amount of the course information. Here, the exam would require the group to prioritize which parts of the question to address, on the basis of its members' personal and collective strengths. Much like the MIT Mystery Hunt, students who take a class one year might design the test for the next cohort, demonstrating their knowledge by what questions they ask.

An exam based on collective intelligence might, moreover, value problem solving, research, and collaboration skills over specific knowledge. Such an approach would value the application of knowledge under innovative conditions over the reproduction of what is already known. Game designer Scot Osterweil (Jenkins 2006b) makes a productive distinction between spelling bees and *Scrabble*. Spelling bees have only one right answer and have clear winners and losers, and thus become the locus of stress. *Scrabble* enables many different possible combinations of letters, encourages active negotiation over acceptable answers, and allows for differing levels of success. Moreover, a test might value students' capacity to address a set of concerns whether or not the knowledge deployed comes from the specific course readings and lectures.

Further, students in such an exam would be evaluated not simply on the information they contributed but on their ability to assess and critique other people's contributions. Producing knowledge would be adversarial in the same way that a court of law is. Every claim would be contested, every assertion would require evidence, and there would be ongoing epistemological reflections about how we know what we know. This new focus on process would require students to show their work, much as on a math test. We would not necessarily be valuing effort rather than results. We could still hold the group accountable for producing a workable solution, but some of what the participants take from the class would be strategies for solving problems and not simply information to be slotted into the problem's framework.

How Do We Constitute the Classroom as a Knowledge Community?

Whereas collective intelligence (or at least Lévy's definition of collective intelligence) has been studied qualitatively, transactive memory systems come from quantitative, empirical literature in the fields of psychology, communication, and organizational behavior, which require the operationalization and measurement of variables. This literature provides an explicit framework of necessary conditions for establishing transactive memory systems.

There are three manifestations of a transactive memory system: specialization, credibility, and coordination (Lewis 2003). First, every group member must have specialized knowledge relevant to the task and every group member must be aware of her teammates' specializations. Second, every group member must find the information she gets from her teammates to be credible. Finally, group members must be able to successfully coordinate their expertise to accomplish a task. All three need to be present in order for a transactive memory system to function. Without specialization, division of cognitive labor will be done at random. Without credibility, group members will not trust teammates enough to delegate tasks to others. Without coordination, the division of cognitive labor cannot be reassembled.

Cognitive Interdependence

In order for a transactive memory system to form, group members must first perceive that they are cognitively interdependent (Brandon and Hollingshead 2004; Hollingshead 2001). Being cognitively interdependent means that group members rely on each other for the learning of information. An individual's success relies not only on what she knows but also on what her teammates know. Three things can lead to the perception of cognitive interdependence: first, a task may have a reward structure that favors the pooling of specialized knowledge as opposed to the utilization of the group's common knowledge. Second, a task may be structured such that one person's output is another person's input; in this case, a group member cannot do her part of a task until other group members have completed their parts of a task. Finally, cognitive interdependence can be established if a task is too complex for any individual to do alone.

Once a group perceives itself to be cognitively interdependent, it must develop a group shared mental model of each other's expertise (Brandon and Hollingshead 2004). Group shared mental models are established through experience and through communication. Groups who have worked together before are more likely to have an established transactive memory system, as they have already learned everybody's expertise (Moreland 1999). They simply must figure out how the task at hand relates to known expertise (Lewis, Lange, and Gillis 2005). Groups who have not yet worked together (or individuals introduced into established groups) must develop models by querying or demonstrating expertise through words and action (Hollingshead 1998a, 1998b; Hollingshead and Brandon 2003). In order for a group shared mental model to work, it must be accurate (the expertise associated with an individual is correct), shared (everybody has the same mental model), and validated (people with known expertise actually utilize the expertise when called upon).

Communication

Communication is essential in transactive memory systems (Brandon and Hollingshead 2004; Hollingshead 1998a, 1998b; Hollingshead and Brandon 2003). It is important early on, as it helps group members learn each other's expertise, and it is important later on, when group members are trying to coordinate activity. The more a team communicates in a longitudinal task, the stronger the transactive memory system is (Jackson and Moreland 2009; Lewis 2004). Also, the percentage of communication that is face-to-face (as opposed to mediated) is also a predictor of transactive memory. The more face-to-face communication, the stronger the transactive memory system is (though there is some evidence to suggest that face-to-face communication is more important earlier on when group members are still learning each other's areas of expertise than later on when group members are utilizing known expertise [Jackson and Moreland 2009]).

Thinking about the manifestations of transactive memory systems, its prerequisites, and the importance of communication raises serious questions about how transactive memory systems can be established for an exam. They have been demonstrated in the university setting for relatively open-ended class projects (Jackson and Moreland 2009; Lewis 2004) and more formulaic lab reports (Michinov and Michinov 2009). Evaluation of a class project is usually based on the final product, without explicitly examining how it relates to class material.

Specialization

One of the biggest questions raised when thinking about transactive memory systems and exams is the role of specialization. In "affinity spaces," members seek out people who bring new skills and knowledge, valuing their individual contributions toward common goals, and thus there is a strong push toward diversity. A large lecture class required for all majors may be intellectually homogeneous. Student's distinctive specializations would more likely be related to skills from hobbies and knowledge from personal interests. Instructors might find it difficult to write an exam where every student could utilize his or her specializations. And it would be necessary to ensure this, both in order to establish cognitive interdependence and to ensure that groups do not default to answering questions about shared knowledge.

Again, there is no one "right answer" to these challenges, given the variety of different kinds of classroom experiences teachers and students are likely to encounter. We might imagine a teacher assigning a much broader array of readings than any given student could master, asking the students to divide responsibility over those readings, as often happens when a group of legal or graduate students are preparing together for their qualification exams. Or we can imagine assigning each student responsibility over different readings on behalf of the group. The students would be expected to know which readings (and which information within those readings) might be relevant to addressing a specific problem. Through a curriculum—"Reading in a Participatory Culture"— Project New Media Literacies experimented with ways of dispersing knowledge across a high school class (Jenkins et al. 2013). In one such approach, each student took a page from *Moby-Dick* to examine closely, annotating and ornamenting core concepts and themes. Each page was arrayed around the room as a shared resource. In another, students identify a core question and become responsible to helping the group recognize where these ideas become relevant to the class's discussion.

Others have assigned students specific roles in the problem-solving process, encouraging them to look at the problem from different angles, even in a context where each student brings similar backgrounds into the class. For example, Antero Garcia (2012) developed *Ask Anansi*, a classroom activity for middle schoolers, which has much in common with alternate reality games. Students work together to formulate questions and interpret clues provided by a trickster spider god. Garcia asked each student to assume a different role, including "diplomats" (who help facilitate group work), "engineers" (who oversee construction activities), "checkered flags" (which keep the group working in a timely manner), "tourists" (who take an outside perspective on the efforts), and "portals" (who ensure communication with those outside the group). By swapping these roles, each student acquires some skills needed to contribute meaningfully to a collaborative process. Garcia notes that learning to take perspectives and to understand the interests of other members is challenging in the early childhood period but comes more naturally to adolescents who are in a developmental phase more focused on peer-based learning. So-called epistemic games, such as those developed by Eric Klopfer (2011), Kurt Squire (2011), or David Williamson Shaffer (2008), often assign specific roles to different group members, giving them different information appliances and different kinds of data the team needs to complete its mission. While assigning such roles may be arbitrary, the specialization ensures that each member must contribute to the collective process.

Credibility

Credibility in transactive memory systems raises other questions. How do we get students to trust each other's expertise? At many universities, students range in academic ability and motivation. Most classrooms have overachieving and underachieving students. Many students have a tendency to dislike group projects because they are afraid of free-riders causing disproportionate divisions of workload. According to our experience, this fear is not unfounded. As a teaching assistant in an empirical research methods class, Adam Kahn provided direct oversight and assistance to student teams completing a full quantitative research project over the course of the semester. While many student groups successfully divided up the workload, other groups struggled with differing academic abilities or motivations. In this particular class, there was some flexibility for penalizing those who did not contribute equally and rewarding those who put in extra work. If we truly want to establish transactive memory systems among students for exams, cognitive interdependence is required, and students must be rewarded on the basis of mutual achievement, not individual achievement.

Online affinity spaces often create mechanisms that encourage novices and experts to work side by side, allowing the newcomers to acquire skills, develop knowledge, absorb shared values, and adopt mutual goals. Here, for example, is how Susan L. Bryant, Andrea Forte, and Amy Bruckman (2005) describe the process of becoming Wikipedian: "Novices and Wikipedians are using the same site. For the most part, they have access to the same set of tools and are cooperating in the same virtual place that has the same set of affordances, with the same group of collaborators." Yet participants understand their contributions in very different ways. Novice users contribute specific bits of information and make localized fixes to articles that reflect their own interests and backgrounds. More experienced Wikipedians, they argue, see the encyclopedia as a whole as more important than any given article. They also view *Wikipedia* as a community and are focused on ensuring the infrastructure that allows its ongoing success. A range of practices, policies, and processes support this gradual integration of some inexperienced participants into the group's ongoing activities, even as others step away once they have satisfied their initial goals. There are multiple potential problems with applying such approaches in an instructional context. There may simply not be enough time for most participants to transition from novice to expert. Students may not be sufficiently motivated to acquire social capital within the group. And there are no mechanisms for allowing those who lack commitment to step aside once more local needs have been met.

Coordination

Coordination, as manifested both in transactive memory and in its more colloquial sense, also raises issues about test design. In order for a transactive memory system to emerge, group members must first learn each other's expertise through shared experience and communication. Once a transactive memory system is established, communication is still necessary to coordinate the members' expertise when implementing a task. In addition, this communication is most effective when done face-to-face. Even at USC, where most students live on or near campus, it is hard to get students in one place unless it is universally scheduled. In the aforementioned research methods class, some groups could not find a single time in a given week where all group members could physically meet—and groups had only three to four students. Even with mediated communication, some students would not reply to teammates' emails right away or show up for prescheduled Skype sessions. If we want our students to learn together, we may need to schedule additional hours when the students are in one place at the same time.

Scalability becomes another coordination problem when dealing with large lecture hall classes. The smaller the group, the less diversity; the larger the group, the greater the coordination costs. Outside of school, game guilds may include several hundred members, though only a small portion of them may go out on any given mission. Similarly, alternate reality games may pool the efforts and knowledge of hundreds of participants, but the larger the group becomes, the more time must be spent in coordinating the distribution of labor. The most innovative use of collective intelligence and transactive memory systems has occurred within smaller-scale seminars and discussion classes—not in large lectures.

The Open Laptop Exam: A Possible Approach

So how might we facilitate the formation of transactive memory systems, collective intelligence, and affinity spaces that produces pedagogical value within the context of a large-scale undergraduate lecture hall class? Here is how we might envision the semester. To some extent this is predicated on USC's structure, but it might be adapted for other schools. This model does not address every concern we have identified here, but it does speak to some core challenges of designing and assessing a classroom knowledge community.

Because students add and drop classes for the first few weeks of the semester, it is important not to form student groups too early, as group turnover can hurt transactive memory (Moreland and Argote 2003). Thus, the semester will begin with core concepts and common texts the instructor feels everybody should know (Lévy's shared knowledge). The course's first midterm would be a traditional, noncollaborative exam, composing a certain percentage of the grade. This diagnostic test can allow the instructors to gauge students' relative abilities when putting together teams. Members should be assigned, with the goal of diversifying skills and knowledge. Allowing students to self-select would almost certainly increase group homogeneity, as membership would be related to existing friendship ties based on similar interests and activities outside the classroom.

After this exam, though, the group becomes important. At this point, the reading list will grow so that it is too much for any individual to read. Students will have to become mutually dependent to survive.

Because transactive memory forms around face-to-face communication, we must provide students a time to meet. Large lecture classes often have smaller discussion sections. Normally a teaching assistant facilitates a discussion or clarifies confusing points from the lecture. However, this hour might be better spent allowing team members to meet to discuss the readings they divided among themselves and relate them to the common lecture themes of the week. The teaching assistant would also stress problem-solving and coordination skills, helping groups refine strategies and learn from their mistakes, more like a coach than like our traditional model of a teacher. Although the ideal team would be self-regulating and self-guiding, the teaching assistant could also help it to assign roles or divide labor, if needed, to ensure that each member contributes equally.

The teaching assistant can provide one question each week that would be representative of those on an exam, allowing group members to synthesize their different readings and learn how the other students think—their strategies for identifying the core stakes of a problem, mobilizing knowledge, testing data, assessing conclusions, and communicating results. These questions could require students to do online searches, tap into knowledge from other classes, or draw on their extracurricular expertise. Through these test runs, students would learn each other's specialization, build trust, and coordinate their efforts on tasks similar to the group exam.

As they enter a collaborative test-taking process, students face the challenge of resolving conflict and committing to a shared answer, especially working under time constraints. Outside of the classroom, affinity groups develop norms, such as those surrounding contributions to *Wikipedia*, to which they can appeal to resolve such conflicts. So, for example, *Wikipedia* articles strive toward neutrality, which is often achieved through inclusion (i.e., featuring all competing perspectives) rather than exclusion (arriving at a consensus response) (Lih

2009). Students' experience of testing may be that there is a right answer the teacher is expecting, and thus they may be less receptive to test-taking strategies that include a broader range of possible answers. Having multiple collaborative activities will allow each group to develop its own norms and protocols for resolving disputes and finding an answer students feel they can stand behind.

The final exam is designed to tap a range of different kinds of expertise. Think of the individual problems as possessing the sense of "meaningful ambiguity," which, McGonigal (2008) argues, motivates the problem-solving activity around alternate reality games "by asking players to cooperate to make meaning out of an ambiguous system, the game-based hive mind celebrates individual perspective even as it embraces the larger, intricate intelligence that emerges only at the scale digital networks afford" (214). For such experiences to be compelling and satisfying, McGonigal (2003) argues, they have to introduce problems that seem within reach of the network of players. She notes that an empowered team often seeks to move beyond the game and tackle real-world social problems, only to be disappointed that such problems may not, in fact, be resolvable given the group's resources and capacities. Exam questions would need to be open-ended enough to allow many different paths to a solution and yet ultimately something that participants can comprehend and resolve.

If the lecture meets twice a week, the questions are given out at the beginning of the first lecture and are due at the end of the second lecture. This will allow students to use the first lecture to start working on the answers and divide the labor. Then students go home and seek more information on their own, and work more on the answers if they so choose. They coordinate efforts so that each student plays to her strengths and so that there is a robust system of checks and balances to identify and eradicate misinformation. Preparing for the exam may be much more like getting ready for a guild raid in *World of Warcraft* than like studying for a traditional test. The second lecture can be used to finalize answers. Also, spanning two lectures affords groups at least two face-to-face opportunities to interact. Students can write their answers using an online tool, such as Google Documents, that allows them to write simultaneously in a single document. In this way, they can make changes to each other's work (knowing who wrote what) and see changes being made to their own work. Changes can be tracked over time and revised if needed.

The group exam will count for 50% of the grade, creating such high stakes that students will hold themselves and each other accountable for their contributions. Questions should rely on multiple readings and lectures so that no one student could answer a question. One possible explanation for the 30 to 40 students getting the same question wrong on the exam mentioned at the beginning of the chapter is that students did not actually study together. Instead, they may have all written the answer to a different sample question and compiled an "answer key" they could use regardless of what questions actually appeared on the exam. There were no mechanisms in place to make sure that errors were not introduced into the system. Students did not take adequate ownership over the integrity of the data they shared. Their process lacked the deliberation at the heart of Lévy's collective intelligence. By training students together as part of a team and having them run through multiple exercises, students will know not only who did which readings but also who grasped which week's lectures best. They will have worked through strategies for consolidating, synthesizing, and vetting information. This process ensures the cognitive interdependence necessary for a transactive memory system.

Of course, some of the literature on gaming implies that a high-stakes test is neither necessary nor desirable: games encourage greater risk taking because the stakes are so low, players are encouraged to learn from their mistakes and improve over time, and playing is an ongoing process and not a one-shot competition. Perhaps this literature would suggest that the grading should be accumulated, with points gained and lost through each of the weekly exercises, and with the final exam simply another opportunity to improve a team's overall performance.

Educational researcher Dan Hickey and his research team at Indiana University (Hickey, Honeyford, and McWilliams 2013) have been exploring what forms assessment needs to take within a participatory learning culture and conclude that assessment should "focus on reflections rather than artifacts." His group has developed a range of activities that might follow a project or exam, asking students to reflect on what strategies they tried and why, rather than simply evaluating them on what they produced. Of course, students will have different capacities to articulate their reflections. McGonigal (2008) has similarly argued that working in large-scale teams to solve alternate reality games encourages "metalevel reflection on the skills and processes that players use to meet new challenges" (222). At the end of the day, the test might function as much as a probe to encourage students to continue to think about the process of their learning as a simple assessment of what they, collectively and individually, know.

Concluding Thoughts

Our thought experiment here may or may not have arrived at a valid solution to the challenges of collaborative testing, but it highlights how the new academic environments of the twenty-first century reframe old questions and create new ones. We have almost certainly not arrived at the best of all possible solutions. For starters, this whole field is so new that we are unlikely to stumble upon the "right" answers the first time we experiment with collaborative testing. Existing modes of examination and assessment emerged over an extended period of time, involving trial and error by many different instructors. If we are going to redesign testing for a networked culture, we must create a space for experimentation and innovation.

At least some of our students—perhaps many of them—are apt to balk if they fear that their grades are being put at risk by an untried system. Perhaps the most conservative force in the undergraduate classroom is the undergraduate. The current generation of students has been subject to standardized testing throughout its education. These students have become very adept at anticipating what is expected of them under these circumstances, and they often become anxious when they are not sure what standards are being applied to evaluate their work. Even though current testing practices are often misaligned to the ways many students learn outside of school and the ways they will work in the future, such practices are familiar and comfortable to those who have excelled in school well enough to enter the college classroom.

And the students would not be totally wrong to be concerned. We have a much clearer sense of which kind of students benefit from traditional testing regimes than we have of which kind of students would excel under the conditions we are describing. Some students may do significantly better, while some may not perform nearly so well. Some of these practices work in play because it *is* play, because play gives us permission to take risks and lowers the consequences for our mistakes. For many of our current generation of students, education is anything but play. So any changes we make have to be introduced carefully and with a fair amount of scaffolding, before they are going to be embraced by even the most adventurous students. This is a key reason why we think the practice of collective problem solving will need to become the central function of the discussion sections when we introduce this process.

Whatever approach we take requires the careful balancing of a range of different factors—including, as we have suggested, ensuring diversity without intensifying operations costs, developing shared norms without constraining the most creative and original participants, designing questions that have the complexity of the real world but also provide challenges that are within the capabilities of a group of students working with the information and skills the class has provided them, and respecting the process while also valuing results. The best balance of these different factors will differ from subject to subject and university context to university context. Rather than providing answers that can simply be followed by other educators, we hope we have asked provocative questions that will push our understanding of these issues to the next level. In this light, on the basis of those concerns and issues presented in part I, we are suggesting that what is needed now is a new framework to answer these questions rather than a reliance on pedagogical frameworks from the past.

What we do know is that the question, Will this be an open-laptop exam? is apt to be a persistent one. As we live more and more fully in a networked culture, we are going to need to factor these new modes of learning, new structures of knowledge, new technical affordances, and new social and cultural processes into our pedagogical practices. As we better understand how collective intelligence and transactive memory operates outside the classroom, we are going to need to deploy those insights to reimagine what we want our students to be able to do and under what conditions they will demonstrate their mastery.

REFERENCES

Austin, John R. 2003. "Transactive Memory in Organizational Groups: The Effects of Content, Consensus, Specialization, and Accuracy on Group Performance." *Journal of Applied Psychology* 88:866–878.

Bartle, Richard. 2003. *Designing Virtual Worlds*. New York: New Riders.

Benkler, Yochai. 2011. *The Penguin and the Leviathan: How Cooperation Triumphs over Self-Interest*. New York: Crown Business.

Brandon, David P., and Andrea B. Hollingshead. 2004. "Transactive Memory Systems in Organizations: Matching Tasks, Expertise, and People." *Organization Science* 15:633–644.

Bryant, Susan L., Andrea Forte, and Amy Bruckman. 2005. "Becoming Wikipedian: Transformation of Participation in an Online Encyclopedia." Paper presented at GROUP '05, Sanibel Island, Florida, November 6–9. http://www.butlercommonplace.org/thoughts/images/8/85/Bryantetal2005.pdf.

Busse, Kristina, and Karen Hellekson, eds. 2006. *Fan Fiction and Fan Communities in the Age of the Internet*. Jefferson, NC: McFarland.

Freire, Paulo. 1970. *Pedagogies of the Oppressed*. Translated by Myra Bergman Ramos. New York: Herder and Herder.

Garcia, Antero. 2012. "Good Reception: Utilizing Mobile Media and Games to Develop Critical Inner-City Agents of Social Change." PhD diss., University of California, Los Angeles.

Gee, James Paul. 2004. *Situated Language and Learning: A Critique of Traditional Schooling.* New York: Routledge.

———. 2007. *What Video Games Have to Teach Us about Learning and Literacy.* 2nd ed. New York: Palgrave Macmillan.

———. 2008. "Learning and Games." In *The Ecology of Games: Connecting Youth, Games, and Learning,* edited by Katie Salen, 21–40. Cambridge, MA: MIT Press.

Hickey, Daniel, Michelle Honeyford, and Jenna McWilliams. 2013. "Participatory Assessment in a Climate of Accountability." In *Reading in a Participatory Culture: Remixing Moby-Dick in the English Classroom,* edited by Henry Jenkins and Wyn Kelley, with Katie Clinton, Jenna McWilliams, Ricardo Pitts-Wiley, and Erin Reilly, 169–184. New York: Teacher's College Press.

Hollingshead, Andrea B. 1998a. "Communication, Learning, and Retrieval in Transactive Memory Systems." *Journal of Experimental Social Psychology* 34:423–442. doi:10.1006/jesp.1998.1358.

———. 1998b. "Retrieval Processes in Transactive Memory Systems." *Journal of Personality and Social Psychology* 74:659–671. doi:10.1037/0022-3514.74.3.659.

———. 2000. "Perceptions of Expertise and Transactive Memory in Work Relationships." *Group Processes & Intergroup Relations* 3:257–267. doi:10.1177/1368430200033002.

———. 2001. "Cognitive Interdependence and Convergent Expectations in Transactive Memory." *Journal of Personality and Social Psychology* 81:1080–1089. doi:10.1037/0022-3514.81.6.1080.

Hollingshead, Andrea B., and David P. Brandon. 2003. "Potential Benefits of Communication in Transactive Memory Systems." *Human Communication Research* 29:607–615. doi:10.1111/j.1468-2958.2003.tb00859.x.

Ito, Mizuko. 2005. "Otaku Literacy." In *A Global Imperative: The Report of the 21st Century Literacy Summit,* 10. Austin, TX: New Media Consortium. http://www.nmc.org/pdf/Global_Imperative.pdf.

Ito, Mizuko, Sonia Baumer, Matteo Bittani, danah boyd, Rachel Cody, Becky Herr-Stephenson, Heather A. Horst, Patricia G. Lange, Dilan Mahendran, Katynka Z. Martinez, C. J. Pascoe, Dan Perkel, Laura Robinson, Christo Sims, and Lisa Tripp. 2009. *Hanging Out, Messing Around, and Geeking Out: Kids Living and Learning with New Media.* Cambridge, MA: MIT Press.

Jackson, Marina, and Richard L. Moreland. 2009. "Transactive Memory in the Classroom." *Small Group Research* 40:508–534. doi:10.1177/1046496409340703.

Jenkins, Henry. 1992. *Textual Poachers: Television Fans and Participatory Culture.* New York: Routledge.

———. 2006a. *Convergence Culture: Where Old and New Media Collide.* New York: New York University Press.

———. 2006b. "Spelling Bees and Scrabble." Confessions of an Aca-Fan, August 22. http://henryjenkins.org/2006/08/spelling_bees_and_scrable.html.

———. 2011a. "A New Culture of Learning: An Interview with John Seely Brown and Doug Thomas." Confessions of an Aca-Fan, January 19. http://henryjenkins.org/2011/01/a_new_culture_of_learning_an_i.html.

———. 2011b. "A Virtual Bullpen? How The USC Cinema School Has Embraced ARGS to Shape the Experience of Entering Students." Confessions of an Aca-Fan, October 17. http://henryjenkins.org/2011/10/a_virtual_bullpen_how_the_usc.html.

Jenkins, Henry, and Wyn Kelley, with Katherine Clinton, Jenna McWilliams, Ricardo Pitts-Wiley, and Erin Reilly, eds. 2013. *Reading in a Participatory Culture: Remixing* Moby-Dick *in the English Classroom.* New York: Teacher's College Press.

Klopfer, Eric. 2011. *Augmented Learning: Research and Design of Mobile Educational Games.* Cambridge, MA: MIT Press.

Knobel, Michelle, and Colin Lankshear, eds. 2010. *DIY Media: Creating, Sharing, and Learning with New Technologies.* New York: Peter Lang.

Lévy, Pierre. (1994) 1999. *Collective Intelligence: Mankind's Emerging World in Cyberspace.* Translated by Robert Bononno. Cambridge, MA: Helix.

Lewis, Kyle. 2003. "Measuring Transactive Memory Systems in the Field: Scale Development and Validation." *Journal of Applied Psychology* 88:587–604. doi:10.1037/0021-9010.88.4.587.

———. 2004. "Knowledge and Performance in Knowledge-Worker Teams: A Longitudinal Study of Transactive Memory Systems." *Management Science* 50:1519–1533.

Lewis, Kyle, Donald Lange, and Lynette Gillis. 2005. "Transactive Memory Systems, Learning, and Learning Transfer." *Organization Science* 16:581–598.

Liang, Diane Wei, Richard Moreland, and Linda Argote. 1995. "Group versus Individual Training and Group Performance: The Mediating Role of Transactive Memory." *Personality and Social Psychology Bulletin* 21:384–393. doi:10.1177/0146167295214009.

Lih, Andrew. 2009. *The Wikipedia Revolution: How a Bunch of Nobodies Created the World's Greatest Encyclopedia.* New York: Hyperion.

McGonigal, Jane. 2003. "This Is Not a Game: Immersive Aesthetics and Collective Play." Paper presented at the 5th International Digital Arts and Culture Conference, Melbourne, Australia, May 19–23.

———. 2008. "Why *I Love Bees*: A Case Study of Collective Intelligence Gaming." In *The Ecology of Games: Connecting Youth, Games, and Learning,* edited by Katie Salen, 199–227. Cambridge, MA: MIT Press.

Michinov, Nicolas, and Estelle Michinov. 2009. "Investigating the Relationship between Transactive Memory and Performance in Collaborative Learning." *Learning & Instruction* 19:43–54.

MIT Mystery Hunt. 2012. "History of the Mystery Hunt." Accessed on March 20. http://web.mit.edu/puzzle/.

Moreland, Richard L. 1999. "Transactive Memory: Learning Who Knows What in Work Groups and Organizations." In *Shared Cognition in Organizations: The Management of Knowledge,* edited by Leigh L. Thompson, John M. Levine, and David M. Messick, 3–31. Mahwah, NJ: Lawrence Erlbaum.

Moreland, Richard L., and Linda Argote. 2003. "Transactive Memory in Dynamic Organizations: Leading and Managing People in the Dynamic Organization." In *Leading and Managing People in the Dynamic Organization,* edited by Randall S. Peterson and Elizabeth A. Mannix, 135–162. Mahwah, NJ: Lawrence Erlbaum.

Moreland, Richard L., and Larissa Myaskovsky. 2000. "Exploring the Performance Benefits of Group Training: Transactive Memory or Improved Communication?" *Organizational Behavior and Human Decision Processes* 82(1):117–133. doi:10.1006/obhd.2000.2891.

Shaffer, David Williamson. 2008. *How Computer Games Help Children Learn.* New York: Palgrave Macmillan.

Sparrow, Betsy, Jenny Liu, and Daniel M. Wegner. 2011. "Google Effects on Memory: Cognitive Consequences of Having Information at Our Fingertips." *Science* 333:776–778. doi:10.1126/science.1207745.

Squire, Kurt. 2011. *Video Games and Learning: Teaching and Participatory Culture in a Digital Age.* New York: Teacher's College Press.

Taylor, T. L. 2008. "Does World of Warcraft Change Everything? How a PvP Server, Multinational Playerbase, and Surveillance Mod Scene Caused Me Pause." In *Digital Culture, Play, and Identity: A World of Warcraft Reader,* edited by Hilde G. Corneliussen and Jill Walker Rettberg. Cambridge, MA: MIT Press.

Walsh, Peter. 2004. "The Withered Paradigm: The Web, the Expert, and the Information Hegemony." In *Democracy and New Media,* edited by David Thorburn and Henry Jenkins, 365–372. Cambridge, MA: MIT Press.

Wegner, Daniel M. 1987. "Transactive Memory: A Contemporary Analysis of the Group Mind." In *Theories of Group Behavior,* edited by Brian Mullen and George R. Goethals, 185–208. New York: Spring-Verlag.

Yuan, Y. Connie, Janet Fulk, and Peter R. Monge. 2007. "Access to Information in Connective and Communal Transactive Memory Systems." *Communication Research* 34:131–155. doi:10.1177/0093650206298067.

Yuan, Y. Connie, Janet Fulk, Peter R. Monge, and Noshir Contractor. 2010. "Expertise Directory Development, Shared Task Interdependence, and Strength of Communication Network Ties as Multilevel Predictors of Expertise Exchange in Transactive Memory Work Groups." *Communication Research* 37(1):20–47. doi:10.1177/0093650209351469.

CHAPTER SEVEN

Games, Passion, and "Higher" Education

JAMES PAUL GEE

Colleges and universities have addressed undergraduate education in different ways (Cole 2009). One way is to offer undergraduate students "mini" versions (called "majors") of what they offer graduate students. Faculty members teach undergraduates a scaled-down version of their disciplinary specialty. A second approach offers undergraduates "big ideas" from the history of thought in Western and other civilizations. This is a liberal arts approach. In most cases, these big ideas are cut off from any real-world applications or projects. A third approach is to make undergraduate education relevant to the future work lives of students. Indeed, the largest major on many campuses today is business (Hacker and Dreifus 2010). And, of course, many community colleges and for-profit colleges engage primarily in vocational education.

Another approach, one that, if not really new, is fast becoming more prevalent (Brandon 2010): colleges offer students exciting social interactions (often beer and bodies) and an environment full of amenities (good food and recreation facilities). In an effort to obtain full-paying students and retain them, academic work is dumbed down and becomes a secondary concern to social interaction. College becomes camp.

Higher Education in Crisis

There are several paradoxes at the heart of colleges and universities today (Hacker and Dreifus 2010; Menand 2010). Our society has decided to make college a goal for all who want it. We have decided that college is a matter of social justice, since, as Perna observes in chapter 2, college graduates earn significantly more than do solely high school graduates across a lifetime. In the past, we backed this goal up with public colleges and universities that were free or inexpensive. Now, however, even many public colleges—let alone private ones—are expensive enough that many students cannot attend them. Other students leave college with mountains of debt.

Another paradox at the heart of colleges and universities is that though they were meant to be "off market" institutions, they are now heavily market-driven (Nussbaum 2010). Today, colleges and universities, with less public support and more competition, have to make money on tuition, new and expanded programs, grants, e-learning, and gifts. There is a push for research that leads to money in the short run, not research that leads to knowledge in the long run. For proponents of free markets, this all seems to the good, and as Tierney observes, perhaps this is all part of what he calls "disruptive technology," which will transform higher education as we have known it. Why not let the market decide which academic areas, research, and faculty should survive (because they make money) and which should not (because they do not)? Why should any college keep losing money in fields or with faculty whose research cannot garner grants?

The answer is—or has been in the past—the same answer as to why we should keep biological diversity around even if we cannot make money on small owls and rare snakes. Diversity—including the stuff that seems useless—is a storage house of possibilities for the future. We cannot know now in the short run what ideas or species may be found crucial in the future in the long run.

No one can tell a student for sure what will be relevant or irrelevant, important or unimportant in the future the student will live in. According to yesterday's model of colleges and universities, students were expected to expose themselves to various ideas and influences and take the risk of being bored or wasting their time in search of what would eventually inspire them to become deep people. Because no one can tell what is relevant or irrelevant, important or unimportant in the long run, markets cannot do so. They can, at best, tell us what is working in the short run. But that may not be good enough for the survival of human society in our complex, high-risk, global world.

The final paradox I want to discuss is one general to all levels of schooling, K–16. It is common today to argue that schools and colleges ought to prepare students for jobs. The problem is that in developed societies like the United States 60% of all the jobs are (often poorly paid) service work (Reich 1992, 2007). So, if the purpose of school is to prepare young people for jobs, then, the purpose of schools is to prepare 60% of their students for bad jobs. Wal-Mart is the biggest employer in the United States. Few teachers with a social conscience really want this to be the goal of their life work, even if they want cheap stores and cheerful service workers.

The argument that schooling should be assessed by its role as job preparation is a moral nonstarter. It is a social nonstarter, as well, because it is dangerous for a society to leave 60% of its citizens seeking dignity and participation in civil life via the skills needed for poorly paid and poorly respected jobs.

There is ample evidence that the greater the degree of inequality (in terms of wealth or status) in a society, the greater the social problems that society has (Marmot 2004; Wilkenson and Pickett 2010). Problems like poor health, less well-being, more anxiety, higher crime, obesity, poor schools, and a lack of social trust ("social capital") are worse in societies with higher degrees of inequality. These problems affect everyone, rich and poor, in highly unequal societies. For example, even better-off people—even the richest ones—have less good health on average in a highly unequal society than they do in ones with less inequality. Today, the United States leads the developed world in inequality and, thus, too, in health problems and other social problems. Inequality in the United States today is as bad as it was in the "Robber Baron" era of the 1890s.

It has been persuasively argued (Wilkenson and Pickett 2010) that the root problem that high inequality causes, the one that helps cause all the other problems, is that in highly unequal societies people judge their status and worth by other people's views of them (which in the United States are primarily based on wealth and power). Many people feel that they do not really count, are not "worthy," and that what they say and do does not really contribute to society. The society becomes full of anxiety and a lack of trust, which harms everyone. A school system that just prepares students for jobs in a highly unequal society can only make the situation worse. For a functioning civil society, schools and colleges must make people feel not just that they count, but actually count. This is not a function that markets in developed societies, societies now often based on short-term gain (and stock prices), can serve.

As the authors in part I point out, nearly everyone agrees that colleges and universities are in crisis, though they disagree what to do about it (Arum and Roska 2011; Kamenetz 2010; Schrecker 2010; Taylor 2010; Tuchman 2009). Each proposed solution stems from the proposer's values and goals in regard to institutions of higher education, goals that are today often about survival and financial success in highly competitive markets (and one where for-profit colleges like the University of Phoenix have hundreds of thousands of students). In this chapter, rather than proposing a solution directly, I discuss how "education" is now working in the world outside of formal institutions. I argue that today's "out of school" learning potentially holds out new paradigms for the reform of colleges and universities should they want to contribute to society beyond being credentialing agents for a job market replete with bad jobs.

A New Formation for Learning

Because massive amounts of effort devoted to school reform have not translated into widespread success, there has been, over the past decade, a great deal of interest in learning out of school. As part of the digital transformation of popular culture, new paradigms for learning have arisen (Gee 2004; Gee and Hayes 2010). There is widespread interest in how some of these new popular culture paradigms might be used to transform learning in libraries, community centers, museums, schools, and colleges without destroying their inherent properties, properties that are often at variance with "business as usual" in our schools and colleges (Gee and Hayes 2011).

I want briefly to characterize one new paradigm in the "school of popular culture." This paradigm has no name and is in no respect standardized across different instances. Rather, different instances of the paradigm constitute at best a "family" of cases with "family resemblances," but not identity. I call the paradigm the "Game/Affinity Paradigm" (GAP for short). My examples from the GAP family involve games, but there are similar paradigms that use other forms of media than games (Gee 2004). What is needed for instantiating the GAP—and what a game supplies—is a well-designed, well-mentored problem-solving space, and as I have said, these spaces could be designed for out of school but also in colleges and universities.

Examples of the GAP raise important issues about access to learning and mastery in twenty-first-century societies in our global world. Good examples of the GAP create, in some cases, stiff competition for formal institutions of learning and even for the credentialed experts who come from them and inhabit them. In some cases, instances of GAP are offering young people twenty-first-century skills of the type sometimes not even on offer in our schools. Who does and does not have access to such skills out of school becomes a crucial equity question. In my own view, the GAP can be brought into such formal institutions, without losing its true power, only at the price of true and deep paradigm change in those institutions. This is a level of transformation that is extremely difficult, given the massive amounts of inertia in our traditional schools and colleges.

Let's look at some examples of GAP. Consider first, then, the highly popular commercial entertainment game *Portal* (there is currently a *Portal1* and a *Portal2*). In *Portal* the player has a "portal gun." The portal gun can make a blue portal and an orange one. If the player's character enters one of the portals, she (the player's avatar in the first game is a female) comes out the other. The player must use the portals to escape from complicated laboratory rooms that in the first game were designed by a robot that said she (yes, she was a she) wanted to test the player's intelligence but, in fact, wanted to kill the player (player's character).

The portals and the virtual world they are in obey certain laws of physics. The player must come to understand this physics well enough to solve various problems that constitute obstacles in the way of escape. For example, the portals obey the law of conservation of momentum, and the player must respect and use this fact in order to solve certain problems in the game.

Portal is not about learning physics, but the player must come to a tacit, embodied understanding of the physics of the portals and the virtual world they operate within. I use the word *embodied* here because in games players often have avatars whose bodies they control. These avatars become "surrogate bodies" in surprisingly powerful ways.

It would be fair to say that even if a player gains some tacit embodied understanding or "feel" for certain principles of physics by playing *Portal*, the player is not learning and need not learn any physics in the sense of being able to articulate (speak and write) knowledge in physics. However, this comment applies only if we view *Portal* solely as a game or a piece of software. However, some players become inspired by *Portal* to join with others on the internet in what I later call *passionate affinity spaces*, but for the time being call *interest-driven sites*. In such spaces they articulate the physics behind *Portal*, discuss how the principles of physics the game uses can be used strategically in gameplay, and even use software to make their own *Portal*-like games that work somewhat differently from the "official" *Portal* games.

For example, some *Portal* players have made a wiki to explicate the physics behind *Portal*. Here is one entry:

> The portals create a visual and physical connection between two different locations in 3-D space. Portal ends are restricted to planar surfaces, but if the portal ends are on nonparallel planes, bizarre twists in geometry and gravity can occur

as the player character is immediately reoriented to be upright with respect to gravity after leaving a portal end. An important aspect of the game's physics is "momentum redirection." Objects retain the magnitude of their momentum as they pass through the portals but in a direction relative to the surface the exit portal is on. This allows the player character to launch objects, or even herself, over great distances, both vertically and horizontally, a maneuver referred to as "flinging" by Valve. (*Wikipedia* 2012)

This is, of course, articulated knowledge, not just tacit knowledge. However, the two are complimentary in science learning. Tacit embodied understanding can give "situated meanings" (meanings based on images, actions, goals, and experience, not just verbal definitions) to the articulated words. Situated meanings are the deepest sort of meanings, because such situated meanings allow people to understand complex language well enough to be able to solve problems in a domain and not just retain information for tests. Indeed, situated meanings are so important to learning that Valve, the company that makes *Portal*, has released the full *Portal* engine so that science educators can use it for science learning more directly.

So players can, if they wish, join an interest-driven site, and work together to discuss the physics of *Portal*. They can redesign the game ("mod it") and, thus, too, learn highly technical design skills and how the physics of game worlds work in general. What this means is that if we want to know what sort of learning goes on in and around *Portal*, we must look not just at the game but at both the game and any and all of its accompanying interest-driven sites. A game and any of its associated interest-driven sites interact with each other to create learning and change over time. So the unit of learning here is "game + interest-driven site." Later I will call certain sorts of interest-driven sites *passionate affinity spaces*, and, thus, we have the Game/Affinity Paradigm (GAP).

It is interesting to note that Valve used the following text to advertise the first *Portal* game: "The game is designed to change the way players approach, manipulate, and surmise the possibilities in a given environment" (The Orange Box 2012). What this means is that the game gives the player a new tool—the portal gun—and learning to use this tool lets the player see the world in a new way and to "surmise" new possibilities for solving problems. I myself cannot imagine a better "vision statement" for an educational institution in our highly complex, fast-changing, high-risk global world. We need to wonder why an ad for a popular culture entertainment product has a better educational vision than many of our schools and colleges.

I have used *Portal* as just one characteristic example of how people can go from games to interest-driven sites and back and forth again and again in a learning process. There are innumerable other examples. For example, consider *The Sims*, the best-selling series of games in history. *The Sims* is a set of games where players build families and communities. They can buy houses, clothes, and furniture in stores or they can make them with design tools that come with the game or by using other tools like *Adobe Photoshop*. They can also create albums with pictures of their "Sims" (their artificial people) accompanied by text.

Some players leave the game to join interest-driven sites where they specialize in designing landscapes, houses, clothes, or furniture that they then share with (or sell to) other players to use in their games. They also give each other challenges to play the game in a certain way (Gee and Hayes 2010). For example, one player who called herself "Yamx" gave other players the following challenge on an interest-driven site devoted to *The Sims*:

Sims 2: Nickel and Dimed Challenge
    This challenge was inspired by, and is named for, the book *Nickel and Dimed* by Barbara Ehrenreich (which has nothing whatsoever to do with Sims, but is nevertheless highly recommended). The idea is to mimic, as closely as possible, the life of an unskilled single mother trying to make ends meet for herself and her kids.

The Goal:
    Raising your kids successfully until they're old enough to take care of themselves. If you can get all children to adult age without anyone dying or being taken away by the social worker, you've made it. (*The Sims*[3] 2012)

Ehrenreich's 2001 book is about how hard it is to be poor, how much struggle, and intelligence it actually takes. Simulating the life of a poor single parent is by no means easy in *The Sims*. The game is a commercial entertainment game, and since being poor is not fun, it is hard to live a life of poverty in the game. So Yamx wrote a long "manual" that stated the rules of the challenge and how players could adapt their gameplay and the technology of the game to better represent a poor life. She and the others had to think carefully about how the rules of play would work and how *The Sims* as a piece of simulation software worked. They debated these matters as a group and made changes as they were needed. Players who "won" the challenge had to use the album function that comes with *The Sims* to write a sort of graphic novel about the story of their family and how the rules of the game and *The Sims* as technological simulation interacted with that story.

This challenge is not a social studies assignment. The players are doing it for "fun" as part of playing and interacting with each other over a commercial entertainment game. Nonetheless, they engaged in a good deal of thoughtful reflection of and discussion on poverty and how one could simulate such a life at the level of emotion and not just physical realities in order to gain a real sense of empathy. Indeed, several women wrote to the discussion board that they are or were poor single parents and that this challenge captured their experiences in powerful ways. One woman even said that she was going to keep the challenge to show her child, when the child gets older, what it was like to be a poor single mother and how she managed the struggle.

Again we might wonder why a commercial product leads to better "social studies" than does the curriculum in many of our schools, where social studies being untested is often untaught. This challenge, in the way it combines social studies, technology, and writing is a better "assignment" than many a high school student or college undergraduate ever undertakes. Yet there is no teacher or professor. There is only a "dungeon master" (Yamx) and players who mentor each other.

As another example, consider the game *Foldit*, a game where players can contribute to science (Foldit 2012). In *Foldit*, players tackle the hard problem of protein folding. Proteins are like small machines in the body that carry out practically all the body's functions. They are made up of chains of amino acids that fold into distinctive three-dimensional shapes. Unfortunately any protein can fold into billions of different shapes. Scientists use super computers to seek to find the optimal fold of a protein (usually its lowest energy state) in order to understand the function of the protein.

Foldit presents players with a model of a protein, the pieces of which they can fold by using a variety of tools. The game scores the player on how good of a fold the player has made. Scores are uploaded to a leaderboard, creating competition between players from all over the world. *Foldit* results have been published in prestigious science journals, including in the leading science journal, *Nature*, in a paper with thousands of authors, a first for the journal (Hand 2010).

In official competitions players have in some cases beaten scientists' super computers in the search for correct protein structures. In 2011 *Foldit* players helped to decipher the structure of the Mason-Pfizer monkey virus (M-PMV), an AIDs-causing monkey virus. While the puzzle was available to play for three weeks, players produced an accurate three-dimensional model of the protein in

10 days. As one media source said: "Video-game players have solved a molecular puzzle that stumped scientists for years, and those scientists say the accomplishment could point the way to crowdsourced cures for AIDS and other diseases" (Boyle 2011).

As in the two cases we just surveyed, players of *Foldit* can join others to study protein science and make suggestions about how to play the game better or even make the game better for scientific discovery. For example, the players have made a wiki that contains a wealth of scientific information and suggestions for ways to discover optimal folds for proteins. Here is one small text from the wiki; players can follow links to learn more and more about protein science, if they choose:

> Amino acids are also the basic units of *FoldIt*. In the structure of a protein, each amino acid contributes one link in the protein *Backbone* and (usually) one *Sidechain*. The backbone establishes the basic structural aspects of the protein, and the sidechains determine the details of its biological function. (Wikia 2012)

Foldit players can, if they choose, go back and forth between interest-driven sites where they can mentor each other in learning protein science and the game where they can apply what they learn, as well as see how the complex scientific language they have learned actually applies to the world and to problem solving. They can—and some have—become domain experts without any formal degrees or credentials. They can even compete with credentialed experts. This phenomenon is more general. The combination of games (and other digital forms of learning) and interest-driven sites is producing a world of "Pro-Ams," people with deep expertise, competitive with credentialed experts, but no "professional" credentials (Anderson 2006; Leadbeater 2004).

My final example is meant to show that this world of games plus interest-driven sites is not merely for the young. And this example will bring us to passionate affinity spaces. This example involves *The Sims* as did one of our earlier examples (Gee and Hayes 2010). Real learning involves passion plus persistence. There is no persistence without passion, since no one would put in thousands of hours of practice for something for which he had no passion. How do people grow passion? We really do not know enough about passion, but let me tell you a story that shows one route to passion and then to persistence.

"Tabby Lou" (her screen name) is a woman who retired in her late 60s in ill health and became homebound. In the old days that could have been the end of the story: a retired shut-in. However, Tabby Lou's daughter and granddaughters played *The Sims*, and she got hooked on playing the game as well.

One day, one of her granddaughters told Tabby Lou she wanted a purple potty to put into her Sims' houses. The game did not come with purple potties. You could not buy one in the stores in the game. But what grandmother would disappoint her grandchild? So Tabby Lou decided she just had to build one for her. But that meant she had to learn to make digital content for *The Sims*, and this at a point in time where one had to master digital design tools that did not then come in user-friendly versions with the game itself. Tabby Lou had to become a designer and not just a player. How could she do this? She needed help and some good, but complicated, digital tools to work with. This, too, in the old days, could have been the end of the story: no help, no tools, or the tools are too hard to learn on one's own.

However, groups of people exist on the internet passionately devoted to designing clothes, houses, furniture, landscapes, and stories for *The Sims*. These people offer sophisticated digital three-dimensional design tools and lucid mentoring. They are organized, when they are at their best, in interesting ways: everyone is accepted (newbies and experts are there together); there is no age grading (old and young are both there); everyone is helped to achieve mastery if they want it; everyone is allowed to get mentored and to mentor others, to learn and teach; everyone is expected to take a proactive stance toward learning that does not, however, exclude asking for help, but help that never undermines one's proactive stance toward learning.

Tabby Lou used one group's resources and made a purple potty. She had a very happy granddaughter. But her granddaughters today are not just happy, they are proud. Tabby Lou got hooked on the interest-driven site and developed a passion for design, not just designing purple potties. Today, more than 13 million people have downloaded her designs. She has won design awards. People have thanked her for her work more than 1 million times in her guest book on the *Sims Resource* site. She is internationally known and respected.

Tabby Lou's story gives us a theory of passion, what I call "the purple potty of passion." The passion starts local and small: Tabby Lou is passionate about making a purple potty for her granddaughter. She finds an interest-driven site (that she eventually comes to love) and its tools to realize that passion. The site is organized in such a way that she becomes passionate about the other people on the site and their shared passion (designing for *The Sims*). Energized by these people, wanting to rise on the site and to serve others who are part of it, she persists through thousands of hours of practice with complex digital tools. She becomes a rock star.

Passionate Affinity Spaces

Thus far I have used the term *interest-driven site* for groups of people organized on the internet around interest in a specific game. In a book I wrote with Elisabeth Hayes (Gee and Hayes 2010), we studied such sites connected to *The Sims*. Different sites worked in different ways, but many of them were well organized to energize learning. We call a subset of interest-driven sites "passionate affinity spaces" (Gee 2004, 2007a, 2007b).

The concept of a passionate affinity space—PAS for short—stresses that the organization of the space (the site and what it links to, including real-world spaces and events in some cases) is as important as the organization of the people. Indeed, the interaction between the two is crucial as well. Using the term *group* overstresses the people at the expense of the structure of the space and the way the space and people interact.

In earlier work, we have outlined features indicative of a PAS (Gee 2004; Gee and Hayes 2010, 2011). However, these features are not absolute. In most cases, a PAS can reflect the "ideal" or prototype to a greater or lesser extent.

There are many different types of affinity spaces on the internet and out in the real world (Shirky 2008, 2010). Some are inclusive, supportive, and nurturing, whereas others are not. Passionate affinity spaces and other sorts of interest-driven groups can give people a sense of belonging, but they can also give people a sense of "us" (the insiders) against "them" (the outsiders). People can be cooperative within these spaces, but they can also compete fiercely for status. They can communicate politely and in a friendly fashion or they can engage in hostile and insulting interaction.

The following list is the set of features associated with *The Sims* passionate affinity spaces we studied in Gee and Hayes (2010). As we list the features of a PAS, it becomes apparent how different schools and colleges are from a PAS. If human learning and growth flourish in passionate affinity spaces, especially nurturing ones, then it is of some concern that educational organizations have so few features of such a space.

Features of Passionate Affinity Spaces

1. *A common endeavor for which at least many people in the space have a passion— not race, class, gender, or disability—is primary.* In a PAS, people relate to each other primarily in terms of common interests, endeavors, goals, or practices—defined around their shared passion—and not primarily in terms of race, gender, age,

disability, or social class. These latter variables are backgrounded, though they can be used (or not) strategically by individuals if and when they choose to use them for their own purposes. This feature is particularly enabled and enhanced in virtual affinity spaces (internet sites) because people can enter these spaces with an identity and name of their own choosing.

What people have a passionate affinity for in a PAS is not first and foremost, at least initially, the other people in the space but the passionate endeavor or interest around which the space is organized. While people may eventually come to value their fellow members as one of the primary reasons for being in the PAS, the shared passion is foregrounded as the reason for being there.

2. *Passionate affinity spaces are not segregated by age.* PAS involve people of all different ages. Teenage girls and older women, and everyone else in between, interact on *The Sims* sites we studied. There is no assumption that younger people cannot know more than older people or that they do not have things to teach older people. Older people can be beginners; indeed, anyone can begin at any time. Older and younger people judge others by their passion, desire to learn, and growing skills, and not by their age.

3. *Newbies, masters, and everyone else share a common space.* Passionate affinity spaces do not segregate newcomers ("newbies") from masters. The whole continuum of people from the new to the experienced, from the unskilled to the highly skilled, from the slightly interested to the addicted, and everything in between, is accommodated in the same space. Different people can pursue different goals within the space, based on their own choices, purposes, and identities. They can mingle with others as they wish, learning from them when and where they choose (even "lurking"). While passion defines a PAS, not everyone in the space needs to be passionate or fully committed. They must, however, respect the passion that organizes the space. The space will offer them the opportunity, should they wish to take it, to become passionate. The passion is the "attractor" for the space.

4. *Everyone can, if they wish, produce and not just consume.* People who frequent a *Sims* PAS often go there to consume, that is, to get content other fans have created, and that is fine. But the space is organized to allow and encourage anyone to learn to build and design. Tools, tutorials, and mentorship are widely offered. In some game-related passionate affinity spaces, fans create new maps, new scenarios for single-player and multiplayer games, adjust or redesign the technical aspects of a game, create new artwork, and design tutorials for other players. In a PAS people are encouraged (but not forced) to produce and not just to consume, to participate and not just to be a spectator.

Most passionate affinity spaces set high standards for the quality of production. There is rarely "social promotion" or lowered expectations. Indeed, as in other groups of real experts (Bereiter and Scardamalia 1993), the standards for production typically rise continuously, as individuals innovate, create new tools, and otherwise push the collective bar for achievement.

5. *Content is transformed by interaction.* The content available in a PAS (e.g., all the *Sims* houses, rooms, furniture, clothes, challenges, and tutorials) is transformed continuously through people's social interactions. This content is not fixed. People comment on and negotiate over content and, indeed, over standards, norms, and values. Most of what can be found in a PAS is a product of not just the designer (and certainly not just the company, e.g., the makers of *The Sims*), but of ongoing social interaction in the group. This is particularly evident in forum discussions around, for example, tutorials, in which people add information, ask questions, and otherwise contribute new information.

6. *The development of both specialist and broad, general knowledge is encouraged, and specialist knowledge is pooled.* Passionate affinity spaces encourage and enable people to gain and spread both specialist knowledge and broad, general knowledge. People can readily develop and display specialized knowledge in one or more areas, for example, learning how to make meshes in *The Sims* or how to tweak a game's artificial intelligence (AI). At the same time, the space is designed in ways that enable people to gain broader, less-specialized knowledge about many aspects of the passion which they share with a great many others in the space. Thus, for example, a *Sims* player may learn that *Milkshape* is a three-dimensional modeling tool that can be used to mod *Sims* content, though not learn how to use the tool. The player will know whom to turn to if she is ever in need of specialist knowledge about *Milkshape*. This fosters the development of people who share knowledge and common ground but who each have something special to offer. To joint endeavors, it also means experts are never cut off from the wider community.

7. *Both individual and distributed knowledge are encouraged.* A PAS encourages and enables people to gain both individual knowledge (stored in their heads) and the ability to use and contribute to distributed knowledge. Distributed knowledge is the collective knowledge accessible through, in this case, the affinity space, and includes knowledge possessed by people, stored in material on the site (or links to other sites), or in mediating devices such as various tools, artifacts, and technologies to which people can connect or "network" their own individual knowledge. Such distributed knowledge allows people to know and

do more than they could on their own. For example, a player who wants to create a new kitchen table for *The Sims* might ask questions on a forum, read tutorials, download modding tools, and analyze tables created by other players. Once the player has created a new table, she may upload it to the site along with instructions for other players. Thus, these spaces encourage and enable people to interact with others and with various mediating devices in such a way that their partial knowledge and skills become part of a bigger and smarter network of people, information, and mediating devices and tools.

Nurturing passionate affinity spaces tends to foster a view of expertise as rooted more in the space itself, or the community that exists in the space, and not in individuals' heads. "Experts" know their expertise is always partial and limited, and they draw on the knowledge stored in the PAS when they need to supplement their individual knowledge or learn new things. The public display of individual expertise is less important than contributing to the collective knowledge of the space. In less nurturing spaces, individuals place more of a premium on establishing their expertise in relation to other people in the space and may vie to lay claim to the possession of unique knowledge or skills. Even nurturing affinity spaces provide opportunities for the recognition of individual achievements and skill but more in the service of encouraging individual growth and contributions to the collective good.

8. *The use of dispersed knowledge is facilitated.* A PAS encourages and enables people to use dispersed knowledge: knowledge that is not actually on the site itself but can be found at other sites or in other spaces. For example, in some *Sims* passionate affinity spaces, there are many software tools available on site made by the designers of *The Sims*, but there are links to all sorts of other groups, software, and sites that have tools to facilitate building and designing for *The Sims*. In a PAS devoted to the game *Age of Mythology*, as another example, people are linked to sites where they can learn about mythology in general, including mythological facts and systems that go well beyond *Age of Mythology* as a game. When a space provides access to dispersed knowledge, it recognizes the value of local and particular knowledge available in other places and created by other groups, and the necessary limitations of its own knowledge base and resources.

9. *Tacit knowledge is used and honored; explicit knowledge is encouraged.* A PAS encourages, enables, and honors tacit knowledge: knowledge participants have built up in practice, but may not be able to explicate fully in words. For example, designers of *Sims* content typically learn primarily through trial and error, not

by memorizing tutorials and manuals. While tutorials (explicit or codified knowledge) are found in abundance in these spaces, designers rely on personal contact, through forums and messaging, to pass on their own craft knowledge and tricks of the trade. At the same time, the PAS offers ample incentives for people to learn to articulate their tacit knowledge in words (e.g., when they contribute to a forum thread or engage in group discussion about a shared problem).

10. *There are many different forms and routes to participation.* People can participate in a PAS in many different ways and at many different levels. People can participate peripherally in some respects and centrally in others; patterns can change from day to day or across larger stretches of time. Sometimes people lead and mentor, and other times they follow and get mentored.

11. *There are many different routes to status.* A PAS allows people to achieve status, if they want it (and they may not), in many different ways. Different people can be good at different things or gain repute in different ways. For example, in the *Sims* passionate affinity spaces we studied, some people are recognized for their skills as content creators, others for their tutorials, and still others for their roles in creating and managing the spaces themselves.

12. *Leadership is porous and leaders are resources.* Passionate affinity spaces do not have "bosses." They do have various sorts of leaders, though the boundary between leader and follower is often porous, because members can become leaders and leaders often can participate as members. Leaders in a PAS, when they are leading, are designers, mentors, resourcers, and enablers of other people's participation and learning. They do not and cannot order people around or create rigid, unchanging, and impregnable hierarchies. Obviously there are degrees of flexibility in leadership, and while nurturing spaces foster respect for experts and those with more advanced skills, they tend toward less hierarchy and a view of leadership as "teaching," with an emphasis on mentoring and providing resources, not necessarily instructing, though this can happen as well.

13. *Roles are reciprocal.* In a PAS people sometimes lead, sometimes follow, sometimes mentor, sometimes get mentored, sometimes teach, sometimes learn, sometimes ask questions, sometimes answer them, sometimes encourage, and sometimes get encouraged. In nurturing spaces, even the highest experts view themselves as always having more to learn, as members of a common endeavor, and not in it only for themselves. They want others to become experts, too.

14. *A view of learning that is individually proactive, but does not exclude help, is encouraged.* Passionate affinity spaces tend to encourage a view of learning where the individual is proactive, self-propelled, engaged with trial and error,

and where failure is seen as a path to success. This view of learning does not exclude asking for help, but help from the community is never seen as replacing a person's responsibility for his or her own learning. Nurturing affinity spaces tends to promote a view of requests for help (when other resources have been exhausted) as a means for enhancing the knowledge base of the space as a whole, as participants engage in collective problem solving.

15. *People get encouragement from an audience and feedback from peers, though everyone plays both roles at different times.* The norm of a nurturing PAS is to be supportive and to offer encouragement when someone produces something. This support and encouragement come from one's "audience," from the people who use or respond to one's production. Indeed, having an audience, let alone a supportive one, is encouraging to most producers. Many *Sims* affinity spaces provide mechanisms for this feedback, such as guest books where people can post messages to content creators.

At the same time, producers get feedback and help (usually also offered in a supportive way) from other creators whom they consider either their peers or people whom they aspire to be like some day. Who counts as a peer changes as one changes and learns new things. Everyone in a PAS may be audience for some people and potential peers for others.

The preceding list is based on the online *Sims* affinity spaces we have studied. Other passionate affinity spaces have these features as well. These features are not easy to achieve, in either nurturing or less nurturing versions, and they can deteriorate over time.

The Future of Colleges and Universities

Students will probably always seek to gain prestige by attending high-status colleges and universities like Harvard and Stanford. But in a world replete with e-learning, lesser-status colleges and universities face intense competition from nearly every quarter. Anything called a "college" can now offer courses and degrees nearly everywhere. Indeed, high-status colleges can and will offer cut-rate, "off brand" versions of their courses and degrees by e-learning so that people can gain some prestige by association with them but without getting their "real" degrees.

In the world outside of formal institutions, people are becoming experts without credentials. They are producing and not just consuming, participating and not just spectating. They are solving problems and preparing themselves for future learning. They are engaged in finding and refining their interests and growing passions that lead to persistence and mastery. Often they are also gaining status—a sense of counting and mattering—outside of markets and jobs, jobs that may be dead ends.

Passionate affinity spaces—like many interest-driven sites—often operate by the Pareto principle (Gee and Hayes 2010, 2011; Shirky 2008): 10–20% of the people in the space make 80–90% of the contributions, and 80–90% of the people in the space make 10–20% of the contributions. This is both good and bad. It is good because everyone's contribution is captured, counts, and might make an important difference. It is potentially bad because not everyone gets (or wants) to be a top contributor.

What this means—if we consider passionate affinity spaces as the breeding grounds of twenty-first-century skills and sites for people to gain a sense of worth in a world that gives too few people a sense of worth "on market"—is that we want people to participate in lots of passionate affinity spaces, in some of which they are in the 80–90% of lesser contributors, but in one or more of which they are in the 10–20% of top producers. It is here that they will have found their true "passion." So, too, people will then become both broad and deep in the way a classical liberal arts education was supposed to ensure.

If there are any colleges and universities that want to take the moral high ground in the face of market forces pushing them to the moral low ground, they will have to get passionate about learning and about creating passionate learners. I am suggesting that colleges—at least some of them—become a large affinity space of many different affinity spaces designed to let all students explore and kindle interests and flame some of them into passions. They may go out of business. And, then, too, they may reinvigorate our frayed public sphere and reinvent the nature of "higher" education. If some do not do it or none can, it will be done "out of school."

REFERENCES

Anderson, Chris. 2006. *The Long Tail: Why the Future of Business Is Selling Less of More.* New York: Hyperion.

Arum, Richard, and Josipa Roksa. 2011. *Academically Adrift: Limited Learning on College Campuses.* Chicago: University of Chicago Press.

Bereiter, Carl, and Marlene Scardamalia. 1993. *Surpassing Ourselves: An Inquiry into the Nature and Implications of Expertise.* Chicago: Open Court.

Boyle, Alan. 2011. "Gamers Solve Molecular Puzzle That Baffled Scientists." Last modified September 18. http://cosmiclog.msnbc.msn.com/_news/2011/09/18/7802623.

Brandon, Craig. 2010. *The Five-Year Party: How Colleges Have Given Up on Educating Your Child and What You Can Do about It.* Dallas, TX: BenBella Books.

Cole, Jonathan R. 2009. *The Great American University: Its Rise to Preeminence, Its Indispensable National Role, Why It Must Be Protected.* New York: Public Affairs.

Ehrenreich, Barbara. 2001. *Nickel and Dimed: On (Not) Getting By in America.* New York: Metropolitan Books.

Foldit. 2012. "Foldit Beta: Solve Puzzles for Science." Accessed August 29. http://fold.it/portal/.

Gee, James Paul. 2004. *Situated Language and Learning: A Critique of Traditional Schooling.* London: Routledge.

———. 2007a. *What Video Games Have to Teach Us about Learning and Literacy.* 2nd ed. New York: Palgrave Macmillan.

———. 2007b. *Good Video Games and Good Learning.* New York: Peter Lang.

Gee, James Paul, and Elisabeth R. Hayes. 2010. *Women and Gaming: The Sims and 21st Century Learning.* New York: Palgrave Macmillan.

———. 2011. *Language and Learning in the Digital Age.* New York: Palgrave Macmillan.

Hacker, Andrew, and Claudia Dreifus. 2010. *Higher Education? How Colleges Are Wasting Our Money and Failing Our Kids—and What We Can Do about It.* New York: St. Martin's Press.

Hand, Eric. 2010. "People Power." *Nature* 466:685–687.

Kamenetz, Anya. 2010. *DIY U: Edupunks, Edupreneurs, and the Coming Transformation of Higher Education.* West River Junction, VT: Chelsea Green.

Leadbeater, Charles. 2004. *The Pro-Am Revolution: How Enthusiasts Are Changing Our Society and Economy.* London: Demos.

Marmot, Michael. 2004. *The Status Syndrome: How Social Standing Affects Our Health and Longevity.* New York: Holt.

Menand, Louis. 2010. *The Marketplace of Ideas: Reform and Resistance in the American University.* New York: Norton.

Nussbaum, Martha C. 2010. *Not for Profit: Why Democracy Needs the Humanities.* Princeton, NJ: Princeton University Press.

The Orange Box. 2012. "Info." Accessed August 12. http://orange.half-life2.com/portal.html.

Reich, Robert B. 1992. *The Work of Nations: Preparing Ourselves for 21st Century Capitalism.* New York: Vintage.

———. 2007. *Supercapitalism: The Transformation of Business, Democracy, and Everyday Life.* New York: Vintage.

Schrecker, Ellen. 2010. *The Lost Soul of Higher Education: Corporatization, the Assault on Academic Freedom, and the End of the American University.* New York: New Press.

Shirky, Clay. 2008. *Here Comes Everybody: The Power of Organizing without Organizations.* New York: Penguin.

———. 2010. *Cognitive Surplus: Creativity and Generosity in a Connected Age.* New York: Penguin.

The Sims[3]. 2012. "Sims 3: Nickel and Dimed Challenge." Accessed August 12. http://forum.thesims3.com/jforum/posts/list/182640.page.

Taylor, Mark C. 2010. *Crisis on Campus: A Bold Plan for Reforming Our Colleges and Universities.* New York: Knopf.

Tuchman, Gaye. 2009. *Wannabe U: Inside the Corporate University.* Chicago: University of Chicago Press.

Wilkenson, Richard, and Kate Pickett. 2010. *The Spirit Level: Why Greater Equality Makes Societies Stronger.* New York: Bloomsbury.

Wikia. 2012. "Amino Acids." Accessed August 29. http://foldit.wikia.com/wiki/Amino_Acids.

Wikipedia. 2012. "Portal (Video Game)." Accessed August 29. http://en.wikipedia.org/wiki/Portal_%28video_game%29.

CHAPTER EIGHT

Game-Like Learning

Leveraging the Qualities of Game Design and Play

KATIE SALEN

Back in the winter of 1891 in the town of Springfield, Massachusetts, James Naismith highlighted the potential of games to educate and engage. Enlisted in December of that year to create an activity that would provide some form of "socially redeeming physical expression" for the working-class youth of the town, Naismith invented the "Guiding Principles of Basket-Ball." Taking cues from the more democratic features of rugby and lacrosse, basketball was soon being played in thousands of gymnasiums across the nation. So well designed were Naismith's guiding principles that within four years the ground rules for the game were in place, giving rise to a unique space of pedagogical possibility—one that elegantly expressed Naismith's belief that the game would teach itself (which it does), and that the players, trying to win, would teach one another (which they do) (Hickey 1997).

Yet, despite (or perhaps because of) these pedagogical leanings, which resulted in millions of young people developing mastery through practice and performance, adults were worried. Several years after Naismith's game took root, the YMCA newsletter *New Era* began running a series entitled "Is Basketball a Danger?" posing questions like: Was basketball getting too rough? Was it too exciting for America's youth? Did youth neglect their studies to "play it all the time?" (Hickey 1997). One hundred twenty years later the questions remain, targeting not basketball—the game seemingly redeemed by a perception that it offers limited but viable pathways toward college and career for a few athletically gifted individuals—but video games and digital media broadly.

As has been noted elsewhere in this book, many parents and educators are deeply conflicted about the potential of games and digital media for learning.

The handwringing centers in part, on a worry not dissimilar to that expressed about basketball in the 1890s; as Gee observes in his chapter, the assumption seems to be that activities that seem to engage young people so wholly cannot be educational too. Following this theory then, learning—school learning— demands something different. That something different has been manifest in policies like No Child Left Behind, which legislates through standardized test scores rather than through learning, and which result in experiences that are socially efficient (e.g., metrics driven) but rarely child-centered. Such an approach to education does not so much discount engagement as a condition of learning as erase it altogether.

What if this theory was flipped on its head to posit that engagement is an absolutely critical condition for learning? In this light, I am extending ideas that the other authors in part II posit in their chapters: engaging a young person in learning is the first step in developing habits and skills that will support them in realizing their academic, civic, and career potential. Can making learning irresistible provide a context that enables young people to survive and thrive?

This chapter takes up this hypothesis, offering a set of guiding design principles for the creation of game-like learning experiences that are socially situated, challenge based, and student centered. Surfaced from within the field of game design, the principles are aligned with a theory of *connected learning*, which seeks to tie together the respected historical body of research on how youth learn best with the opportunities made available through today's networked and digital media (Ito et al. 2013). This approach to learning also draws from what a close analysis has shown that games do best: drop players into inquiry-based, complex problem spaces that are leveled to deliver just-in-time learning and use data to help players understand how they are doing, what they need to work on, and where they need to go next.

As a framework, the design principles for game-like learning pivot on a central axis of engagement rooted in the power of play. Fullerton, as illustrated in her chapter, has affinities with this perspective, as do Jenkins and Gee. I build on their respective ideas by developing a design framework that aligns games and their affordances with the best of what connected learning has to offer.

The first part of this chapter explores the values and assumptions underlying connected learning; a set of guiding design principles is then built from this foundation. The chapter concludes by speculating on how connected, game-like learning might be leveraged to change how parents, educators, and policy makers think about the purposes of education and the challenges young people face to survive and thrive in an increasingly complex, globalized world.

Connected Learning

Connected learning offers a way of thinking about where, when, and how learning might take place, given the massive changes in how people create, use, and share information and expertise (Ito et al. forthcoming). Developed by members of the MacArthur Foundation Connected Learning Research Network in conjunction with many fellow travelers from a range of fields and sectors, the model acknowledges Dewey while building on innovations in technological and social processes that were unimaginable even 15 years ago. The theory calls on today's interactive and networked media in an effort to create learning experiences that are more effective, better integrated, and broadly accessible for more youth. It builds on the presence of the kind of participatory culture outlined by Henry Jenkins, John Seely Brown, and others where young people are

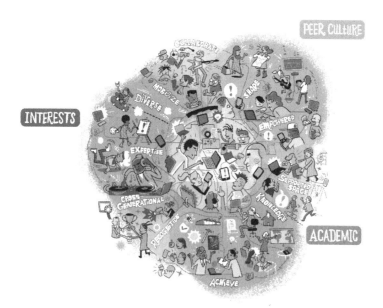

Figure 8.1. Connected learning links learning across interests, academics, and peer culture. *(Courtesy of the DML Hub [dmlcentral.org]; XPLANTIONS @2012 Dachis Group for ConnectedLearning.tv)*

supported in becoming producers of knowledge and culture but does so in ways that connect the oft-segregated spheres of formal and informal learning. Further, it is an approach to learning that seeks to integrate learning experiences that take place in peer, interest, and academic contexts, harnessing and translating popular peer culture and community-based knowledge for academic relevance (figure 8.1). Within the model, school is not the only place where learning is valued; rather, it is one of several linked contexts in which learning is made resilient.

Connected Learning in Action

Imagine a young woman named Tal, who likes to write and draw and who socializes with a close-knit group of cousins about her same age. One of the cousins goes to her same school and is a gamer—his current game of choice being a video game called *Minecraft*. He found out about the game from one of his teachers at school and quickly fell in love with it. The game is played on a computer and is primarily about creativity and building. Players can modify the terrain of *Minecraft*'s three-dimensional world in different ways to build shelters or other enclosures to survive attacks from monsters. The game has some strategic components as well. Players have to mine elements like stone, water, various ores, and tree trunks and manage those resources while attending to their hunger and health.

Tal started playing *Minecraft* at her cousin's house. They decided to help form a *Minecraft* club at school, and soon many more students had joined. Lunchtime was spent sharing building tips, playing each other's levels, and talking about what they were going to do in the game when they got home. The teacher who had originally told them about the game set up a *Minecraft* server that the club could access, and the community of players continued to grow and diversify to include younger and older siblings, friends from other schools, parents, and other teachers.

Tal got the idea to write scripts for her and her friends to film as animated plays in the game from a post on a *Minecraft* player's forum; she got support for doing so from her social studies teacher, who had noticed Tal's interest in creative writing. While the teacher was not a *Minecraft* player herself, she did recognize that the game created a socially rich and creatively driven context for nurturing Tal's writing interests. Tal was allowed to include her *Minecraft* productions in the school's online student magazine, as did other members of her production team, many of whom went to different schools. The status and recognition she gained from these outlets fed her confidence and supported her burgeoning identity as a creative writer.

In addition, Tal started writing more frequently and found that the practice paid off in her writing for class assignments, mostly because her teacher challenged her to develop her own voice, no matter what the topic. She still went to the *Minecraft* club at school, but usually spent the sessions working on her scripts and getting ideas for new stories from the levels created by other players on the server. By the end of her sixth-grade year, Tal was writing every day and sharing her work with the community that had developed around the school's *Minecraft* server. Her parents were amazed at her persistence and initiative and were looking for summer writing programs for young authors that she could take part in to support her interest over break.

This story is inspired by the activities of students and teachers at Quest to Learn, a New York City public middle school created by the Institute of Play in partnership with the NYC Department of Education. The school was designed from the ground up, to support connected learning, and has done so through the lens of game design and play. Helping students to make connections between areas of interest that they may be pursuing out of school with academic outcomes is a core feature of the school, as is a desire to build bridges between online and offline activities that have peer, interest, and academic relevance. The flurry of activity, spaces, and communities that have grown up around *Minecraft* at Quest is just one example of connected learning in action. There are certainly many more that could be explored, but they will be saved for later. First a few more words on basketball.

Where Does Learning Take Place?

When Naismith invented basketball, it is likely that he never considered the extent to which players would learn how to play the game in spaces beyond the court. While a player new to the game surely honed skills during games and practice sessions in the gym, it is equally certain that much of the player's expertise was developed elsewhere. A player intent on improving his or her skills would have most certainly watched numerous games with friends, debated technique with other enthusiasts, listened to or read stories about the exploits of star players, and sought out practice resources in the form of family or friends. And while initial skills may have been learned with the help of a coach, learning to play basketball—really learning it—required a player to leverage the expertise of an entire network of participants who were helping to grow the game bottom-up. Expertise in basketball, then as now, is developed most fully in the communities that form around the game.

As we see in his chapter, James Paul Gee (2004) calls this space of community an affinity space and points to online communities like those connected to games like *The Sims*, a PC-based simulation-style game where players control the life activities of miniature people, and *Portal 2*, a puzzle-style video game where players grapple with the physics of teleportation, as exemplars of environments in which players create, share, and develop expertise. This model is important to the argument being developed here as game-like learning focuses on the creation of learning experiences that look beyond the design of a game or media artifact into the affinity space that surrounds it. The design of game-like learning, then, is also the design of community.

The concept of affinity spaces acknowledges that learning is both socially situated—expertise resides in the community, mediated through exchanges between participants—and networked. Learning to play basketball occurs in multiple, overlapping spaces—connected spaces—across which an individual's skills, knowledge, interests, and identities develop. It is therefore critical that supports, be they technological, human, or economic, are in place to enable individuals to both access and make sense of the various experiences they are having in spaces that are likely separated in space, time, and institutional domain. Creating such supports, however, is no simple task, given the dominant view of education as institutionally "owned" by schools. This has not always been so.

LEARNING ECOLOGIES

As Lawrence Cremin (1979) notes in *Traditions of American Education*, "Individual institutions and individual variables are important, to be sure; but it is the ways in which they pattern themselves and relate to one another that give them their educational significance, and in ways in which their outcomes confirm, complement, or contradict one another that determine their educational effects" (128). The project of learning at the time of basketball's invention was "owned" by a whole host of institutions that made up the life world of a young person: home, church, school, and community. This configuration of learning institutions included both formal and informal learning opportunities; the learning biography of any individual was made up of the patterns created by the changing relationships of these institutions to each other and to the learner over time.

Today a learner's biography, while similarly patterned, likely contains barriers erected by the learning institutions themselves, which limit participation. Many schools consistently block access to Web 2.0 technologies, and access to social and commercial entertainment content is generally frowned upon in formal educational settings. After school programs or online communities designed to provide alternative spaces of engagement for young people have no way of validating these forms of knowledge and participation within federally sanctioned assessment regimes. Cultural institutions with educational missions routinely create innovative curriculum that is shared only within the walled networks of their closed education communities.

Many learning institutions are trapped in an old paradigm—one that emphasizes learners as individual consumers of content, recognizes traditional lines of institutional authority, and prioritizes the ownership of intellectual property (Ito et al. forthcoming). As a result, they have very few mechanisms for responding in adaptive ways to innovations in learning technologies and networks. Innovation is stymied by outdated infrastructures and policies, as well as by hardened boundaries between schools and other sites of learning. In many cases, an institution's urge to protect its organizational position and reputation, as well as its legacy and assets, overshadows the growing awareness that its youth constituents increasingly live their lives across multiple physical and digital spaces guided by norms of creative collaboration, flexible engagement, and open access. Rather than embrace the learning capacities of connected learning networks, schools have tended to exclude games and online media from their repertoire and fight an uphill battle to capture young people's attention.

Connected learning argues for the very patterns of engagement that emerge from participation across experiences and institutions but are blocked by many schools. Today's social media and web-based communities provide exceptional opportunities for learners, parents, caring adults, teachers, and peers in diverse and specialized areas of interest to engage in shared projects, creative production, and inquiry (Ito et al. forthcoming). Learning environments must therefore be designed to be openly networked in order to link together institutions and groups across various sectors; learning resources, tools, and materials should be made abundant, accessible, and visible across these settings. The principles guiding the design of connected learning environments therefore center on learning that is production centered, organized around a shared purpose, and supported within open networks.

SUPPORTING CONNECTED LEARNING

How complex is it to create such designed environments? Think back to the example of Tal and the types of supports that had to be in place to enable her writing across home, afterschool, and school contexts. She needed to have access to online environments like the game *Minecraft*, which allowed her to actively create, experiment, and design. The barrier to entry had to be low, since she was not a hard-core gamer, and the game had to connect to something she enjoyed doing—in this case, spending time with her cousin. The online environment had to provide ways for her to hang out, socialize, lurk, and learn the norms of the game, helped along by the teacher who moderated the school's *Minecraft* server. Tal had to see examples of what other players were doing with *Minecraft*—YouTube fit the bill—which gave her models to follow and learn from. More importantly, she had to be able to easily search for, view, and reference these examples as she was working so that she could continually improve her ideas by reviewing the work of others.

Tal had to have access to a laptop, software like iMovie and GarageBand, and ideally support at school for using these tools, since she could not count on having access to those resources at home. She had to have a teacher who was open to her interests and willing to help Tal connect these interests to academically relevant activities, like class assignments.

Tal had to discover a shared purpose with other members of the community—the creation of animated plays in *Minecraft*—and have access to tools and settings in which this shared interest could be made visible. Even more importantly, she needed ways to make her work visible to others across a range of contexts that mattered to her, in order to build reputation and status as a writer. Last, she had to have access to learning environments that gave her problems to discover and solve, around an existing or cultivated interest.

Patterns of interaction within networks, when seen from a learner's perspective, matter most when they center on an area of interest. Research has shown that having a passion for a topic or activity has a strong correlation with higher learning outcomes (Halpern 2002). It makes sense that, when an individual or group becomes interested in something, whether a subject area, a hobby, or a person, engagement translates into a motivation to learn. Often it does not even *feel* like learning, so powerful is the interest.

Games model this effect well, offering up irresistible problems to solve in some of the unlikeliest domains. A player does not necessarily need to have an interest in spelling and grammar to get deeply involved in games like *Super*

Scribblenauts, a puzzle game for the Nintendo DS, or *Words With Friends*, a *Scrabble*-like social network site game. The beauty of these two games is that the complex problem space offered up is so engaging that players end up learning about adjectives and other parts of speech, even if they never cared about them in school. Further, interest does not have to be innate—it can be cultivated via a set of learning experiences that help learners develop not only interests or passions but also a diverse set of identities. This is one reason that an alignment can be found between connected learning and a game-like approach—each places the learner in the center of the experience; each values engagement as a necessary condition for learning; and each situates learning within a set of overlapping experiences where understanding and expertise can be developed at differing rates. If the guiding design principles of connected learning advocate for production-oriented communities, open networks, and a shared sense of purpose, what might games and their design add to the mix?

What Is Known and Unknown about the Potential of Games?

Data and outcomes from various studies—identified in part III of this volume, as well as in publications such as *Learning Science through Computer Games and Simulations*, published by the National Academy of Sciences, and the *Synthesis Report on the Games, Learning, and Assessment Workshop* (Shute et al. in press; Shute, Ventura, and Kim 2011)—highlight several reasons for games' connected potential.

First, games are situated. They support learning by doing, not by rote memorization of facts. With games, players move from level to level by implementing strategies and concepts they learn as they play the game. Learning is the result of interaction with an interesting problem context where learners construct meaning (Gee 2008; Klopfer, Osterweil, and Salen 2010; Schaffer 2006; Squire 2006). *Minecraft* players learn how to build shelters not because the game provides tools for building and an environment in which to build. They do so because the monsters come out at night—if a player has not built a shelter in which to hide by the time night falls in the game, they will not survive until morning. And so players learn what can be mined from the landscape to build a rudimentary shelter within the first 15 minutes of play. This learning grows in sophistication as their building skills do, and players are challenged to constantly reimagine what they want their *Minecraft* world to be. The possible solutions

are gloriously diverse and deeply rooted in individual player's interests and design sensibility.

Second, problem discovery and solving in games require players to apply
various competencies to succeed, such as thinking about different relationships among variables to solve a complex problem. Additionally, the challenges
offered up by games tend to be differentiated. Struggling players can repeat levels until they master skills and concepts, and advanced players can move forward by attempting increasingly challenging levels. Educators must think
about differentiation daily, and one of the tenets underlying this work is a belief
in the idea that there are the similarities between a good game designer and a
good teacher. Each thinks deeply about ways of igniting inquiry and curiosity;
each is a master of motivation by creating challenges (momentarily) just out of
reach.

As this book attests, education is one area where individuals are looking to
games for new approaches to the design of learning. Some city governments are
exploring game-like models of participatory budgeting that have shown success in Canada and Latin America. Participatory budgeting allows members of
a community to make decisions on spending priorities for their city. This budgeting process can often look and feel very much like a large, multiplayer game.
Topcoder Inc., a software company that uses a competition-based software development approach, is leading the way in integrating game design thinking
into the space of entrepreneurial innovation (Lakhani 2008).

Yet despite the interest in games from a range of sectors, the research and
literature on their potential are equally notable for what is not yet well understood or well demonstrated. There are few examples, for instance, of digital
games being used in academic settings as formative or summative assessment
tools, despite their data-rich nature. It is not yet known, for example, how and
in what ways simulation- and game-based measures of learning might be more,
less, or equally valid than paper-and-pencil measures. There is a weak understanding of how games might be mobilized in educational settings to support
development of isolated concepts and skills, as well as concepts that are interdependent and that operate across domains. And few examples exist of how
games and the application of their underlying principles can help teachers assess learning that is collaborative and connected to hard-to-measure skills like
teamwork, creativity, and problem solving.

These gaps in knowledge are perhaps not unexpected, given the relative
youth of the games and learning field. But they point to a need for greater application of the core principles that have been documented in settings that model,

to a greater or lesser degree, the day-to-day demands of education. The gaps highlight a need to move beyond the approaches of traditional educational technology and children's software development, where games have been most often seen as content-delivery mechanisms, much like textbooks or worksheets. Instead, an approach is required that recognizes and builds on their key properties as designed systems—the structures of interactivity and engagement that underlie a game's ability to support players in progressing successfully and persistently through the space of its design.

The design of the Quest school model, as noted earlier in the chapter, was a response to this challenge—an attempt to better understand and by default, begin to expose both the promises and limitations of games. One strategy taken was to move beyond the idea of games as discrete artifacts in the classroom that students would play to learn content, much like they would use a textbook, video, or online learning resource. Instead, the model argues for a pedagogical approach that frames the design of learning activities over time as both connected and game-like. This meant developing a model for the creation of learning experiences that drew from the core design principles organizing games and their play.

The design of learning, as a result of this focus, is centered on the creation of well-structured and engaging challenges that give rise to a "need to know" in students. The game-like challenges offer a space of possibility for learners to tinker, explore, hypothesize, and test assumptions. They build in opportunities for authority and expertise to be shared and made reciprocal among learners, mentors, and teachers. And they support multiple, overlapping pathways toward mastery. Depending on the domain, challenges might be worked on over a series of weeks or several days; they might focus on a specific content area or skill or require an interdisciplinary integration. Groups of students within a class might be assigned different parts of the challenge to work on, depending on their level and interest. The following section offers a snapshot of the model in action.

Game-Like Learning in Action

Teachers in the Quest schools work with game designers to create 10-week-long "missions." The missions pose difficult and often enigmatic challenges for students to solve. Quests of 1 to 5 weeks in length break down the bigger challenge into smaller ones whose solutions contribute tools, knowledge, and skills to the larger mission. Here is a good example.

Last year a mission called "Ghost vs. Ghost" challenged Quest to Learn's seventh graders to grapple with the question of how it could be possible for a group of individuals to experience the same event but come away with competing points of view. A group of fictional ghosts of various lineages, all present at the events surrounding the founding of the American colonies, were trapped in the sub-, sub-, subbasement of the Natural History Museum. They were fighting over the "correct" interpretation of historic events. The question posed was a critical one: How might someone know what and who to believe when everyone's story is different?

Over the course of the mission—which connected history, social studies, and writing and tackled a robust set of required learning standards—students dug into primary documents to uncover evidence supporting various versions of the contested events. They wrote individual memoirs from the point of view of their favorite colonial ghost, and they ultimately produced persuasive essays that were grounded not only in a respect for the rigors of narrative and history but in the power of empathy to allow for the coexistence of competing points of view.

Creating opportunities for learners to fail productively—to discover what they need to know through a process of trial and error—is a trait shared among inquiry-oriented teachers and game designers. One key property of these types of experiences is that they require that individual expertise be applied within a collaborative context. Members of a team must work together on a problem by contributing different forms of skill and expertise.

Sports video games like *FIFA Soccer* or *Madden NFL 12*, which are based on the popular sports of soccer and football respectively, are good examples, but so are games like *Starcraft*, a military science fiction real-time strategy game, and *Legend of Zelda*, an action-adventure game, in which successful players learn how to leverage the knowledge and skills of others to accomplish different goals. The idea that teamwork and collaboration are skills critical to success in the twenty-first-century workplace is not new, of course, but game-like learning has some potential to become a key space for these skills to develop. Here's one more example, to illustrate this point.

The New York City Math Olympiad Tournament provides teams of middle school students from schools around the city the chance to demonstrate their not insignificant mathematical chops. Teams meet weekly throughout the year to practice and come to the tournament prepared to compete. In 2010, Quest to Learn fielded a team of sixth and seventh graders, in contrast to the mostly eighth-grader makeup of the other teams. Members of the team had come to

Quest from different elementary schools across the city, and all shared a passion for math.

Traditionally, teams focus their practice sessions on individual training—in the competition students compete as individuals in the initial rounds, so individual performance is critical. But because of Quest to Learn's focus on game-like learning, members of the team were also trained in collaboration as part of their regular classes. As a result, participants had deep experience in what might be called "teaming and competing": groups of individuals working together to achieve both individual and group success.

Quest's team won the Olympiad and most who witnessed the victory said simply, "They were the team who worked together best."

Game-Based Assessment in Action

The fact that game-like learning gives students experience in applying individual expertise to the solving of collaborative problems is both a promise and a potential limitation of the model, owing to the way learning is most commonly assessed in schools. Assessment tools like standardized tests tend to focus on the knowledge and understanding demonstrated by individuals, not groups. Most teachers are trained to use data in the classroom to assess student learning in contexts where all students are expected to know and master the same thing, exemplified by the reproduction of facts or content knowledge that can fit easily into a standardized worksheet. Now, this is not true of all teachers or all classrooms, but the point is that the most commonly used approaches to assessment are not very good at measuring group learning or valuing differences in what any particular student might know and be able to contribute to the solving of a collaborative problem.

Games, on the other hand, give players access to many different kinds of data that can be used to understand not only their own progress and performance against a set of goals but also the very nature of the problems they are trying to solve. Digital games in particular can collect enormous amounts of data from players and then use that corpus of data to dynamically change gameplay in an engaging way. These data can be mined in a multitude of ways for real-time assessments and to look at different groups: small groups to millions of players in a specific demographic, for example. For the purposes of illustrating this potential, take the following scenario, which is based on the use of a commercial off-the-shelf game in a science-and-math-based class at Quest to Learn called *The Way Things Work*. The game was integrated into a larger mission the students were working on that challenged students to create disaster relief plans for a large, geologically unstable American city.

A young woman and two of her fellow classmates exchanged text messages early one Monday, making a plan to meet at school at 8:00 a.m. They planned to spend 15 minutes reviewing the plan each had put together around the "moves" they wanted to make that day in the simulation-style game *SimCity 4*, a digital game they have been playing in their science class for the past several weeks. They had to think like urban planners in the game, designing and building a settlement that could grow into a city. There were many different kinds of planning decisions they had to make as they worked to manage the environment, quality of life, and finances of their simulated cities.

After each play session, the game provided each student with several screens worth of data showing the state of their current resources (e.g., funding, population, food, work force), a log of resource management over time, and a mapping of resource management to changes in things like population growth, energy consumption, and environmental impact. The students had made a habit of asking their teacher to print out these screens for them during class so that they could get together before school and during lunch to strategize.

Each discovered how important these shared strategy sessions were when one student added so many factories to her city in an attempt to decrease unemployment that it was likely that the areas neighboring hers would become polluted. Few of the students in the class up to that point had understood that all of their cities were part of a linked urban ecology the teacher had created as part of the overall challenge rules—changes in one city had the potential to affect change in the others. At the end of each class, students would report out on the status of their city, whose data were input into a Google spreadsheet that showed each city's effect on surrounding communities.

Their teacher had been tracking student understanding of learning standards (reading topographical maps and making inferences, recognizing and analyzing the cause and effect relationships) and meta cognition skills by observing the in-game resource management data for each of her students, and observing the sequences of choices the students were making over time in an effort to manage the growth of their cities. Some of these observations were made as she walked around during class observing students at play; others came from a review of the spreadsheet where daily outcomes were being tracked for each student's city.

These data gave her information on *when* students begin to make choices demonstrating their understanding of the interdependencies of the city systems (i.e., how long into the play of the game and in the context of what set of decisions and outcomes). This moment was an important performance indicator of student understanding of the dynamic and interconnected nature of systems; the teacher could compare her notes on when this moment came for each player, giving her data on how her students were progressing comparatively against the competencies and skills she was using the game to teach and assess. They had studied the human body last year in another class, and the teacher was looking for students to make a similar connection to the way in which connected systems influence each other.

Examples like this can help connect the dots between connected and game-like learning. They can also highlight many of the features of games discussed here, as well as in other chapters in this book, including the way in which games offer up contexts for problem solving that challenge both individual and collective forms of knowing. The sharing of strategies by the students in The Ways Things Work class described earlier point to the presence of a shared purpose and need to share and collaborate. Each of these qualities is a component of a connected, game-like learning plan, yet none can be taken for granted—each must be intentionally designed into the overall system. This is true at the level of any game or game-like activity that is created, and at the level of the types of interactions that take place between students, teachers, and other participants in any of the communities into which the activity extends.

Guiding Principles of Game-Like Learning

Game-like learning, when embedded within a connected learning framework, has the potential to enable new engagement models that not only support learning with academic, civic, and career implications but also cultivate peer exchange and the building of mentor networks. These models include teaming and competing structures that mix collaborative and competitive elements; real-time data to support just-in-time learning; rewards and incentive structures that are communally defined and reinforced; and multiple, overlapping expressions of recognition and reputation. But are there larger ideas that help hold these various elements together in ways that move them beyond a kind of "gamification" of the classroom? Are there design principles that can be expressed as elegantly as those developed by Naismith for basketball that enabled the game to be taken up and played in ways that may have been stylistically different yet fundamentally the same?

My colleagues and I at the Institute of Play were faced with this very question in 2011 when the institute started work on the design of a second public school—CICS ChicagoQuest. We challenged ourselves to distill the institute's game-like learning model into a set of guiding design principles that expressed the essence of the model without defining exactly how it would be instantiated on the ground. This restriction was important for the following reason. Design can be defined as the practice of exploring the tension between the existing and the potential. It is a mode of transformative action that design historian Clive Dilnot (1998) has noted allows us to see "how we negotiate the limits of what we understand, at any moment, as the actual." Game design pushes this concept even further by legislating through the design of possibility spaces that arise from a set of rules. These rules give shape to the limits of the actual and provide opportunities for players to discover these limits by pushing against them in creative ways. When this happens, the experience of play is born, in all of its transformative potential.

As such, we did not want to create a second school that simply replicated the on-the-ground design of Quest to Learn. Rather, we saw the design challenge as one of remix, where the core model, described by a set of guiding principles, was adapted to the needs of a local context. In order to do this, however, we needed to articulate the principles in such a way that their transformative potential was actionable. We needed to choose principles that worked like the rules of a game: defining a space of possibility that was inscribed with a set of features that, when realized, would give rise to connected, game-like learning experiences.

Following are the set of seven guiding design principles that emerged from a process of reflection on the Quest school model. In some respects, these dovetail with Gee's comments about passionate affinity spaces and in others they do not insofar as both commentaries are provisional and designed to stimulate conversation rather than frame ideas into concrete. Embedded within each of the seven principles are several design features. These features point to specific elements that can be designed in support of the larger guiding principle. Design features represent our thinking on the types of mechanisms that need to be present to support realization of the larger principle within a designed learning context. Much of the original thinking around the design features was developed in collaboration with my colleagues from the Connected Learning Research Network, including Mimi Ito, Kris Gutiérrez, Sonia Livingstone, Bill Penuel, Jean Rhodes, Juliet Schor, and Craig S. Watkins.

One caveat: while the principles offered up here continue to be play-tested daily by Quest teachers, school leaders, curriculum developers, game designers, and students, they are a work in progress. In attempting to describe the defining contours of a dynamic system, the model most surely errs on the side of simplicity, in order to allow for uptake and revision of the principles by a diverse group of stakeholders. The approach mirrors the design of games—start with a simple set of rules that, in combination, produce an experience that is rich in meaningful choice for the player. These choices are the means by which the player engages with the system and ultimately transforms it.

In designing a set of rules, the onus is on making sure that the space of possibility that arises from them is not too big, too complex, or too restraining: too big and players get lost; too complex and players are unable to parse out the relationship between their actions and outcomes in the game; too restraining and players lose all sense of agency. The sweet spot sits somewhere in between.

1. *Everyone is a participant.* Create a shared culture and practice where everyone contributes, which may mean that different students contribute different types of expertise. Design learning experiences that invite participation and provide many different ways for individuals and groups to contribute. Build in roles and supports for teachers, mentors, outside experts, and instructors to act as translators and bridge builders for learners across domains and contexts. Make sure barriers to entry are low and that there are opportunities for students, especially new students, to lurk and leech (i.e., observe and borrow); peer-based exchange, like communication and sharing, should be made easy and reciprocal. Develop a diverse set of resources to support teaching and mentorship activities. Consider developing challenge-based experiences that invite networks of experts in to collaborate with students; design problem sets in ways that capitalize on global expertise.

2. *Feedback is immediate and ongoing.* Create structures for students to receive ongoing feedback on their progress against learning and assessment goals. Feedback should include structures for guidance and mentorship, which may take place via the online communities associated with the curriculum or in classroom, after school, or home settings. Create ways for this feedback to increase in depth and richness as the types of contributions students make or the roles they take on grow and change. Provide opportunities for students to take on leadership roles, based on expertise and interest. Make sure there are plenty of ways for them to share their work with their peers, solicit feedback, teach others how to do things, and reflect on their own learning. One key aspect of

this is allowing every student's contribution to be visible to everyone else in the group. Utilize the tools associated with the school's social network platforms to enable communication and exchange between peers, who may or may not be part of the same group or setting.

3. *Challenge is constant.* One of the more powerful features of challenge-based experiences is that they create a *need to know* by challenging students to solve a problem whose resources have been placed just out of reach. Students must develop expertise in order to access the resources. They are motivated to do so either because the learner finds the problem context itself engaging or because it connects to an existing interest or passion. Make sure that learning activities support situated inquiry and discovery so that students have rich contexts within which to practice with concepts and content. Consider including "gates," levels, or other structures that limit access to highlight opportunities for advancement. As students advance against a challenge, provide a diverse array of opportunities for them to build social and cultural capital around their progress. Explore teaming and competing structures like competitions and collaborations that mix collaborative and competitive elements in the service of problem discovery and solving.

4. *Learning happens by doing.* Learning is participatory and experiential. Students learn by proposing, testing, playing with, and validating theories about the world. Challenge-based learning experiences should be designed around performance-based activities that give rise to authentic learning tasks. Make sure that learners have access to robust mechanisms for discoverability; resources supporting problem discovery and solving are easy to find, diverse, and easily sharable across networks. Peer-produced tutorials, frequently asked questions, and other materials should be easy to find, use, and share. Think of ways to situate problem sets within a context that has meaning or relevance for participants, be this peer, interest, or academic in orientation. Provide students with multiple, overlapping opportunities to interact with experts and mentors who model expert identities associated with the problem space. Allow students to collaborate in many different ways, as they explore different roles or identities related to the design project at hand.

5. *Everything is interconnected.* Students should be provided with multiple learning contexts for engaging in game-like learning—contexts in which they receive immediate feedback on progress, have access to tools for planning and reflection, and are given opportunities for mastery of specialist language and practices. Create infrastructures for students to share their work, skill, and knowledge with others across networks, groups, and communities. These

channels might take the form of online public portfolios, streamed video or podcasts, student-led parent conferences, or public events where work is critiqued and displayed, to name but a few. Allow students to make interest-, peer-, and academic-based identities, status, and achievement visible across settings of home, school, afterschool, and peer group. Build in roles and supports for teachers, mentors, outside experts, and instructors to act as translators and bridge builders for learners across domains and contexts. Provide diverse forms of recognition and assessment, which might take varied forms, including prizes, badges, rankings, ratings, and reviews. A social network platform can play a key role in supporting this principle.

6. *Failure is celebrated as iteration.* Create many opportunities for students and teachers to learn through failure. All learning experiences with a game-like learning model should embrace a process of prototyping and iteration, based on a game design methodology: students work through multiple versions of any idea or solution, integrating ongoing feedback into the learning process, and developing debriefings that identify strengths and weaknesses of both process and solution. In some cases, students may choose to build on previous solutions or approaches of other students, seeing themselves as contributors to a larger body of collaboratively generated knowledge. Participants build both cultural and intellectual capital as a result.

7. *It kind of feels like play.* Create learning experiences that are fundamentally engaging, learner centered, and organized to support inquiry and creativity. Rules create limits: learning experiences invite interaction and inquiry into the limits and possibilities of the platform, tools, problem spaces, or media in which students are working. Challenges organize inquiry so that learning experiences pose challenges for participants to overcome in ways that are engaging and aligned with interest and ability level. Support learners in defining goals that structure the nature of their interaction and inquiry from moment to moment, as well as longer term. Align core mechanics with learning goals; in other words, the ways in which participants interact with the learning environment—the mechanics or "verbs" of their interaction—align with core learning outcomes. Action is therefore never *not* in the service of the learning taking place. Design choice is to be meaningful: participants power movement through the experience via choices they make along the way. Help students reflect on the choices they are making in the design or transformation of a system—empower them to see themselves as agents of change.

Table 8.1 offers a view of the seven principles at-a-glance. It is important to call attention to the fact that the model is systemic—no single principle or fea-

TABLE 8.1
Seven Guiding Principles of Game-Like Learning

Design Principle	Supporting Design Features	Guiding Reflections
Everyone is a participant	• Low barriers to entry and access • Varied participation opportunities and ways to contribute • Diversity in level and type of expertise supported • Sharing is easy and reciprocal • Incentives and rewards for learner support • Integrated professional development programming	• Do all students have a role to play, which allows them to contribute? • Is peer-based exchange like communication and sharing easy and reciprocal? • Are a diverse set of resources to support teaching and mentorship available?
Feedback is immediate and ongoing	• Guiding feedback and mentorship • Increasingly rich feedback and support for specialization • Leadership development opportunities • Visibility of contributions enables communication and exchange between peers	• Are students using data as tools to inform their learning? • Are there opportunities for students to take on leadership roles, based on expertise and interest? • Are contributions visible to everyone in the group?
Challenge is constant	• Challenges create a "need to know" • A need to share enables peer exchange • Embedded infrastructure for sharing across individuals, groups, and communities • Structured access • Contributions organized around a shared culture, knowledge base, or purpose • Infrastructure to support collaborations and competitions	• Is a "need to know" created by organizing learning around solving complex problems set in engaging contexts? • Does the design of the challenge create both a reason and an opportunity for sharing? • Is a shared interest being pursued via the challenge? • Do students have opportunities to both team and compete?
Learning happens by doing	• Participatory and experiential contexts • Performance-based and authentic task design • Robust mechanisms for search and discoverability • Abundant learning resources organized around challenges	• Are students involved in hands-on inquiry? • Are students being challenged to tinker, explore, hypothesize, and test assumptions? • Does the learning experience allow students to show understanding in multiple ways?

(continued)

TABLE 8.1
(*continued*)

Design Principle	Supporting Design Features	Guiding Reflections
	• Ongoing interaction with experts and mentors • Varied opportunities to build social capital	• Are support resources linked to challenges and easy to find and share? • Do students have access to mentors who are modeling best practices within the domain?
Everything is interconnected	• Diverse forms of recognition and assessment are visible across communities • Cross-site sharing mechanisms for credentialing, mentoring, and assessment • Feedback loops reinforce activity across spaces and sites • Support multiple, overlapping pathways toward mastery	• Does the experience build in opportunities for authority and expertise to be shared and made reciprocal among learners/mentors/teachers? • Is there a way for students to share their work, skill, and knowledge with others across networks, groups, and communities? • Are adults helping students to make connections across contexts and communities?
Failure is celebrated as iteration	• Easy to use prototyping tools • Numerous structured opportunities for reflection • Student-level controls for making work public • Low-risk "messing around" spaces afford opportunities to see many examples of possible outcomes • Rubrics are leveled through novice, apprentice, senior, master stages	• Are students prototyping and iterating to improve ideas and understanding? • Do students have control over when and to whom they share their work? • Are students allowed to remix and build on the work of others to meet a shared goal? • Is evidence of progress toward goals visible to students?
It kind of feels like play	• Rules create limits • Challenges organize inquiry • Goals provide purposeful interaction • Choice is meaningful • Core mechanics align with learning goals • Reflection is integrated throughout	• Is the learning experience engaging, learner centered, and organized to support inquiry and creativity? • Are students making choices that matter? • Are students given opportunities to reflect on their understanding of the current and future state of a system?

ture is seen as acting on its own accord. The fact that the principles are listed separately here, with associated design features that seem isolated, should be understood as a limitation of the page, not as a rule of the model. The narrative examples that have been included throughout the chapter are one attempt to show the principles and features in action.

Conclusion

Engagement is, first and foremost, a way into learning, as the examples included throughout this chapter and the chapters of Gee, Fullerton, and Jenkins have attempted to show. The design of engagement is really a problem of the design of learning experiences, whether or not these experiences occur in the classroom or in spaces beyond its walls. And designing for connected, game-like learning requires a mindset that sees the various spaces of formal and informal learning opportunities as integrally linked. A designer's job, as creator of the contexts, activities, and connectors linking each, be they assessment or credential systems, mentor networks, communities, or tools and technologies, is to attend first to an invitation to participate.

In my own research and practice, I have long worked to understand the role game design might play in creating invitations to participate. The design of the Quest schools began with the question of how the design of a school could be reimagined as an invitation to engage. Research showed that many young people did not see school as a place that cared anything at all about whether or not they were engaged and, by turn, successful. It seemed clear that many teachers were not being given opportunities to see that the design of learning experiences fit into their domain of expertise. Reports like "Faster and Fancier Books: Mapping the Gaps between Expert and Public Understandings of Digital Media and Learning," by the FrameWorks Institute (Kendall-Taylor, Lindland, and Mikulak 2010) showed that most parents had very little reason to believe that the type of engagement they were seeing in their children around games and social media had any connection at all with an institution called school.

In response to these observations and following the principles outlined in this chapter, learning experiences within Quest to Learn were inspired by a process of prototyping and iteration, based on a game design methodology: students work through multiple versions of any idea or solution, integrating ongoing feedback into the learning process, and developing debriefings that identify strengths and weaknesses of both process and solution. In some cases, students may choose to build on previous solutions or approaches of other students, seeing themselves as contributors to a larger body of collaboratively generated knowledge. Participants build both cultural and intellectual capital as a result.

Teachers and students alike are encouraged to manage and reflect on their evolving identities as learners, producers, peers, researchers, and citizens. As a result, the focus is on learning how to *produce meaning*—for themselves and for external audiences—within complex, multimodal contexts. Creativity, expression, and innovation underlie this learning as students practice through the coding and decoding of linguistic, numeric, social, and cultural systems. This approach challenges traditional barriers among consumer, producer-viewer, and designer, allowing students to gain the skills to act as full citizens within a connected, participatory landscape (Salen et al. 2011).

As noted earlier, there is still a tremendous amount of work to be done to understand the promises and limitations of a game-based framework for the design of learning in higher education. Despite the existence and relative success of both Quest to Learn and CICS ChicagoQuest (students at Quest to Learn have tested slightly above average across the city on standardized tests in its first two years while showing gains in twenty-first-century skills like systems thinking, teamwork, and time management; no data are yet available for CICS ChicagoQuest, as it is in its first year), it will take years to understand the kind of effect that game-based pedagogy might ultimately have on the lives of students. Many more examples are needed of game-like learning environments, of game-based assessments, of models of mentorship and coaching that take their cues from game design and play. A robust research agenda must be more fully developed and informed by ongoing work in the learning sciences to understand exactly what it is about game-like environments that support or get in the way of good learning.

Both formal research and anecdotal evidence from the schools collected thus far show this: many of the students are changing. They are becoming more agile in their thinking, more creative in their problem solving, and more attuned to their skills as collaborators. Like Naismith's players, they are learning to pivot away from notions that school has to be boring and solely driven by adult voices, away from the idea that learning cannot be hard and engaging at the same time, and away from a belief that school is not a place for them.

Ultimately connected, game-like learning seeks to enable individuals to learn to work effectively across networks designed for educational, social, and civic purposes and to develop strategies to establish and mobilize social networks for their own purposes. If done well, such designs would provide opportunities for young people to learn and work within connected networks, rather than within isolated educational institutions, supported through innovative uses of social media. Young people within such experiences would be assessed in interacting with tools, resources, and collaborators; developing capacities to find information and judge its credibility; building reputations; and trusting while forming youth-centered identities. Young people would be creatively constructing new learning networks as they reflect on how learning is connected to their interests, passions, and life goals. Last, they would be engaged with others, via game-like learning and the connected networks it enables—growing, building, learning, and being.

REFERENCES

Cremin, Lawrence A. 1979. *Traditions of American Education*. New York: Basic Books.
Dilnot, Clive. 1998. "The Science of Uncertainty: The Potential Contribution of Design Knowledge." Paper presented at the Ohio Conference, Doctoral Education in Design, Pittsburgh School of Design, Carnegie Mellon University, Pittsburgh, October 8–11.
Gee, James Paul. 2004. *Situated Language and Learning: A Critique of Traditional Schooling*. New York: Routledge.
———. 2008. "Learning and Games." In *The Ecology of Games: Connecting Youth, Games, and Learning*, edited by Katie Salen, 21–40. Cambridge, MA: MIT Press.
Halpern, Diane F. 2002. "Cognitive Science and the Work of Reform." *New Directions for Higher Education, Special Issue: Building Robust Learning Environments in Undergraduate Science, Technology, Engineering, and Mathematics* 119:41–44.
Hickey, Dave. 1997. *Air Guitar: Essays on Art & Democracy*. Los Angeles: Art Issues Press.
Ito, Mizuko, Kris Gutiérrez, Sonia Livingstone, Bill Penuel, Jean Rhodes, Katie Salen, Juliet Schor, Julian Sefton-Green, and S. Craig Watkins. 2013. *Connected Learning*. Irvine, CA: Digital Media and Learning Research Hub.
Kendall-Taylor, Nathaniel, Eric Lindland, and Anna Mikulak. 2010. "'Faster and Fancier Books': Mapping the Gaps between Expert and Public Understandings of Digital Media and Learning." Washington, DC: FrameWorks Institute.
Klopfer, Eric, Scot Osterweil, and Katie Salen. 2010. "Moving Educational Games Forward." Cambridge MA: MIT Education Arcade. Accessed September 4, 2012. http://education.mit.edu/papers/MovingLearningGamesForward_EdArcade.pdf.
Lakhani, Karim R. 2008. *InnoCentive.com (A)*. Cambridge, MA: Harvard Business School Publishing.
Salen, Katie, Robert Torres, Loretta Wolozin, Rebecca Rufo-Tepper, and Arana Shapiro. 2011. *Quest to Learn: Developing the School for Digital Kids*. Cambridge, MA: MIT Press. Accessed August 16, 2013. http://mitpress.mit.edu/sites/default/files/titles/free_download/9780262515658_Quest_to_Learn.pdf.

Schaffer, David Williamson. 2006. *How Computer Games Help Children Learn.* New York: Palgrave Macmillan.

Shute, Valerie, Vanessa P. Dennen, Yoon Jeong Kim, Oktay Donmez, and Chen-Yen Wang. In press. "21st Century Assessment to Promote 21st Century Learning: The Benefits of Blinking." In *Games, Learning, Assessment*, edited by James Paul Gee. Boston: MIT Press.

Shute, Valerie, Matthew Ventura, and Yoon Jeon Kim. 2011. "Synthesis Report on the Games, Learning, and Assessment (GLA) Workshop." Paper prepared for the Gates and MacArthur Foundations. Accessed September 4, 2012. http://myweb.fsu.edu/vshute/pdf/GLA%20report.pdf.

Squire, Kurt. 2006. "From Content to Context: Video Games as Designed Experiences." *Educational Researcher* 35(8):19–29.

PART THREE

What Do We Know about Games and What Do We Need to Learn?

CHAPTER NINE

Assessing Learning in Video Games

VALERIE SHUTE, MATTHEW VENTURA,
YOON JEON KIM, AND LUBIN WANG

As others have noted throughout the book, video games are hugely popular. For instance, revenues for the video game industry reached $7.2 billion in 2007, and overall 72% of the population in the United States plays video games (Entertainment Software Association 2011; Fullerton 2008). The amount of time spent playing games also continues to increase (Escobar-Chaves and Anderson 2008). Considering the fact that many college students are avid game players, it is not surprising that institutions of higher education have begun to acknowledge the power of video games (Jones 2003). That is, to meet the needs of a new generation of students entering college, educators and researchers have begun searching for ways to creatively incorporate video games into their courses.

Besides being a popular activity, playing video games has been shown to be positively related to a variety of cognitive skills (e.g., visual-spatial abilities, attention), personality types, academic performance, and civic engagement (Chory and Goodboy 2011; Ferguson and Garza 2011; Green and Bavlier 2007; Shaw, Grayson, and Lewis 2005; Skoric, Teo, and Neo 2009; Ventura, Shute, and Kim 2012; Witt, Massman, and Jackson 2011). As Ragusa notes in her chapter, games also have gender-related facets that can be exploited to encourage equity. Video games also motivate students to learn valuable academic content and skills, within and outside of the game (Barab et al. 2010; DeRouin-Jessen 2008). Finally, studies have shown that playing video games can promote pro-social and civic behavior (Ferguson and Garza 2011).

In this chapter, we describe how well-designed video games can be used as vehicles to assess and support learning across a variety of knowledge and skills.

We also present a framework for designing such embedded assessments into video games and illustrate the approach with examples from a physics game. We conclude with our thoughts on future research in this area. Throughout the chapter, we use the term *video games* to refer to games that are played on gaming consoles, computers, and mobile devices. Our chapter stands in contrast to Weiland's; we appreciate the caution that he provides. Our focus, however, is based on the assumption that games and learning have unique contributions to make for educational progress. The challenge is to understand how to first assess the learning outcomes of games and then improve games so that their learning potential might be more fully exploited.

Educational Benefits of Video Games

Before discussing ways to use games to assess learning, we first need to define what we mean by learning. Our conception of learning is that it is a lifelong process of accessing, interpreting, and evaluating information and experiences, and then transforming those into knowledge, skills, conceptualizations, values, and dispositions. This is a broader and more fluid view of learning compared to more conventional (e.g., cognitive, behavioral) perspectives, which tend to ask: "Did the student remember X and Y on the test?"

Learning also represents a change from one point in time to another in terms of knowing, doing, believing, and feeling. Learning is not necessarily linear; that is, knowledge can start off very shallow and then quickly explode into a rich knowledge base over a relatively short period of time. For example, in language learning people start by learning a few words, but in a span of a year that number can increase to hundreds of words and phrases, in addition to grammatical knowledge (Smith 2002).

The learning theories that best suit educational game design include socioconstructivism and situated learning (Lave and Wenger 1991; Vygotsky 1978). On the basis of these theories, the learner is active in the learning process, where "doing" is more important than listening, and the learner determines the pace of learning. Moreover, learning in many cases is the result of interactions with a problem context where learners actively construct meaning in the process of solving problems, large and small.

How can video games foster learning? Video games can be seen as vehicles for exposing players to intellectual activities. Much like taking a course in college or playing a sport, video games engage players in activities that require intellectual effort. People who want to excel at something—from athletes to dancers to surgeons to computer programmers—spend countless hours practicing their craft. By continually refining techniques and developing new maneuvers to enhance their skills, they manifest the belief that practice is critical to improvement. There is considerable support in the literature, going back more than 100 years, for the idea that "practice makes perfect" or, in its less extreme form, that "practice makes better" (Bryan and Harter 1899; Newell and Rosenbloom 1981; Schneider and Shiffrin 1977; Shiffrin and Schneider 1977; Shute, Gawlick, and Gluck 1998; Thorndike 1898; Underdahl, Palacio-Cayetano, and Stevens 2001). The common conclusion across all of this work is that people become more accurate and faster the more often they perform a task. Content learning or skill acquisition thus represents a change in a person that occurs as a function of experience or practice. But practice can be boring and frustrating, causing some learners to abandon their practice and hence learning. This is where the principle of game design comes in—good games can provide an engaging environment designed to keep practice interesting.

Can important skills, like problem solving, really be improved by playing video games? Polya (1945) has argued that problem solving is not an innate skill but something that can be developed: "Solving problems is a practical skill, let us say, like swimming. . . . Trying to solve problems, you have to observe and imitate what other people do when solving problems; and, finally, you learn to solve problems by doing them" (5). Students are not born with problem-solving skills. Instead, these skills are cultivated when students have opportunities to solve problems proportionate to their knowledge. Additionally, cognitive complexity theory predicts that video games should lead to learning because they simultaneously engage players' affective and cognitive processes (Tennyson and Robert 2008). These affective processes can be seen as dependent on how engaging a video game is, where engagement is a function of the core principles of good game design working in concert (Fullerton 2008; Shute, Rieber, and Van Eck 2011). Some of the features of good games include adaptive challenges, goals and rules, interactive problem solving, control (of learning and the game environment), ongoing feedback, and sensory stimuli.

Given the feature of presenting adaptive challenges to players, video games can actually cause a state of frustration (or "pleasant frustration") (Gee 2007). In good games, obstacles, constraints, and generally wicked problems become something that we want to resolve because reaching for goals and ultimately succeeding are highly rewarding. McGonigal (2011) has referred to this as a positive kind of stress, called eustress, which is actually good for us, providing us with a sense of motivation and desire to succeed. We see this pleasant frustration (or eustress) as a positive aspect of video games because it shows that students are being pushed to their limits, a requirement for teaching in the zone of proximal development (Vygotsky 1978). This repeated frustration can also prepare students for tolerating frustration, a common emotional response in higher education.

Consider, for example, the popular game *Portal 2*. In *Portal 2*, the player has to navigate through a three-dimensional environment with a "portal gun" that allows the player to teleport by shooting "portals" into special walls. In the game, the player must first determine the spatial environment and then use various tools and the portal gun to open a door. Frustration can arise quickly from: (a) not knowing the spatial environment, (b) not understanding the problem, (c) not knowing how to the use various tools to open the door, and (d) a recurring character in the game that taunts the player with insults. In many cases this frustration can be overwhelming after repeated failures. However, this type of failure and frustration is important to experience (and overcome) because it helps students prepare for the challenges of higher education, and life in general. Thus, video games have the power to help students cope with frustration by repeated exposure to challenging intellectual activities. Educators who wish to take advantage of the potential of video games to support their students' learning may not know how to employ assessment in (or with) the game to capture information concerning what, how, and to what extent players are learning from the games.

Developing Good Educational Video Games

Video games typically require a player to apply various competencies to succeed in the game (e.g., creativity, problem solving, persistence, and collaboration). The competencies required to succeed in many games also happen to be the same ones that are needed to succeed in higher education and that companies are looking for in today's highly competitive economy (Gee, Hull, and Landshear 1996). But for video games to gain a footing in education there needs to be more collaboration among educators, researchers, and game designers. Having a shared understanding of these rather isolated specialty areas is critical in order to move forward with the design of engaging educational games.

Collaborative research and development should include the right balance of educators and researchers—with expertise in assessment, learning, and content—as well as game designers to optimize the development of well-designed educational games. These games would allow for the assessment and support of learning in an engaging way within a rich and authentic context. Knowing what (and how well) students are learning in a video game is a function of sound assessment practices. That is, the primary purpose of an assessment is to collect information that will enable the assessor to make inferences about a person's competencies—what they know, believe, and can do and to what degree. Evidence-centered design (ECD) is one such approach that is suitable for building valid and reliable assessments that ultimately may be embedded in video games to monitor and support learning (Shute 2011; Shute et al. 2009).

ECD is an assessment design framework that consists of three main models that work in concert: competency model, evidence model, and task model. A good assessment (which could be a video game) elicits behavior that bears evidence about key competencies, and it must also provide principled interpretations of that evidence in terms that suit the purpose of the assessment (Mislevy, Almond, and Lukas 2004; Mislevy, Steinberg, and Almond 2003). To build an ECD assessment, the competency model is first defined. This represents a set of psychological constructs on which inferences are based (Almond and Mislevy 1999). These constructs can be knowledge, skills, dispositions, beliefs, or whatever you want to assess.

The evidence model attempts to answer the question about what behaviors or performances serve as evidence for variables within the competency model. Task models describe features of situations that will be used to elicit performance. The main purpose of tasks, such as levels or quests in a game, is to elicit dynamic evidence (which is observable and empirical) about competencies (which are unobservable and theoretical). Results from the task model in a traditional assessment consist of a set of items or problems; but in the context of video game-based assessments, task modeling produces a collection of problems designed to capture particular types of performance data that would then inform the targeted learning goals or competencies. Because individuals learn in action, assessment should be situated within this learning process (Gee 2003; Salen and Zimmerman 2005). The ECD framework helps operationalize what learners do in complex contexts and how it relates to constructs of interest. Additionally, ECD helps us link specific learner actions within games to constructs, without interrupting what learners are doing or thinking (Shute 2011).

In summary, the ECD framework is based on the assumption that assessment is, at its core, an evidentiary argument. Its strength resides in the development of performance-based assessments where what is being assessed is latent or not apparent (Rupp et al. 2010). The ECD framework begins by determining what we want to assess (i.e., the claims we want to make about learners) and clarifying the intended goals, processes, and outcomes of learning. This information about the student can be used to support learning. That is, it can serve as the basis for delivering timely and targeted feedback to the student-player, as well as presenting a new task or quest that is right at the cusp of the student's skill level, in line with flow theory (Csikszentmihalyi 1990) and Vygotsky's (1978) zone of proximal development.

Stealth Assessment in Video Games

In addition to the ECD methodology for assessment development, new assessment technologies are needed to capture the vast amounts of data that can come from video gameplay. One technology we developed and currently use is called *stealth assessment*. Stealth assessments are performance-based assessments embedded within games to dynamically, unobtrusively, accurately, and transparently measure how players are progressing relative to targeted competencies (Shute 2011; Shute et al. 2009). Embedding performance-based assessments within games provide a way to monitor a player's current level on valued competencies and then use that information as the basis for support, such as adjusting the difficulty level of challenges.

How does stealth assessment work? During gameplay, students naturally produce rich sequences of actions while performing complex tasks, drawing on a variety of competencies. Evidence needed to assess the competencies is thus provided by the players' interactions with the game itself (i.e., the processes of play), which can be contrasted with the end product(s) of an activity—the norm in most educational environments. Thus, stealth assessment is built within the game (without changing fundamental game mechanics) and statistically aligns the game problems and players' interactions in the game with the underlying competencies of interest.

Currently, we are exploring the validity of stealth assessments in the video game *Newton's Playground*. In this research, we are evaluating the degree to which our stealth assessments yield valid and reliable measures of the targeted competencies (e.g., creativity, persistence, and conceptual physics).

Newton's Playground

Newton's Playground emphasizes two-dimensional physics simulations, including gravity, mass, potential and kinetic energy, and transfer of momentum. The

Figure 9.1. Golf problem in *Newton's Playground*.

objective of each problem in the game is to guide a green ball from a prede-
termined starting point to a red balloon. All movement obeys the rules of
physics relating to Newton's three laws of motion. The primary game mechanic is drawing physical objects on the screen that "come to life" once the
object is drawn. For example, in figure 9.1, the player must draw a golf club on a
pin (i.e., little circle on the cloud) to make it swing down to hit the ball. In the
depicted solution, the player also drew a ramp to prevent the ball from falling
down a pit.

The speed of (and, importantly, the impulse delivered by) the swinging golf
club is dependent on the mass distribution of the club and the angle from which
it was dropped to swing. The ball will then fly at a certain speed and trajectory. If drawn properly, the ball will hit the balloon. The various problems in
Newton's Playground require the player to create and use pendulums, levers,
springboards, and so forth to move the ball. All solutions are drawn with color
pens using the mouse.

Agents of Force and Motion

Newton's Playground requires players to create and use the following devices to
help the ball reach the balloon:

1. *Ramp*: A ramp can be employed to change the direction of the motion of the ball (or another object). In some cases, other tools (e.g., a pendulum or nudge) are needed to get the ball to start moving.

2. *Lever*: A seesaw or lever involves net torque. A lever rotates around a fixed point usually called a fulcrum or pivot point. An object residing on a lever gains potential energy as it is raised.

3. *Pendulum*: A swinging pendulum directs an impulse tangent to its direction of motion. The idealized pendulum is a specialized case of the physical pendulum for which the mass distribution helps determine the frequency. One can draw a physical pendulum in *Newton's Playground*, and the motion will be determined by the mass distribution.

4. *Springboard*: A springboard (or diving board) stores elastic potential energy provided by a falling weight. Elastic potential energy becomes kinetic as the weight is released.

5. *Pin*: A pin allows the position of one body to be fixed in space. Like a nail, it supplies a force large enough to resist motion of the point it is attached to. Two pins hold a body immobile against a background.

6. *Rope*: Ropes generally transmit tension between objects. If a rope is draped over a pulley with masses attached at both ends and the masses are equal, their weights are equal, and the net force on each will be the difference between the tension pulling up on the mass and the force of gravity pulling down. Ropes can also act like trampolines, generating forces on objects by stretching the rope and then removing the force (by deleting objects) to produce upward momentum on the ball.

7. *Nudge*: An arrow in *Newton's Playground* allows the user to poke or nudge an object into motion.

Newton's Playground is a game that we developed to support stealth assessment of focal competencies (i.e., conceptual physics understanding, conscientiousness, and creativity). This game was inspired by and modeled after a popular physics game called *Crayon Physics Deluxe* by Petri Purho. *Newton's Playground* has the same basic game mechanics as *Crayon Physics Deluxe* (e.g., draw objects that serve to move the ball to an end point), and our game uses the same physics engine (i.e., Box2D).

Developing stealth assessments in *Newton's Playground* required a comprehensive delineation of player actions that would count as varying levels of success in the game (i.e., defining the evidence model). It also entailed creating new problems in the game in line with the task model to meet specific needs of the assessments. We are currently implementing stealth assessments for two competencies (conceptual physics understanding and persistence).

Conceptual Physics

Over the past several decades it has become very clear that many students who have gotten acceptable grades in one or more physics courses actually have very limited practical understanding of the physics involved. Numerous studies have shown that a passing grade does not mean that a student has an appreciation of physical principles (Crouch and Mazur 2001; Hake 1998; Halloun and Hestenes 1985). For instance, Halloun and Hestenes (1985) found that only 15% of their 478 college physics students showed an accurate understanding of the relationship between unbalanced forces and acceleration (i.e., Newton's second law: $F = ma$). This has led to widespread adoption of the text *Conceptual Physics* by Paul Hewitt (2009) and the development of two instruments, the Force Concept Inventory (Hestenes, Wells, and Swackhamer 1992) and the Mechanics Baseline Test (Hestenes and Wells 1992), now widely used to compare student mastery of the concepts of mechanics. Recognition of the problem has also led to a renewed interest in the mechanisms by which physics students make the transition from naive or folk physics to Newtonian physics (DiSessa 1982) and to the possibility of video game playing assisting in the process (White 1984).

Physics engines are becoming pervasive in gaming environments, providing a sense of realism in a game (e.g., Havok engine). Within these gaming environments, players can experiment with principles of physics such as impulse, inertia, vector addition, elastic collision, gravity, velocity, acceleration, free fall, mass, force, and projectile motion. The degree that players apply these principles correctly in *Newton's Playground* constitutes evidence for conceptual understanding of physics.

Following Hewitt's textbook on foundational conceptual physics (Feynman 1964; Feynmann, Leighton, and Sands 1964), we interpret competency in conceptual physics to involve the following:

1. *Conceptual understanding of Newton's three laws of motion.* Newton's three laws of motion provide a conceptual understanding of how objects interact in the environment. The first law tells us that an object in rest stays in rest in the absence of any forces, and an object in motion stays in motion in the absence of any forces. The second law ($F = ma$) tells us how the

motion of the particle (object) evolves when it experiences a nonzero net force. Here F is the net force applied (i.e., the vector sum of all the forces acting on the object), m is the mass of the object, and a is the object's acceleration. Thus, the net force applied to an object produces a proportional acceleration. That is, if an object is accelerating, then there is a net nonzero force on it. Any mass that is gained or lost by the system will cause a change in momentum that is not the result of an external force. In simple terms, it takes less force to accelerate an object that has less mass compared to one with more mass. The third law states for every action there is an equal and opposite reaction. This is commonly described by hitting a tree with a baseball bat. The force exerted on the tree by the swinging bat is equal to the force exerted back on the person swinging the bat.

2. *Conceptual understanding of potential and kinetic energy.* Potential energy exists when a force acts on an object to restore the object to its resting point (or "lower energy configuration"). For example, when a springboard (like in *Newton's Playground*) is bent downward, it exerts an upward force to return to its unbent position. The action of bending the springboard down requires energy, and the force acting on the springboard to return it to its resting point is potential energy. When the bent springboard is released, the stored energy will be converted into kinetic energy.

3. *Conceptual understanding of conservation of angular momentum or torque.* The angular momentum of a system of objects about any point of reference can be computed from the position and momentum of each of the objects. A useful mental image is that of a figure skater or gymnast. Figure skaters will begin an elegant spin with arms outstretched. Once they start spinning, they typically draw their hands inward so that they can spin more rapidly. The sum of the mass of each object making up the skater times the square of the (perpendicular) distance to the axis of rotation is called the skater's *moment of inertia*. For a rotating object, the angular momentum is the product of the moment of inertia and the angular velocity. With negligible friction between skater and ice, decreasing the moment of inertia by moving the arms inward increases the rotational velocity. Similar considerations apply to a gymnast doing somersaults while dismounting, or a diver on the way down to the water. A torque with a short moment arm can counterbalance the torque exerted by a much smaller force with a larger moment arm and vice versa. Consider an ordinary lever. The force of support at the fulcrum is not directly given, but

the relation between torque and angular acceleration can easily be exploited by measuring torques from the fulcrum.

Newton's three laws constitute a parent principle that is pervasive in almost all problems in *Newton's Playground*. Successful use of each agent of force and motion is an indicator for a particular physics principle. Additionally, there are micro-indicators that inform each agent and principle as well. Table 9.1 displays our current set of micro-indicators for each conceptual physics principle.

All of the problems that are used in our stealth assessments require the player to create and use one or more agents of force and motion in the solution. A successful solution thus informs one or more of the competencies that we hope to develop in the student. As an illustration, consider the problem called *ballistic pendulum*, shown in figure 9.2.

This problem was inspired by an actual experiment often conducted in introductory physics courses in college to teach physics concepts. It requires the student to create a pendulum positioned so it hits the ball into a trajectory that ultimately hits the balloon. Successfully solving this problem suggests that the student has an intuitive concept of torque, linear, and angular momentum.

Consider another problem shown in figure 9.3. This problem specifically requires the player to use a springboard solution. The springboard is a variant of the lever in which one flat board rests on an object that is pinned in place

TABLE 9.1
Micro-indicators for Agents of Force and Motion

Agents	Micro-indicators
Ramp	1. Number of bends (or tubes, i.e., tortuosity) 2. Angle of each bend 3. Length of ramp
Lever	1. Length of the lever 2. Position of fulcrum 3. Height through which object falls before hitting lever 4. Mass of object 5. Location of the dropped object on lever (distance from fulcrum)
Pendulum	1. Angle of pendulum relative to horizontal fulcrum (180 degrees max) 2. Length between the axis point and the fulcrum (moment of inertia) 3. Mass (important when the pendulum hits something) 4. Position of pin
Springboard	1. Length of springboard 2. Mass of the object to weight it down 3. Position of the ball at release 4. Delete object or let fall off springboard 5. Angle of springboard at release (90 degrees max)

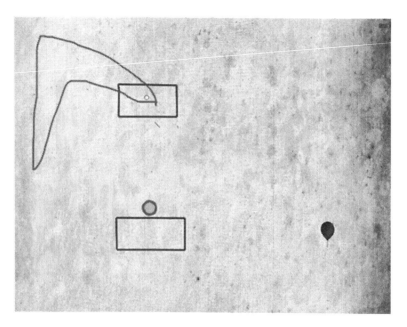

Figure 9.2. Ballistic pendulum problem in *Newton's Playground.*

but hangs over one edge. As shown in figure 9.3, a weight is affixed onto the free end of the springboard. The edge acts as an instantaneous axis of rotation, and the board experiences an angular acceleration that can be used to launch objects up into space. This requires knowledge of potential and kinetic energy, and conservation of angular momentum. As table 9.1 indicates, there are certain micro-indicators that we look for in a springboard problem. For example, understanding potential energy entails maximizing the "spring" of the springboard. This requires adding sufficient weight to exert a downward force on the springboard and can be accomplished either by dropping an object onto the springboard or by attaching an object to the springboard and then deleting the object once the springboard has bent down to a sufficient angle. In the latter case, knowing when to delete the object from the springboard requires knowledge of angular momentum in order to maximize the upward force on the ball.

Conscientiousness and Persistence

Persistence is the disposition to try hard, particularly in the face of failure (Shute and Ventura 2013). It is one of the main facets of conscientiousness,

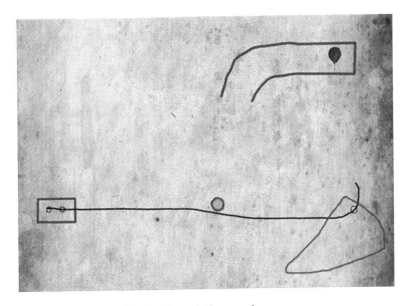

Figure 9.3. Diving board problem in *Newton's Playground.*

which has emerged as an important competency in predicting academic performance (Poropat 2009) as well as positive life outcomes (Roberts et al. 2007). Conscientiousness is a multifaceted competency that commonly includes tendencies related to being attentive, hardworking, careful, detail-minded, reliable, organized, productive, and persistent (Roberts et al. 2005).

Various studies and meta-analyses have shown the importance of self-report measures of conscientiousness in predicting a variety of important outcomes while controlling for cognitive ability. Conscientiousness has consistently been found to predict academic achievement from preschool to high school, to the postsecondary level and adulthood (Abe 2005; De Fruyt and Mervielde 1996; Noftle and Robins 2007; O'Conner and Paunonen 2007; Poropat 2009; Shiner, Masten, and Roberts 2003; Trapmann et al. 2007). Meta-analyses have linked conscientiousness with grades between $r = .21$ and $.27$, and the relationship is independent of intelligence (Noftle and Robins 2007; Proporat 2009).

Assessing persistence in a game such as *Newton's Playground* is primarily based on seeing how long players spend trying to solve difficult problems. The challenge in this assessment design is that different ability levels can preclude a player from solving a problem. To address this issue, we created difficulty indexes for all of the *Newton's Playground* problems. This allows us to incrementally increase the difficulty of problems to ensure that students will eventually get to problems they will have trouble solving. Difficulty indexes include the following:

1. *Relative location of ball to balloon.* If the balloon is positioned above the ball in a problem, this forces the player to use a lever, pulley, springboard, or pendulum to solve the problem (0–1 point).
2. *Obstacles.* This refers to the pathway between the ball and balloon. If the pathway is obstructed, this requires the player to project the ball in a very specific trajectory to hit the balloon (0–2 points).
3. *Distinct agents of force or motion.* (See previous section on Agents of Force and Motion.) A problem may require one or two agents to get the ball to the balloon (0–1 point).
4. *Novelty.* This addresses whether a problem is novel relative to other problems played. Problem solution is not easily determined from experience with other problems (0–2 points).

Each problem was evaluated under all of the rubrics to yield a total difficulty score (i.e., ranging from 0 to 6). Consider a problem called *Cave Story* shown in figure 9.4. This problem gets a difficulty score of 5, as the balloon is above

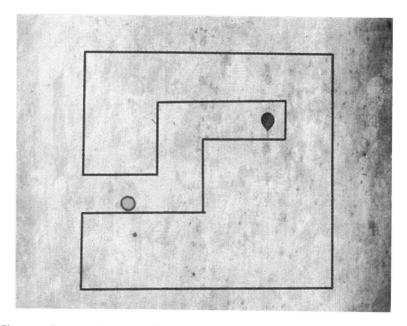

Figure 9.4. Cave story in *Newton's Playground.*

the ball (1), there's one obstacle which is a narrow pathway (1), two agents are typically needed to solve it (1), and there is no other problem like that in the game (2). Thus the problem in figure 9.4 would be a good problem to assess persistence as it will likely be unsolvable by many students.

Conclusion

As described in this chapter, games often require a player to apply various competencies to succeed. Many of these competencies are considered to be valuable for college graduates to succeed in the twenty-first-century work force (Casner-Lotto and Barrington 2006). For instance, in a strategy-based game like *Starcraft*, players must engage in causal reasoning and systems thinking. That is, they need to consider the ramifications of their actions in the game—not only on aspects of building their own interstellar galaxy but also in relation to other players' interstellar galaxies (e.g., how to strategically collect resources that will grow faster than those of competing players). In addition, many games require divergent thinking to solve hard problems (e.g., *Crayon Physics Deluxe*), encourage players to thoroughly explore a space before moving on (e.g., *L.A. Noire*), and call for players to work in teams to solve complex problems (e.g., *World of Warcraft*).

We encourage researchers and educators to look at how video games can be used to assess key skills needed in the twenty-first century. These skills are important in today's society, and video games have the power to assess and to help improve these skills through providing an engaging medium to practice the skills over extended periods of time.

Good game design coupled with a robust assessment approach should be the starting point for any research project focused on building a video game for educational purposes. That is, such research should combine game design with assessment methodologies such as ECD at the outset of the game design process rather than considering assessment as an afterthought. These assessments should be grounded in theory and should start with defining what competencies are important and how a video game can be used to assess and improve these competencies. Finally, more attention should be given to figuring out specifically how video games can help improve important new competencies. Because good video games hold such an engagement value, they are useful (and fun) tools for players to practice skills over extended amounts of time, especially for today's college students who grew up playing such games.

REFERENCES

Abe, Jo A. 2005. "The Predictive Validity of the Five-Factor Model of Personality with Pre-school Age Children: A Nine Year Follow-Up Study." *Journal of Research in Personality* 39:423–442.

Almond, Russel G., and Robert J. Mislevy. 1999. "Graphical Models and Computerized Adaptive Testing." *Applied Psychological Measurement* 23:223–237.

Barab, Sasha, Tyler Dodge, Adam Ingram-Goble, Patrick Pettyjohn, Kylie Peppler, Charlene Volk, and Maria Solomou. 2010. "Pedagogical Dramas and Transformational Play: Narratively Rich Games for Learning." *Mind, Culture, and Activity* 17:235–264.

Bryan, William L., and Noble Harter. 1899. "Studies on the Telegraphic Language: The Acquisition of a Hierarchy of Habits." *Psychological Review* 6:345–375.

Casner-Lotto, Jill, and Linda Barrington. 2006. *Are They Really Ready to Work? Employers' Perspectives on the Basic Knowledge and Applied Skills of New Entrants to the 21st Century Work Force.* New York: Conference Board.

Chory, Rebecca M., and Alan K. Goodboy. 2011. "Is Basic Personality Related to Violent and Non-violent Video Game Play and Preferences?" *Cyberpsychology, Behavior and Social Networking* 14:191–198.

Crouch, Catherine H., and Eric Mazur. 2001. "Peer Instruction: Ten Years of Experience and Results." *American Journal of Physics* 69:970–977.

Csikszentmihalyi, Mihály. 1990. "The Domain of Creativity." In *Theories of Creativity*, edited by Mark A. Runco and Robert S. Albert, 190–212. Newbury Park, CA: Sage.

De Fruyt, Filip, and Ivan Mervielde. 1996. "Personality and Interests as Predictors of Educational Streaming and Achievement." *European Journal of Personality* 10:405–425.

DeRouin-Jessen, Renée E. 2008. "Game On: The Impact of Game Features in Computer-Based Training." PhD diss., University of Central Florida.

DiSessa, Andrea A. 1982. "Unlearning Aristotelian Physics: A Study of Knowledge-Based Learning." *Cognitive Science* 6:37–75.

Entertainment Software Association. 2011. *2011 Sales, Demographic and Usage Data: Essential Facts about the Computer and Video Game Industry.* Washinton, DC.

Escobar-Chaves, Soledad L., and Craig A. Anderson. 2008. "Media and Risky Behaviors." *Future of Children* 18:147–180.

Ferguson, Christopher J., and Adolfo Garza. 2011. "Call of (Civic) Duty: Action Games and Civic Behaviors in a Large Sample of Youth." *Computers in Human Behavior* 27:770–775.

Feynman, Richard P. 1964. *The Character of Physical Law.* Ithaca, NY: Cornell University Press.

Feynman, Richard P., Robert B. Leighton, and Matthew Sands. 1964. *The Feynman Lectures in Physics.* Redwood City, CA: Addison-Wesley.

Fullerton, Tracy. 2008. *Game Design Workshop: A Playcentric Approach to Creating Innovative Games.* Burlington, MA: Elsevier.

Gee, James Paul. 2003. *What Video Games Have to Teach Us about Learning and Literacy.* New York: Palgrave Macmillan.

———. 2007. *Good Video Games + Good Learning: Collected Essays on Video Games, Learning and Literacy.* New York: Peter Lang.

Gee, James Paul, Glynda Hull, and Colin Landshear. 1996. *The New Work Order: Behind the Language of the New Capitalism.* Boulder, CO: Westview.

Green, Shawn C., and Daphne Bavlier. 2007. "Action-Video-Game Experience Alters the Spatial Resolution of Vision." *Psychological Science* 18:88–94.

Hake, Richard R. 1998. "Interactive-Engagement versus Traditional Methods: A Six-Thousand-Student Survey of Mecahnics Test Data for Introductory Physics Courses." *American Journal of Physics* 66:64–74.

Halloun, Ibrahim, and David Hestenes. 1985. "The Initial Knowledge State of College Physics Students." *American Journal of Physics* 53:1043–1055.

Hestenes, David, and Malcolm Wells. 1992. "A Mechanics Baseline Test." *Physics Teacher* 30:159–166.

Hestenes, David, Malcolm Wells, and Gregg Swackhamer. 1992. "Force Concept Inventory." *Physics Teacher* 30:141–158.

Hewitt, Paul. 2009. *Conceptual Physics*. 11th ed. San Francisco: Addison Wesley.

Jones, Steve. 2003. *Let the Games Begin: Gaming Technology and Entertainment among College Students*. Washinton, DC: Pew Research Center.

Lave, Jean, and Etienne Wenger. 1991. *Situated Learning: Legitimate Peripheral Participation*. Cambridge: Cambridge University Press.

McGonigal, Jane. 2011. *Reality Is Broken: Why Games Make Us Better and How They Can Change the World*. New York: Penguin Press.

Mislevy, Robert J., Russel G. Almond, and Janice F. Lukas. 2004. *A Brief Introduction to Evidence-Centered Design*. Los Angeles: Center for Research on Evaluation, Standards, and Student Testing.

Mislevy, Robert J., Linda S. Steinberg, and Russel J. Almond. 2003. *On the Structure of Educational Assessment*. Los Angeles: UCLA Center for Research on Evaluation, Standards, and Student Testing.

Newell, Allen, and Paul S. Rosenbloom. 1981. "Mechanism of Skill Acquisition and the Law of Practice." In *Cognitive Skills and Their Acquisition*, edited by Jone R. Anderson, 1–51. Hillsdale, NJ: Lawrence Erlbaum Associates.

Noftle, Erik E., and Richard W. Robins. 2007. "Personality Predictors of Academic Outcomes: Big Five Correlates of GPA and SAT Scores." *Journal of Personality and Social Psychology* 93:116–130.

O'Connor, Melissa, and Sampo V. Paunonen. 2007. "Big Five Personality Predictors of Post-Secondary Academic Performance." *Personality and Individual Differences* 43: 971–990.

Polya, George. 1945. *How to Solve It*. Princeton, NJ: Princeton University Press.

Poropat, Arthur E. 2009. "A Meta-analysis of the Five-Factor Model of Personality and Academic Performance." *Psychological Bulletin* 135:322–338.

Roberts, Brent W., Oleksandr S. Chernyshenko, Stephen Stark, and Lewis R. Goldberg. 2005. "The Structure of Conscientiousness: An Empirical Investigation Based on Seven Major Personality Questionnaires." *Personnel Psychology* 58:103–139.

Roberts, Brent W., Nathan R. Kuncel, Rebecca L. Shiner, Avshalom Caspi, and Lewis R. Goldberg. 2007. "The Power of Personality: The Comparative Validity of Personality Traits, Socioeconomics Status, and Cognitive Ability for Predicting Important Life Events." *Perspectives on Psychological Science* 4:313–345.

Rupp, André A., Matthew Gushta, Robert J. Mislevy, and David W. Shaffer. 2010. "Evidence-Centered Design of Epistemic Games: Measurement Principles for Complex Learning Environment." *Journal of Technology, Learning and Assessment* 8(4):4–47.

Salen, Katie, and Eric Zimmerman. 2005. "Game Design and Meaningful Play." In *Handbook of Computer Game Studies*, edited by Joost Raessens and Jeffrey Goldstein, 59–80. Cambridge, MA: MIT Press.

Schneider, Walter, and Richard M. Shiffrin. 1977. "Controlled and Automatic Human Information Processing: I. Detection, Search, and Attention." *Psychological Review* 84:1–66.

Shaw, Rebecca, Andy Grayson, and Vicky Lewis. 2005. "Inhibition, ADHD, and Computer Games: The Inhibitory Performance of Children with ADHD on Computerized Tasks and Games." *Journal of Attention Disorders* 4(8):160–168.

Shiffrin, Richard M., and Walter Schneider. 1977. "Controlled and Automatic Human Information Processing: II. Perceptual Learning, Automatic Attending and a General Theory." *Psychological Review* 2(84):127–190.

Shiner, Rebecca L., Ann S. Masten, and Jennifer M. Roberts. 2003. "Childhood Personality Foreshadows Adult Personality and Life Outcomes Two Decades Later." *Journal of Personality* 6(71):1145–1170.

Shute, Valerie J. 2011. "Stealth Assessment in Computer-Based Games to Support Learning." In *Computer Games and Instruction*, edited by S. Tobias and J. D. Fletcher, 503–524. Charlotte, NC: Information Age Publishers.

Shute, Valerie J., Lisa A. Gawlick, and Kevin A. Gluck. 1998. "Effects of Practice and Learner Control on Short- and Long-Term Gain and Efficiency." *Human Factors* 2(40):296–310.

Shute, Valerie J., Lloyd Rieber, and Richard Van Eck. 2011. "Games . . . and . . . Learning." In *Trends and Issues in Instructional Design and Technology*, edited by R. Reiser and J. Dempsey, 321–332. Upper Saddle River, NJ: Pearson Education.

Shute, Valerie J., and Matthew Ventura. 2013. *Stealth Assessment: Measuring and Supporting Learning in Games*. Cambridge, MA: MIT Press.

Shute, Valerie J., Matthew Ventura, Malcolm I. Bauer, and Diego Zapata-Rivera. 2009. "Melding the Power of Serious Games and Embedded Assessment to Monitor and Foster Learning: Flow and Grow." In *Serious Games: Mechanisms and Effects*, edited by Ute Ritterfeld, Michael Cody, and Peter Vorderer, 295–321. Mahwah, NJ: Taylor and Francis.

Skoric, Marko M., Linda L. Teo, and Rachel L. Neo. 2009. "Children and Video Games: Addiction, Engagement, and Scholastic Achievement." *CyberPsychology & Behavior* 12:567–572.

Smith, Geoff P. 2002. *Growing Up with Tok Pisin: Contact, Creolization, and Change in Papua New Guinea's National Language*. London: Battlebridge Publications.

Tennyson, Robert D., and Jorczak L. Robert. 2008. "A Conceptual Framework for the Empirical Study of Instructional Games." In *Computer Games and Team and Individual Learning*, edited by Harold F. O'Neil and Ray Perez, 3–20. Amsterdam: Elsevier.

Thorndike, Edward L. 1898. "Animal Intelligence: An Experimental Study of the Associative Processes in Animals." *Psychological Review* 5:551–553.

Trapmann, Sabrina, Benedikt Hell, Jan-Oliver W. Hirn, and Heinz Schuler. 2007. "Meta-analysis of the Relationship between the Big Five and Academic Success at University." *Journal of Psychology* 215:132–151.

Underdahl, Jennifer, Joycelyn Palacio-Cayetano, and Ron Stevens. 2001. "Practice Makes Perfect: Assessing and Enhancing Knowledge and Problem-Solving Skills with IMMEX Software." *Learning & Leading with Technology* 28(7):26–31.

Ventura, Matthew, Valerie J. Shute, and Yoon J. Kim. 2012. "Video Gameplay, Personality and Academic Performance." *Computers & Education* 58:1260–1266.

Vygotsky, Lev. 1978. *Mind in Society: The Development of Higher Psychological Processes.* Cambridge, MA: Harvard University Press.

White, Barbara Y. 1984. "Designing Computer Games to Help Physics Students Understand Newton's Laws of Motion." *Cognition and Instruction* 1:69–108.

Witt, Edward A., Adam J. Massman, and Linda A. Jackson. 2011. "Trends in Youth's Videogame Playing, Overall Computer Use, and Communication Technology Use: The Impact of Self-Esteem and the Big Five Personality Factors." *Computers in Human Behavior* 27:763–769.

CHAPTER TEN

Implications and Applications of Sociable Gaming for Higher Education

NICOLE B. ELLISON, DONGHEE YVETTE WOHN, AND CARRIE HEETER

Over the past few years, games that are played on social media platforms have garnered attention from game designers and game scholars—and, most recently, from higher education scholars and practitioners as well. Because they are embedded in social media platforms, these games have been dubbed *social games* (although, of course, any game that involves interpersonal interaction is inherently social). We thus use the term *sociable gaming* to refer to gameplay that is accompanied by some type of social interaction. This social interaction, which lies at the heart of sociable gaming, can take various forms. It can occur within a game or outside of a game and can be synchronous or asynchronous, verbal or nonverbal, co-located or remote. In this chapter, we focus on social network games—games that are embedded as applications in social network sites such as Facebook. We argue that academic institutions and especially those who work with students (administrators, faculty, and staff) should consider the social capital benefits of sociable gaming for students and capitalize on their social and technical affordances in order to help young people be more successful in their pursuit of higher education.

How can social network games help students successfully apply to, attend, and graduate from college? We believe the primary explanatory mechanism is *communication*. Communication enables student socialization processes through activities such as making friends on campus, accessing information, and developing social support networks. Most games encourage communication, but games that are played on social network sites are especially good at supporting social interactions because they enable players to easily connect and communicate with friends, friends of friends, and strangers. Social network games provide a low-barrier context for interaction (Wohn et al. 2011) and can act as a "social lubricant" (Ellison, Steinfield, and Lampe 2011) giving players something to talk about. These conversations can then lead to interactions that are not game-related, potentially supporting relationship development and interaction among players. Teens from different social circles may start talking about their crops in the Facebook game *FarmVille* move on to chatting about something that happened in class that day, and end up talking about a class assignment. Research shows that many college students use Facebook to get class-related questions answered (Lampe et al. 2011), and we suspect that students benefit twice from this practice—once when their informational needs are met, and a second time when these exchanges become social.

Social network sites such as Facebook, Myspace, and Twitter are extremely popular among young people. Social network games can benefit from social features and practices that are specific to the social network site they are hosted on. For instance, people who play games in Facebook can identify others with shared interests through their profiles and find common ground (shared experiences and affiliations) with one another (Ellison, Steinfield, and Lampe 2011). We believe these interactions can provide the foundation for exchanges of informational and social support, which are important in the context of students' psychosocial development and college success.

Although they are more complicated to measure than explicit outcomes like grades, interpersonal communication skills and the ability to maintain a supportive social network are important for college students to master. *Social capital* gives us a framework for describing the benefits of social relationships in regard to emotional and informational support, and research has identified social capital as being an important factor predicting successful college access and persistence (e.g., Coleman 1988; Dika and Singh 2002).

Social Capital

Social capital describes the different tangible and intellectual resources held by people we know, such as a friend's knowledge about plumbing or a parent's ability to help with a down payment. Social capital does not speak to the resources held directly by an individual but rather describes the resources in one's social connections that have the potential to be accessed when needed. Bourdieu (1986) and Coleman (1988) introduced the concept of social capital as a new dimension of capital, in addition to human capital and physical capital. Physical capital is material that helps create a tangible product (e.g., natural resources, money), while human capital refers to the knowledge and skills held by people (Coleman 1988). Social capital describes an individual's ability to tap into both physical and human capital through networked connections including friends, family, acquaintances, online communication partners, and neighbors. Social capital reflects not the resources (such as access to information or funds) an individual possesses directly but those available through his or her social network. Of course, we both give to and expect to receive support from others, and reciprocity norms are an important component of what makes social capital work.

There are two different types of social capital: bridging and bonding (Putnam 2000). Bridging social capital describes social connections that may be able to provide novel information and access to different perspectives and ways of thinking about the world. Bridging social capital is typically associated with connections or relationships that are less close, such as acquaintances or "friends of friends." This is because we tend to have these weaker relationships with people who are different from us and know different kinds of things, as opposed to our close friends who are more likely to be similar to us. Although it is often assumed that closer friends are more helpful than acquaintances, in situations where information is not well known but valuable, weaker ties can actually be more useful. For younger people, activities that bring together students from different schools—such as debate competitions, sporting events, or 4-H fairs—can be valuable because exposure to different kinds of people can encourage the open-mindedness and more expansive worldviews associated with bridging social capital (Williams 2006). Thinking of college students, we know that the years between 18 and 25 constitute an important stage of psychosocial development known as "emerging adulthood" (Arnett 2000), and researchers have speculated that exposure to new and diverse ideas during the college years (bridging social capital) may be especially powerful (Steinfield, Ellison, and Lampe 2008). In addition to representing new perspectives and worldviews, our weaker ties are also more likely to know information that we do not already know. Novel information is often more valuable than commonly shared information—think of a stock tip that only a few people know versus one that is common knowledge. The sociologist Mark Granovetter (1973) found that adults were more likely to report hearing about a job opportunity from a weak tie than a strong one—a phenomenon dubbed the "strength of weak ties." In summary, the structure of one's social network—specifically the number of connections that represent a wider array of information and perspectives—helps to define one's potential bridging social capital (Burt 1992).

Bonding social capital, on the other hand, is associated with close relationships such as family and friends. Robert Putnam (2000) describes bonding social capital as a limited resource—something of tangible or social value—that is valuable to both the giver and the receiver, such as emotional support or a sense of belonging (Williams 2006). For young people, examples of bonding social capital are found in close friends who offer a shoulder to cry on or family members who are willing to drive long distances at inconvenient times. In the context of postsecondary success, bonding social capital is related to social support, an important predictor of student adjustment and persistence.

Social Capital as a Lens for Explaining Academic Outcomes

Social capital is a construct often used to examine educational phenomena and outcomes because it takes into account not only the resources explicitly held by an individual (the student) but also those available to the individual via his or her social relationships with teachers, parents, friends, coaches, and others. Social capital offers us a conceptual framework for considering the effects of various individual and environmental factors on academic outcomes.

James S. Coleman (1988) was one of the first scholars to use social capital as a framework for explaining academic achievement. He noticed that Catholic high schools had lower dropout rates than nonreligious schools, even those that were privately run, and suggested that the religious community created an atmosphere that made high school completion a highly expected norm. He also found that social capital was actually more important than socioeconomic status (SES) in predicting high school retention. For example, students from families that had average SES but low social capital had higher dropout rates than those from families that had lower SES but higher levels of social capital. This work spurred a profusion of scholarship on how social capital acquired through family, community, and peer networks affects different dimensions of academic achievement, including grades in middle and high school, college enrollment, and college adjustment.

Sociable Gaming and Social Capital

Sociable games are potentially powerful tools for maintaining and building social capital. Games are often very compelling, fun experiences that can serve as a mechanism for meaningful social interaction—a way to spend enjoyable time with friends and even to make new friends. Game emotion researcher Nicole Lazzaro (2004) identified what she refers to as four keys to fun in gaming: hard fun (overcoming difficult obstacles), easy fun (curiosity, discovery, and exploration), altered states (thinking or feeling something different from everyday life), and people fun (competition, cooperation, performance, and spectacle). Three forms of people fun are amusement, *Schadenfreude* (a German word for pleasure from a rival's misfortune), and naches (the pleasure or pride a parent or mentor experiences at the success of her child or mentee). People fun is one of the essential sets of emotions that make games engaging and enjoyable. Very often, playing games is a social activity, whether it involves playing with other people (such as opponents and teammates) or playing in the presence of others (such as spectators and fans).

Gaming is a part of most teens' social lives. Sociable gaming by teens includes "people fun" involving peers, siblings, parents, and sometimes strangers. Ninety-seven percent of teens in a 2008 study for the Pew Internet & American Life project reported that they play games (Lenhart et al. 2008), and most play games with other people. Lenhart et al. (2008) confirm that gaming is a social activity for most teens, reporting that only one-fourth of teens plays games exclusively when they are alone and three-fourths sometimes or always game with others, either with people who are physically present in the same room, with distant others over the internet, or both. Teens who play multiplayer online games tend to play online with people they already know rather than with people they met online. A 2011 survey from Capital One Financial Corporation found that half of the parents of teens they studied reported that they play online games with their teen (Fenton Report Global 2011).

Forms of Sociable Gaming

Sociable gaming provides opportunities for "people fun" and the development of bonding and bridging social capital. Some of the most popular forms of sociable gaming occur when the people involved are co-located. Because the people are together in the same physical space, communication can easily occur inside or outside of the game itself. Games on many gaming platforms are designed to be played by two or more players who are physically together, including *Wii Bowling*, *Mario Kart* (a go-cart-style racing game for two to four players), *Carcassonne* (a classic board game in which players strategically place "territory tiles" to score points, now available on the iPad), and *Guitar Hero* (a music video game in which players use a guitar-like controller to try to match notes and rhythm of rock music songs).

Yet another form of co-located sociable gaming is playing games in the presence of other people. This may involve simply being in the same room with a roommate or friend while playing a game, or the nonplaying other(s) may be paying attention to the game. For instance, *Just Dance* is a dancing game that requires mimicking movements on the screen. Although the game can be played only by a few players at a time, others can still enjoy watching as spectators. As with the co-located games, these kinds of experiences can support relationship development and, potentially, bonding social capital.

Co-located sociable gaming can also involve strangers, although opportunities to build bridging social capital by making new connections are limited. Less direct forms of sociable gaming often occur around online games, in the form of leader boards (lists of top scoring players) and discussion forums where players can go to talk about the game. For example, users can play the role of Flo, a waitress who must keep a growing number of impatient customers happy in the online single-player game *Diner Dash* by Playfirst. Playfirst publishes a leaderboard and supports a very active player discussion forum. Other forms of social interaction tied to single-player games continue to be developed. For example, in the single-player game *Spore* by Electronic Arts, players design creatures using the creature editor and then evolve them through levels of increasing complexity to galactic domination. After players create a creature, they can upload and share their creation with other players and keep track of how many people use their creature. Players can also upload videos of gameplay directly to YouTube. Research has shown that teens' participation in these kinds of game-related activities can be a gateway to mastery of digital tools and a trajectory to developing information technology expertise (Hayes 2008). Figuring out how to use the tools tends to involve communication with expert strangers, potentially contributing to bridging social capital.

Multiplayer gaming over a network brings together players who are usually not physically together. Networked multiplayer games often connect players who do not even know each other outside of the game. MMOGs (massively multiplayer online games) such as *World of Warcraft* and *Star Wars Galaxies* bring players together from anywhere on the internet. High school students play against or with professionals from all walks of life. However, players play in character, using a pseudonym, and communication opportunities during gameplay are often focused on what is happening in the game, potentially limiting social capital development opportunities.

Games played on social network sites such as *FarmVille* on Facebook provide a different slant on playing in the presence of others. Friends may be physically together, each logged in to Facebook. More often, friends are separated in time and space, yet they can use Facebook to invite friends to be neighbors, visit each other's farm, help each other take care of crops, and send gifts.

Another example of a multiplayer social network game is *Facebook Scrabble*. One player logs in to Facebook to complete a turn. The game notifies the opposing player or players about their opponent's action and informs the player who is up next that it is his or her turn. Whenever the next player is ready, he or she logs in to Facebook and completes his or her turn. The time between turns is completely under control of the players. Finishing a game may take weeks, days, hours, or minutes. Social network games can also be massively multiplayer. In *The Sims Social*, a Facebook life simulator game, players design and control semiautonomous beings known as Sims. Like other social network games, *The Sims Social* takes advantage of the social features of Facebook to enable users to interact with their Facebook friends (or friends of friends, or strangers), helping them to complete quests and enacting relationships among their Sims.

Sociable gaming can help build and maintain social capital by providing new, far-reaching venues for informal sociability that extend beyond the family, peers, and neighbors whom youth encounter in day-to-day life. Sociable gaming can act as virtual "third places" (in addition to home or work/school) for informal sociability, similar to community centers, churches, parks, and other places young people gather. Third places are places other than the workplace or the home that bring together people from different walks of life and serve a critical function in promoting informal sociality in communities (Oldenburg 1999). Steinkuehler and Williams (2006) argue that "by providing spaces for social interaction and relationships beyond the workplace and home, MMOGs have the capacity to function as one form of a new 'third place' for informal sociability. Participation in such virtual 'third places' appears particularly well suited to the formation of bridging social capital—social relationships that, while not usually providing deep emotional support, typically function to expose the individual to a diversity of worldviews" (885). Social network games can provide a low-barrier liaison to other types of social interaction that could potentially lead to increased social capital that would benefit academic aspirations and behavior. For instance, young people with fewer connections on social network sites may be less likely to use these sites, but social network games could function as a kind of social "bait" that encourages users to spend more time on the social network site and either connect with new people or deepen existing weak tie relationships.

Massively Multiplayer Online Games

Research has shown that playing MMOGs can contribute to players' social capital, especially through team-based activities and creation and maintenance of relationships. MMOGs bring large numbers of geographically and demographically diverse players together into a virtual game world. These players, about one-quarter of whom are teens (Yee 2006), have at least one thing in common: interest in playing that MMOG. Of course, the more different they are in other respects, the more opportunities they represent for bridging social capital gains.

Research shows that participation in MMOGs does tend to increase players' bridging social capital (Steinkuehler and Williams 2006). This effect was strongest within guilds, a special type of group MMOG players join either to develop community among members or to focus on achieving larger and riskier game-related goals than an individual player can achieve alone. Guilds are automatically given a group chatting channel for members only. Guilds vary in size and can adopt informal or formal organizational structures.

Additionally, MMOG players who become intensely involved with their guild do appear to form social capital ties with other members of their guild (Ratan et al. 2010; Steinkuehler and Williams 2006). Ratan and colleagues (2010) found that guild members were significantly more likely to feel trust for each other than they were to feel trust of others in the game. However, players trusted MMOG players who were not guild members more than they trusted general individuals on the internet. Because trust and expectations of reciprocity are components of social capital, being a registered player of an MMOG could be said to support social capital development.

Multiplayer Games

In addition to MMOGs, local Wi-Fi networks, now common in public spaces as well as college campuses, make it possible for individuals on the same local network to find and game with each other, without ever knowing the other's offline identity or exact physical location. Heeter, Sarkar, Palmer-Scott, and Zhang (2012) conducted a field experiment in which they connected pairs of coffee shop visitors who were sitting alone to play a Wi-Fi-connected two-player game with a stranger who was also at the coffee shop. They simulated what might occur if a local Wi-Fi gaming portal that connected co-present players were available. Initially the two parties were anonymous. Each was given an iPad, and the game was launched. Neither player knew where the other was located within the café. If the two participants happened to be in the same room facing each other they could notice their opponent. This was classified as high visibility. Otherwise one's opponent was a mystery. The game, *Carcassonne*, had a built-in chat system so it was possible to play together and to chat while you played within the game. Disclosing one's location or name was optional. High-visibility pairs rarely used the text chat but did make eye contact, speak to each other, and expressed visible emotions. Low visibility pairs relied on text chat within the game.

The researchers applied Duck's (1983) concept of friendship drive in their analysis. Duck showed that once someone amasses a certain number of friendships (which he refers to as their critical mass, which may be different for different individuals), that person loses the desire to seek out new friends. Friendship drive may be a confounding factor in building new sources of social capital because it influences whether someone is interested in forming new social bonds. Friendship drive is highest in young adults, declining sharply after the age of 30, with an upsurge again just before retirement (Duck 1983). Thus, precollege and college students are at an age when they are particularly interested in making new friends. Heeter and colleagues' (2012) study found that participants who were interested in making new friends (who experienced friendship drive) were more interested in the idea of playing the game with someone they did not already know. Those experiencing friendship drive were more likely to say they would like to play with the same partner again and that they hoped to see their partner again. They were also more open to the idea of playing again with someone they did not know in the future. In other words, Wi-Fi gaming with a stranger in a public place was a more attractive experience for those experiencing friendship drive than for those who were socially satisfied. These findings suggest that gaming that facilitates meeting new people, such as local Wi-Fi gaming, may be especially attractive to incoming college students who are highly motivated to form new relationships on campus.

Sociable Single-Player Games

Single-player online games can introduce social mechanisms by creating opportunities to form community surrounding the game. Earlier in this chapter we gave examples of social mechanisms in the single-player games *Diner Dash* and *Spore*. Cooper et al. (2011) studied how players of *Foldit*, a crowd-sourcing protein folding game, used the game's social mechanisms to share, run, and modify code "recipes" to automate the protein-folding strategies they developed to increase gameplay efficiency and effectiveness. *Foldit* provides a series of tutorials to teach players how to use the game interface to manipulate three-dimensional protein-like structures. The game presents a series of puzzles based on real proteins.

Foldit attracted international attention in 2011 when players succeeded in deciphering the structure of the Mason-Pfizer monkey virus (M-PMV) retroviral protease, an AIDS-causing monkey virus (Science Daily 2011). Gameplay is complex, and the game provides a means for players to write and share recipes (bits of code) to accomplish complicated tasks. Despite the capacity to share recipes, Cooper found that players usually kept their code recipes private, for their own exclusive personal use. A small subset of recipes was shared by the creator with a small group of other players (akin to bonding social capital connections). Another subset of recipes was shared publicly by the creator, visible to and usable by all players (more akin to bridging social capital dynamics). Although there were comparatively few public recipes, some were very widely used. By virtue of being a *Foldit* player, anyone could access these recipes, which had been shared with the world by their creator. The *Foldit* case illustrates the benefits of having sharing mechanisms for members of an online gaming community and highlights the challenge for game designers of motivating players to engage in public sharing. Educational institutions have an opportunity to use gaming to build local communities in order to support institutional goals such as learning, a sense of belonging, mentoring, sharing, and outreach.

Co-located Play

Yet another form of social interaction during gaming is co-located play. Individuals in the same physical location can each play single-player games, yet experience "people fun" by playing alongside each other, and sometimes simply watching someone else play. Coffee shops, cybercafés, and on-campus public computer labs and computer labs at museums provide this form of co-located play, as do after school gaming clubs. People using separate computers can log on to separate games. Alternatively, they can log in to the same online environment, resulting in a complex, mixed-mode environment where players can engage in face-to-face communication in the physical room as well as interacting with one another and other virtual world inhabitants in the online setting.

Fields and Kafai (2010) conducted ethnographic research of online gameplay of *Whyville*, a science-related virtual world for tweens, in the context of playing in an after school club in which 20 after school club members were physically together while they logged in on individual computers to play. By structuring the after school club so that the tweens navigated two overlapping social spaces—the game world and the club—learning was scaffolded, and the researchers had the opportunity to observe both in-game and in-room social behaviors. Club members interacted with each other in *Whyville*, where they also interacted with other "Whyvillains" (members of the virtual world) who did not belong to the after school club. This unusual blend of interacting with co-present, known others and online, pseudonymous others facilitated building close relationships among the physically co-present players and also potentially building weak ties with pseudonymous online players in the space. The authors acknowledge that learning how to play in a virtual world is a complex and time-consuming challenge. Co-located players were observed helping each other figure out how to play. For example, the researchers observed how knowledge of how to teleport (jump to other locations) in *Whyville* spread via social interactions within the club because players could talk to and look at the screen of someone who had already figured it out and thus see how to teleport (Fields and Kafai 2010). They also examined how the practice of throwing projectiles (a key way to socialize in *Whyville*) was discovered and evolved within the group, noting a strong influence of the shared physical space on the spread of projectile throwing.

Sociable Gaming in the Classroom

Teachers increasingly use digital games in the classroom. A recent survey found that 32% of K–8 teachers use games two-to-four times per week, and 18% do so every day (Millstone 2012). Game usage is higher in K–5 (57%) than middle school (38%). These teachers believe that games help motivate and engage low-performing students and that games foster collaboration among students and help them sustain focus on learning tasks.

Social interaction to support collaborative learning in classroom games can occur in each of the different modalities discussed earlier. Massively multi-player learning games such as *Quest Atlantis* use co-located play, assigning each student to a computer (Barab et al. 2005). Learners solve quests together within the game world. Some learning games are designed to be played by groups of students, such as *The Great Solar System Rescue*, which uses one computer and designates a specific role for each member of the five-person team (Jackson 1997). Social interaction before and after playing a single-player game can rein-force learning content and build upon players' enjoyment, cooperation, and competition experiences. Single-player learning games can be played in teams or pairs, with players sharing a single computer and planning gameplay moves together.

A different approach to introducing "people fun" through social interaction in single-player games is having two people play an electronic game together, either taking turns using the mouse or otherwise sharing decision making in the game. Looking at co-play of commercial games, Lim and Lee (2007) found that co-playing led to a significant increase of the player's physiological arousal during nonviolent gameplay. Furthermore, co-playing enhanced the players' sense of presence and identification. Some learning games are designed as mul-tiplayer experiences. Pedagogical arguments in favor of team rather than indi-vidual learning games derive from collaborative learning research, which shows that small group work is associated with more learning and better reten-tion than learning through other forms of instruction (Davis 1993). When stu-dents are put in learning situations where they must explain and discuss their beliefs, students report that some of their thoughts become clearer and that other beliefs may be challenged by peers or a teacher (Linn and Burbules 1991).

Co-play is a sociable gaming classroom strategy that teachers can use to in-troduce social interaction into a single-player game. For example, Werner, Denner, and Bean (2004) developed guidelines for paired programming that can be easily adapted to paired play. One player is assigned to control the mouse for a defined period (such as the first level of a game). The pair then switches seats and hands off the mouse for the next level. The partner who is not control-ling the mouse is assigned to watch and provide guidance and help minimize mistakes. Paired play introduces a social dimension to single-player games, in-creasing the likelihood of pro-social (and antisocial) play. Benefits for learning could come from cooperation in the form of discussion and shared decision mak-ing within the team. Competition between teams might also motivate efforts to earn a good score. Potential drawbacks include bullying, added distractions, stereotypical expectations that interfere with concentration (such as girls being self-consciously aware of a perceived expectation that girls are bad at games), and even a "fear of winning" barrier, which can occur when competing publicly instills a desire not to win.

Sociable Gaming, Civic Engagement, and Leadership

The Association of American Colleges and Universities reports that colleges and universities increasingly emphasize civic learning and civic engagement (Association of American Colleges and Universities 2012). These skills, attitudes, and behaviors are considered essential for a twenty-first-century citizenry. Sociable gaming has been linked with a variety of pro-social benefits including learning, civic engagement, and leadership. A recent study of college students also found a relationship between gaming and civic engagement. Specifically, college students who play MMOGs also reported being more civically engaged than did their non-MMOG playing peers (Hartshorne, VanFossen, and Friedman 2012). Kahne, Middaugh, and Evans (2008) examined civic dimensions of teen video gameplay. They identified six "civic gaming experiences" (activities players engage in when they play games) that parallel in-school activities found to encourage civic engagement (Carnegie Corporation of New York 2003). These civic gaming experiences include helping or guiding other players; learning about a problem in society; exploring a social issue the player cares about; thinking about moral or ethical issues; helping to make decisions about how a community, city, or nation should be run; and organizing game groups or guilds.

The researchers measured civic engagement and interest by assessing behaviors such as searching for information about politics and current events online, volunteering, raising money for charity, protesting, trying to persuade others how to vote, or demonstrating (Kahne, Middaugh, and Evans 2008.). They found that the overall quantity of teen gameplay was unrelated to civic engagement and interest. Gameplay that included civic gaming experiences was highly related to civic engagement and interest. Sociable gaming (playing games alongside others in the same room) was also highly related to civic interest and engagement, whereas playing games online alone was not. Proactive engagement with the game outside the boundaries of the game (such as commenting on websites or contributing to discussion boards related to the game) was also associated with civic interest and engagement. Boys were twice as likely to experience civic gaming experiences as girls, regardless of frequency of play.

Sociable gaming has also been linked to leadership skills. Nick Yee's (2006) research found that MMOG players believe they learn a lot about leadership, including conflict mediation, group motivation, and persuasion when a change in goals was necessary. Younger players were more likely to report learning leadership skills from MMOG play. Corporations increasingly recognize that multiplayer gaming and particularly playing MMOGs helps players develop leadership skills. A team of researchers used the Sloan Leadership Model as a guide for analyzing 50 hours of MMOG gameplay across five different MMOGs. They found all four key leadership qualities from the Sloan Model in the behavior of MMOG guild leaders. According to researchers associated with the project, the behavior of MMOG guild leaders provides a good window into what business leadership may look like three to five years in the future (IBM 2007). The implications of this argument suggest that today's teen and college-age MMOG players may be better prepared to become business leaders than their nongaming elders.

In summary, the social skills and relationships that players develop through and around gameplay can teach numerous social skills such as teamwork, leadership, social support provision and requests, collaborative learning, and information seeking.

Social Media and Social Network Games

In this section, we focus on the ways in which social media games and sociable gaming might support college student development and learning practices, especially related to communication skills and social capital development. The term *social media* describes a broad category of communication technology which has a specific set of social and technical affordances designed to promote user-to-user interaction. Although there is not a universally accepted definition of social media (also associated with "Web 2.0" tools and technologies), the term is typically used to describe a set of online tools and spaces that incorporate the exchange of user-generated content, in contrast to earlier traditional media and earlier web technologies which relied on a one-to-many broadcast model. Social media emphasize the sharing of user-created knowledge (such as *Wikipedia*), opinions (such as Yelp!), and content exchange (such as Flickr).

This chapter is primarily concerned with games embedded in one genre of social media, social network sites (SNSs). Ellison and boyd (2013) write, "A social network site is a networked communication platform in which participants: (1) have uniquely identifiable profiles that consist of user-supplied content,

content provided by other users, and/or system-provided data; (2) can publicly articulate connections that can be viewed and traversed by others; and (3) can consume, produce, and/or interact with streams of user-generated content provided by their connections on the site" (158).

Several general characteristics of social media may support social capital formation, maintenance, and accrual. Nan Lin (1999, 2001) outlines three important components of social capital: the resources embedded in a social structure, the accessibility of these resources, and the ability to utilize or mobilize these resources. Although it is not explicated in this definition, the ability to provide resources to others is a critical component of social capital, and this expected reciprocity is implicitly embedded in Lin's definition. We believe two characteristics of social media are important for social capital accrual and maintenance: reshaping networks, and facilitating information and support requests and provisions.

First, social media—specifically SNSs but other forms of social media as well—can reshape social networks by reinvigorating relationships that might otherwise be dormant. Sites like Facebook, which has various technical features that allow users to locate ties from previously inhabited contexts (such as high school or preview jobs), interact with these ties and find common ground. One example of such a feature is the friend-suggesting tool, which is an algorithm that recommends connecting with people with whom one has a mutual connection (a Facebook friend in common).

These relationships, or ties, can be useful sources of information. First, the networks supported by SNSs may be larger, broader, and more diverse than those supported by traditional means of communication. Because SNSs facilitate the maintenance of weaker ties, they may be better able to provide access to diverse perspectives and worldviews, as suggested by the work of Mark Granovetter (1973) and others. One of the early pieces to examine SNSs noted that with SNSs "the number of weak ties one can form and maintain may be able to increase substantially, because the type of communication that can be done more cheaply and easily with new technology is well suited for these ties. If this is true, it implies that the technologies that expand one's social network will primarily result in an increase in available information and opportunities— the benefits of a large, heterogeneous network" (Donath and boyd 2004, 80). In that social capital speaks to the resources held in one's network, the fact that SNSs may both reshape one's network (by enabling maintenance of a larger network) and increase the visibility of resources already held in the network are important. For instance, through profile information, SNSs surface important information about individuals (e.g., friends in common, past employment history, shared common ground) and also gives individuals greater awareness of those in their wider network and the ability to access "friends of friends." A recent memo from the Facebook Data Team found that Facebook users are exposed to novel information from their weak ties (Bakshy 2012).

Second, SNS features—such as the "status update," which is broadcast to one's network—enable users to request information from and provide information to their social network connections. Research has examined the ways in which individuals rely on social network sites to complement information seeking through other channels. For instance, Morris, Teevan, and Panovich (2010) surveyed 624 Microsoft employees and interns and found that half reported using their status update to ask a question. Teens and college students are also using SNSs to ask questions of their classmates about academic work and to organize study groups and projects. For example, EDUCAUSE reports that more than half of U.S. college students use SNSs for tasks such as communicating with classmates about school (Salaway, Caruso, and Nelson 2008), and more than one-quarter used an SNS as part of a class (Smith, Salaway, and Caruso 2009). Many college students use the site for activities such as organizing study groups (Lampe et al. 2011) and believe their SNS use is associated with positive academic outcomes (Dahlstrom et al. 2011). The low-income high school students participating in Greenhow and Robelia's (2009) study used a SNS to request help with school-related tasks, including asking questions about instructions or deadlines, broadcasting or requesting educational resources, and planning study groups. Although less research addresses this directly, there is also evidence that certain aspects of SNS use are related to social support benefits. For instance, Vitak, Ellison, and Steinfield (2011) found that certain Facebook behaviors, such as having a family member on Facebook, was related to perceptions of social provisions related to close friends and family, although more research needs to be done to contextualize these findings.

Social Network Games

The benefits we have explicated, however, are more salient for individuals who are able to proactively engage with their network via social media. Those who do not have many connections or do not engage in communication with their network may be less able to access these social capital resources. However, games embedded within social media can be a low-barrier means of communication that act as a springboard for further communication between individuals.

These games are referred to in the academic literature as *social network games* (Wohn et al. 2010). Social network games are digital games that are applications within existing social network sites. They are a unique type of online game because the games facilitate communication both within the game and also on whatever social media site the game is hosted (Wohn et al. 2011). For example, in many games on Facebook, players are encouraged to post requests and achievements on their Facebook Wall, which can be viewed and commented on by members of their broader social network, not just those friends who are also playing the game. Unlike MMOGs, whose population is limited to registered players of the game (Steinkuehler and Williams 2006), social network games are situated in the context of the vast, complex social graph articulated in social network sites by hundreds of millions of diverse users. Playing a social network game may begin with play or sharing with known others but can cross over into different clusters in an individual's network, becoming an open house where these groups can commingle. In other words, social network games exist in a richly social context that is a mix of past and present connections and social, professional, and academic pursuits (Radoff 2011). Each social network participant constructs her own unique social graph, which is the history of connections and activities she engages in within the network. A 2010 survey of 1,202 U.S. and U.K. internet users who play social games at least once a week showed that most social gamers also interact with fellow gamers outside the gaming environment, with only 22% indicating gameplay was their only form of interaction with fellow social game players (Pop Cap Games Information Solutions Group 2010).

Although many of the popular social network games are simple in nature, it is important to note that social network games are not defined by their content or game mechanics. They can range from single-player arcade games that are reminiscent of the earliest arcade and computer games (e.g., *Tetris*) to adaptations of turn-based board and card games (e.g., *Words With Friends*, an SNS version of the board game *Scrabble*). The most popular games that have emerged as a new content genre are simulation games about resource allocation and space customization and have garnered millions of players around the world. As of March 2012, 9 of the top 10 applications on Facebook, not counting internet browsers or embedded code, were games (Inside Network 2012). Each had more than 19 million average monthly users globally with *CityVille*, a multiplayer city simulation game, topping the list at 46 million.

Social network games have been criticized by popular media (and, until very recently, even the mainstream game industry), as being addictive and mindless and for forcing players to "use" (exploit) one's social network to play the game. Many social network games are difficult to play without cooperation from other players: for example, when building a house, one would need an array of different building materials, some of which can be acquired only through social connections. Although this type of gameplay facilitates social interaction, it can sometimes put a strain on relationships if one player starts making excessive requests (Wohn et al. 2011). Nonetheless, these characteristics highlight the major features of social network games. First, most of the popular social network games have short "levels" that do not require much time to play; players are often given limited "energy" that runs out with each action performed in the game and must be replenished over time. This feature prevents players from playing long hours at a time, but encourages them to come back frequently. Because most social network games are very easy to learn and can be played in short intervals throughout the day, these characteristics can be inviting for people who are uncomfortable with new technology, new users of social network sites, and people who do not have many online connections. In other words, social network games may be a "killer app" (an irresistible experience that draws people into a technology) for some kinds of users, such as those who do not have many friends on Facebook.

Second, most of the games do not have complicated game mechanisms and involve repetitive clicking (or touching, if played on a touch screen) behavior. This can induce routine behavior—in fact, studies have shown that most of the time people spend playing social network games is purely habitual and that players are not consciously thinking about why they are playing the games at the time they are engaged in them (Wohn 2011a, 2011b). This makes these games a popular means of coping when relieving stress or boredom (Wohn et al. 2011). The simplicity of the games has also attracted an older female demographic. Whereas the typical traditional console videogame player used to be a teenaged boy, casual games—many of which are hosted on social network sites—have expanded the game player demographic such that in the United States, women over 18 years of age are one of the fastest-growing player groups in the games industry (Entertainment Software Association 2011). Players of social network games are diverse in terms of age, cultural orientation, and motivations for why they play (Hou 2011; Lee and Wohn 2012; Wohn et al. 2011). This is important to note because it means that players have access to a more diverse population of potential connections, an important component of bridging social capital.

As illustrated earlier, many actions in social network games that rely on social interaction are in fact orchestrated by the game mechanics. Many social network games, especially the games developed by Zynga, require players to constantly ask favors of their social network in order to continue playing the game. Despite the fact that this type of interaction is motivated by the "selfish" reasons of advancing in the game rather than a desire to interact with other players in a meaningful social manner (Wohn et al. 2011), facilitated interaction can still lead to positive relationship results. One of the mechanisms that enhances these social bonds is reciprocity—the expectation that others will respond in a likewise fashion. Expectations about reciprocity are a critical component of social capital dynamics. In a controlled experiment that involved players engaging in reciprocity in one condition but not the other, Wohn (2011a, 2011b) found that even among strangers, the act of nonverbal exchange, such as helping out the other player through simple clicking behaviors, contributed to higher levels of trust and perceptions of social support. This experiment showed that some components often associated with bonding social capital (such as trust) can be developed even without verbal communication. In another study, interviews with adult Facebook users showed that even if people connect with others for the selfish reasons of advancing in the game, the in-game interaction encourages conversation about topics unrelated to the game (Wohn et al. 2011). Such relationship enhancements were particularly salient among players who only vaguely knew each other (e.g., spouse of a distant cousin) or were introduced to each other by a mutual contact. Social network games can act as a water cooler or icebreaker in that the content of the game serves to highlight common ground among participants, especially for more distant or weaker ties, such as old friends or colleagues, because the game provides players with a topic to discuss and an interest that they both share (Wohn et al. 2011). In fact, those people who choose to play social network games for the purpose of building common ground are more likely to publish their game achievements on their Facebook Wall (Wohn et al. 2011), which could be interpreted as an effort to reach out to people in their network who are not game players. In a survey of U.S. and U.K. social network game players, more than half (56%) said that gaming made them feel more connected with members of their social network, and 52% made new friends through the game (Pop Cap Games Information Solutions Group 2010). Also in this survey, 50% reported that they correspond more with friends and family, while 48% have reconnected with old friends as a result of their gameplay. Moreover, aside from direct interaction related to the game content, many social network games support "person fun" by having social incentives, such as badges, bragging rights, and leaderboards, and incorporating social interactions into gameplay, allowing for shared experiences (Radoff 2011).

Implications for Higher Education

Social network games have many potential benefits related to teamwork, leadership, how to engage in social support provision and requests, collaborative learning, and information seeking. By developing or becoming associated with social network games as part of a larger social network presence, colleges can leverage relationships with potential future students, current students, and alumni. In 2010, 53% of more than 500 million Facebook users played games, and half of Facebook logins were specifically to play games (O'Neil 2010). According to Pew Internet & American Life Project research (Lenhart et al. 2011), 95% of teens aged 12 to 17 were online, and 80% used social media sites such as Facebook, Myspace, and Twitter. Of older teens (14- to 17-year-olds), 88% use social network sites, as do 87% of young adults age 18 to 29. Facebook is the dominant social network site for teens; 93% of social network site users have a Facebook account. Half of teens who use social network sites play social network site games. Younger teens are more likely to play games on social network sites (69% of 12- to 13-year-old social network site users do so, compared to 44% of teens aged 14 to 17).

Higher-education institutions and educators could harness the social capital and interaction affordances of games, especially social network games, in several ways. For instance, social network games may provide branding opportunities, where low barriers to entry could be used to increase affiliation to the institution. Growing numbers of prospective future students, current students, alumni, faculty, and staff belong to and utilize a common social network platform (Facebook). This provides unprecedented potential for an institution to build a relationship with prospective students long before they are ready to make college choices. Social networking and social network games also may provide a means of staying connected to alumni. Cross-generational connections (between alumni, current students, and incoming students) could be facilitated through gameplay. Finally, building connectivity among different university stakeholders could be utilized for event promotion, fundraising, and other tasks.

Grumpy Snowmen is an example of a university using a casual game to build brand awareness and brand loyalty (Pohl 2012). The game is a parody of the popular casual game *Angry Birds*, but instead of birds attacking pigs, the player is a Spartan (the school mascot) defending Michigan State University from attacks by its Big Ten rivals who have set up snow forts populated with Grumpy Snowmen. There have been 14,000 downloads and an estimated 150,000 levels played in the first two months since the game was launched. Players include current students and faculty, alumni, and potential future students. This game is currently a downloadable game; if it were a social network game, players of the game not only would be able to play with other people related to the institution but might also form connections that extend to nongame arenas. In another example, MSU Green League is an internal competition that was developed using game-design principles to motivate players to engage in sustainability practices including recycling and reducing energy use.

Another example of social network game application to educational contexts is using the games for learning. The *Mission: Admission* game mentioned by Tracy Fullerton in chapter 5 of the book, for example, illustrates how a card game increases efficacy about college application processes and can inform a Facebook version targeting the same learning objectives. While the basic gameplay may be the same, the Facebook game increases accessibility to nontraditional audiences (e.g., home-schooled students) and introduces a broader "person fun" element by enabling students to share their activities with others through Facebook.

Social network games may not have a direct effect on educational outcomes but can have an indirect effect by helping students' social adjustment to new environments, such as in the case of high school students transitioning to college. Because most students who drop out of college do so during their first year, social acclimatization is critical during this period. Numerous studies have shown that loneliness, lack of friends, and other major life transition factors can negatively affect an individual's academic motivation. Social network games might help students stay connected with old friends and family, as well as connect on an interpersonal level with new acquaintances, thus developing social capital.

In addition, social network games could help broaden the network of high school or college students who do not have many social resources, such as first-generation college students, international students, and out-of-state students. Compared to other methods of connecting with new communication partners, social network games have relatively low barriers. They are typically easy to learn and master, enjoyable to many, and free or inexpensive. Past research suggests that usage of social network sites is related to increases in bridging social capital, and we would expect these gains to be associated with social network games use as well. From an institutional perspective, these qualities make social network games optimal for connecting with unconventional audiences, such as older people and women (who are less likely to play other kinds of online games), youth who are not technologically savvy, and youth from low-income families who have access to public technology resources.

Social network games exist in richly populated social spaces. For example, social network games on Facebook facilitate the possibilities for a player to connect and play with college student peers, university staff, and people who already graduated from college. For those students who do not feel a social connection to their institution, playing these games virtually with current and former members of their institution could help build a sense of affiliation and provide a smooth transition into other types of social interaction.

Prior research on social software can help to set expectations for participation in social network games for college and universities. Two especially relevant concepts are power laws of equality and power laws of participation. Media and community expert Clay Shirky (2003) describes the predictable imbalance in human systems known as power law, or the 80:20 rule. In fact, human systems do not follow bell curves of participation. Instead, according to Shirky (2003), using the example of a website, page views and the traffic from referring sites will follow power laws. Furthermore, increasing the size of the system, whether it is number of users or amount of content, increases the gap between the number one spot and the median spot (Shirky 2008). We can expect that social network games for higher education will follow these patterns of activity. A few players will account for most of the game activity. Most members will play one or a few games. This will not mean that the games are a failure. What is critical is offering low threshold forms of participation that can engage broad participation. Administrators should keep in mind that games will not appeal to all stakeholders, but those who do engage are likely to be highly engaged, which could translate to institutional benefits.

In summary, we have outlined some of the ways in which social network games can support student interaction and other positive social capital outcomes. Following what we know about SNS use and social capital, the types of interaction that social network games facilitate may be especially helpful for students who have less social capital resources, such as first-generation students. Although the feature sets of these games are still being defined, organizations seeking to use social network games and designers who create them have begun to codify the process, benefits, and elements that go into making them. We are very excited to see how the next generation of social network games will be utilized by institutions of higher education.

REFERENCES

Arnett, Jeffrey Jensen. 2000. "Emerging Adulthood: A Theory of Development from the Late Teens through the Twenties." *American Psychologist* 55:469–480.

Association of American Colleges and Universities. 2012. "Civic Learning Resources." Accessed May 31. http://www.aacu.org/resources/civicengagement/index.cfm.

Bakshy, Eytan. 2012. "Rethinking Information Diversity in Networks." Accessed January 25. http://www.facebook.com/notes/facebook-data-team/rethinking-information-diversity-in-networks/10150503499618859.

Barab, Sasha, Michael Thomas, Tyler Dodge, Robert Carteaux, and Hakan Tuzun. 2005. "Making Learning Fun: Quest Atlantis, a Game without Guns." *Educational Technology Research and Development* 53:86–107.

Bourdieu, Pierre. 1986. "The Forms of Capital." In *Handbook of Theory and Research for the Sociology of Education*, edited by John G. Richardson, 241–258. New York: Greenwood Press.

Burt, Ronald. 1992. *Structural Holes: The Social Structure of Competition.* Cambridge, MA: Harvard University Press.

Carnegie Corporation of New York. 2003. "The Civic Mission of Schools." New York. http://www.civicyouth.org/PopUps/CivicMissionofSchools.pdf.

Coleman, James S. 1988. "The Creation and Destruction of Social Capital: Implications for the Law." *Notre Dame Journal of Law, Ethics, & Public Policy* 3:375–404.

Cooper, Seth, Firas Khatib, Ilya Makedon, Hao Lu, Janos Barbero, David Baker, James Fogarty, Zoran Popovic, and Foldit players. 2011. "Analysis of Social Gameplay Macros in the Foldit Cookbook." Paper presented at the Foundations of Digital Games Conference, Bordeaux, France, June 29–July 1.

Dahlstrom, Eden, Tom de Boor, Peter Grunwald, and Martha Vockley. 2011. *ECAR National Study of Undergraduate Students and Information Technology.* Boulder, CO: EDUCAUSE.

Davis, Barbara Gross. 1993. *Tools for Teaching.* San Francisco: Jossey-Bass.

Dika, Sandra L., and Kusum Singh. 2002. "Applications of Social Capital in Educational Literature: A Critical Synthesis." *Review of Educational Research* 72:31–60.

Donath, Judith, and danah boyd. 2004. "Public Displays of Connection." *BT Technology Journal* 22:71–82.

Duck, Steve. 1983. *Friends, for Life: The Psychology of Close Relationships.* New York: St. Martin's Press.

Ellison, Nicole B., and danah boyd. 2013. "Sociality through Social Network Sites." In *The Oxford Handbook of Internet Studies*, edited by William H. Dutton, 151–172. Oxford: Oxford University Press.

Ellison, Nicole B., Charles Steinfield, and Cliff Lampe. 2011. "Connection Strategies: Social Capital Implications of Facebook-Enabled Communication Practices." *New Media and Society* 13:873–892.

Entertainment Software Association. 2011. *Essential Facts about the Computer and Video Game Industry.* Washington, DC. http://www.theesa.com/facts/gameplayer.asp.

Fenton Report Global. 2011. "Survey Suggests Time Teens Spend Playing Video and Online Games Can Be Used to Teach Important Life Lessons." Last modified August 9. http://www.fentonreport.com/technology-trends/survey-suggests-time-teens-spend-playing-video-and-online-games-can-be-used-to-teach-important-life-lessons.

Fields, Deborah, and Yasmin Kafai. 2010. "Knowing and Throwing Mudballs, Hearts, Pies, and Flowers: A Connective Ethnography of Gaming Practices." *Games and Culture* 5:88–115.

Granovetter, Mark S. 1973. "The Strength of Weak Ties." *American Journal of Sociology* 78:1360–1480.

Greenhow, Christine, and Beth Robelia. 2009. "Old Communication, New Literacies: Social Network Sites as Social Learning Resources." *Journal of Computer-Mediated Communication* 14:1130–1161.

Hartshorne, Richard, Philip VanFossen, and Adam Friedman. 2012. "MMORPG Roles, Civic Participation and Leadership among Generation Y." *International Journal of Gaming and Computer-Mediated Simulations* 4:55–67.

Hayes, Elisabeth. 2008. "Girls, Gaming, and Trajectories of IT Expertise." In *Beyond Barbie and Mortal Kombat: New Perspectives in Gender and Games*, edited by Yasmin Kafai, Carrie Heeter, Jill Denner, and Jen Sun, 217–230. Cambridge, MA: MIT Press.

Heeter, Carrie, Dan Sarkar, Becky Palmer-Scott, and Shasha Zhang. 2012. "Engineering Sociability: Friendship Drive, Visibility, and Social Connection in Anonymous Co-located Local Wi-Fi Multiplayer Online Gaming." *Journal of Games and Computer-Mediated Simulations* 4(2):1–18.

Hou, Jinhui. 2011. "Uses and Gratifications of Social Games: Blending Social Networking and Game Play." *First Monday* 16(7). http://firstmonday.org/htbin/cgiwrap/bin/ojs/index.php/fm/article/view/3517/3020.

IBM. 2007. *Virtual Worlds, Real Leaders: Online Games Put the Future of Business Leadership on Display. A Global Innovation Outlook 2.0 Report*. Armonk, NY. http://www.ibm.com/ibm/files/L668029W94664H98/ibm_gio_gaming_report.pdf.

Inside Network. 2012. "AppData." Accessed June 20. http://www.appdata.com/logged_out.

Jackson, David. 1997. "Case Studies of Microcomputer and Interactive Video Simulations in Middle School Earth Science Teaching." *Journal of Science Education and Technology* 6:127–141.

Kahne, Joseph, Ellen Middaugh, and Chris Evans. 2008. "The Civic Potential of Video Games." Cambridge, MA: MIT Press. http://www.civicsurvey.org/White_paper_link_text.pdf.

Lampe, Cliff, Donghee Yvette Wohn, Jessica Vitak, Nicole Ellison, and Rick Wash. 2011. "Student Use of Facebook for Organizing Collaborative Classroom Activities." *International Journal of Computer-Supported Collaborative Learning* 6:329–347.

Lazzaro, Nicole. 2004. "Why We Play Games: Four Keys to More Emotion without Story." Last modified March 8. http://xeodesign.com/xeodesign_whyweplaygames.pdf.

Lee, Yu-Hao, and Donghee Yvette Wohn. 2012. "Are There Cultural Differences in How We Play? Examining Cultural Effects on Playing Social Network Games." *Computers in Human Behavior* 4:1307–1314.

Lenhart, Amanda, Joe Kahne, Ellen Middaugh, Alexandra Macgill, Chris Evans, and Jessica Vitak. 2008. *Teens, Video Games, and Civics: A Pew Internet and Family Life Report*. Washington, DC: Pew Internet & American Life Project. http://www.pewinternet.org/Reports/2008/Teens-Video-Games-and-Civics.aspx.

Lenhart, Amanda, Mary Madden, Aaron Smith, Kristen Purcell, Kathryn Zickuhr, and Lee Rainie. 2011. *Teens, Kindness and Cruelty on Social Network Sites: A Pew Internet and Family Life Report.* Washington, DC: Pew Internet & American Life Project. Last modified November 9, 2011. http://pewinternet.org/Reports/2011/Teens-and-social-media .aspx.

Lim, Sohye, and Jong-Eun Lee. 2007. "Effects of Coplaying on Arousal and Emotional Responses in Videogame Play." Paper presented at the International Communication Association Conference, San Francisco, May 24–28.

Lin, Nan. 1999. "Building a Network Theory of Social Capital." *Connections* 22:28–51.

———. 2001. "Building a Network Theory of Social Capital." In *Social Capital Theory and Research*, edited by Nan Lin, Karen S. Cook, and Ronald S. Burt, 3–30. New Brunswick, NJ: Transaction Publishers.

Linn, Marcia, and Nicholas Burbules. 1991. "Construction of Knowledge and Group Learning." In *The Practice of Constructivism in Science Education*, edited by Kenneth Tobin, 91–119. Washington, DC: AAAS Press.

Millstone, Jessica. 2012. "Teacher Attitudes about Digital Games in the Classroom." New York: Joan Ganz Cooney Center at Sesame Workshop. http://www.joanganzcooneycenter .org/images/presentation/jgcc_teacher_survey.pdf.

Morris, Meredith Ringel, Jaime Teevan, and Katrina Panovich. 2010. "What Do People Ask Their Social Networks, and Why? A Survey Study of Status Message Q&A Behavior." Paper presented at CHI, Atlanta, April 10–15.

Oldenburg, Ray. 1999. *The Great Good Place: Cafes, Coffee Shops, Bookstores, Bars, Hair Salons and Other Hangouts at the Heart of a Community.* New York: Marlowe & Company.

O'Neil, Nick. 2010. "10 Mind Blowing Facebook Games Statistics." Last modified September 22. http://www.allfacebook.com/facebook-games-statistics-2010-09.

Pohl, Scott. 2012. "Grumpy Snowmen: MSU's Answer to Angry Birds." Accessed March 18. http://wkar.org/post/grumpy-snowmen-msus-answer-angry-birds.

Pop Cap Games Information Solutions Group. 2010. "2010 Social Gaming Research." Accessed June 20, 2012. http://www.infosolutionsgroup.com/2010_PopCap_Social_Gaming _Research_Results.pdf.

Putnam, Robert. 2000. *Bowling Alone: The Collapse and Revival of American Community.* New York: Simon & Schuster.

Radoff, Jon. 2011. *Game On: Energize Your Business with Social Media Games.* Indianapolis, IN: Wiley.

Ratan, Robby, Jae Eun Chung, Cuihua Shen, Dmitri Williams, and Marshall Pool. 2010. "Schmoozing and Smiting: Trust, Social Institutions, and Communication Patterns in an MMOG." *Journal of Computer-Mediated Communication* 16:93–114.

Salaway, Gail, Judy Caruso, and Mark Nelson. 2008. *The ECAR Study of Undergraduate Students and Information Technology, 2008.* Boulder, CO: EDUCAUSE Center for Applied Research.

Science Daily. 2011. "Gamers Succeed Where Scientists Fail: Molecular Structure of Retrovirus Enzyme Solved, Doors Open to New AIDS Drug Design." Last modified September 19. http://www.sciencedaily.com/releases/2011/09/110918144955.htm.

Shirky, Clay. 2003. "Power Laws, Weblogs, and Inequality." *Clay Shirky's Writings about the Internet.* February 8. http://shirky.com/writings/powerlaw_weblog.html.

———. 2008. *Here Comes Everybody: The Power of Organizing without Organizations.* New York: Penguin Books.

Smith, Shannon, Gail Salaway, and Judy Caruso. 2009. *The ECAR Study of Undergraduate Students and Information Technology, 2009*. Boulder, CO: EDUCAUSE Center for Applied Research.

Steinfield, Charles, Nicole B. Ellison, and Cliff Lampe. 2008. "Social Capital, Self-Esteem, and Use of Online Social Network Sites: A Longitudinal Analysis." *Journal of Applied Developmental Psychology* 29:434–445.

Steinkuehler, Constance, and Dmitri Williams. 2006. "Where Everybody Knows Your (Screen) Name: Online Games as 'Third Places.'" *Journal of Computer-Mediated Communication* 11:885–909.

Vitak, Jessica, Nicole B. Ellison, and Charles Steinfield. 2011. "The Ties That Bond: Reexamining the Relationship between Facebook Use and Bonding Social Capital." Paper presented at 44th Annual Hawaii International Conference on System Sciences, Kauai, Hawaii, January 4–7.

Werner, Linda, Jill Denner, and Steve Bean. 2004. "Pair Programming Strategies for Middle School Girls and Boys to Reduce the Gender Gap." Paper presented at the 7th IASTED International Conference Computers and Advanced Technology in Education, Kauai, Hawaii, August 16–18.

Williams, Dmitri. 2006. "On and Off the 'Net: Scales for Social Capital in an Online Era." *Journal of Computer-Mediated Communication* 11:593–628.

Wohn, Donghee Yvette. 2011a. "Reciprocity in Social Network Games and Generation of Social Capital." Paper presented at the Association for Education in Journalism and Mass Communication (AEJMC) Conference, St. Louis, August 10–13.

———. 2011b. "The Role of Habit Strength in Social Network Game Play." *Communication Research Reports* 29:74–79.

Wohn, Donghee Yvette, Cliff Lampe, Rick Wash, Nicole Ellison, and Jessica Vitak. 2011. "The 'S' in Social Network Games: Initiating, Maintaining, and Enhancing Relationships." In *Proceedings of the Hawaii International Conference of System Sciences (HICSS)*, edited by Ralph H. Sprague Jr., 1–10. Washington, DC: IEEE Computer Society.

Wohn, Donghee Yvette, Yu-Hao Lee, Jieun Sung, and Tor Bjornrud. 2010. "Building Common Ground and Reciprocity with Social Network Games." Poster presented at CHI, Atlanta, April 10–15.

Yee, Nick. 2006. "The Demographics, Motivations and Derived Experiences of Users of Massively-Multiuser Online Graphical Environments." *PRESENCE: Teleoperators and Virtual Environments* 15:309–329.

CHAPTER ELEVEN

Gender, Social Media, Games, and the College Landscape

GISELE RAGUSA

To fully understand the role that gender plays in social media and its effect on higher education, we must first contextualize the changing landscape of technology in colleges and universities. This chapter offers a research-informed future forecasting of gender differences associated with new media. The foci are two connected types of socially focused technologies used in postsecondary education: social networking and socially mediated games. The chapter explores the strengths, challenges, power issues, and biases associated with gender in social media. It provides directions and recommendations for understanding relationships between social media on gender roles and identity development, and in particular how it manifests itself on college campuses.

Gender, Media, and Twenty-First-Century Technologies

As Tracy Fullerton describes in her chapter, the growth of new media applications has facilitated development of online social networks for individuals with common interests of communicating, socializing, and collaborating (Shen et al. 2010). Social media genres connect people for social and professional purposes, and these experiences provide new meaning for friends, acquaintances, and collegial relationships, casting people's social net far beyond geographic and traditional sociopolitical boundaries. This is especially important on college campuses because it is in these environments where friendships and support structures can develop.

As Zoë Corwin discusses in part I, social media have enabled people to communicate casually and professionally in ways that were only imagined a decade ago. For college-aged individuals, this practice has become a part of everyday life. This is particularly evident for those considering college enrollment (Zick-uhr and Smith 2012), as these groups "live" in media-saturated worlds. In a recent survey by Roberts, Foehr, and Rideout (2005), college-aged students spend more than 7.5 hours daily using some form of electronic media, with more than one-fourth of that time spent in "multi-media" situations, which accounts for overall exposure exceeding 10 hours per day, an amount of time that far surpasses time spent during a weekday at school or with family members.

Early gender and media research indicates that males and females have historically accessed media at different rates. In studies of computer use by Much-erah (2003), Kay (1992), and Koch (1994), males were found to be more likely to use computers than females. Importantly, contemporary research counters this finding, as access to and availability of technology is no longer gender-bound, because basic technology (e.g., internet) is now close to "universally accessible" (Horrigan and Smith 2007; Jackson et al. 2001). Internet use has doubled between 2000 and 2011. In 2000, half of all men used the internet and 45% of women used the internet, and in 2011, internet use by women increased to 76% and by men to 80% (Zickuhr and Smith 2012, 2). Currently, 26% of all women and 24% of all men are smartphone users. Such statistics indicate that technology usage across genders is now virtually "equal" in spite of early reported gender inequities.

The proliferation of changing media and increased access requires that individuals and groups make choices about media use. Both research and marketing data have indicated that young adult media choices are often associated with social position and identity aspiration (Brown and Bobkowski 2011; Steele 1999). Media-preference-related research has uncovered significant differences in use patterns associated with identity including age, gender, race, and ethnicity. As examples of this, college students spend more time listening to digitized music and using the internet, while younger teens watch television and movies and play video and online games (Brown and Bobkowski 2011, 2). College-aged women are more likely to use cell phones, text message, and send messages via social networking sites (Lenhart et al. 2008), while college-aged males spend more time playing computer games (Roberts, Foehr, and Rideout 2005).

Males and females have been found to use technology media, and specifically email and the internet, for different purposes (Hartsell 2005; Jackson et al. 2001). For example, Jackson and colleagues examined gender differences in purposes of internet use of young adults and explored cognitive, motivational, and other affective factors responsible for these differences. They determined that women utilize social media primarily for communicating, while men use social media for gathering information. Psychosocial factors predicted social media use across genders in their research. Similarly, Hartsell (2005) explored interaction patterns among genders in online discussion posts, and in particular those connected to college courses. She noted, when examining the quantity and quality of the socially mediated interaction, women engaged in purposeful interaction more frequently than men and that men's interactions were more "direct" and of a reporting nature, while women's interactions were supportive with less direct reporting and more communicative foci. This finding is supported by other research on gender and online interaction patterns among college students (Arbaugh 2000; Shaw and Gant 2002); female interaction is primarily communication focused and male interaction is information-centric. These findings are especially important on college campuses because differences in technology use across genders need to come under consideration when student affairs personnel, faculty, and college administrators make decisions about the media they will use for information sharing. For example, given that research has indicated that males are more likely to spend time on games, these media may serve as motivation for engaging college men in academic activities for which they may have limited interest. Games could serve as media for tutoring and developmental education. Social networks and group communication through social media may also serve as a means to bridge gender differences. Deliberate interactive activities could be set up on networks that provide structured or semistructured opportunities to work in cross-gender team building to bridge gaps in technology preferences and purposes. Alternatively, gender-specific network sites may assist in developing college students' gender identity particularly if younger students are paired with same-sex role models and mentors of older ages as a means of support and role modeling during critical college transition periods.

Motivation, Power, and Gender: Theoretical Models Predicting Social Media Interaction on College Campuses

More than a decade ago and before the advent of contemporary social networks and games, Jackson and colleagues (2001) proposed a model of internet use in which motivational, affective, and cognitive factors served as "both antecedents and consequences of (internet) use" (364). The model posited that people use the internet because it meets their purposes, elicits positive affect, and meets or challenges their cognitive abilities. This model was particularly pertinent when considering learning through technology in colleges and universities. However comprehensive and forthcoming the model was for its era, it was conceptualized before the advent of contemporary social media and in particular social networking and socially mediated games. It missed critical factors that necessitate inclusion when studying contemporary media interaction and especially in studies of gender on college campuses. Jackson's model does provide necessary building blocks for analyses of impacts of contemporary social network and game interactions, mediating factors, and potential gender-latent challenges and dilemmas that are pertinent to college students.

Ellison, Steinfield, and Lampe (2007) highlight the role of "bridging and bonding" social capital in their study of Facebook (one of the social network sites most widely used by college students). This perspective is detailed by Ellison and her colleagues here, and its frame provides a useful theoretical element that capitalizes on Jackson's early work and reframes analyses with foci on contemporary technology-mediated interaction and associated learning. Social capital per Ellison and colleagues (2007) are "resources accumulated through relationships among people" (1145) and viewed as a means of achieving positive outcomes. In the context of social networks and games, social capital increases community commitment and allows participants "to draw on resources from other members of the networks to which he or she belongs" (1145). This builds on the work of Paxton (1999) and Putnam (2000) whereby social bonding refers to strong ties among individuals or groups that occur in emotionally connected relationships, while social bridging refers to "weak ties" that are associated with loose connections most often related to information or new perspectives rather than support (Ellison et al. 2007, 1146). While the research of Ellison and colleagues (2007), Paxton (1999), and Putnam (2000) was not originally focused on gender, in this chapter I build on their work, include the scholarship of critical studies researchers (Kinder 1991; Willis 1991), and consider feminist pedagogy as defined by Luke and Gore (1992) in the development of a new theoretical model related to college students and gender. This model, when applied to contemporary social media and specifically to networks and games on college campuses, provides an analytical framework by which we can understand the impact of social media on gender identity and associated

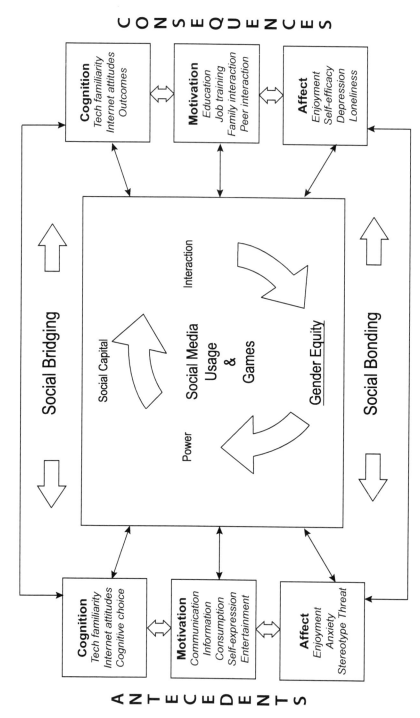

CONSEQUENCES

ANTECEDENTS

Cognition
Tech familiarity
Internet attitudes
Outcomes

Motivation
Education
Job training
Family interaction
Peer interaction

Affect
Enjoyment
Self-efficacy
Depression
Loneliness

Social Bridging

Social Bonding

Interaction

Social Capital

Social Media
Usage
&
Games

Gender Equity

Power

Cognition
Tech familiarity
Internet attitudes
Cognitive choice

Motivation
Communication
Information
Consumption
Self-expression
Entertainment

Affect
Enjoyment
Anxiety
Stereotype Threat

Figure 11.1. Theoretical model associated with gender, social media, and games on college campuses.

development and, most importantly, factors associated with college student learning. This in turn can shift game, network, and other social media design away from that which is at times biased against women and girls toward media that is equitably supportive of both genders and facilitates pro-social development and learning across genders using an equity pedagogy (Bandura 2002; Gentile et al. 2009; Luke 1994; Luke and Gore 1992). From this vantage point, social networks and games can play a pronounced, contributory role in achieving gender equity (figure 11.1).

The model incorporates historical and contemporary theories associated with technology mediation, learning, social media, feminism, and game theory principles. New to the model are the interactions among the constructs: motivation, cognition, learning, and affect, as these constructs are necessary to assess the impacts of social media on users and especially on college students' learning. These constructs affect one another, thus impacting development, learning, and full participation with social media and especially social networks and learning-focused games (Bandura 2002). The introduction of feminist pedagogy to the model requires that we challenge how representations of gender and sexuality disempower some groups while privileging others. Importantly, gender equity is used to describe both the principle and practice of fair and equitable allocation of resources to and opportunities for college students facilitated by socially rich media. Gender equity eliminates discriminatory practices that are barriers to full participation for either gender on college campuses. This is of particular importance in postsecondary networking (and even gameplay) and its links to college access, as we have yet to equalize playing fields in terms of college admissions, full participation, and retention on college and university campuses nationally. Learning-focused media and games could play an influential role in such equity if we are deliberate in the way we design network sites focused on college learning, access, and support.

Notably, the practice of gender equity does not necessarily imply that everyone is treated universally in the model because universal treatment is unlikely to yield equal opportunities for males and females within existing power structures in contemporary media. Instead, equity equates to changing responses to and treatment of both genders to ensure that gender is a neutral factor when accessing resources and technology-mediated opportunities. This represents the primary change feature in the theoretical model and provides the context for gender impacts.

Contemporary Media: Social Networking Opportunities and Challenges

New media choices offer opportunities for young people to no longer experience media passively. Ample research examining behavior patterns of specific groups in media interaction and use has been initiated. Because the focus of the chapter is on gender at the postsecondary level, the review that follows is restricted to comparisons between adolescent and young adult males and females in contemporary media use, behaviors, and experiences on college campuses.

In the most commonly used social networking sites, such as Facebook and LinkedIn, an individual creates a profile that uniquely identifies her or him and allows for dynamic, integrated images, video, and audio components, thus enabling sharable and flexible construction of identity (Ellison, Steinfield, and Lampe 2007). Within these sites, users keep public chronologies and diaries, send public and private messages, ask for comments from others associated with their posts, and uniquely identify themselves with preferences that publicly display their profile for all networked members to view.

Social media enable college students to maintain contact with high school and other neighborhood friends while they transition to college; at the same time, such media also allow them to connect with students on their own college campus. Colleges and universities now utilize these networks as a means of communicating with students while they prepare for entrance to college and once they arrive on campuses. However convenient this is for college personnel, gender-related needs and motivation among students are often ignored in the current use of sites. Typically, networks are used for information sharing, while not fully capitalizing on the flexibility, interactivity, and existing resources available through the media. To improve interaction from student to student, student to faculty, and student to support personnel, groups could be deliberately structured on social networks that facilitate mentorship and cross-aged role modeling for college students before their arrival on campus and that assist in retention support once students enroll. This networking is very powerful for incoming college freshman and transfer students, during times when students' social, identity, and academic vulnerability is paramount.

Recent research has indicated that the two genders engage in social media identity construction in different ways. This speaks to the importance of frontloading student support that leverages social media as students prepare to enter college. Mikami and colleagues (2010) examined the communication and friendship development of teens and college students on social networking sites. Network use was compared longitudinally to face-to-face interaction, and friendship patterns were the primary targets of this research. Participants' social network web pages were examined and compared using instrumentation that quantified friendship relationships and identity developmental patterns. Mikami and colleagues (2010) found that adolescent youth who display greater negativity in their face-to-face peer interactions are significantly less likely to have social networking pages in college, and those who have a network site among this subgroup post items at lower rates. Additionally, college-aged students who describe more positive attributes in their close relationships are more likely to have social networking pages. Participants reporting positivity also have more friends posting comments on their network page(s). Mikami and colleagues (2010) found that young women have significantly more people posting positive comments on their network in addition to this subgroup posting more supporting comments on their web pages than young men have. This study's results on differentiated gender patterns in network behaviors is supported by others (Hartsell 2005; Jackson et al. 2001) and confirms that not only do genders have different interaction patterns in networks, but they also have different motivations and perhaps even different perceived roles during interaction. These findings are important to faculty and student affairs personnel because they suggest that network patterns can be used to provide caution to college staff where social struggles may be emerging in students. Network interaction patterns can trigger the need for planned social interventions among students that may serve as an important prevention strategy to alleviate social difficulties before they escalate.

Social networks can enable informal and formal mentorship opportunities to occur within and across genders. Girls Educational and Mentoring Services (GEMS), a national network that uses Facebook and Twitter as outreach to exploited girls, serves as a profound example of this opportunity. GEMS has, through deliberate processes of networked virtual mentorship, enabled girls and young women to experience collective female leadership and lessened isolation on college campuses nationally. The Stepup Women's Network (2012), a second example of such work, has a goal to "bridge communities of professional women and underserved teen girls through mentorship, networking, and advancement."

Baldwin (2011) and Austrian (2011) describe the critical need for "safe spaces" for adolescent girls as they develop into adulthood, much of which occurs on college campuses. Safe spaces are "girl only" spaces where women and girls can receive peer mentorship and support from others of the same gender and develop career and life skills that enable lifelong independence. Baldwin (2011) and Austrian (2011) view gender-specific experiences as important "safe spaces" for women and girls to interact and grow. I view social networking as a means of expanding upon built environments that enable these efforts, so that women and girls can reach across social and geographic boundaries and provide and receive mentorship and education including financial literacy and career development and engage in meaningful friendship and partnerships in virtual "safe space" environments that have international impact that is unsurpassed by previous face-to-face mentored efforts. These environments enable collaboration among women and girls and facilitate collective intelligence among gender groups (Brown and Lauder 2000). This process is of upmost importance in postsecondary education as these efforts can serve as means for adolescent girls to have access and retention support in college and university settings that may not be bound by the brick and mortar of traditional campuses.

However powerful social networking may be when directed at improving the lives of traditionally marginalized subgroups of college students and providing access to resources, skills, and support, some social network interactions have recently received significant negative media attention. One rather dramatic negative interaction pattern emerging in social networks (and in other social media) is cyberbullying. According to the National Crime Prevention Council (2012), cyberbullying refers to when networks (or other internet media) are used in cruelty to others by posting text or images intended solely to hurt or demean another person. The Pew Internet & American Life Project (Lenhart and Madden 2007) posits that one-third (32%) of American online teens have been the victim of cyberbullying and 39% of social network users have been cyberbullied, as opposed to 22% of teens not using social networking sites in the past five years. These alarming statistics provides ample warning that social networking warrants watchful monitoring and perhaps secure restructuring to alleviate this emergent problem.

Cyberbullying differs from the more traditional forms of bullying in that it can occur at anytime, 24/7 (Hinduja and Patchin 2012). Messages, videos, and images can be distributed instantaneously to a worldwide audience with the perpetrator remaining anonymous, often making the "bully" very difficult to trace. Although research on cyberbullying is scarce, approximately 30% of students in grades 6–16 report they recently have been cyberbullied or have cyberbullied someone, indicating that cyberbullying begins in K–12 and extends on to college campuses. Hinduja and Patchin's (2012) research reveals that females are twice as likely as males to be victims and perpetrators of cyberbullying. Hence, gender differences associated with cyberbullying have important implications both for potential female victimization and for empowerment depending upon the role in which women and girls are situated within the media. As youth venture on to college campuses, cyberbullying takes on new meaning, because college goers are no longer monitored by their families and therefore must be armed to protect themselves when parental monitoring is no longer present. This has important implications for training needs in college student affairs staff. Cyberbullying has not been a typical training topic for student affairs personnel; however, given the impact of this challenge, it certainly warrants targeted training efforts.

Cyberbullying is one example of how networking can go terribly wrong. This societal challenge is becoming pervasive and is especially problematic for girls and young women. It presents us with a call for strategic monitoring of network sites, particularly on college campuses, and the need for development of deliberate review mechanisms that student affairs administrators and college counselors can use to determine the worth and appropriateness of social network sites for their college students. Criteria are needed to determine the appropriateness of sites, and college support providers need tools to help their students to develop skills to confront cyberbullying and to proactively avoid it. The good news about this contemporary social problem is that there are new resources available for parents, college students, and college staff to learn about protecting against cyberbullying and other similar negative dilemmas in social networking. One such resource, *Our Space*, in a collaboration sponsored by the GoodPlay Project, provides a venue in which young people engage in ethical thinking and pro-social conduct in online simulation environments. This project enables young people to become "cyberwise" as they practice venturing into new media environments using safe spaces in which to practice protecting themselves and others. This is being used for both K–12 and college students and could be expanded or specialized to meet the campus-specific needs of college students. These tools can be quite valuable as students venture independently onto college campuses where they are no longer under the watchful eye of their parents and must make informed choices about media use to protect themselves and those with whom they interact online.

However compelling social networking environments can be for college students, networks can have both positive and negative impacts on the gender depending on how individuals are situated in the network contexts and the roles in which they situate themselves. Both young men and women need tools to engage in pro-social and equity-minded behaviors online and to avoid victimization. These tools can be delivered or facilitated by college faculty, college counselors, community members, or facilitated by the social networking environment itself, especially if it is deliberately structured with support and equity foci.

Gender, Game Environments, and College Play

Games are one particular type of social media in which gender differences are magnified. Educators, families, and others interested in human development have long recognized the importance of play in child development but have not extended such importance to college-going groups. Importantly, games have been identified as critical mediators for youth's social, cognitive, and moral development (Okagaki and Frensch 1994). This perspective dominates childhood literature; however, play in young adulthood has been sparsely studied using a sociodevelopmental lens (see figure 11.1). Ironically, most technology-mediated and especially socially mediated games cater to adolescent players, as this group is a primary user of the genre, suggesting, from both a marketing and an educational perspective, that play is an arena that warrants continued study focused on postsecondary populations. Given that research on social media use has indicated that college students are making choices to participate in socially mediated spaces, games provide an important genre where both males and females may thrive and where gender equity could be supported.

Both men and women play games; however, the gender-related pattern varies by age. At almost every age level, males spend more time playing games than females do; however, by combining computer and video games, a recent Kaiser Family Foundation Report (Roberts, Foehr, and Rideout 2005) found that a steady drop in gameplay occurs between the ages of 8 and 18. Boys play an average of 1 hour and 34 minutes per day and girls less than half as long (about 40 minutes). The pattern indicated an even steeper drop as young women and men enter college. Researchers posit that this is likely associated with the time it takes to focus on college. While game use in college is less than that (particularly for women) of adolescents, college students (particularly men) do play socially mediated games. Winn and Heeter (2009) studied gender and game use with a slant toward gender difference in "use of time" in adulthood and how this interfaces with gameplay. They found distinct differences in the way the two genders use leisure time in college and posit that gameplay difference among genders could be related to time use differences associated with grade point average (GPA) and employment while in college. This is of particular importance among college students because time use is critical among students who have very little free time available overall. In this study, male students were found to spend five times as much time on games as females in college.

While gameplay in college is far less frequent in women than men (Winn and Heeter 2009), games designed to meet the unique needs of women and those that promote gender equity can serve as a powerful social force for both genders. Gender-neutral games and games in which females are portrayed in power and with strength in decision making are a vantage point for gender equity in girls and women. Gender-neutral games are becoming more prevalent in the gaming world. Games that include massively multiplayer online role-playing games (MMORPGs) in virtual worlds like *FarmVille*, *Whyville*, and *CityVille* and other massively multiplayer online games (MMOGs) accessed via smartphone applications include *Hanging With Friends* and *Draw Something* are community-focused games that do not involve gender roles. These games foster "virtually" limitless collaboration and "friendly" competition with gender anonymity during play. They also improve equity among players; they promote community and vocabulary development and have been found to be attractive to college-aged female players as they build upon their social media behavior preferences for community (Shaw and Gant 2002) and communication (Shen et al. 2010).

To further explore the usage of these type of games, a game based on the role designation game *FarmVille* could be developed, which requires decision and choice making, in which genders could be assigned nonstereotypic roles that promote advanced decision making and nontraditional career choice to promote gender equity. Alternatively, *Words With Friends*, another gender-neutral game, could be expanded upon to include equity-focused words so that the equity-focused vocabulary is targeted. These examples provide males and females with equity mindsets that could promote pro-social behavior. Additionally, gameplay between genders in which female and males are portrayed as equals may facilitate development of such equity. This is especially important on college campuses because it is during this time period that students are developing their ideals independent from their families, exploring altruism, engaging in independent decision making (often for the first time in their lives), and beginning to take activist stances on behalf of themselves and their peers (Kohlberg 1973).

Game Design and Gender Empowerment

Games that promote feminist perspectives are far less prevalent than gender-neutral games. Currently, there are many web-based "games for girls"—games that are designed specifically for female players. Upon careful review of such games at their advertised sites, however, I note that most (ca. 82%) of these games depict activities such as "dress up," with foci on physical appearance, makeup and beauty, cooking, and other traditionally stereotypic activities. Most reviewed games are advertised on pink, flowery websites, also characteristic of traditional, stereotypic gender identification. Further, these games purport to exemplify "girl power" but do not attempt to defy tradition and reframe gender identity in power roles.

One game suite of interest from a feminist perspective is titled *Girl Power*, in which female heroes in history are embedded in activities and other game functions. Unfortunately, even among these types of games in which feminist heroism is promoted, game features depict traditional elements associated with gender stereotypes, with girls in traditional garb. Even games that claim to be about "girl power" present stereotypic roles for women and girls (Guy 2007). There are other educational games that are relatively nonstereotypic including those situated in network sites (as described as gender neutral); however, few of these are designed to meet the unique identity and empowerment needs of young women and girls (Flanagan 2003). So, what does this mean for college students? First, it signals that additional development is warranted in games. This genre provides opportunity for college students to play a gender equity role in improving the types of games available to society through game development.

In line with this premise, research on feminist technology calls for gendered analyses that explore the mutual shaping of gender and technology in which technology is viewed as both a source and a consequence of gender relations, and in which gender shapes the way in which technology is used. This is important in game design whereby involving women and girls, especially college students, in game design could set direction of design efforts in favor of the needs and preferences of women and girls. This perspective is supported by Cunningham's (2011) work, in which females were engaged in game design. This research resulted in granting females "agency" in game design, thus enabling them to design "gender neutral" characters for games, indicative of their desire to challenge the traditions of gender stereotypic game characters. This contemporary scholarship serves as a model for future feminist-centric design and research that informs college careers for girls and young women that is of particular importance because in STEM (science, technology, engineering, and mathematics) research, access to STEM careers for women lags far below males.

Hypersexuality in Games

Ample game research focused on character depiction, role, and gender impact emerged in the late 1990s and early 2000s. Scholars began having concerns over the impact of the media on gender stereotypes in the late 1990s (Sherman 1997) and applied this concern to game character depiction shortly thereafter (Eastin 2006). The concerns involve gender inequity, potential effects on females with regard to victimization, and socialized gender-biased practices in game story lines. Since the advent of video games that have "human-like" characters or avatars, hypersexuality in video game characters is of significant concern. Hypersexuality appears in avatars' clothing, in both type and amount of clothing. Most often, female avatars are depicted in highly sexualized costumes, bearing frightened or submissive facial expressions. In contrast, male avatars are often portrayed as hypermasculine, extremely muscular, aggressive, and often violent (Downs and Smith 2010). This is very prominent in action-oriented games and war strategy games, which constitute half of the top 10 most popular and commonly purchased games among college students (Entertainment Software Association 2011). Unfortunately, when contemporary games depict player avatars in stereotypic roles, the games reinforce traditional and often marginalized roles for women and girls. While only 10% to 14% of all video game characters are females (Dietz 1998; Dill et al. 2005; Downs and Smith 2010; Mou and Peng 2008; Wohn 2011) in today's games, when the female gender is represented, it is often hypersexualized. Images in these games send messages to male and female game players that females are weaker than males and that women are not in positions of power. They legitimize hypersexualization that, in the case of college student players, provide formative information for gender identity development during a time when body image is especially vulnerable.

Not only are female characters hypersexualized; male figures are similarly depicted in some games. Male characters are often draped with weaponry representing warrior imagery suggestive of violence. These types of avatar depictions are particular to action or war genre games; however, these images permeate a highly popular category of contemporary action games that college students commonly play (Entertainment Software Association 2011). The depictions accentuate power differentiation and present women in a marginalized role. On college campuses, student affairs staff must counter these images and the messages that they send to students during a developmental period when students are very vulnerable with regard to body image. These characters have similar effects to that of magazine model images that occurred during the "Twiggy era" (1960s and early 1970s), which resulted in a dramatic rise in eating disorders among both high school and college students. These are powerful forces for student support providers to reckon with that could result in compromising situations for both male and female college students.

Gender stereotypic avatar depiction in games is especially problematic when consideration is given to self-concept, a construct that is typically fragile in college goers (Bandura 2002; Behm-Morawitz and Mastro 2009; Peter and Valkenberg 2008). While Bandura's framework for efficacy and identity suggests that certain media characteristics enhance learning, research has indicated that pronounced exposure to violence and sexualized media leads to victimization of females (Noll et al. 2009). Accordingly, challenges associated with principle features of the games and character or avatar development, in addition to the experience in the game, should be carefully considered during game design. These phenomena cannot be ignored if we have hope that gender equity in social media will be achieved. The good news is that gender-neutral game development is becoming pervasive, particularly with increased use by teens and young adults of smartphones and the ease of use of gender neutral MMOGs on such apparatus.

Games, Networks, and Gender: Where Do We Go From Here?

This chapter has argued that we have much work to do to improve development of mutually supportive social media and specifically social network sites and equitable games for college goers. While contemporary social networks in which individuals form communities may support gender equity and development on equal playing fields for college students, stereotypic gender roles are currently present in some features in social media across genres. Cyberbullying has taken on a new flavor in social networking sites, particular for female college students. Females are far more likely to be cyberbullied on social networking sites than males. Players of both genders encounter sexualized, stereotypical messages from female avatars with exaggerated sexualized clothing and submissive victimized facial features, and violent and overly masculine messages from male avatars with exaggerated muscular physiques and overpowering demeanors. As college faculty and student affairs staff and counselors, we can play an authoritative role in advising media designers in changing the "face" of networks and games literally and figuratively for the sake of college students across genders. We must engage in pro-social behavior to facilitate this important change (Anderson and Bushman 2001) as these changes have consequences associated with college access, persistence, and comfort. Efficacious, confident, empowered young women and men can make sound college-related choices and will be armed to persist in college even when faced with potential isolation and adversity, if this stance is facilitated (Gentile et al. 2009).

Pro-Social Networks and Games: A Movement Toward Equity for All

Given the potential for gender inequity in social media and in particular in games, challenges for which we need college-focused solutions include: (1) determination of which experiences are mutually supportive of male and female college goers; (2) pro-social review of games and other social media experiences for gender neutrality or biases (Anderson and Bushman 2001; Gentile et al. 2009); and (3) recommendations for improving situations that promote gender equity in social networks, games, and other social media.

As described, social media genres can serve as means to empower young women and men and certainly can provide equity across genders. This involves rethinking the design of network sites and involving different folks from those who are typically involved in design processes in testing (in the case of games, "play testing") with gender equity as a goal. Decisions made during design (and redesign) for each of the highlighted type of social media must keep gender equity on the forefront.

In terms of social networking, sites and applications for sites that support opportunities for both genders to engage in activities that promote equity should be supported, and usage of such site features should be encouraged by those who influence college students, including college faculty, coaches, student affairs staff, and other college support providers with whom male and female college students interact regularly. Sites that support mentorship and career development for young women are of utmost import for college-bound girls as these sites can have worldwide impact in college access.

Changing traditional sociocultural norms involving gender are also critical, and therefore engaging male college students in efforts to reduce discrimination against women is important. This can be effectively facilitated via social networking sites and through educational gameplay. Currently international philanthropic causes are added to Facebook, Twitter, and LinkedIn. We must add gender equity and in particular equity in college access, retention, and student support to such network causes.

Addressing gender stereotypes requires focusing on men as well as working with women at the college level. Enlisting male role models for young men, identifying male allies, and establishing partnerships and initiatives via social networks and games that are designed to educate both men and women on the benefits of gender equity can help to improve understanding, communication, and cooperation and lay a strong foundation for future development efforts among college students as they enter the work force. This, too, can be accomplished via social networking sites and could be especially effective if we play an active role in encouraging and participating in network-facilitated mentoring opportunities that promote equity of men and women. Effectively designed and supported social networking sites can help to reduce the social isolation and exclusion that both genders experience on college campuses and among those seeking to find out information about college-going processes.

Supported and monitored social network sites can provide male and female college students with safe places to gather, help them to build gender-specific social networks, offer social support and mentorship, build leadership, and connect them to information, services, and opportunities that address and end marginalization in society and support equitable career support, particularly in careers that are underrepresented by women, including STEM careers. By involving community leaders in gender-network-facilitated and enabled education, changes to gender norms can benefit both genders.

Games have related but slightly different issues operationally to promote gender equity. Given that games have "gone viral," we must capitalize on this and alter the way in which games are designed and play-tested to be certain that gender equity is achieved. This can be accomplished by involving both female and male college students in game design (Cunningham 2011). Effectively designed and supported socially focused games can enhance the empowerment process by deliberately challenging gender norms, reducing restrictions, and offering college women access to typically "male" spaces and more opportunities for their intellectual and social development. Groups including Women-Gamers.com are setting the stage for this proactive stance in game design by seeking to increase female gamer demographics by providing scholarships to girls who are interested in computer science and other game-development-related careers (Flanagan 2003). This in turn increases college and career opportunities for women in fields that have been traditionally dominated by males. We need to build upon these efforts and promote both gender-neutral game development and feminist perspective games.

Both social networking design and game development can be used to promote gender equity and empower both genders on virtual and built college campuses. We need to expand upon the contemporary research and practices in social media that promote this stance and use new media and modern technology to enable gender equity to go viral across college campuses.

REFERENCES

Anderson, Craig A., and Brad J. Bushman. 2001. "Effects of Violent Videogames on Aggressive Behavior, Aggressive Cognition, Aggressive Affect, Physiological Arousal, and Prosocial Behavior: A Meta-analytic Review of Scientific Literature." *Psychological Science* 12:353–359.

Arbaugh, John B. 2000. "An Exploratory Study of the Effects of Gender on Student Learning and Class Participation in an Internet-Based MBA Course." *Management Learning* 31:503–519.

Austrian, Karen. 2011. *Expanding Safe Spaces, Financial Education, and Savings for Adolescent Girls in Kenya [Brief No. 29]*. New York: Population Council. http://www.popcouncil.org/pdfs/TABriefs/29_KenyaGirlsSavings.pdf.

Baldwin, Wendy. 2011. *Creating Safe Spaces for Adolescent Girls [Brief No. 39]*. New York: Population Council. http://www.popcouncil.org/pdfs/TABriefs/39_SafeSpaces.pdf.

Bandura, Albert. 2002. "Social Cognitive Theory of Mass Communication." In *Media Effects: Advances in Theory and Research*, edited by Jennings Bryant and Dolf Zillmann, 121–153. Mahwah, NJ: Lawrence Erlbaum Associates.

Behm-Morawitz, Elizabeth, and Dana Mastro. 2009. "The Effects of the Sexualization of Female Video Game Characters on Gender Stereotyping and Female Self-Concept." *Sex Roles* 62:808–823.

Brown, Jane D., and Piotr S. Bobkowski. 2011. "Older and Newer Media: Patterns of Use and Effects on Adolescents' Health and Well-Being." *Journal of Research on Adolescence* 21:95–113.

Brown, Phillip, and Hugh Lauder. 2000. "Collective Intelligence." In *Social Capital: Critical Perspectives*, edited by Stephen Baron, John Field, and Tom Schuller, 34–37. New York: Oxford University Press.

Cunningham, Carolyn. 2011. "Girl Game Designers." *New Media & Society* 13:1373–1388.

Dietz, Tracy L. 1998. "An Examination of Violence and Gender Role Portrayals in Video Games: Implications for Gender Socialization and Aggressive Behavior." *Sex Roles* 38:425–442.

Dill, Karen E., Douglas A. Gentile, William A. Richter, and Jay C. Dill. 2005. "Violence, Sex, Race and Age in Popular Video Games: A Content Analysis." In *Featuring Females: Feminist Analyses of the Media*, edited by Ellen Cole, Jessice D. Henderson, and Jessica Henderson Daniel, 115–130. Washington, DC: American Psychological Association.

Downs, Edward, and Stacy Smith. 2010. "Keeping Abreast of Hypersexuality: A Video Game Character Content Analysis." *Sex Roles* 62:721–733.

Eastin, Matthew S. 2006. "Video Game Violence and the Female Game Player: Self- and Opponent Gender Effects on Presence and Aggressive Thoughts." *Human Communication Research* 32:351–372.

Ellison, Nicole B., Charles Steinfield, and Cliff Lampe. 2007. "The Benefits of Facebook 'Friends': Social Capital and College Students' Use of Online Social Network Sites." *Journal of Computer-Mediated Communication* 12:1143–1168.

Entertainment Software Association. 2011. *Essential Facts about the Computer and Video Game Industry.* Washington, DC. http://www.theesa.com/facts/pdfs/ESA_EF_2011.pdf.

Flanagan, Mary. 2003. "'Next Level': Women's Digital Activism through Gaming." In *Digital Media Revisited*, edited by Gunnar Liestøl, Andrew Morrison, and Terje Rasmussen, 359–388. Cambridge, MA: MIT Press.

Gentile, Douglas A., Craig A. Anderson, Shintaro Yukawa, Nobuko Ihori, Muniba Saleem, Lim Kam Ming, Akiko Shibuya, Albert K. Liau, Angeline Khoo, Brad J. Bushman, L. Rowell Huesmann, and Akira Sakamoto. 2009. "The Effects of Prosocial Video Games on Prosocial Behaviors: International Evidence from Correlational, Longitudinal, and Experimental Studies." *Personality and Social Psychology Bulletin* 35:752–763.

Guy, Hannah. 2007. "Women Video Gamers: Not Just Solitaire." Accessed September 11, 2012. http://www.asiancanadian.net/2007/03/women-video-gamers-not-just-solitaire.html.

Hartsell, Taralynn. 2005. "Who's Talking Online: A Descriptive Analysis of Gender and Online Communication." *International Journal of Information and Communication Technology Education* 1:42–54.

Hinduja, Sameer, and Justin W. Patchin. 2012. "Ten Ideas for Youth to Educate Their Community about Cyberbullying." Accessed September 11. http://www.cyberbullying.us/teens_cyberbullying_prevention_activities_tips.pdf.

Horrigan, John B., and Aaron Smith. 2007. *Home Broadband Adoption, 2007.* Washington, DC: Pew Internet & American Life Project.

Jackson, Linda A., Kathryn S. Ervin, Paul D. Gardner, and Neal Schmitt. 2001. "Gender and the Internet: Women Communicating and Men Searching." *Sex Roles* 44:363–379.

Kay, Robin H. 1992. "Understanding Gender Differences in Computer Attitudes, Aptitude, and Use: An Invitation to Build Theory." *Journal of Research on Computing in Education* 25:159–172.

Kinder, Marsha. 1991. *Playing with Power in Movies, Television, and Video Games: From Muppet Babies to Teenage Mutant Ninja Turtles.* Berkeley: University of California Press.

Koch, Melissa. 1994. "Opening Up Technology to Both Genders." *Education Digest* 60:18–23.

Kohlberg, Lawrence. 1973. "Continuities in Childhood and Adult Moral Reasoning Revisited." In *Life-Span Developmental Psychology*, edited by Paul B. Baltes and K. W. Scharie, 179–204. New York: Academic Press.

Lenhart, Amanda, Sousan Arafeh, Aaron Smith, and Alexandra Rankin Macgill. 2008. *Writing, Technology and Teens*. Washington, DC: Pew Internet & American Life Project. http://www.pewinternet.org/~/media//Files/Reports/2008/PIP_Writing_Report_FINAL3.pdf.pdf.

Lenhart, Amanda, and Mary Madden. 2007. *Social Networking Websites and Teens*. Washington, DC: Pew Internet & American Life Project. http://www.pewinternet.org/~/media//Files/Reports/2007/PIP_SNS_Data_Memo_Jan_2007.pdf.pdf.

Luke, Carmen. 1994. "Feminist Pedagogy and Critical Media Literacy." *Journal of Communication Inquiry* 18:30–47.

Luke, Carmen, and Jennifer Gore. 1992. *Feminism and Critical Pedagogy*. New York: Routledge.

Mikami, Amori Y., David E. Szwedo, Jonathon P. Allen, Martin A. Evans, and Amanda L. Hare. 2010. "Adolescent Peer Relationships and Behavior Problems Predict Young Adults' Communication on Social Networking Websites." *Developmental Psychology* 46:46–56.

Mou, Yi, and Wei Peng. 2008. "Gender and Racial Stereotypes in Popular Video Games." In *Handbook of Research on Effective Electronic Gaming in Education*, edited by Richard E. Ferdig, 922–937. Hershey, PA: Information Science Reference.

Mucherah, Wilfridah. 2003. "The Influence of Technology on the Classroom Climate of Social Studies Classrooms: A Multi-dimensional Approach." *Learning Environments Research: An International Journal* 6:37–57.

National Crime Prevention Council. 2012. "Cyberbullying." Accessed September 11. www.ncpc.org/topics/cyberbullying.

Noll, Jennie G., Chad E. Shenk, Jaclyn E. Barnes, and Frank W. Putnam. 2009. "Child Abuse, Avatar Choices, and Other Risk Factors Associated with Internet-Initiated Victimization of Adolescent Girls." *Pediatrics* 123:1078–1083.

Okagaki, Lynn, and Peter A. Frensch. 1994. "Effects of Video Game Playing on Measures of Spatial Performance: Gender Effects in Late Adolescence." *Journal of Applied Developmental Psychology* 15:33–58.

Paxton, Pamela. 1999. "Is Social Capital Declining in the United States? A Multiple Indicator Assessment." *American Journal of Sociology* 105:88–127.

Peter, Jochen, and Patti M. Valkenberg. 2008. "Adolescents' Exposure to Sexually Explicit Material on the Internet." *Communication Research* 33:178–204.

Putnam, Robert D. 2000. *Bowling Alone: The Collapse and Revival of American Community*. New York: Simon and Schuster.

Roberts, Donald F., Ulla G. Foehr, and Victoria Rideout. 2005. *Generation M: Media in the Lives of 8–18 Year-Olds*. Washington, DC: Henry J. Kaiser Family Foundation.

Shaw, Lindsey H., and Larry M. Gant. 2002. "Users Divided: Exploring the Gender Gap in Internet Use." *CyberPsychology and Behavior* 5:517–527.

Shen, Aaron, X. L., Matthew K. O. Lee, Christy M. K. Cheung, and Huaping Chen. 2010. "Gender Differences in Intentional Social Action: We-Intention to Engage in Social Network–Facilitated Team Collaboration." *Journal of Information Technology* 25:152–169.

Sherman, Sharon R. 1997. "Perils of the Princess: Gender and Genre in Video Games." *Western Folklore* 56: 243–258.

Steele, Jeanne Rogge. 1999. "Teenage Sexuality and Media Practice: Factoring in the Influences of Family, Friends, and School." *Journal of Sex Research* 36:331–341.

Stepup Women's Network. 2012. "About." Accessed January 4. http://www.suwn.org/.

Willis, Susan. 1991. *A Primer for Daily Life*. New York: Routledge.

Winn, Jillian, and Carrie Heeter. 2009. "Gaming, Gender, and Time: Who Makes Time to Play?" *Sex Roles* 61:1–13.

Wohn, Donghee Y. 2011. "Gender and Race Representation in Causal Games." *Sex Roles* 65:198–207.

Zickuhr, Kathryn, and Aaron Smith. 2012. *Digital Differences*. Washington, DC: Pew Internet & American Life Project.

CHAPTER TWELVE

How Much Technology Is Enough?

STEVEN WEILAND

We do not think of the mechanical clock as an advanced form of technology, but its invention was one of Neil Postman's favorite episodes in the mixed meanings of innovation. For the thirteenth-century Benedictine monks who invented it, the clock was to be used to regulate daily prayers. It worked so well that it soon became a device for synchronizing and controlling what people did far from monasteries. As Postman (1993) explains, a century after it appeared the clock allowed for scheduled work, industrial standardization, and economic transformation. "Without the clock, capitalism would have been quite impossible. And so, here is a great paradox: the clock was invented by men who wanted to devote themselves more rigorously to God; and it ended as the technology of greatest use to men who wished to devote themselves to the accumulation of money" (15).

The most important consequences of any technology do not become clear until many years after its introduction. In the case of this century, with the extraordinarily rapid pace of technological innovation and application, education is a scene of ferment and exhortation. Thus, as one account of the meaning of the "digital age" for schooling put it, "This is the time for educational visionaries to act" (Collins and Halverson 2009, 127). At the same time, responding to what, in their view, are unwelcome features of the new technologies like declines in attention and the reflective habits and knowledge-building features of reading, critics of "action" without a better understanding of its consequences see a different kind of urgency: "This is the moment, while the digital age is still young, to recoup these losses" (Powers 2010, 210).

In what follows, the claims of leading advocates for technology-based edu-cational reform—from K–12 through the postsecondary years—are presented as part of a debate they themselves barely recognize as having any interest for the students whose lives and work they intend to influence, and for college and university faculty and administrators who are under increasing pressure to re-examine their roles. The chapter begins with an account of the "new literacies" (or the "new media literacies") and how they represent for their advocates the most compelling way that technology can redefine teaching and learning. The next section is devoted to the widely recognized demographic dimension of technology and education. Thus, the "Net Generation," those born after 1990, is seen as an essential force in the realignment of educational values and prac-tices, particularly in the preference for games and social media. Profiles of two successful students belie the belief that Net Generation experience is uniform in responding to what the latest technologies offer. The chapter's third section is aimed at making a place in this book for the views of those who contest claims for reform by technology, or who would stay its impact while faculty and stu-dents join in efforts to better understand what it will mean. For those worrying about learners of all ages encountering the increasingly digital world, reading and solitude—the subjects of the chapter's fourth section—represent two forms of experience in particular need of attention. The section offers posi-tions—"stewardship" and "partnership"—worth incorporating into relations between students and teachers. A fifth section continues in the vein of moder-ating the impact of technology, this time via the uses of history, or the experi-ences of exemplary figures who succeeded in mediating change in their time. The conclusion proposes that the interaction of new digital practices and criti-cism of them be seen first in the context of yet another feature of the postsec-ondary landscape—the uses of Open Educational Resources—and then, in the form of "technology education," as an obligation that can be a fruitful part of teaching and learning in the transition to the digital age.

This chapter is inspired by remarks by Mark Bauerlein and Sherry Turkle, two of the most insistent skeptics about claims made for the necessary applica-tions of technology to education. From Bauerlein (2008a): "Digital technology has become an imperial force and it should be met with more antagonists." And from Turkle (2010): "I think it is for a generation of professors to not be intimi-dated and say 'Oh, this must be the way of the future.'" And the chapter displays more faith in our current institutions—and prospects for modification accord-ing to technology rather than wholesale transformation—than is the case gen-erally in those seeking to advance the role of technology in education. For James

Gee and Elisabeth Hayes (2010), an influential team of game and social media theorists, schools are certain to be "relic institutions" (64). And a statement from Cathy Davidson and David Theo Goldberg (2009) presents postsecondary education's history as a useless artifact of the predigital world. Thus, "the future of conventional learning institutions is past—*it's over*—unless those directing the course of our learning institutions realize, now and urgently, the necessity of fundamental and foundational change" (14–15; emphasis in original).

The chapter reflects the view that *it is not over*, and that "digital maximalism" (in the apt phrase of William Powers, whose work is considered herein) can be challenged with countervailing claims about cognitive development and learning, alternative images of the Net Generation in its educational and social relations, and forms of faculty work that bring students into the debate about the digital future. Thus, education can be seen as a scene of change and also as a location for reflecting from different positions on its consequences. In doing so, I am explicitly raising questions about some of the assumptions the authors have made in the previous chapters. As Corwin and her colleagues noted in the introduction, how social media and games will impact higher education is not yet resolved; what really needs to occur is a fulsome debate about the changes swirling around us, and this chapter is one additional component.

Literacy, New versus Old: A Cambrian Moment?

The cornerstone of triumphalist claims for the uses of technology in learning is in the case for the "new literacies," featuring games, social media, and other digital resources or tools associated with the internet and Web 2.0. Of course, with the so-called Net Generation now in its third decade, and with unceasing innovation in technology, particularly in mobile devices, the new literacies cannot be denied as forces for change, a challenge to fundamental activities of learning in and out of school.

Until late in the past century the term *literacy* could be understood to refer simply to the ability to read and write. But E. D. Hirsch's program for "cultural literacy" had an impact beyond its controversial claims for the advantages of the traditional curriculum (Hirsch 1987). It made literacy a general ability, as in competence or knowledge in a particular area of activity (e.g., "emotional literacy" or "financial literacy"). Still, reading remains essential in the expansion of the term to refer to the ability to understand a medium, and to communicate in it. When the National Research Council (1999) and Association of College and

Research Libraries (1999) identified "information technology literacy" and then (more simply) "information literacy" as a necessary new educational ability, they intended to guide the development of students in navigating the rapidly expanding internet and its proliferating resources. By then, of course, "media literacy" had a place in K–12 education, but it was limited to the ability to understand and, to the degree possible for young students, think critically about television, movies, and advertising. Newer forms of media-based literacy recognized the emerging power of digital formats and the internet. It was no accident that it fell to an association of libraries to specify new "standards" for the literacy required by the information-rich web.

In the next decade there followed a host of proposals allied to the intentions of the NRC and ACRL, each in its way seeking to name an urgent and growing domain for learning and the abilities necessary for educational and career success. The proposals reflected increasing attention to what the internet offered beyond conventional information, or the emergence of what came to be called Web 2.0. And the new demands have been configured for understanding in different ways, with the forms of literacy expanding to reflect new applications: "multimedia literacy" (Mayer 2001), "silicon literacy" (Snyder 2002), "digital literacy" (Eshet-Alkalai 2004), "multi-literacies" (Selber 2004), "ITC [Information and Communication Technology] Literacy" later changed to "iSkills" (Educational Testing Service 2012), "digital competence" (Krumsvik 2008), "new media literacy [or literacies]" (Jenkins 2009), "21st century social media literacies" (Rheingold 2010), and, in the now favored formulation, simply the "new literacies" (Baker 2010; Knobel and Lankshear 2007; Wilber 2008).

The linguist and game theorist James Gee (2010), who penned a chapter for part II, has outlined the path to the new literacies from a different but overlapping direction; his work, along with the scholarship of literacy theorists, colleagues in adjacent fields such as education, psychology, and media studies, helped formulate what came to be called the "New Literacy Studies." This movement, still influential in the theorizing of reading and what it supplies, for example, to teacher education programs, focuses on what is social about literacy, or how language must be understood in the circumstances of its production and use. Inevitably, the New Literacy Studies have had to recognize the digital media, though there is not yet a consolidated program representing what has been "new" in literacy since the 1980s (Gee [2010] proposes research in that direction with consequences for K–12 and postsecondary education). But complementary research interests have encouraged the steady expansion of the operations of literacy in accord with social and technological meanings (for a comprehensive review, see Mills 2010). Cathy Davidson's (2011) identification of no less than 17 "Twenty-First Century Literacies" represents the most extensive account yet and includes "Network Awareness," "Global Consciousness," "Data Mining," and "Sustainability" in a shared project of K–12 and postsecondary education. Approaches to understanding the role of new literacies in postsecondary education are gathering around the impact of those new practices of communication and entertainment that challenge the foundations of traditional postsecondary literacy in reading (especially "long-form" texts) and writing (especially in expository forms).

However redefined by what is offered by screens (see Carr 2010), reading as an activity of finding meaning in digital multimedia represents only one feature of the new literacies for theorists who focus on what is participatory about them, particularly in games and social media, where video and audio are welcome tools for "content creation" (in the popular phrase that recognizes the change from "consumption" to "participation"). That is the key theme in research and curriculum projects sponsored by the *Digital Media and Learning* initiative launched in 2007 by the MacArthur Foundation and represented in a series of books published by the MIT Press (e.g., Davidson and Goldberg 2010; Ito et al. 2009; Jenkins 2009; Salen 2011). These constitute empirical and theoretical work in advancing a Web 2.0–based program for what it means to have "21st Century Literacies." In effect, they represent a joint effort of advocacy as much as a scholarly project of inquiry.

A coauthor of the chapters on games and passion in part II, Henry Jenkins, named by Gee (2010) as the most important new literacies scholar of our time, wrote (with others) the influential white paper that is the foundational and guiding statement for the MacArthur Initiative. He organized his position around a group of abilities reaching far beyond reading and writing, reflecting his belief that it would be new creative opportunities—via digital practices outside school with the affordances of Web 2.0—that would force a fundamental reorganization of education (a revised version appeared as Jenkins 2009). Jenkins acknowledges the role of "judgment" in selecting and using online information, and of "networking" in synthesizing hypermedia resources. But for him the new literacies are chiefly "participatory" and a matter of "cultural competencies" and "social skills." They derive from producing digital work via "simulation" and "appropriation," reflecting what is learned from collaboration or "collective intelligence." Jenkins wishes to steer educational attention away from "individual accomplishment" (i.e., in activities like solitary reading and traditional writing) toward student production and distribution of media.

Accordingly, he dismisses the "information-focused" uses of the internet and welcomes the "communication and entertainment-focused" abilities that make young users "content creators." They are the vanguard in an emerging "participatory culture." For Jenkins and others, learners adept with the new media will demonstrate to formal educational institutions what must change in the curriculum and routines of teaching. Thus, many of my colleagues in this book are among the most respected scholars in the field who have helped define the emergent fields of new media literacies; while their work is admirable, I am less certain that their impact on higher education will—or should be—as far-reaching as they suggest.

The MacArthur Initiative has been slow to have a direct impact on postsec-ondary education, the chief exception being at Duke where the vocabulary de-veloped by Jenkins supports the Humanities, Arts, Science, and Technology Advanced Collaboratory (HASTAC) (with Davidson its leader). But, suitably enough, in the domain of traditional postsecondary literacy, expressive for-mats are changing to reflect the impending reign of the visual and social. Writ-ing programs have moved quickly in the undergraduate curriculum to embrace the new norms for learning, reflecting what students prefer in Web 2.0–based literacy. According to a reformer of university composition, priority can now go to the "extracurricular writing curriculum," presumably everything from text messaging to forms of online opinion and expression (e.g., blogs and wikis), and how they alter our thinking about utility and students' need for instruction. "They need neither self-assessment nor our assessment: they have a rhetorical situation, a purpose, a potentially worldwide audience, a choice of technology and medium—and they write" (Yancey 2004). And what they should be en-couraged to leave behind is "essayistic literacy" (Clark 2010). Indeed, stu-dent writing is a primary place for the digital vanguard to promote the prior-ity of the visual and the "vernacular" in learning (DeVoss, Eidman-Aadahl, and Hicks 2010).

Gee also sees traditional essayist literacy as the primary obstacle to reform-ing the curriculum with what he and others find as the cognitive opportunities in games and other digital learning tools. A decade ago he named the chief domain of the new literacies "affinity spaces" (see chapter 7 for a complete ac-count), or locations where, for example, game players and hobbyists, or at least those with the strongest "passion" for an activity, can capitalize on networked communications. These, again, signify forms of out-of-school learning, largely from popular culture, and the results are "complex, deep, and knowledge pro-ducing" (Gee and Hayes 2010, 69). But, as spokesmen for institutional reform,

Gee and Hayes see in such spaces the demise of conventional postsecondary education: "Does anyone think that a college organized as a plethora of passionate affinity spaces devoted to academic knowledge and complex systems, spaces with everyone in them (faculty and students alike), would not be as good as or better than many, or perhaps better than all of our current colleges" (88)?

A discourse of transformation typifies accounts of the new literacies and their necessary and inevitable impact on education at all levels. It is featured in the MacArthur Initiative; the programs and publications of the Sloan Foundation Consortium (or Sloan-C); the postsecondary service organization EDU-CAUSE; the New Media Foundation, which produces the annual and influential *Horizon Report* guiding institutions toward adoption of the latest and anticipated technologies; and in the Pew Internet & American Life Project, through the public presentations (often to educational associations) of its survey research. All make distinctive contributions to the case for adapting teaching and learning to the new literacies while speaking in a single voice about the urgency of such an effort. The report from the U.S. Department of Education, Office of Education Technology (2010), *Transforming American Education: Learning Powered by Technology*, consolidates these activities and spares nothing in its confidence in the digital future of education: "The challenge for our education system is to leverage the learning sciences and modern technology to create engaging, relevant, and personalized learning experiences for all learners that mirror students' daily lives and the reality of their future . . . . The opportunities [represented by students' out of school mastery of new media literacies] are limitless, borderless, and instantaneous" (4). So too are contributors to *Hacking the Academy* incredulous that there might be any reasonable doubts about the complete digital reorganization of the university (Cohen and Scheinfeldt 2011).

If "limitless" describes what can be expected in applications of the new literacies to education, then their impact must be transformational. Nothing less than a "sea change in thinking, knowing, learning, and teaching" and "a seismic shift in epistemology" are ahead (Dede 2007, 2008). According to Jenkins, we must embrace a "new paradigm." Others insist that a "new mindset" is necessary to move beyond traditional ideas and practices (Knobel and Lankshear 2007). Thus, the old and the new in literacy are presented in binary form, a familiar rhetorical strategy among digital utopians. Perhaps the best known is the opposition of "digital natives" to "digital immigrants" (Prensky 2001), with the former representing everything as fruitful in the electronic habits and preferences of the young, or those who have grown up as the so-called Net Generation, and the latter, older and slower learners (the "immigrants" burdened by an outdated educational discourse), seen as unlikely to be able to capitalize on what the digital age offers (see Bennett, Mason, and Kervin 2008 for the case, made by several others, for the overestimation of the abilities of "natives").

John Seely Brown (2011), a widely admired technology visionary who inspired Davidson's version of the new literacies, says we are at a "Cambrian moment," offering an image of profound geological change (of about 500 million years ago) when there was a vast increase in diverse and complex forms of life. Thus, ours is a time for "world building," now with digital technology. And why stop there? *Second Life*, a game increasingly used in postsecondary education, offers opportunities via its organization around avatars to be someone other than who we actually are. Digital tools can equip us with unprecedented powers: "We really are talking about something that has never happened on earth before. For most of human history, one's fate was eternal and there was no second chance at life. But [players of *Second Life*] have broken, albeit in a small way and only for a moment, the skein of fate. This is, indeed, the stuff of the gods" (Gee and Hayes 2010, 38). With such strong statements, and such widespread support from foundations and government agencies, the purpose of this book seems clear and warranted; what I wonder, however, is if there is as complete a basis for such claims as is being made. My purpose is less to be the Luddite at the digital party and more to provoke a sense of caution by raising questions that have yet to be answered.

Net Generation Students: Expectations and Experience

While federal support for education has been defined in the past decade by a preference for "evidence-based" interventions and inquiry, the standard has been hard to apply in the digital realm. Still, the Department of Education report cited earlier, with its claims for "limitless" educational benefits of technology, says this: "Social media content created by teachers and learners, from blogs to podcasts to YouTube videos, or creations and performances in virtual worlds, enrich on-demand learning" (U.S. Department of Education, Office of Education Technology 2010, 17). Predictably enough, Jenkins's work and a *Horizon Report* are cited with a study by the Organization for Economic and Cultural Development (OECD) (2009). But the OECD, while acknowledging increasing use of new media, actually claims the opposite. It says that there is "no conclusive evidence about the effects of technology on academic achievement" (7).

The OECD report names many reasons why empirical research has not caught up with the claims made for learning with technology, including the difficulty (if necessity) of mounting longitudinal studies. The essence of the OECD report, ignored in *Transforming American Education,* is the claim that empirical research on the long-term educational value of technologies is not now "coherent" enough to provide "useful knowledge" for parents, educators, and policy makers. We have a "very scattered field" with only "inconclusive results" (7). That is the case too in postsecondary education. Empirical studies of the role of social media are inclusive. They direct us—no surprise—to their uses in socialization, or students' "adjustment to college" (e.g., DeAndrea et al. 2011). But their impact has been "negative" on "academic integration," or success in the classroom and the curriculum (e.g., Kord and Wolf-Wendel 2009).

For Gee, Davidson, and others, the problem is that the current view of academic ability and achievement is out of date, too narrow to recognize what digital technologies offer in problem solving, critical thinking, and cognitive teamwork. Davidson's *Now You See It* (2011)—which includes her program for "21st Century Literacies"—is rich in evidence for the plasticity of the brain. She makes the case for how neurobiology shapes attention, or, as she prefers, redesigns itself for learning by multitasking. But what a new view of attention means for higher education is undocumented. What must be recognized, Davidson insists, from accounts of the popularity of teenage game playing, is that "these digital natives happen to be the happiest, healthiest, most social, most civic-minded, best adjusted, and least violent and self-destructive teens since large demographic surveys began at the end of World War II" (154–155). She adds that they "are having fun and learning too." This is not the conclusion of Richard Arum and Josipa Roksa (2011) in *Academically Adrift,* where they argue, on the basis of extensive survey data, that college students today are studying and learning less than ever. But Davidson trusts her experience, particularly a new course she devised titled, "This Is Your Brain on the Internet," which, with its lack of a "standard syllabus, method, or conclusion," is represented as a groundbreaking exercise in the reform of postsecondary teaching and learning based on demonstrating how "accident, disruption, and distraction increase the motivation to learn and to solve problems" (102). The only record of student learning is in Davidson's enthusiasm for it. Authoritative studies demonstrating the cognitive inefficiencies of distraction and multitasking (summarized by Glenn 2010), features of the new literacies favored by Davidson as essential for learning, have no place in her account of the prospects for a postsecondary digital utopia.

Even as empirical studies of the impact of games and social media on learning emerge, accounts of individual learners can direct us to the interaction of our expectations for what some students can gain from "affinity spaces" and what experience can reveal to others about the limits of social media. Gee and Hayes profile the Net Generation with the story of "Sam," a teenager whose childhood featured his skill at games and cultivation of an affinity space with them. Even as a two-year-old he had played simple computer games. And when he was seven he began a long period of interest in *The Age of Mythology* (AOM), in which he became "expert" at "customizing," a sign that he was "in charge of his own learning." That means revising relations between old and new media: "Games were not something to 'waste time' on, unrelated to more 'important' matters, no more than books" (Gee and Hayes 2010, 26). We never hear from Sam himself, presumably because his own views of his digital story correspond to Gee's (who appears to be his father). The case is well suited to what Gee and Hayes believe should encourage us to welcome the new literacies. That is, they are anything but threats to the traditional ones. Thus: "Sam made deep connections between games . . . and reading and writing. He did not see them as separate or competing activities. When Sam grew passionate about a game, as he had about [AOM], he wanted to read and write about it and eventually connect it to other activities and interests" (23).

We are left to anticipate Sam's unlimited success in consolidating the new and the old literacy—all gain, no loss. Gee and Hayes specify a host of "potential" benefits to learning represented by Sam's experience, including higher-order literacy skills, production with digital technology, and adept use of social media. But these are, of course, abilities observed from the perspective of unqualified enthusiasm for games. There are no gaps in Sam's digital history, only signs that games can meet every educational reformer's expectation for "engaged" students who operate flawlessly with the newest tools.

Sam's college years are ahead, and by then, when his dedication to social media is likely to match what he takes from games, there may be reasons for him to think and speak about his digital life from a more reflective position than the one in which he is presented. That is what we see in another recent portrait of the Net Generation. Katie Davis's (2011) "Anna" is an undergraduate who has blogged for some years and is of course adept too at other social media. Like Sam, Anna is a successful student, and she is at a demanding university. The log of online experience she agrees to keep to support Davis's research shows her new media use to be (in Anna's words) "all throughout the day." That is evident even in Davis's office when Anna responds to text messages as she is being interviewed. Davis acknowledges her multitasking ability, noting that while Anna is engaged in two conversations, "she is in control of both."

Still, there is plain tension between what Davis names as "meaningful connection" deriving from Anna's high school blogging and what can be observed of her digital life in college. Davis (2011) detects "ambivalence," and Anna reports that, while she welcomes the ease of constant connectivity, she worries over the "real time tradeoff," or her attention to the "places on the internet that aren't so valuable to me." It is a "tradeoff" too, she says, in "having the constant stream of information" and what it contributes to her sense of her life as "fragmented." Anna tells Davis:

> Last year I was actually reading a book most of the time, or at least I was in the middle of something. Right now, I'm not really in the middle of anything. That makes me sad, but I just end up turning to the Internet instead of a book. It's a lot more manageable. It's there, it's easy, you can finish an article and move on to something else. If somebody interrupts you on the phone or something, it's easy to get off of it. Whereas, once I actually start reading I want to be reading for a period of time. I just want to be curled up in a book and not a part of everything else. It's hard to do that when everything is so permeated by communication.
> (1974)

The internet as a limitless resource and unending distraction is now a familiar figure in representations of the digital age (e.g., Jackson 2008; Richtel 2012). The new popularity of tablets serving as e-readers has exacerbated the difficulty with their internet connectivity. A college senior and iPad owner reports trying to maintain her habits of reading only to find it challenging to focus on a new novel: "I've tried to sit down and read it in Starbucks or the apartment, but I end up on Facebook or Googling something, and then the next thing you know I've been surfing for 25 minutes" (Bosman and Richtel 2012).

So too does Anna's precollege blogging flag, with shorter and shorter entries and little self-reflection as, in Davis words, she is consumed by "a life lived in bits and bytes." Davis and Anna acknowledge the rewards of digital technology, its flexibility and immediacy, but neither sees any signs of more discernment in choosing and finishing books following from the struggle with distraction (as reported by another tablet reader to Bosman and Richtel [2012]).

Taken together, Sam and Anna reveal how "gain and loss"—the most favored figure in accounts of the digital age—can be represented for different purposes. In Gee and Hayes's optimism there is the case for making a complete (or nearly so) educational platform of youthful dedication to games. But they insist too, with informal play in mind, that "the problems of school are being solved out of school" (Gee and Hayes 2010, 64). The answer is in adopting "lessons" in literacy from popular culture particularly in the ways they appear to empower "participants." Sam's "passion" and success cannot be denied.

But the experience of the Net Generation, as the costs of youthful preferences are better understood by many college students themselves, hardly means an uncomplicated relation to digital technologies. Davis (2011) sees her research role as recording "appreciation" for the relational features of the new digital media and "regret" about their cognitive impact. "Bouncing from Web site to Web site exposes [Anna] to a broad range of information but makes it difficult to process any of it in a meaningful way" (1979). Information theorist David Levy and colleagues (2011) have found allied problems in survey research begun in 2010. Of more than 300 students at several kinds of institutions, a majority reports dismay about the time spent online, about being "continually connected," feeling "preoccupied" with devices, and giving less-than-appropriate attention to academic work, including of course what is required in reading.

Reading and Solitude, Stewardship and Partnership

Perhaps no feature of the digital age with meaning for education has had more attention than reading. When the *New York Times* headlined the first in what has been a regular series of reports on the subject, "Online, R U Really Reading" (Rich 2008), it signified the threat of screens to traditional literacy, a question of increasing significance with the popularity of dedicated e-readers and other mobile devices.

For many partisans of the new literacies, games and other digital tools pose no threat to book reading since its limits have already been revealed by schooling, with its tradition of cultivating individual efforts in literacy. In his MacArthur white paper, Jenkins (2009) sees little chance for school reading to be as "compelling" as games, where there is a justifiably more appealing "rationale for learning," or "what players learn is put to use immediately" (38). Thus, as Gee and Hayes (2011) present them, nineteenth-century unschooled readers are our best models for learners today, who can find in games the deinstitutionalized autonomy in learning they desire. But life in the "late age of print" (Striphas 2009) has prompted great interest in the nature of reading on screens, or what the peculiar demands of books, now observable from outside the print revolution, mean for depth of cognitive experience and comprehension (Wolf

2007). There is no shortage of accounts of the historical meanings of printed books and traditional reading (e.g., Darnton 2009). And the prestigious Morgan Library is conducting a project for elementary school children giving them firsthand experience in the design and production of illuminated books in the manner of the Renaissance. "Book time" is presented as an alternative to "screen time," with the goal of prompting appreciation of print and solitary reading without "trying to stop the flow of technology" (Jones 2012).

The speed of development of new mobile devices—smart phones and tablets—and increasing consumer devotion to them have made it plain that whatever differences there are between reading print and screens will matter less and less to most readers. And for some observers, technology supports reading in ways unacknowledged by its critics, including the opportunities in using social media to produce and read texts, even the briefest and most casual ones. For Harvard English professor Leah Price (2007), any form of reading contributes to digital literacy. We worry too much, she believes, about the decline of reading and judge ourselves against an unrealistic view of the practices and standards of the past.

From the time of Neil Postman's (1993, 1995, 1999) jeremiads of the late twentieth-century, critics of the impact of technology have specified worrisome features of its educational influence (e.g., Gitlin 2007; Oppenheimer 2003). But skepticism and resistance today have been scaled up (so to speak, in the vocabulary of campus technology) in accord with the expansion of technology into every domain of life. As much as anything else, Nicholas Carr's (2008) question in a widely cited 2008 *Atlantic* article—"Is Google Making Us Stupid?"—invited recognition that there was another side to celebrations of the internet and the space it represents for communicating, including access to the resources an historian of technology like Carr welcomed for his work. Changes prompted by the web in his cognitive habits—the kind endorsed by Davidson as fruitful and mind-expanding distractions—felt to him like obstacles to the thinking necessary to make something durable from what his online searching produced. Google was friend and enemy, a structure for the intellectual uses of the internet registered by other scholars (e.g., Bell 2005). But the problem, as Carr suggests, was larger than the anxieties of professional readers and writers.

The PBS Frontline documentary *Digital Nation* (Frontline 2010), admirably balanced in presenting different perspectives about technology, is still forthright in identifying threats to our mental powers, or what traditional literacy contributes to abilities for reflection, discrimination, and reasoned judgment.

There is some irony, of course, in using media (*Digital Nation*'s website is rich in multimedia resources) to protest their overuse. But the program shows the dangers of uncritical promotion of the new literacies, or just what can be seen, alas, in another PBS documentary.

For Mark Bauerlein (2008a), featured in *Digital Nation*, the condition of reading, particularly "long form texts" like canonical novels, reflects postsecondary complacency about the impact of technology. In an account of the problems of online reading, Bauerlein specifies the habits of the new literacies as obstacles to the liberal education curriculum. Technology is devoted to "devices of acceleration" and "the shape and tempo of online texts differ so much from academic texts that e-learning initiatives in college classrooms can't bridge them." Thus, students can speak with pride of their new literacy while standing secure in what they take to be necessary generational change: "My dad is still into the whole book thing. He has not realized that the internet kind of took the place of that" (Bauerlein 2008b, 41). Bauerlein relied on data from many studies of learning, at all levels of the system, and anticipated the case made in *Academically Adrift*.

Questions of reading are now presented too as neurological (Wolf 2007) with biological evidence for text-oriented brain structures serving indispensable mental abilities (e.g., those which shape attention). Still, the brain is adaptive, and there can only be speculation about the impact of the internet in learning based on texts. But the growing preference for the visual and the briefest of informational fragments, and habits of constant person-to-person connectivity, might well undermine even e-reading, with print left behind as an antiquarian taste, like fountain pens. When Amazon's Kindle appeared, early adopters expressed disappointment that users could only read on the devices and that without internet connectivity they were being denied what was necessary (in their view) for a complete textual experience (Lankes 2010). Now, with the iPad and its competitors, e-reading can be seen as simply one among many forms of connectivity, an "app" with no special digital status. According to Bauerlein (2008b), mindful of the screen-reading behavior of his students (like Anna),

> Forming reading and thought patterns through screens prepares individuals for only part of the communications demands of the twenty-first century, the information retrieval and consumer-behavior parts. The abilities to concentrate upon a single recondite text, to manage ambiguities and ironies, to track an inductive proof . . . screen reading hampers them. (148)

Studies now show that with extensive instruction students can read for intelligibility on screens (e.g., Coiro 2011), but this view vies with the case made for "skill transfer" from experience with out-of-school media use (Gasser et al. 2012). In effect, we are between what David Weinberger (2012) synthesizes as "long form and web form" texts. His fair-minded if critical account of Carr's argument sees the interactivity of the web as gaining in priority over print but not without the uses of understanding the independent affordances of the two. Still, the "reality," Bauerlein (2008b) insists, thinking of his classroom experience, is that the most common of internet reading habits—"fast scanning, page hopping, associative thinking, no unfamiliar content"—will undermine the "scrupulous reading" necessary for successful study and work (150).

The future of reading is the primary question, I believe, associated with the new literacies. Bauerlein is wary of teen and young-adult peer culture as a distracting cognitive force. And psychologist Sherry Turkle (2008), who has been studying technology's impact on student identities for decades, sees now an allied problem of the online "self" as it is reflected in game playing and the uses of social media. With mobile devices has come "continuous co-presence" or the "tethered self" with "always-on" digital connectivity, an impediment to learning as much as a resource for it. In Turkle's (2010) view, we are too driven by "what technology wants" instead of cultivating the cognitive abilities necessary, for example, in the reading of serious books: "What technology makes easy is not always what nurtures the human spirit." And she rejects the assumptions, among advocates for the new literacies, that online "interactivity" and "collaboration" always mean that "exciting things are happening educationally." Instead, Turkle urges solitary reading and the "complex interaction" books can offer without having "things exploding on the screen." In effect, solitude is an element of intellectual independence.

In the new literacies, collaboration is the way for students to overcome old educational habits of individual achievement and to learn via "participation" in the manner of social constructivism. And in the vocabulary of online learning, perhaps no term is more honored than "interactivity." But "active learning" via student-to-student interaction can be the subject of critical inquiry, with research asking for recognition of undergraduate and graduate student claims for greater autonomy and opportunities for "self-direction" in their work, or less reliance on required group activities (Cuthrell and Lyon 2007) and the "norming" of learning in compulsory participation in online discussions (Gulati 2008). A class designated as a "learning community" will test its members' taste for mutuality and timely cooperation. Arum and Roksa (2011) in *Academically Adrift* state that their data show that in common academic tasks like preparing for examinations, "studying alone is beneficial, but studying with peers is not" (100). And as Susan Cain (2012) asserts, the cultural bias toward collaboration and group work—symbolized by the recent popularity of the open-office configurations in corporations—can actually inhibit the creative thinking and problem solving (two favorites of the new literacies) deriving from solitary reflection.

Turkle directs us to images of autonomous academic work where responsibility is generated from within. And *Wikipedia* co-founder Larry Sanger (2010), surprisingly perhaps, has made the case for the individual learner, particularly (as Bauerlein does) in relation to what is necessary to liberal education. The lesson in the protests against imposing group work on students—including digital "participation"—is that in order to think *for* yourself you must also think *by* yourself. That does not mean all the time. But the ideology of Facebook, captured in the pronouncement of the company's chief operating officer—"We want everything to be social"—is unworthy of the intellectual traditions represented by colleges and universities (Morozov 2012). The social and the solitary are two complementary forms of character and learning, hardly reducible to competing "mindsets" (as in Knobel and Lankshear 2007) or a definitive choice to be made in the competition between the old and the new.

The momentum of the new can appear unstoppable; after all, if our moment is "Cambrian," then uncontrollable geological forces will determine our fate. If school is a "relic" and "it's over" for our colleges and universities, then is it worth intervening? Bauerlein (2008a) insists on the responsibility at all educational levels to protect traditions of reading: "We need an approach that doesn't let teachers and professors so cavalierly violate their charges as stewards of literacy." In Bauerlein's use of this rich term, a steward is someone who works to preserve something of great cultural value and helps to guarantee its sustainability. But what is at stake is not a matter of cultural nostalgia. For institutions and academic programs, there is the task of reconciling the boundless optimism and reform urgency in accounts of the Net Generation, and the abilities made necessary by technology, with recognition of what is still distinctive about reading as it has been practiced for centuries. We are all now new readers, to the degree at least that we capitalize on the links in networked information of all kinds. And Bauerlein himself is an industrious blogger, often showing his range as an online reader (at the *Chronicle of Higher Education*). Thus, when he urges asking questions of technology as an "imperial force," it is to claim a space for exploring how educational authority in the digital age can reflect old as well as new practices and values.

Turkle (2010) also proposes faculty resistance, or guidance for students about a complacent gain and loss way of thinking about the new habits of attention represented in compulsive multitasking: "Look, there really are important things you cannot think about unless you're only thinking about one thing at a time. There are just some things that are not amenable to being thought about in conjunction with 15 other things. And there are some kinds of arguments you cannot make unless you're willing to take something from beginning to end." There is no need to reject technology, just the need "to put it in its place." But that is likely more than most students can accomplish, influenced as they are by the marketplace and their peers, not to mention what they take from postsecondary reformers predicting digital transformation. When Turkle (2011) says, "they need our help . . . [and] we must be their partners" (295), it is to suggest a shared interest in reflection aimed at moderating the "enchantment" of technology. The goal is "to move forward as generations together in embrac[ing] the complexities of our situation." In Bauerlein's *stewardship* and Turkle's *partnership*, there is much teaching and learning to do about our technology.

David Levy and colleagues (2011) too propose making a virtue of the generation gap and the apparent limits of the "Digital Immigrants." Thus, their experience of the predigital world, with its different conditions of attention and attitudes toward time, can be valuable resources for students, particularly those like Anna who have important questions to ask about the uses of technology in their lives and learning. Levy, with his colleagues (2011) who have been surveying students at all types of postsecondary institutions, believes that the faculty can capitalize on student interest in such a "conversation," however much we may assume about youthful dedication to the latest mobile devices and digital experience.

A "Big Story" and a Vocabulary for "Fighting Back"

What kind of vocabulary might make such a conversation fruitful? Bauerlein is wary, as his critics say he should be, about being read simply as a "grouch" who resents the young and defends educational tradition only from habit (the provocative title of his 2008 book, *The Dumbest Generation*, was the perfect resource for his antagonists). But the unwelcome news he brings merits the tone of his criticism. And in the end, it is not, again, students themselves who can be expected to probe on their own the complex effects of the digital age. They need the intellectual and instructional direction rejected by new literacies reformers with their claims for the democratization of educational authority. Postman

(1999) named the task as a narrative one: "Our old ways of explaining ourselves to our selves are not large enough to accommodate a world made paradoxically small by our technologies, yet larger than we can grasp" (115). He urged the need for framing our circumstances with a "big story."

In *Hamlet's BlackBerry* that is what we find. William Powers (2010) historicizes our problems with constant connectivity and debilitating distraction with portraits of creative adaptation to technological change in history. The sequence reaches from ancient Greece to our own time, and it features the story of literacy, or how the interaction of new forms of reading and writing have presented opportunities for communications and knowledge and prompted strategies for managing them consistent with durable human values and practices. Powers gives us a history of individual actions, or ways that technological innovation has prompted equally inventive responses reflecting the conditions of social life. The sequence constitutes a "big story" in the sense that it presents events and ideas across time in a way that gives them collective meaning. It is a tale that takes shape and is visible in the form that Powers tells it only in the context of the problems we face in our own time.

Powers's (2010) encountered his subject—it stands at the middle of the story he was ultimately to tell—at a "revelatory" 2006 exhibit at the Folger Shakespeare Library (Washington, D.C.) devoted to technologies of writing. It demonstrated that "the advent of printing was a radical incitement to write, rather than a signal of the demise of handwritten texts." One reason was a phenomenon we know very well—information overload. We do not usually associate it with the Renaissance, but in the view of historians the phrase conveys how Shakespeare and his contemporaries experienced the new world of print and the abundant information it had already produced. An artifact on display at the exhibit takes Powers to *Hamlet* and to the image that gave him the title for his book.

Powers is interested in the habit of writing by hand as it persisted long after print. And, of course, even in our own digitalized time, students still take notes that way, and the sale of modern versions of the Elizabethan "table" are flourishing (the popular Moleskine notebooks). But this is more than an antiquarian taste. Powers (2010) compares the notebook to radio, which was supposed to have disappeared (or nearly so) with the advent of television. Who would want only audio without the visual? "Today, in our information-jammed world, many of us enjoy radio precisely because it produces only sound—no text, images, or video—and can relieve media overload" (149). Relief came in Shakespeare's time in the form of the "table" (an ancestor of the "tablet"). It was common in

Elizabethan England to carry around what was then called a "writing table" (or simply a "table") that functioned as a kind of pocket-sized notebook, a means of controlling the noticeable increase in information in Shakespeare's time, much like the function of our portable digital devices (Powers writes at the peak of popularity of the BlackBerry, which was to lose significant "market share" to the Apple iPhone and its clones). For Elizabethans who could write, the device could "lighten the burdens of the post-Gutenberg mind . . . an antidote to the new busyness, a portable, easy-to-operate device that allowed the user to impose order on the clamorous world around him" (150).

Hamlet's unconnected "BlackBerry" is for Powers (2010) one in a long historical line of tools for "pushback," devised to provide a "sense of mental order and control." A notebook can address the complex cognitive situation of digital life with "utter simplicity." It is living unplugged. Because a paper notebook is not connected to the grid, it is independent and need not be "defensive" in relation to all that is available online. "The selectivity is autonomous and entirely self-directed. I'm the search engine, the algorithm, and the filter" (152).

With the other historical exemplars in *Hamlet's BlackBerry*, Powers (2010) finds related tactics for finding distance. Plato favored walking outside the city in developing the argument of the *Phaedrus* and its case against the new and, to his mind, disabling technology of writing. For Seneca it was, paradoxically, the activity of writing—in a long series of personal and philosophical letters—that offered "inner distance" from cosmopolitan Rome. Difficult as it may be, the goal is to find what Powers calls, in the case of Thoreau, a "Walden zone" where "simplicity and inwardness reign—a sanctuary from the crowd" (191). He does not dismiss the value of interactivity—including even the popular idea of the "wisdom of crowds"—but he urges that we cultivate enough self-consciousness always to measure our interests against the form it often takes in "digital maximalism," or the "always-on" mentality. Summarizing the "big story" he narrates, Powers says, "Over and over in our history, new technologies arrive that play to our natural maximalist tendencies. At the same time, quietly but persistently, there's a need to find balance. The best solutions serve as a kind of bridge to the tech future, one that ensures that we'll arrive with our sanity intact" (155).

Conclusion: Postsecondary Lessons in Technology

In the first decade of this century, games and social media were claimed to be the new digital resources certain to transform education. That may remain the case in K–12 learning. But in postsecondary education, it is the advent of online Open Educational Resources (OER) that could mean the "disruption" named by some observers as necessary to reforms that will guarantee more access and efficiency in teaching and learning (Christensen et al. 2010; Lewin 2012; Walsh 2011). Stanford University president John Hennessy, whose institution is pioneering in the OER movement via the MOOC (a massively open online course), is now convinced that online learning should have priority in any consideration of the future of postsecondary education. "There is," he says, "a tsunami coming" (Auletta 2012).

A tsunami signifies powerlessness before an unexpected and overwhelming force, and the fear that prompts action with little time for thought or planning. The metaphor may be unusual, but there is nothing exceptional about Hennessey's claim, a familiar one among those urging the transformation of education by technology. What makes it different is that it comes from the leader of one of our premier research universities, which are typically preoccupied with matters of research funding, scientific innovation, and graduate and professional education, with little interest in undergraduate distance learning. Hennessy is also aware of the pressures on access and affordability in higher education, whatever the status and prospects of his own institution's students. And in work force development, as William Tierney makes plain in the first chapter in this book, the urgency of our situation is itself a case for "disruption" in making the abilities of current and future generations suitable to new and emerging opportunities for learning and work.

Thus, as anticipated by reformers in different domains, the new educational landscape would include in OER the formal routines of postsecondary coursework (often featuring lectures, the most reviled of pedagogies among new media advocates), as they are central now to organizational innovations based at Stanford, MIT, and Harvard and in new media-based opportunities reflecting out-of-school "interest driven" learning, challenges to virtually every tradition of postsecondary education. This chapter has focused on the second category and the debate it has prompted about how much technology is enough in our educational system. But any account of *disruption* (favored by those interested in online learning) or *transformation* (the favored term of those committed to games, social media, and the new literacies) will have to address the relations between the two as institutional structures, curricula, and student and faculty preferences change (or do not) in the context of what appears will be a long period of adaptation to volatility in national and global economic and social conditions.

However change comes to be configured, education in the digital age, including new understandings of literacy, will redefine relations between postsecondary faculty and students. That begins with recognizing that educational technology is itself an essential subject (if generally a "hidden" one), deserving attention to its history, uses, and meanings. In effect, the next task for the faculty, as reflected in the oppositional positions displayed in this chapter, can be named in a pedagogical paradox: teaching *with* technology and (to a degree) *against* it.

But, as Bauerlein and Turkle advise, this is an intellectual project—with its own lessons in technology and education—to be shared with students. Web 2.0 is barely a decade old and, inevitably, research on its uses and impact is lagging behind the optimism of those who see it as the touchstone of educational transformation. Or, even if learning and teaching, and institutions, are transformed, we can ask: "In what direction will change move?" Will it be in a straight line toward the digital future or, to adopt the most popular technological metaphor, in a network of educational practices, where the old interacts with the new, and teaching and learning reflect such relations. To be sure, Jenkins offers signs of such a view when he says that new media literacies should complement traditional ways of reading and writing. But in his accounts of new media (and in those which focus on games), books are hardly made to look appealing in relation to other kinds of informal (or "interest driven") learning, which are always identified, unlike book reading, as essential to the twenty-first-century workplace.

Consider just one more demurral about seeing too much in the uses of new forms of literacy in the social media. Andrew Sullivan (2008), one of the most influential of bloggers (formerly of the *Atlantic* and the *Daily Beast*, now at the *Dish*), resists the "triumphalist notion" that blogging can stand in for traditional writing.

> A blogger will air a variety of thoughts or facts on any subject in no particular order other than that dictated by the passing of time. A writer will instead use time, synthesizing these thoughts, ordering them, weighing which points count more than others, seeing how his views evolved in the writing process itself.... The result is almost always more measured, more satisfying, and more enduring than a blizzard of posts.

New literacy advocates will say, of course, that they intend no such replacement. But, as students are encouraged to take up what is newest on behalf of being literate for the twenty-first century, what signs do we see in projects of the new literacies that forthrightly promote the slow-paced and contemplative precision that Sullivan endorses?

We can be wired for learning to the degree that we choose affordances consistent with our values, likely to be a combination of the old and the new. In this, *Hamlet's BlackBerry* (Powers 2010) offers timely lessons in the history of technology, or how change can be managed according to the example of our philosophical forbears (Seneca, Thoreau, and others) who learned to manage cultural transformations with practical self-consciousness. Digital visionaries may prefer the rapid and complete digitalization of teaching and learning, but experience will also guide faculty and students toward everyday and incremental change, where the new complements the old instead of displacing it.

The problem remains, though, for those who would slow the installation of the new literacies in postsecondary education as the cornerstone of the curriculum, of responding to the scale of change in how we find, organize, store, and apply knowledge. Whatever any scholar thinks about the new literacies, there is the need in every field for a workable epistemology for the digital age. If, as Weinberger (2012) has proposed, the internet represents a world "too big to know," then the new conditions of knowledge suggest the need to understand what it means to scale up, so to speak, in our projects of inquiry and teaching even as we scale down (in Powers's vocabulary) what we want in our personal experience of technology. Weinberger, like other technovisionaries, sees generational change as our best resource for educational reform, with what that assumes about the abilities of today's (and tomorrow's) young reflecting their digital immersion. But other observers are asking about how those growing up with games and social media—the postsecondary students of the next decade—will overcome what appear to be digital threats to their wellbeing (Pea et al. 2012).

In his search for a way into the technological future Postman (1995) urged that a place in the curriculum be made for exploring our circumstances, desires, and doubts. Technology is to be a subject for study, with a historical accent. "Technology education" would help students find their place in the long journey from print to screens with recognition of how every new technology influences practices and values in a ratio of gains and losses. Postsecondary students can only know what choices for learning remain in the "late age of print" with faculty restraint in representing the latest opportunities. The effort Postman imagines, like *Hamlet's BlackBerry*, cannot, he says, be "negative," toward either the past or the future. His program can help students to learn about "what technology helps us to do and what it hinders us from doing; it is about how technology uses us, for good and ill, and about how . . . technology creates new worlds for good or ill" (192).

However we come to what is next, as personal and professional uses of technology continue to expand, it will reflect our learning about the emerging digital world, including recognition of competing positions (Gopnick 2011). In this, oddly enough, we are near the situation named by Albert Manguel (2008), in our relations with print.

> The love of libraries, like most loves, must be learned. No one stepping for the first time into a room made of books can know instinctively how to behave, what is expected, what is promised, what is allowed. One may be overcome by horror—at the clutter or the vastness, the stillness, the mocking reminder of everything one doesn't know, the surveillance—and some of that overwhelming feeling may cling on, even after the rituals and conventions are learned, the geography mapped, the natives found friendly. (4–5)

Apart from the "stillness," which is hard to find in the fast-paced world of the internet, Manguel's recognition of what a library demands reminds us of the durability of reading, with some of it solitary, as the essence of literacy. It is hard won, and particularly so when there is electronic competition for cognitive attention, with high-volume claims for compulsory change in the direction of new digital abilities, and what they claim for the social. Their value is plain. And so is the utility of educating ourselves, while we teach and learn, in the conditions of technology we have made and can remake.

REFERENCES

Arum, Richard, and Josipa Roksa. 2011. *Academically Adrift: Limited Learning on College Campuses*. Chicago: University of Chicago Press.

Association of College and Research Libraries. 1999. *Information Literacy Competency Standards for Higher Education*. Chicago: ACRL.

Auletta, Ken. 2012. "Get Rich U." *New Yorker*, April 30.

Baker, Elizabeth, ed. 2010. *The New Literacies: Multiple Perspectives on Practice and Research*. New York: Guilford.

Bauerlein, Mark. 2008a. "Online Literacy Is a Lesser Kind." *Chronicle Review*, September 19.

———. 2008b. *The Dumbest Generation: How the Digital Age Stupefies Young Americans and Jeopardizes Our Future*. New York: Penguin.

Bell, David. 2005. "The Bookless Future: What the Internet Is Doing to Scholarship." *New Republic*, May 2.

Bennett, Sue, Karl Mason, and Lisa Kervin. 2008. "The 'Digital Natives' Debate: A Critical Review of the Evidence." *British Journal of Educational Technology* 39:775–786.

Bosman, Julie, and Matt Richtel. 2012. "Finding Your Book Interrupted . . . by the Tablet You Read It On." *New York Times*, March 4.

Brown, John Seely. 2011. Commencement Speech, Department of Communication, Stanford University. June 12. Accessed February 19, 2012. http://www.johnseelybrown.com/stanford2011.pdf.

Cain, Susan. 2012. *Quiet: The Power of Introverts in a World That Can't Stop Talking.* New York: Crown.

Carr, Nicholas. 2008. "Is Google Making Us Stupid?" *Atlantic*, July–August.

———. 2010. *The Shallows: What the Internet Is Doing to Our Brains.* New York: Norton.

Christensen, Clayton, M., Michael B. Horn, Louis Caldera, and Louis Soares. 2011. *Disrupting College: How Disruptive Innovation Can Deliver Quality and Affordability to Postsecondary Education.* Washington, DC: Center for American Progress.

Clark, J. Elizabeth. 2010. "The Digital Imperative: Making the Case for a 21st Century Pedagogy." *Computers and Composition* 27:27–35.

Cohen, Dan, and Tom Scheinfeldt. 2011. *Hacking the Academy: A Book Crowdsourced in One Week.* Ann Arbor: University of Michigan Press. http://www.digitalculture.org/hacking -the-academy/.

Coiro, Julie. 2011. "Talking about Reading as Thinking: Modeling the Hidden Complexities of Online Reading Comprehension." *Theory Into Practice* 50:107–115.

Collins, Allan, and Richard Halverson. 2009. *Rethinking Education in the Age of Technology: The Digital Revolution and Technology.* New York: Teachers College Press.

Cuthrell, Kristen, and Anna Lyon. 2007. "Instructional Strategies: What Do Online Students Prefer?" *Merlot Journal of Online Learning and Teaching* 3:357–362.

Darnton, Robert. 2009. *The Case for Books: Past, Present, and Future.* New York: Public Affairs.

Davidson, Cathy N. 2011. *Now You See It: How the Brain Sciences of Attention Will Transform the Way We Live, Work, and Learn.* New York: Viking.

Davidson, Cathy N., and David Theo Goldberg. 2009. *The Future of Learning Institutions in a Digital Age.* Cambridge, MA: MIT Press.

———. 2010. *The Future of Thinking: Learning Institutions in the Digital Age.* Cambridge, MA: MIT Press.

Davis, Katie. 2011. "A Life in Bits and Bytes: A Portrait of a College Student and Her Life with Digital Media." *Teachers College Record* 113:1960–1982.

DeAndrea, David, Nicole Ellison, Robert Larose, Charles Steinfield, and Andrew Fiore. 2011. "Serious Social Media: On the Use of Social Media for Improving Students' Adjustment to College." *Internet and Higher Education* 15:15–23.

Dede, Christopher. 2007. *A Sea Change in Thinking, Knowing, Learning, and Teaching: The ECAR Study of Undergraduate Students and Information Technology, 2007.* Boulder, CO: EDUCAUSE.

———. 2008. "A Seismic Shift in Epistemology." *EDUCAUSE Review*, May–June, 80–91.

DeVoss, Dànielle Nicole, Elyse Eidman-Aadahl, and Troy Hicks. 2010. *Because Digital Writing Matters: Improving Student Writing in Online and Multi-media Formats.* San Francisco: Jossey-Bass.

Educational Testing Service. 2012. "The iSkills Assessment from ETS." Retrieved September 17. http://www.ets.org/iskills/about/.

Eshet-Alkalai, Yoram. 2004. "Digital Literacy: A Conceptual Framework for Survival Skills in the Digital Era." *Journal of Educational Multimedia and Hypermedia* 13:93–106.

Frontline. 2010. *Digital Nation*. Washington, DC: PBS.

Gasser, Urs, Sandra Cortesi, Momin Malik, and Ashley Lee. 2012. *Youth and Digital Media: From Credibility to Information Quality*. Cambridge, MA: Berkman Center for Internet and Society, Harvard University.

Gee, James Paul. 2010. *New Digital Media and Learning as an Emerging Area and "Worked Examples" as One Way Forward*. Cambridge, MA: MIT Press.

Gee, James Paul, and Elisabeth R. Hayes. 2010. *Women and Gaming: The Sims and 21st Century Learning*. New York: Palgrave Macmillan.

———. 2011. *Language and Learning in the Digital Age*. New York: Routledge.

Gitlin, Todd. 2007. *Media Unlimited: How the Torrent of Images and Sounds Overwhelms Our Lives*. Rev. ed. New York: Picador.

Glenn, David. 2010. "Divided Attention: In an Age of Classroom Multitasking, Scholars Probe the Nature of Learning and Memory." *Chronicle Review*, February 28.

Gopnick, Adam. 2011. "The Information: How the Internet Gets inside Us." *New Yorker*, February 14.

Gulati, Shalni. 2008. "Compulsory Participation in Online Discussions: Is this Constructivism or Normalization of Learning? *Innovations in Education and Teaching International* 45:183–192.

Hirsch, E. D. 1987. *Cultural Literacy: What Every American Needs to Know*. New York: Vintage.

Ito, Mimi, Sonja Baumer, Matteo Bittanti, danah boyd, Rachel Cody, Becky Herr-Stephenson, Heather A. Horst, Patricia G. Lange, Dilan Mahendran, Katynka Z. Martinez, C. J. Pascoe, Dan Perkel, Laura Robinson, Christo Sims, and Lisa Tripp. 2009. *Hanging Out, Messing Around, and Geeking Out: Kids Living and Learning with New Media*. Cambridge, MA: MIT Press.

Jackson, Maggie. 2008. *Distracted: The Erosion of Attention and the Coming Dark Age*. Buffalo, NY: Prometheus.

Jenkins, Henry. 2009. *Confronting the Challenges of Participatory Culture: Media Education for the 21st Century*. Cambridge, MA: MIT Press.

Jones, Karen. 2012. "Teaching Children the Value of Pre-Web Pages." *New York Times*, March 14.

Knobel, Michelle, and Colin Lankshear, eds. 2007. *A New Literacies Sampler*. New York: Peter Lang.

Kord, JoLanna, and Lisa Wolf-Wendel. 2009. "The Relationship between Online Social Networking and Academic and Social Integration." *College Student Affairs Journal* 28:103–123.

Krumsvik, Rune. 2008. "Situated Learning and Teachers' Digital Competence." *Education and Informational Technology* 13:279–290.

Lankes, R. David. 2010. "The Missing Links: Ereaders, the iPad, That's It? The Device Industry Is Blowing a Great Opportunity to Revolutionize Reading." *School Library Journal* 56:32–34.

Levy, David M., Daryl L. Nardick, Jeanine Turner, and Leanne McWatters, L. 2011. "No Cellphone? No Internet? So Much Less Stress." *Chronicle of Higher Education*, May 8.

Lewin, Tamar. 2012. "Instruction for Masses Knocks Down Campus Walls." *New York Times*, March 4.

Manguel, Albert. 2008. *The Library at Night*. New Haven, CT: Yale University Press.

Mayer, Richard. 2001. *Multimedia Learning*. New York: Cambridge University Press.

Mills, Kathy Ann. 2010. "A Review of the 'Digital Turn' in the New Literacy Studies." *Review of Educational Research* 80:246–271.

Morozov, Evgeny. 2012. "The Death of the Cyberflâneur." *New York Times*, February 4.

National Research Council. 1999. *Being Fluent with Information Technology*. Washington, DC: National Academy Press.

Oppenheimer, Todd. 2003. *The Flickering Mind: The False Promise of Technology in the Classroom and How Learning Can Be Saved*. New York: Random House.

Organization for Economic Co-operation and Development (OECD). 2009. *New Millennium Learners: Initial Findings on the Effects of Digital Technologies on School Age Learners*. Paris. http://www.oecd.org/dataoecd/39/51/40554230.pdf.

Pea, Roy, Clifford Nass, Lyn Meheula, Marcus Rance, Aman Kumar, Holden Bamford, Matthew Nass, Aneesh Simha, Benjamin Stillerman, Steven Yang, and Michael Zhou. 2012. "Media Use, Face-to-Face Communication, Media Multitasking, and Social Well Being among 8–12 Year-Old Girls." *Developmental Psychology* 30:1–10.

Postman, Neil. 1993. *Technopoly: The Surrender of Culture to Technology*. New York: Knopf.

———. 1995. *The End of Education: Redefining the Value of School*. New York: Knopf.

———. 1999. *Building a Bridge to the 18th Century: How the Past Can Improve Our Future*. New York: Knopf.

Powers, William. 2010. *Hamlet's BlackBerry: Building a Good Life in the Digital Age*. New York: Harper.

Prensky, Marc. 2001. "Digital Natives, Digital Immigrants, Part 1." *On the Horizon* 9(5):1–6.

Price, Leah. 2007. "You Are What You Read." *New York Times Book Review*, December 23.

Rheingold, Howard. 2010. "Attention and Other 21st Century Social Media Literacies." *EDUCAUSE Review*, September–October.

Rich, Motoko. 2008. "Literacy Debate: Online, R U Really Reading." *New York Times*, July 27.

Richtel, Matt. 2012. "Wasting Time Is New Divide in Digital Era." *New York Times*, May 29.

Salen, Katie. 2011. *Quest to Learn: Developing the School for Digital Kids*. Cambridge, MA: MIT Press.

Sanger, Lawrence. 2010. "Individual Knowledge in the Internet Age." *EDUCAUSE Review* March–April, 14–24.

Selber, Stephen. 2004. *Multiliteracies for a Digital Age*. Carbondale: Southern Illinois University Press.

Snyder, Ilana, ed. 2002. *Silicon Literacies: Communications, Innovation, and Education in the Electronic Age*. New York: Routledge.

Striphas, Ted. 2009. *The Late Age of Print: Everyday Book Culture from Consumerism to Control*. New York: Columbia University Press.

Sullivan, Andrew. 2008. "Why I Blog." *Atlantic*, November 1. http://www.theatlantic.com/magazine/archive/2008/11/why-i-blog/307060/.

Turkle, Sherry. 2008. "Always-on/Always-on-You: The Tethered Self." In *Handbook of Mobile Communications Studies*, edited by James E. Katz, 121–138. Cambridge, MA: MIT Press.

———. 2010. Interview. *Frontline: Digital Nation*. Washington, DC: PBS.

———. 2011. *Alone Together: Why We Expect More from Technology and Less from Each Other*. New York: Basic Books.

United States Department of Education, Office of Educational Technology. 2010. *Transforming American Education: Learning Powered by Technology.* Washington, DC.

Walsh, Taylor. 2011. *Unlocking the Gates: How and Why Leading Universities Are Opening Up Access to their Courses.* Princeton, NJ: Princeton University Press.

Weinberger, David. 2012. *Too Big to Know: Rethinking Knowledge Now That the Facts Aren't the Facts, Experts Are Everywhere, and the Smartest Person in the Room Is the Room.* New York: Basic Books.

Wilber, Dana. 2008. "College Students and New Literacy Practices." In *Handbook of Research on New Literacies,* edited by Julie Coiro, Michelle Knobel, Colin Lankshear, and Donald Leu, 553–581. Mahwah, NJ: Erlbaum.

Wolf, Marjorie. 2007. *Proust and the Squid: The Story and Science of the Reading Brain.* New York: Harper.

Yancey, Kathleen. 2004. "Made Not Only in Words: Composition in a New Key." *College Composition and Communication* 56:297–328.

The Shape of Things to Come

WILLIAM G. TIERNEY AND ZOË B. CORWIN

Those who suggest that academe never changes are largely mistaken. Through similes such as "governing faculty is like herding cats" or "changing the curriculum is like moving a graveyard," too often the picture gets painted of colleges and universities in stasis, wedded to the status quo. We appreciate why such portraits occur. Shared governance, in particular, is a deliberative process where conversations take place over one or another issue for much of the academic year, if not years. The pace of change can seem very slow, indeed.

And yet, since the dawn of the past century American higher education has undergone remarkable changes. In 1900 very few U.S. institutions would have been considered in the top-tier of the world's universities. According to admittedly subjective rankings tables, a century later well over half of the world's top 100 great universities are found in the United States. Most of the scientific research and publication outlets are found in North America. How academics do their research also has changed; large scientific teams from multiple disciplines now routinely work together in ways that would have been impossible only a half century ago. Scientific advancements also have continued unabated, which has fostered the rise of new disciplines and the demise of others.

But as we mentioned in part I, what has not changed very much is the nature of teaching and learning. Because the forms of teaching have not changed very much, what one expects of students has remained relatively the same. To be sure, courses, majors, and degrees are updated and texts change from year to year, but the overall substance of learning in the academy is more similar than different from a century ago, and that is about to change.

There is a classic Abbott and Costello skit called "Who's on first?" where Costello gets befuddled by the names of his friend's team. "Who" plays first base, "What" plays second, and "I don't know" plays third. Linguistic confusion ensues as Costello asks Abbott "Who plays first base" and Abbott responds, "Yes." We are close to getting into that situation in academe without half as much humor in terms of academic offerings. Not so long ago if individuals wanted a bachelor's degree, the student attended a four-year institution; if they wanted an associate's degree or a certificate they went to a community college. By the early twenty-first century, however, the country has reached a point where four-year institutions are offering two-year degrees and two-year institutions are offering four-year degrees. Both institutions offer certificates.

Although for-profit institutions have been around for more than a century, the reality is that until recently if someone spoke of "going to college," the meaning was clear. Someone attended either a private institution or a public institution. But public institutions now get as little as 7% of their moneys from public funds. For-profit institutions may get as much as 90% of their funds from the public sector. In some states for-profit institutions educate and train more students than private institutions. Some private non-profit institutions such as National University act more like for-profits in their behavior (and do a better job) and some for-profits have been taking their institutions into the nonprofit world. The fastest-growing degree in higher education is a certificate that requires neither accreditation nor faculty with doctoral degrees. Companies are a major provider of certificate training programs.

And now a situation exists where neither two- nor four-year institutions will be offering courses because of legislation in California and elsewhere. As noted in part I, a capacity problem exists in much of the country. Part of the problem is the recession that occurred, which caused state budgets to constrict so that public institutions received less state support. But the public institutions also have had little appetite for radically redesigning how they teach and how students learn. The result has been an inability to increase capacity by traditional means. The country needs to educate more students, but too many students cannot get the classes they need. Potential students are effectively closed out of the local public institutions because courses still mean "seat-time," and there are limited seats. Some of the most innovative strategies that are being developed to deal with capacity are in neither traditional public or private institutions nor for-profit colleges and universities. Start-up companies are increasingly able to offer classes that can be transferred to a public institution. The course offerings could be done by a for-profit institution, but they also could be supplied by a company such as Sylvan Learning, or even "Bill and Zoë's Best Buy." Thus, according to the scenarios we outlined in part I, the sorts of issues discussed in part II are increasingly commonplace rather than unique.

And then there is the issue of how college students navigate their social lives and, relatedly, their learning. Recently, Corwin asked her qualitative methods master's students to spend their class break jotting down observations. Her students returned amazed by just how many other students they had observed on their phones—sitting in groups, walking alone, riding bikes, while studying; most students were connected to someone or to some activity on their mobile device. Students currently served by postsecondary institutions are perpetually connected. They have grown up with Google at their fingertips. If they have a question, they "google" the answer. They take an active role and create online content by "liking" posts, commenting, and creating blog entries or adding to existing resources. As Gee and Jenkins and Kahn discuss, students have grown up with access to massive online communities. Many are adept at navigating online social relationships and evaluating how and where to find information and support. As a consequence, they problem-solve in different ways and with a much wider network than adults did when they were in college. In the well-received *Hanging Out, Messing Around, and Geeking Out*, Mizuko Ito and colleagues (2010) share findings from ethnographies that capture the spirit and habits of new media usage of youth. From everyday participation in networked publics to newly conceptualized peer networks (i.e., friending an individual on Facebook) to interest-driven affiliations, youth culture has changed. And in turn, the way to think about literacies and the way institutions structure social interactions and learning opportunities must change as well.

To be sure, multiple hurdles need to be overcome before games and social media are entirely integrated into the postsecondary fabric. Regulatory structures need to be developed and put in place to guarantee that flimflam artists do not sell the consumer a set of poor learning experiences. If courses are to be offered, they have to be done in a manner that is cheaper than if the taxpayer just gave the additional moneys to the public institutions for additional "seats"; the courses have to be of a quality equivalent to what students would find on those traditional campuses. What seems irreversible, however, is that games and social media are here to stay, and the pace of change and integration into the fabric of postsecondary education is going to continue at an extremely fast pace.

Such changes can be exciting, as the authors in part II have conveyed. To those in the traditional higher-education world, these changes have the potential to be transformative. Too often, however, the changes are portrayed by using disaster metaphors. As individuals and think tanks have tried to analyze these innovations, authors have predicted "avalanches," "tsunamis," and end-of-world metaphors. Interestingly, such reports have been commonplace when writing about K–12 education—the nation has been portrayed as "at risk" and the like because of a poor primary and secondary system. The current reports about higher education, however, do not go so far as to claim widespread malaise or ineffectiveness (although problems such as learning outcomes are commonly noted). Rather, the "avalanche" reports express concerns about capacity, cost, and, of consequence, technology. The consensus is that more students need to be educated at a lower cost, and the best means to do that is by way of technology.

We share those concerns and some of the solutions, but we are not convinced that the best way to go about talking about difficult problems is by way of shouting, "The sky is falling!" Such language did not help Chicken Little very much, and we do not think it helps academe. In an emergency, the need is for calm heads and clear-headed thinking. Calm does not suggest dismissing problems or staying wedded to the status quo. What academe needs right now is a sustained, systematic discussion about the problems—and opportunities—that exist. And for that discussion to be productive, we need calm language rather than those who prefer to draw cataclysmic portraits. This book has been one such effort at a levelheaded analysis of the potential that exists. We have highlighted ways in which games and social media might stimulate innovation and reflection in postsecondary settings. And yet, we also have included in Steve Weiland's chapter a caution that widespread euphoria is unwarranted until there is a more fulsome debate. Just as we are uncomfortable with "end-of-the-world" analogies, we are also more circumspect than simply suggesting that an academic version of the New Jerusalem is right around the corner.

Unquestionably, the authors in part II are proponents for meaningful usage of games and social media in higher education. We included chapters from these authors because they have worked on games and social media in various capacities—Fullerton and Salen as game designers, and Gee and Jenkins as two of the leading thinkers about new media literacies. All of them work in higher education. They have been involved in the game and social media worlds long enough to remember a primitive start where only early adapters found pleasure and excitement in a particular game or new invention. As Tierney noted in part I, however, disruptive technologies always begin with early adapters who are intrigued by the invention, even if they cannot always see how the invention will develop or if it will become mainstream. However, those with a history are also able to see how these changes advance understanding in one domain or another, whereas those who use sustainable technologies are either unaware or dismissive of these new inventions.

Distance learning was once heralded with great promise—a promise that was never really realized because the technology was ineffective and inefficient. If a student had the choice between a class at a traditional institution and a class by way of a television monitor, the traditional class always won. The result was that distance learning was the choice of last resort. In the 1970s, when Tierney worked on the Fort Berthold Indian Reservation that covered over a million square miles and had a population of 6,000 residents, distance learning was an option so that the faculty at the local community college did not have to travel for hours simply to teach a class. But the technology was so poor that driving four hours to teach a class rather than having to use the televisions and related equipment became commonplace.

Even as the technology improved, analogies frequently delineated the caliber of different types of education where traditional education was thought of as "Armani" and online courses were "Armani-X." If one could afford an Armani, then why buy the cheaper product? The assumption had been until recently that games and social media simply were doing what traditional entities such as teachers or college counselors did and, for one reason or another, no longer did. From this perspective, a course online was better than no course at all. Indeed, until about 2010 such thinking was the norm in the academy. The known purveyors of online learning and games also did not help insinuate themselves into the rarefied halls of the academy. If online courses were primarily utilized by for-profit institutions that subscribed to an array of sketchy activities, then the technology was of little value. If companies that produced violent games such as *Grand Theft Auto* had profit as their primary motive, then games had no place in the educational mainstream.

What Jenkins and Kahn observed in their chapter, however, was not a second-rate usage of social media but questions about how these technologies might improve teaching and learning, and most definitely change the paradigm. Gee's chapter echoes this point by observing how different technologies and games enhance learning insofar as, with technology, students do not simply learn better but learn differently. The arc of progress that Salen and Fullerton discuss in their chapters suggests that games and social media are no longer in the purview of simply the converted geeks but, as has been shown over the last few years, are now ready for mass consumption. And when the masses utilize social media and games in academe, they are no longer thinking of the technology as the weak link; instead, as Salen and Gee point out, it now enables users to do things that previously were impossible. The result is that the teaching and learning side of academe has reached a point that researchers reached a generation ago with the widespread use of email and laptops. Rather than type a paper on a typewriter and post it in the mail to a colleague thousands of miles away or across campus, now with a click of button the colleague will receive the text in seconds. As Corwin mentions in part I, the implications for how knowledge is created and disseminated are significant.

The challenge for those who work in traditional public and private (and to a certain extent for-profit) institutions is to think about how these new technologies might be employed in their organizations. Decreasing numbers of individuals remain in denial (albeit many of them remain in a critical group—the faculty); larger numbers are, like Weiland, intrigued by the possibilities but remain skeptical. His concerns are useful not as stumbling blocks or a nostalgic call to a return to yesteryear but as foundation upon which to think about how to proceed. As we mentioned at the outset, the point is neither to assume that the "sky is falling" nor to argue that such changes will never impact academic work. Some Jeremiahs believe that the end of higher education is near; too many faculty members wish to believe that the way they have taught can be preserved. Obviously, we disagree. The end is not near, but a new beginning is close. The challenge is to consider how to harness these bright new ideas and technologies and utilize them in a manner that enables academics to improve the teaching and learning of postsecondary education.

In part III, Gigi Ragusa reminds readers that there are potential downsides of a fully functioning social media. Gender inequities and cyberbullying are but two examples of problems that new technologies provide. What Ragusa points out, however, is a way forward with regard to how to assess learning. She points out the related threats associated with new media and then offers ways to improve the technologies not simply so they might work more efficiently but also more effectively. In the other two chapters, the authors discuss viable ways to think about and assess what goes on in games. Valerie Shute and colleagues highlight strategies such as stealth assessment to measure the development of targeted competencies during gameplay. Nicole Ellison, Donghee Yvette Wohn, and Carrie Heeter highlight the value of better understanding the social networks and related social capital made possible through sociable games. The discussions are important because games and social media are entering postsecondary education at a time of fiscal shortfalls. If new media are going to reach their potential, there has to be an evaluative component attached to them.

To be sure, just as one could not have predicted iPads when the first laptops came out, how social media and games will evolve in higher education is unclear. What we have been arguing here is that their place is now firmly established; the potential for using each to enhance learning, engage students, and promote cost-effective scalability is considerable. Social media, the internet, and online games have the potential to blur the boundaries of class, race, age, and gender. The potential also exists to foster collaboration across space and time. Those of us working in postsecondary organizations and related entities need to learn the new vocabularies, make smart use of the tools that are prevalent in youth culture, and move forward with a clear-headed optimism about what the future may provide.

REFERENCE

Ito, Mimi, Sonja Baumer, Matteo Bittanti, danah boyd, Rachel Cody, Becky Herr-Stephenson, Heather A. Horst, Patricia G. Lange, Dilan Mahendran, Katynka Z. Martinez, C. J. Pascoe, Dan Perkel, Laura Robinson, Christo Sims, and Lisa Tripp. 2010. *Hanging Out, Messing Around, and Geeking Out: Kids Living and Learning with New Media*. Cambridge, MA: MIT Press.

Glossary

affinity spaces. A place where informal learning takes place, often occurring online, but not exclusively. Affinity spaces encourage knowledge sharing because of a strong, shared interest in a common activity.

collective intelligence. A theory that describes shared or group intelligence stemming from the activity of many individuals working on a common problem or idea.

connected learning. A model of learning that highlights the potential for information and online collaboration available to youth in their daily lives. This model emphasizes multiple contexts for learning and a distributed network of people and institutions, including schools, libraries, museums, and online communities made possible by digital technologies.

disruptive technology. A new technology that displaces an established technology.

games. A form of play with goals and structure. It is often colloquially used to mean computer or video games, which enable computer mediated play.

gamification. The infusion of game design techniques, game mechanics, or game rewards into existing systems and structures, for example, the creation of badges within learning situations to motivate students.

massively multiplayer online games (**MMOGs**). Games that are capable of supporting large numbers of players simultaneously. Some games maintain persistent worlds so that players may develop characters, items, and experiences over months or years of play.

massively open online courses (**MOOCs**). Large-scale open courses offered, accessed, and managed via the web, sometimes featuring crowd-sourced interaction and feedback, peer review, and group collaboration.

Open Educational Resources (**OER**). Freely accessible, usually openly licensed documents and media that are useful for teaching, learning, educational assessment, and research purposes.

play. Voluntary, intrinsically motivated activity often associated with toys and games. Sometimes dismissed as frivolous, play can also be a transformative experience, especially when linked to learning.

situated learning. A model of learning within a community of practice such that it takes place in the same context in which it is applied and so is authentic and more easily transferable.

social capital. A term used to describe potential or actual resources accessed through social networks given norms of social reciprocity.

social games (also *sociable games*). Online games that include social interaction, especially those that are embedded within a social network such as Facebook and feature multi-player gameplay mechanics. Popular games of this type include *FarmVille*, *CityVille*, and *The Sims Social*.

social media. Web and mobile applications that allow the creation and exchange of user-generated content such as text, images, audio, and video.

social network. A mobile or online site or service that facilitates connections among individuals, including sharing messages and media. It is often focused on a specific use profile, such as LinkedIn for business networking or Classmates.com for connecting fellow graduates.

transactive memory system. A mechanism that enables groups to collectively encode, store, and retrieve knowledge.

Web 2.0. A second generation in the development of the World Wide Web, conceived as a combination of concepts, trends, and technologies that focus on user collaboration, sharing of user-generated content, and social networking.

Contributors

David Conley is a professor of educational methodology, policy, and leadership at the University of Oregon. He is the author of *College and Career Ready: Helping All Students Succeed beyond High School* and *College Knowledge: What It Really Takes for Students to Succeed and What We Can Do to Get Them Ready*. Conley is currently conducting research on issues related to college readiness, college and high school course content analysis, high school–college alignment and transition, and large-scale diagnosis and assessment of college readiness. His most recent book, *Getting Ready for College, Careers and the Common Core: What Every Educator Needs to Know*, was published in fall 2013 by Jossey-Bass.

Zoë B. Corwin is associate professor of research at the Pullias Center for Higher Education at the University of Southern California. Corwin has conducted research on college preparation programs and access to financial aid for underserved students, college pathways for foster youth, and the role of social media and games in postsecondary access and completion. She is co-editor of *Preparing for College: Nine Elements of Effective Outreach* with SUNY Press. In addition to academic articles, she has published several monographs designed for practitioners outlining effective college preparation strategies. Corwin currently directs the *Collegeology Games* project for the Pullias Center.

Nicole B. Ellison is an associate professor in the School of Information at the University of Michigan. Her research addresses issues of self-presentation, social capital, relationship development, and identity in online environments, most recently exploring the role of social media for supporting college-going activities among low-income and first-generation youth. A list of her publications is available at http://www-personal.umich.edu/~enicole/pubs.html.

Tracy Fullerton is the Electronic Arts Endowed Chair in Interactive Entertainment at the USC School of Cinematic Arts, where she directs the USC Game Innovation lab, a design research center for experimental games including *Cloud, flOw, Darfur Is Dying*, and *The Night Journey*, a collaboration with media artist Bill Viola. Tracy is the author of *Game Design Workshop: Designing, Prototyping and Playtesting Games.* Current projects include *Walden*, a game simulation of Henry David Thoreau's experiment at Walden Pond, and the Collegeology Games project in collaboration with the Pullias Center.

James Paul Gee is the Mary Lou Fulton Presidential Professor of Literacy Studies at Arizona State University. He is a member of the National Academy of Education. His book *Sociolinguistics and Literacies* (1990; 3rd ed., 2007) was one of the founding documents in the formation of the "New Literacy Studies," an interdisciplinary field devoted to studying language, learning, and literacy in an integrated way in the full range of their cognitive, social, and cultural contexts. His book *An Introduction to Discourse Analysis* (1999; 2nd ed., 2005; 3rd ed., 2011) brings together his work on a methodology for studying communication in its cultural settings, an approach that has been widely influential over the past two decades. His most recent books include *What Video Games Have to Teach Us about Learning and Literacy* (2003; 2nd ed., 2007), *Situated Language and Learning* (2004), *Good Video Games and Good Learning: Collected Essays* (2007), *Women and Gaming: The Sims and 21st Century Learning* (2010), and *Language and Learning in the Digital World* (2011), the latter two written with Elizabeth Hayes.

Carrie Heeter is professor of telecommunication, information studies, and media at Michigan State University and coordinator of the fully online graduate certificate program in serious games. Her most recent serious game, *DNA Roulette*, is part of The Tech Museum's permanent collection of online exhibits and was awarded "most innovative game" at the 2012 Meaningful Play conference. She is currently exploring ways to create technology-supported meditation micro-experiences that can be used to enhance daily life.

Henry Jenkins is the Provost's Professor of Communication, Journalism, Cinematic Art, and Education at the University of Southern California. He is the author or editor of 15 books, including the recently released *Spreadable Media: Creating Meaning and Value in a Networked Culture* (coauthored with Sam Ford and Joshua Green). His work on education includes *Confronting the Challenges of a Participatory Culture* and *Reading in a Participatory Culture: Remixing Moby-Dick in the Literature Classroom* (coauthored with Wyn Kelley, Katie Clinton, Jenna McWilliams, Ricardo Pitts-Wiley, and Erin Reilly). He blogs regularly at henryjenkins.org.

Adam S. Kahn is a doctoral candidate in communication at the Annenberg School for Communication and Journalism at the University of Southern California. He is interested in social and psychological aspects of human-computer interaction, computer-mediated communication, and video games. Drawing on theories of transactive memory systems, social presence, and embodied cognition, his research examines expertise coordination in avatar mediated groups. Kahn holds a B.S. in computer science, a B.A. in history, and an M.A. in media studies, all from Stanford University, and an M.A. in communication from USC Annenberg.

Yoon Jeon Kim is a doctoral candidate in the Educational Psychology and Learning Systems Department at Florida State University. She specializes in designing assessments for twenty-first-century skills. She has also been involved in several projects that apply evidence-centered design (ECD) in video game environments. She is currently completing her dissertation investigating influences of game design choices on psychometric features of game-based assessments.

Laura W. Perna is professor in the Graduate School of Education and Faculty Fellow of the Institute for Urban Research at the University of Pennsylvania. Recent publications include *Understanding the Working College Student: New Research and Its Implications for Policy and Practice*, *Preparing Today's Students for Tomorrow's Jobs in Metropolitan America: The Policy, Practice, and Research Issues*, and *The State of College Access and Completion: Improving College Success for Students from Underrepresented Groups* (with Anthony Jones).

Gisele Ragusa is an associate professor at the University of Southern California with a faculty appointment in the Viterbi School of Engineering's Division of Engineering Education. Ragusa has extensive experience in engineering education, instrument design, measurement, mixed-approach research design, and advanced statistical analyses. Ragusa has expertise in teacher education, instructional practices at K–12 and university levels, and publishes research in engineering education and K–12 STEM. She has designed and tested instruments that measure university students' preparedness for global work forces, college-related efficacy, and teachers' instructional performance metrics at the K–12 and university levels. Her most recent psychometric project is to assist the National Science Foundation in designing, testing, and implementing an instrument that measures STEM university students' creativity and innovation. She is currently principal investigator of several National Science Foundation, Department of Education, and National Institute of Health grants with primary foci on STEM education, K–12 pipeline/access programs, educational outreach, and engineering education and serves as project evaluator on several federally funded projects.

Katie Salen locates her work in the field of game design and serves as the executive director of the nonprofit Institute of Play, which is focused on games and learning. She is also professor of games and digital media at DePaul University, and learning director of GlassLab, a lab focused on developing game-based assessments created via a partnership between Electronic Arts, the Electronic Software Association, and the Institute of Play. Katie led the team that founded Quest to Learn in 2009, a grade 6–12 public school in New York City, as well as ChicagoQuest, a 6–12 charter school that opened in the fall of 2011 in Chicago. Salen is coauthor of *Rules of Play* (2003), a textbook on game design, *The Game Design Reader* (2005), *Quest to Learn: Growing a School for Digital Kids* (2011), and editor of *The Ecology of Games: Connecting Youth, Games, and Learning* (2008), all from MIT Press. She has worked as a game designer for more than 12 years and is a former coeditor of the *International Journal of Learning and Media*. She was an early advocate of the then-hidden world of machinima and continues to be interested in connections between game design, learning, and transformative modes of play.

Mary Seburn is founder and principal of Quantiful, a research and analytics consultancy, and is principal research scientist at the Educational Policy Improvement Center. She has authored numerous technical reports for U.S. and State Departments of Education and has published in journals including *Applied Psychological Measurement*, *Personality and Social Psychology Bulletin*, and *Assessment for Effective Intervention*.

Valerie Shute is the Mack & Effie Campbell Tyner Endowed Professor in the Department of Educational Psychology and Learning Systems at Florida State University. Her current research involves using immersive games with stealth assessment to support learning—of cognitive and noncognitive knowledge, skills, and dispositions. Her research has resulted in numerous grants, journal articles, books, chapters in edited books, a patent, and a recent book, *Innovative Assessment for the 21st Century: Supporting Educational Needs*, coedited with Betsy Becker.

William G. Tierney is Co-Director of the Pullias Center for Higher Education at the University of Southern California, University Professor, and the Wilbur-Kieffer Professor of Higher Education at the Rossier School of Education. Former president of the American Educational Research Association, Association for the Study of Higher Education, and the USC Academic Senate, Tierney is an expert in higher-education policy analysis, governance, and administration; college access; and qualitative methods. His work has been funded by the Irvine Foundation, Atlantic Philanthropies, the Ford Foundation, the U.S. Department of Education, the Lumina Foundation of Education, and the Bill & Melinda Gates Foundation, among others. Recent publications include *Trust and the Public Good: Examining the Cultural Conditions of Academic Work*; *New Players, Different Game: Understanding the Rise of For-Profit Colleges and Universities* (with Gilbert Hentschke); *Financial Aid and Access: Understanding the Public Policy Challenges*; and *Building the Responsive Campus: Creating High Performance Colleges and Universities*.

Matthew Ventura is a senior research scientist in the College of Education at Florida State University. His current research involves how video game use can improve a variety of skills, including spatial reasoning, problem solving, persistence, qualitative physics, and computational thinking. His work has resulted in numerous publications spanning the areas of assessment, cognitive science, and education.

Lubin Wang is a doctoral student in the program of Instructional Systems at the Florida State University. She has been working on two research projects with her adviser, Dr. Valerie Shute. The projects related to using games as a vehicle to assess and augment learning. Lubin has developed her own research interests in using games to enhance problem-solving skills and examining the relationship of players' "gaming the system" behaviors to cognitive flexibility.

Steven Weiland is professor of higher education at Michigan State University, where he teaches courses in education in the digital age, adult career development, educational inquiry, and other subjects. He has taught online for a decade in MSU's graduate degree programs. Before joining the faculty at MSU, he taught and held administrative positions at the Universities of Michigan, Iowa, and Minnesota, and he served for nine years as Director of the National Federation of State Humanities Councils. His published work is in American intellectual history, literary studies, adulthood and aging, academic careers, and other subjects.

Donghee Yvette Wohn is a postdoctoral researcher at Northwestern University. She studies the social and psychological effects of social media usage and is particularly interested in nonconscious behaviors, such as media habits. Her research on games focuses on social network games and so-called casual games.

Index

Page numbers in *italics* indicate figures and tables.

librarians and knowledge production, 113–15
libraries, love of, 305
Lim, Sohye, 247
Lin, Nan, 250
literacy: academic, 77; digital, and digital citizenship, 117–19; new literacies, 285–90, 297–98, 303–4
loans for postsecondary education, 83–84
Luke, Carmen, 265
Lumina Foundation, 23
lures of games, 128–31

MacArthur Foundation, 192, 287, 288
majors: as approach to undergraduate education, 171; "impacted" or oversubscribed, 28
Manguel, Albert, 305
market-driven, postsecondary institutions as, 172, 173–74. *See also* for-profit higher education
massively multiplayer online games. *See* MMOGs
massively multiplayer online role-playing games (MMORPGs), 273–74
massively open online courses (MOOCs), 6, 116, 302
matriculation knowledge and skills, 84–87
McGonigal, Jane, 155, 164, 165, 219
meaning: production of, 212; situated, 176
media ideologies, 104
mediated communication, 112
membership organizations, 34
mentoring, 79, 84, 136, 269, 270, 278
Middaugh, Ellen, 248
Mikami, Amori Y., 269
Minecraft, 193–94, 197, 198–99
Mission: Admission (game): assessment and feedback, 139–40; described, 4–5, 85, 89–90; lure and, 130–32; sharing knowledge, 141; as social network game, 256; underlying structure, 135–36
MIT Mystery Hunt, 156
MMOGs (massively multiplayer online games): civic engagement and, 248; leadership skills and, 249; learning and, 111; sociable gaming and, 241–42, 243
MMORPGs (massively multiplayer online role-playing games), 273–74

MOOCs (massively open online courses), 6, 116, 302
Morris, Meredith Ringel, 251
Mucherah, Wilfridah, 263
multimediated networks, 113–14
multiplayer games, 149, 240–41, 243–44. *See also* MMOGs

Naismith, James, 190
Nam, Yunju, 51
Ness, Erik C., 59
Net Generation, 284, 285, 290–94. *See also* digital natives
network interaction patterns and gender, 269
new literacies, 285–90, 297–98, 303–4
Newton's Playground: agents of force and motion in, 223–25, 227; ballistic pendulum problem in, 227, 228; *Cave Story* problem in, 230, 230–31; conceptual physics assessment in, 225–28; conscientiousness and persistence assessment in, 228–31; diving board problem in, 227–28, 229; overview of, 222–23, 223
New York City Math Olympiad Tournament, 201–2
New York Nearest Subway, 90
No Child Left Behind, 191
nontraditional partnerships, developing, 41–42
norms of college and workplace, 42, 80–81
Norvig, Peter, 39

Obama, Barack, 7, 23
occasions to play games, 131–33
OECD (Organization for Economic and Cultural Development), 290–91
online counseling and mentoring programs, 84
online courses, 36, 38, 39, 315. *See also* MOOCs
online universities, 10
Open Educational Resources (OER), 302
open-laptop exams: approach to, 162–65; challenges of, 146–47; collective intelligence and, 155–57; overview of, 13; reactions to change and, 166–67; transactive memory systems and, 157–62
Organization for Economic and Cultural Development (OECD), 290–91
organizations and disruptive technologies, 32–36
Osterman, Paul, 47